Great Women OF THE BIBLE

Great Women of the Bible

NEW TESTAMENT

JIMMY SWAGGART

Jimmy Swaggart Ministries
P.O. Box 262550 • Baton Rouge, Louisiana 70826-2550
Website: www.jsm.org • Email: info@jsm.org
(225) 768-7000

ISBN 978-1-934655-94-8
09-121 • COPYRIGHT © 2014 Jimmy Swaggart Ministries®
19 20 21 22 23 24 25 26 27 28 / CM / 12 11 10 9 8 7 6 5 4 3

TABLE OF CONTENTS

INTRODUCTION

When I undertook this effort, I had felt to do so in only one volume. However, I soon found out that there is so much material as it regards the great women of the Bible that it would be far best to do this in two volumes: "Great Women of the Bible, Old Testament" and "Great Women of the Bible, New Testament."

I will begin with Mary, the Mother of our Lord, even though chronologically she follows Elisabeth. As well, the two, Mary and Elisabeth, are so intertwined that it is imperative, we thought, to address both of them together.

The manner and way in which the Holy Spirit worked as it regards the Mother of our Lord and the Mother of John the Baptist, who introduced Christ, proclaims, I think, the necessity of, in a sense, addressing the two as one.

THE WORD OF THE LORD

Once we begin to study the great women of the Bible, and the contribution they made to the great Work of God, we start to realize just how important that contribution was and is.

The Holy Spirit is the One Who inspired the Holy Text, therefore, He allotted the space He so desired as it regards each one of these great personalities. We find to our Blessing that the information given is far more than we realize, especially when we begin to make a study of these very important personalities.

I pray that this volume, "Great Women of the Bible, New Testament," will be received as readily as was our first volume, "Great Women of the Bible, Old Testament."

I personally feel this study opens up a new vista of understanding as it regards the great Plan of

Redemption. It is very sobering to realize that in this Plan of Redemption, the Lord chose a woman to bring the Redeemer into the world even though it could have been done in many other ways.

It is also sobering to realize that the Lord chose a woman, Mary Magdalene, to be the very first one to herald the Resurrection of our Lord.

Then, we think of Paul's first Convert on European soil as being Lydia, actually, a businesswoman, with, in fact, her house becoming the first Church on European soil. This was the first thrust of the Gospel taken westward, which would mean so much to the future of the world.

As you peruse and hopefully study the contents of this book, I believe that your understanding of the Word of God, as well as the Ways of the Lord, will be greatly enhanced.

Once again, as with Volume 1, I want to dedicate this effort to Frances, with whom I celebrated our 60th wedding anniversary on October 10, 2012.

As I said in the first volume, I say again: when the both of us one day stand before the Lord, if there is any credit whatsoever to be given, 90 percent of that credit will go to Frances.

Her Faith has always amazed me!

In everything the Lord has instructed us to do, He has, without exception, given Frances an insight into that Call that was and is remarkable, to say the least. She has an amazing ability to discern things, far more than I ever could think of doing so, and she's almost never wrong.

So, with every line I write and every personality in this book that is addressed, irrespective of the tremendous way that dear lady, whomever she might be, was used by God, Frances will always be in my thoughts.

"Glorious things of thee are spoken,
"Zion, City of our God,
"He, Whose Word cannot be broken,
"Formed thee for His Own Abode:
"On in the Rock of Ages founded,
"What can shake thy sure repose?
"With Salvation's walls surrounded,
"Thou mayst smile at all thy foes."

"See, the streams of living waters,
"Springing from eternal love,
"Well supply thy Sons and Daughters,
"And all fear of want remove:
"Who can faint, while such a river,
"Ever flows their thirst to assuage?
"Grace which, like the Lord, the Giver,
"Never fails from age to age."

"Round each habitation hovering,
"See the cloud and fire appear,
"For a glory and a covering,
"Showing that the Lord is near!
"Glorious things of thee are spoken,
"Zion, City of our God;
"He, Whose Word cannot be broken,
"Formed thee for His Own Abode."

Great Women of the Bible

NEW TESTAMENT

Chapter One

MARY AND ELISABETH

ZECHARIAH AND ELISABETH

"There was in the days of Herod, the king of Judaea, a certain Priest named Zacharias, of the course of Abia: and his wife was of the daughters of Aaron, and her name was Elisabeth" (Lk. 1:5).

It is said that the first four Verses of this Gospel written by Luke are written in pure classical language; the sentences are balanced, almost with a rhythmical accuracy. It is stated that they are evidently the words of a highly-cultured mind that is well versed in Greek thought. Such was Luke.

However, with the Fifth Verse, Luke writes in the manner in which these experiences and information were given unto him. The information came from wonderful, simple people, and he will report it in the same manner. In this, it is easy to note that not only was the relating of these accounts to be absolutely accurate, but, as well, the very color and flavor were to be maintained.

HEROD THE GREAT

The phrase, *"There was in the days of Herod, the king of Judaea,"* pertains to *"Herod the Great."* The event concerning the birth of John the Baptist took place toward the end of his reign.

Besides Judaea, his dominion included Samaria, Galilee, and a part of Peraea.

Luke's description of him as *"king of Judaea"* is totally accurate in that the Roman senate had, on the recommendation of Antony and Octavius, granted to him this title.

H.D.M. Spence says that it was a strange and sad state of things. The Land of Promise, Israel, was ruled over by an Edomite, with the Temple on Mount Zion in his custody. Actually, the entirety of Israel had now been ruled by the Gentiles for some 600 years.

Spurning the clarion call of Jeremiah the Prophet, Israel rebelled against God until her supremacy was taken away. The sacred writer said, *"But they mocked the messengers of God, and despised His Words, and misused His Prophets, until the Wrath of the LORD arose against His People, till there was no remedy"* (II Chron. 36:16). At that time, the scepter of power was taken from the faltering hands of the kings of Judah and given to the Gentiles where it has remained ever since.

With Israel's rebellion against Christ, which was the crowning blow of all, these people called *"Jews"* would lose everything. In 70 A.D., Titus, the Roman general, destroyed the whole of Israel. Then, their very reason to exist was lost, and, consequently, they were made to wander as outcasts all over the world until finally becoming a Nation again in 1948.

Despite the abject failure, they will still fulfill the Plan of God, finally accepting Christ, which will be at the time of the Second Coming. So, when one reads of *"Herod, the king of Judaea,"* one is actually reading the abject failure of Israel.

ZACHARIAS

The phrase, *"A certain Priest named Zacharias,"* should actually be pronounced *"Zechariah."* It means, *"Remembered of Jehovah."*

Never was a man more aptly named.

For about 400 years, Israel had not heard the voice of a Prophet. The Lord will now *"remember Israel"* and give a son to Zechariah and Elisabeth, who will be the first Prophet after that long silence. As well, he will be the greatest Prophet who has ever lived because he was privileged to introduce to the entirety of the world,

"The Lord Jesus Christ, King of kings, and Lord of lords."

THE COURSE OF ABIA

The phrase, *"Of the course of Abia,"* pertained to the courses instituted by David for Temple service.

Each of the 24 courses performed their duties for one week (I Chron. 24). Then another group of Priests would come in to do the same weekly service; consequently, not any of the Priests had to stay away from their homes very long. From Eleazar and Ithamar, the two surviving sons of the first High Priest, Aaron, had descended these 24 families. Consequently, their forefathers had been carrying out these same duties for nearly one thousand years, minus the years of the Babylonian dispersion. It continued until the fall of Jerusalem and the burning of the Temple in 70 A.D. According to Josephus, the Jewish historian, Zechariah was especially distinguished by belonging to the first of the 24 courses, or families.

The phrase, *"And his wife was of the daughters of Aaron, and her name was Elisabeth,"* means that both the husband and wife traced their lineage back to Aaron, the first High Priest — a coveted distinction in Israel.

However, we shall see that despite this honored distinction, Zechariah and Elisabeth placed little stock in their distinguished position, rather seeking and serving God for the Righteousness that He Alone could give.

RIGHTEOUS

"And they were both Righteous before God, walking in all the Commandments and Ordinances of the Lord blameless" (Lk. 1:6).

The phrase, *"And they were both Righteous before*

God," tells us something remarkable about these people.

By this time, the Pharisees and religious leaders of Israel had become so lifted up within themselves that they actually thought that being a child of Abraham constituted Salvation. Of course, as stated, those who held the coveted positions, as Zechariah and Elisabeth, generally thought very highly of themselves. Actually, their son, John the Baptist, would direct his attention to this, saying, *"... and begin not to say within yourselves, We have Abraham to our Father: for I say unto you, That God is able of these stones to raise up children unto Abraham"* (Lk. 3:8). To be sure, the religious leaders did not take too kindly to John the Baptist declaring that they needed to repent.

And yet, there were some few in Israel, as Zechariah and Elisabeth, who did not fall into this self-righteous group. Their *"Righteousness"* was not self-righteousness but that imputed by the Lord.

BLAMELESS

The phrase, *"Walking in all the Commandments and Ordinances of the Lord blameless,"* although given by Luke, is sanctioned by the Holy Spirit and proclaims a lifestyle of Righteousness, which not many had. What an honor to be called by the Holy Spirit, *"Blameless."* Of course, that meant *"blameless"* as it regarded endeavoring to keep the Law. It did not mean they were sinless, for no one fits that description except Christ.

As it regards our present consecration, if the Holy Spirit likewise wrote an account of us, what would that account be?

BARREN

"And they had no child, because that Elisabeth was

barren, and they both were now well stricken in years"
(Lk. 1:7).

The phrase, *"And they had no child,"* is said simply but with great portent.

The idea is that they desperately wanted children but had not been able to have any.

The phrase, *"Because that Elisabeth was barren,"* placed her in the same category as Sarah and Abraham (Gen. 11:30; 17:17).

In Israel, a childless house was looked on as a mark of Divine displeasure, possibly the punishment of some grave sin. Consequently, due to this, very few in Israel would have referred to Zechariah and Elisabeth as *"blameless."* However, God did!

The modern church, as well, is so prone to judge when it has little knowledge of the actual truth of the situation. That is at least one of the reasons Jesus said, *"Judge not, that you be not judged"* (Mat. 7:1).

As well, *"Man looks on the outward appearance, but God looks on the heart"* (I Sam. 16:7).

The phrase, *"And they both were now well stricken in years,"* means that Elisabeth was past the age of childbearing. Consequently, John's birth was just as miraculous as that of Isaac as it regarded Abraham and Sarah (Rom. 4:17-21; Heb. 11:11).

THE PRIEST'S OFFICE BEFORE GOD

"And it came to pass, that while he executed the Priest's office before God in the order of his course" (Lk. 1:8).

The phrase, *"And it came to pass,"* is of far greater consequence than immediately meets the eye.

It referred not only to the time when Zechariah would go to Jerusalem regarding his week of duties in the Temple but, as well, the passing of the entire 400 years of prophetic silence, which was now to be remedied. Even more so, it spoke of the way being prepared for the Advent of Israel's Messiah, the Lord Jesus Christ. In other words, this is one of the most important moments in human history!

The phrase, *"That while he executed the Priest's office before God,"* means that Zechariah took his duties very seriously before God. He considered that what he did was as *"unto the Lord."*

In truth, and considering how the Lord would use the father of John the Baptist, it was imperative that Zechariah be this type of man. To be sure, inconsistency, slothfulness, and little attention to duty will never characterize one used by God.

The phrase, *"In the order of his course,"* as stated, concerned *"The course of Abia"* (Abijah — I Chron. 24:10).

Some think this was the month of July. If that is so, Jesus was conceived six months later (Lk. 1:26), which would have been in January, consequently, being born nine months later in October. It is fairly certain He was not born on December 25th because shepherds were continuing to keep their flocks out at night, which would have hardly been the case in late December.

THE ANGEL OF THE LORD

"And there appeared unto him an Angel of the Lord standing on the right side of the Altar of Incense" (Lk. 1:11).

This *"Angel of the Lord"* referred to *"Gabriel"* (Vs. 19).

Angels are mentioned quite often in Luke (1:11, 26; 2:9, 15, 21; 12:8; 15:10; 16:22; 22:43; 24:4, 23).

The word or name, *"Angel,"* is used generically of *"God, Christ, men, and certain spirit beings."* One has to look at the context to ascertain to whom is referred. The word literally means, *"Messenger."*

The one referred to as *"Gabriel,"* undoubtedly one of the greatest Angels ever created by God, would fall into the class that is referred to as *"Angels"* as we think of the term.

This Angel will have a message for Zechariah that is astounding, to say the least.

"Standing on the right side of the Altar of Incense," is the side of propitiation, which, in effect, means that God accepts the sacrifice. Consequently, the *"right side"* was spoken for purpose (Mat. 25:33; Mk. 16:5; Jn. 21:6).

FEAR

"And when Zacharias saw him, he was troubled, and fear fell upon him" (Lk. 1:12).

This Passage expresses extreme startlement on the part of this Priest, and no wonder!

The phrase, *"He was troubled, and fear fell upon him,"* expresses pretty well the reaction of most all at being placed in the presence of such a Being.

The spirit world is very real, affecting all people, whether they know it or not, either in a negative or a positive way.

Of course, demon spirits from the world of darkness can only affect in a negative sense, and, in one way or the other, they come to *"steal, kill, and destroy"* (Jn. 10:10).

However, Angels from God come either to bless or to warn. According to Scripture, Believers are surrounded by Angels, although unseen (II Ki. 6:17; Ps. 34:7).

Angels were prominent during the Lord's Earthly Ministry and in connection with His Death and Resurrection.

Their presence proves that the Messiah was not an Angel but the Lord of Angels.

FEAR NOT

"But the Angel said unto him, Fear not, Zacharias: for your prayer is heard; and your wife Elisabeth shall bear you a son, and you shall call his name John" (Lk. 1:13).

The phrase, *"But the Angel said unto him, Fear not, Zacharias,"* proclaims that this appearance pertains to Blessing. The fear and agitation of Zechariah, no doubt, was obvious. I cannot conceive that any other person would have acted any differently. Any contact with the other world of eternal Light is something extraordinary, to say the least! It has not happened to many, and yet, this is the world in which all righteous souls will live forever.

As well, I cannot help but believe that when Gabriel (and this was Gabriel) said, *"Fear not,"* a great calming effect came over Zechariah. The *"fear"* does not so much derive from the glorious presence as the lack of spiritual knowledge on our part in this area and, more particularly, the personal unworthiness of man. These Beings, such as Gabriel, have never sinned and, consequently, are perfectly righteous.

The evidence seems clear that man was originally created even higher than the Angels. David asked of the Lord, *"What is man, that You are mindful of him? and the son of man, that You visit him?*

"For You have made him a little lower than the Angels, and have crowned him with glory and honor" (Ps. 8:4-5).

The Hebrew word, *"Elohim,"* here translated, *"Angels,"* should have been translated, *"God,"* or, *"Godhead."* It should never have been translated, *"Angels,"* in this Verse. All of this means that man was originally created higher than the Angels, but, by sin, he was brought very low and made subject to death. Now, man, in his lessened state (short of God's Glory, Rom. 3:23), is below Angels. However, in the coming Kingdom Age, this will be rectified, with man, because of the Cross, rightly regaining that which was lost with Adam's fall.

A SON

"And your wife Elisabeth shall bear you a son": how old they were at this time is not known, but the Scripture says, *"They both were now well stricken in years."*

When nature is feeble, broken, and dead, it is then possible for God to act in Power.

JOHN

The phrase, *"And you shall call his name John,"* has the meaning, *"Jehovah shows favor."*

John was one of the seven persons in the Bible named before birth (Ishmael, Gen. 16:11; Isaac, Gen. 17:19; Solomon, I Chron. 22:9; Josiah — 325 years before birth, I Ki. 13:2; II Ki. 22:1; Cyrus — named 175 years before his birth, Isa. 44:28-45:1; John the Baptist, Lk. 1:13, 60-63; Jesus, Mat. 1:21).

In effect, the name, *"John,"* means, *"Grace,"* and was an apt description of the one who would introduce the Lord of Glory, the One Who would bring *"Grace and Truth"* (Jn. 1:17).

JOHN THE NAZARITE

"For he shall be great in the Sight of the Lord, and shall drink neither wine nor strong drink; and he shall be filled with the Holy Spirit, even from his mother's womb" (Lk. 1:15).

The phrase, *"For he shall be great in the Sight of the Lord,"* constitutes the only true greatness.

Regrettably, he would not be great in the eyes of the religious leaders of Israel.

Actually, *"greatness"* from God is seldom recognized by the world or even the church. Regrettably, most seek for *"greatness"* in the sight of man instead of God.

The phrase, *"And shall drink neither wine nor strong drink,"* means that he was a *"Nazarite."*

The *"Nazarite"* had to abstain from intoxicating drink of all kinds in order that no spirit, other than that of Jehovah (Prov. 20:1), would control him.

As well, he was not to cut his hair during the time of consecration, which, in the time of John the Baptist, was the entirety of his life. Long hair on a man denoted weakness and, in essence, was meant to say that God was his strength.

Also, he must not go near a dead body, even that of his nearest relation. Death signified the terrible results of sin and was its perfect picture. Consequently, the Nazarite, who was to epitomize life, must abstain from any association with death. There is, for example, the consecration of Samuel (I Sam. 1:11). Actually, in the Qumran Text, I Samuel 1:22 ends with the words, *"A Nazarite forever all the days of his life."*

Chapter 6 of Numbers provides the fullest and most detailed account of the Nazarite.

FILLED WITH THE HOLY SPIRIT FROM HIS MOTHER'S WOMB

The phrase, *"And he shall be filled with the Holy Spirit, even from his mother's womb,"* has no reference to the Acts 2:4 experience, which had not yet come to pass.

The word, *"Filled,"* in the Greek Text means, *"To furnish or supply."* It actually means that from his mother's womb, he was called and designated for a particular task. As well, even from his mother's womb, the Holy Spirit would furnish and supply Direction,

Leading, and Guidance. In other words, the Holy Spirit watched over him extensively, even as an infant, and with Personal Guidance once he reached the age of understanding. The proclaiming of the Message of Repentance to Israel was absolutely necessary respecting the coming of the Messiah.

Due to the significance of this task and, above all, the Introduction of the Messiah, there was an unusual or even a singular help given, which had never been afforded to another.

HE DEPARTED TO HIS OWN HOUSE

"And it came to pass, that, as soon as the days of his ministration were accomplished, he departed to his own house" (Lk. 1:23).

The phrase, *"And it came to pass,"* referred to the conclusion of the week of his duties.

"That, as soon as the days of his ministration were accomplished," proclaims his faithfulness to his task.

I wonder what his fellow Priests thought of his inability to speak. More so yet, did he relate by writing that he had seen and spoken with the Angel Gabriel, or did he keep it to himself?

I think it is obvious that the news spread that he had had a Vision, but I doubt that he related very much as to the particulars of the Vision. He would want to wait and tell his wife first of all!

"He departed to his own house," would have indicated a time of unparalleled joy. What a message he would have for Elisabeth!

That which they had sought for so long, even giving up hope, was now about to happen despite their advanced age. What a joyful moment between these two that must have been when he related by writing (Vs. 63) that which the Angel had spoken unto him.

CONCEPTION

"And after those days his wife Elisabeth conceived, and hid herself five months, saying" (Lk. 1:24).

Elisabeth's conception proclaims this coming to pass exactly as the Angel Gabriel had foretold. There is no way of knowing how old she was, just *"well stricken in years."*

However, the Lord would renew her youth in order that this Miracle child would be brought into the world. As the Lord through Abraham and Sarah brought forth the Miracle child Isaac, who would begin the family through which the Messiah would come, likewise, the Lord brings forth another Miracle child to announce that He has come (Jn. 1:29).

The phrase, *"And hid herself five months, saying,"* proclaims her fully realizing the magnitude of this moment.

Every indication is that she hid herself in order to seek the Face of the Lord regarding how this child was to be raised and how it should be trained.

THE REPROACH IS TAKEN AWAY

"Thus hath the Lord dealt with me in the days wherein He looked on me, to take away my reproach among men" (Lk. 1:25).

"Thus hath the Lord dealt with me in the days wherein He looked on me," proclaims the Lord spelling out to Elisabeth during this five months who her son would be and what he would do. Her task was very special, and every indication is that she carried it out exactly as the Lord demanded of her.

The phrase, *"To take away my reproach among men,"* proclaims her gratitude to the Lord, not only for doing this thing, but for making her the most blessed mother in the world, other than the Virgin Mary, and for all time.

Every indication is that in noting her barrenness, her neighbors had long since concluded that it was a Judgment from God. How so wrong they were! As previously stated, this situation had been brought about not because of sin or wrongdoing in the lives of her and her husband, but rather because of right doing. The Holy Spirit said of them, *"And they were both Righteous before God"* (Vs. 6).

THE ANGEL GABRIEL

"And in the sixth month the Angel Gabriel was sent from God unto a city of Galilee, named Nazareth" (Lk. 1:26).

"And in the sixth month," refers to six months after Elisabeth had conceived; consequently, John was six months older than Jesus.

Matthew alludes to the Birth of Jesus, but only Luke gives us the announcement of that Birth as well as details concerning the actual event. More than likely, these details were provided to either Luke or Paul, or both, by Mary personally.

Other than the account given by Luke, fantastic stories have arisen concerning Mary, mostly fostered and nurtured by the Catholic church. However, these are utterly unknown to Scripture and should be ignored. It is wrong to be wise beyond what is written in the Word of God.

"The Angel Gabriel was sent from God," concerns the announcement of the greatest event in human history, the coming Birth of the Redeemer of man, the Lord Jesus Christ.

This is the Story of the Incarnation as prophesied by Isaiah (Isa. 7:14; 9:6-7).

GALILEE

Under Roman domination, Israel was divided into Judaea, Samaria, Peraea, and Galilee. Galilee comprised the territory of the Tribes of Zebulun, Naphtali, and Asher. Josephus, the Jewish historian, tells us that this area was rich and populous and covered with flourishing towns. Nazareth is some 24 miles east of the Sea of Galilee.

It is said that at this time or, at least, a little later, a Roman garrison was located near Nazareth, which, among other things, caused strict Jews to hold the place in scorn (Jn. 1:46).

So, it was at this place, ridiculed and despised, which God would choose for the upbringing of His Son. However, the Glory of Jesus Christ easily erased that stigma and has given this little town a fame unlike any other place in the world.

A VIRGIN

"To a virgin espoused to a man whose name was Joseph, of the house of David; and the virgin's name was Mary" (Lk. 1:27).

The words, *"To a virgin,"* in the Greek Text, is *"parthenos,"* which refers to a pure virgin who has never known a man and never experienced marriage relationship (Mat. 1:23; 25:1, 7, 11; Lk. 1:27; 2:36; Acts 21:9; I Cor. 7:25, 28, 34, 36-37; II Cor. 11:2; Rev. 14:4). In Mary's case, it is plainly stated that she had never known a man (Vs. 34), and so, no one has a right to question the Virgin Birth.

In the Hebrew, the word is *"Ha-alma,"* which means,

"The virgin — the only one who ever was, or ever will be a mother in this way."

Some have contended that these original words, especially the Hebrew Text, simply mean any young woman, but this is blatantly untrue! It means only one who is a pure and undefiled virgin — any maid who has never known man.

JOSEPH, OF THE HOUSE OF DAVID

The phrase, *"Espoused (engaged) to a man whose name was Joseph, of the house of David,"* proclaims Joseph being in the direct lineage of David through Solomon.

Actually, Mary was of the house of David, as well, but through another of David's sons, Nathan. If the Davidic throne had continued, Joseph would now be the king of Judah.

As recorded by Matthew, Joseph, at first, had difficulty accepting Mary's story concerning her conception but was given a dream by the Lord which clarified the situation (Mat. 1:18-25). Luke does not mention this situation.

AND THE VIRGIN'S NAME WAS MARY

The phrase, *"And the virgin's name was Mary,"* is proclaimed in Luke, Chapter 1, and, as stated, to also be of the house of David. Mary was a cousin of Elisabeth, the mother of John the Baptist (Vs. 36). It is said that her mother's name was Anne. It is also said that she surpassed the maidens of her own age in wisdom and that there were many young men who sought her hand in marriage.

Scholars say that the absence of any mention of her parents in the Gospels suggests the thought that she was an orphan, and the whole narrative of the nativity presupposes poverty. The name, *"Mary,"* is the same as *"Miriam" or "Marah."* Unfortunately, Mary's name has been supplied because of the unscriptural devotion and even worship given to her by Catholicism.

This has exacerbated greatly in the last few years due to the influence of the late Pope John Paul II, who claimed that Mary appeared to him years ago, telling him he would be Pope.

Due to this error, and gross error it is, I think the following information concerning Catholicism and Mary would be helpful.

MARY, THE MOTHER OF GOD?

The Catholic people pray to Mary as mediatrix: *"Hail, Mary, full of Grace, the Lord is with you. Blessed are you among women and blessed is the fruit of your womb, Jesus. Holy Mary, Mother of God, pray for us sinners, now at the hour of our death. Amen."*

A former Catholic priest wrote:

"I can personally testify that the Jesus Christ I knew, loved and served as a Roman Catholic is not the same Jesus Christ I know, love and serve today. The Jesus I once knew was a wafer of bread and a cup of wine — and He had a mother called Mary who stood between Him and me. I couldn't get through to Him except through her, and He couldn't get through to me except through her.

"In other words, my religion back then was tantamount to — let's say — Buddhism or the Muslim religion. There was no difference, objectively speaking between me as a Catholic Priest and a Muslim Priest, for example."

These words are sad, yet, they describe the situation perfectly. How many times do we see bumper stickers that say: *"Can't find Jesus? Look for His Mother!"* Mary dominates every aspect of Catholic religious life. Unfortunately, this is the opposite of Biblical Christianity. In these statements, we want to look at Mary as the Catholic sees her, Mary as the mediator between Jesus Christ and man, and Mary as the Bible describes her.

MARY — AS THE CATHOLIC SEES HER

"Oh Mary, my Queen and my Mother, I give myself entirely to you. And to show my devotion to you, I consecrate to you this day, my eyes, my ears, my mouth, my heart, my whole being without reserve. Wherefore, oh, good Mother, as I am your own, keep me and guard me as your property and possession" (Prayer of Consecration to Mary as enjoined by Catholics).

Catholics feel that Mary occupies a unique and tremendously influential position as a result of her role as Christ's Human Mother. They are taught that they can safely instruct all of their problems to her. She provides, they say, the spiritual key to Salvation of the soul and to receiving miraculous answers to prayers concerning earthly problems.

Catholics are taught (although many will deny this) that Mary is to be given worship equal to God — and higher even than worship afforded the Angels and Saints. She is to be addressed as *"My Mother."* Even casual observation of Catholics reveals that both conversations and services bring forth more references to the *"Blessed Virgin"* than to the Three Persons of the Holy Trinity — God the Father, God the Son, and God the Holy Spirit. Obviously, the Catholic religion is strongly oriented toward veneration of Mary.

She is called the following:
• The Mother of Divine Grace
• Help of Christians

- Ark of the Covenant
- Queen of Angels
- Morning Star
- Health of the sick
- The Gate of Heaven

CULT OF MARY

The Catholic *"cult of Mary"* is based fundamentally on her sacred motherhood. The fourth century title bestowed upon her by that which would ultimately become the Catholic Church — Theotokos (Greek for *"bearer of God"*) — was equivalent to *"Mother of God."*

Rome evidently reasoned this way:

"Mary is the Mother of Jesus. Jesus is God. Ergo, Mary is the Mother of God."

Furthermore, Catholics state and believe that to deny honor to Mary actually is to deny the Deity of Christ. Of course, if a person accepts this, he opens a floodgate of ensuing theological absurdities that must be accepted as logical development of the original fallacy.

IS MARY THE MOTHER OF GOD?

No! Mary is not the Mother of God.

Mary was the Mother of the Human Being, Jesus. Mary served a biological function that was necessary to bring about a unique situation. The preexistent Son of God was to take on human form. As He walked the Earth (in human form), He was Very God and Very Man. His *"God"* component, if we are to use that term, had always been. As God, He had no beginning, was not formed, created, or made, but always has been, always is, and always shall be.

While Mary was essential to harbor His Developing Human Form (for nine months), she had nothing whatsoever to do with His Godhood! Mary was, therefore, the Mother of Jesus, the Man. She was not, by any stretch of the imagination, the Mother of God.

God has no mother! If one understands the Incarnation, one understands that God, while never ceasing to be God, became completely Man.

"Wherefore when He comes into the world, He said, Sacrifice and Offering You would not, but a Body have You prepared Me" (Heb. 10:5).

It was this Body that God prepared for His Son — Jesus Christ — Who would become Man.

Of necessity, He would be born into the world as are all other human beings, but with one tremendous difference, His Virgin Birth:

"Therefore the Lord Himself shall give you a sign; Behold, a virgin shall conceive, and bear a Son, and shall call His Name Immanuel" (Isa. 7:14).

This virgin was the teenage maiden called Mary. She was to bring the Son of God into the world. However, it was not God Who would be born; it was *"the Man Christ Jesus"* (I Tim. 2:5).

THE ANNUNCIATION OF JESUS

The Bible tells us that the Angel Gabriel was sent from God to a virgin named Mary.

"And the Angel came in unto her, and said, Hail, you who are highly favored, the Lord is with you: blessed are you among women" (Lk. 1:28).

Using this Passage, the Catholic church has altered the words to read:

"Hail, Mary, full of Grace." The church then interprets its own words by advancing the argument that since Mary is full of Grace, she must have been the finest in holiness of all created beings. Further, Catholic doctrine concludes that through the Grace bestowed

on her, she received from God the degree of purity and holiness necessary to be worthy of serving in the role of *"Mother of God."*

Now, let us pause to examine for a moment the *"Hail, Mary"* prayer, which is quoted in its entirety at the beginning of this dissertation. Because this prayer is based (albeit loosely) on Scripture (Lk. 1:28), it seems to Catholics to place God's Stamp of Approval on the Catholic position in regard to Mary.

The *"Hail, Mary"* begins:

"Hail, Mary, full of Grace, the Lord is with you. Blessed are you among women and blessed is the fruit of your womb, Jesus."

THE STUDY OF LANGUAGE

Language changes constantly. Word meanings change constantly. For example, a few years ago, a person who was *"gay"* was *"happy."* Today, a *"gay"* person is a *"homosexual,"* with the old definition having fallen completely out of usage.

By the same token, the word, *"Blessed,"* has, through usage, taken on two meanings. *"Blessed"* — pronounced as one syllable — describes someone who has received a blessing. When someone is blessed, he has come suddenly into money, he has been cured of all illness, etc. On the other hand, *"Blessed,"* pronounced as two syllables (bless-ed), implies a person of superior spirituality or someone who is more saintly in moral character; for example, *"That bless-ed man returned a lost wallet and wouldn't even accept a reward."*

At the time the Bible was written (and when it was translated by the King James translators), the word, *"Blessed,"* had only one meaning — referring to one who had received a blessing.

Similarly, the word, *"Grace,"* has come to have a

meaning, as well, that is not the Biblical definition. *"Grace"* — within Scripture — means a Gift from God that is undeserved. *"Grace"* is a free gift from God, with no preconditions or strings attached. However, today, *"Grace"* has come to be used to imply an inherent human quality of goodness that is closely allied to bless-ed-ness.

So, the wording of the *"Hail, Mary"* prayer, taken in the context of today's language usage, appears to give Scriptural support to Catholic contentions that Mary was eternally without sin. Turning to the actual words of Scripture, however, we receive a different picture. The Angel Gabriel's actual words were:

HIGHLY FAVOURED

"Hail, you that are highly favoured, the Lord is with you: blessed are you among women" (Lk. 1:28).

Mary was unquestionably highly favored by God in that He chose her to receive this honor. It was certainly a Blessing to be singled out to hold such a distinctive position in the history of the world. However, all the rest of the words within this prayer simply were proposed by the Catholic church and have no basis in Scripture whatsoever.

Delving further into this matter, we read where Mary's cousin Elisabeth said:

"And whence is this to me, that the Mother of my Lord should come to me?" (Lk. 1:43)

Here, Elisabeth called Jesus, *"Lord."* She was talking about the unborn Holy Child then occupying Mary's womb. He definitely is Lord. He is called *"the Lord Jesus Christ"* many times within the Word of God.

However, once again, it must be emphasized that it was not God Who was born of Mary; it was the human Child — the Lord Jesus Christ.

The unbiblical worship of Mary has its perverted foundation in the insupportable misnomer, *"Mother of God."*

The correct Scriptural description of Mary is the simple Biblical expression, *"Mary the Mother of Jesus"* (Acts 1:14).

THE IMMACULATE CONCEPTION

This erroneous (and confusing) term does not refer to the Conception of Jesus Christ as most non-Catholics and many Catholics believe. It refers to the conception of Mary in her mother's womb.

The Catholic Catechism says:

"The Blessed Virgin Mary alone, from the first instant of her conception, through the foreseen merits of Jesus Christ, by a unique privilege granted her by God, was kept free from the stain of original sin . . . from the first moment of her conception she possessed justice and holiness, even the fullness of Grace, with the infused virtues and the Gifts of the Holy Spirit."

This doctrine, a total fiction with no Scriptural support, was *"infallibly"* defined by Pope Pius IX as part of the *"Revealed deposit of Catholic Faith"* in 1854. There was great opposition to this pronouncement at the time within the Catholic church.

The doctrine of the Immaculate Conception implies that for Mary to be born without original sin, her mother also had to be a sinless virgin. The only other alternative is that God granted her a unique immunity to the all-persuasive original sin that is in an estimable element of the human condition.

To be frank, Roman Catholic theologians lamely defend their assertion of the Immaculate Conception by saying that *"God could have done it,"* or, *"It was fitting that He should do so — and therefore He did it."*

Of course, if God had decided on such a course, it would have meant that He was replacing the Plan of Salvation described in the Bible with a totally new concept. If this had happened, we would have a *"Quadrinity"* instead of the *"Trinity,"* which Pope John Paul II tried to institute.

Then, God's Word would have stated that the Godhead consists of God the Father, God the Son, God the Holy Spirit, and Mary, the Mother of God. The Bible does not so state, so we can then conclude that this aberrant and ridiculous doctrine is not of God.

THE ORIGIN OF THE STATEMENT, *"MARY, THE MOTHER OF GOD"*

The veneration of Mary and the use of the term, *"Mother of God,"* originated about 381 A.D.

It was officially decreed by the Council of Ephesus in 431 A.D.

Prayers began to be directed to Mary, as well as to the other Saints, about 600 A.D.

The Immaculate Conception of Mary, as stated, was proclaimed by Pope Pius IX in 1854 A.D.

In 1931, Pope Pius XI reaffirmed the doctrine that Mary is the *"Mother of God,"* as if an infallible statement needs to be confirmed!

In 1950, Pope Pius XII pronounced the doctrine of the *"Assumption of Mary."* This states that Mary, at the completion of her earthly life, was bodily taken up into Heaven without knowing death. Oddly enough, this mystical belief had been a peripheral precept within the Catholic church since the Middle Ages but was only given official certification in 1950.

There was a great deal of resistance to the issuance of this doctrine by Pope Pius XII, but he insisted that it was his infallible right to declare such a *"fact."*

THE BABYLONIAN CULT

Fundamentally, the worship of Mary originated with the worship of *"the Queen of Heaven"* — a pagan deity. It seems that the Roman church — in altering its doctrines to conform to those formally observed by conscripted pagans — saw that it would be politically desirable to supply the populace with a satisfying parallel figure within their newly imposed Christian religion. Thus was Mary elevated to Divine status.

The image of mother and child had been a primary object of Babylonian worship centuries before the Birth of Christ.

From Babylon, this spread to the ends of the Earth. The original mother figure in this tableau was Semiramis — the personification of unbridled lust and sexual gratification. Once we begin to study the worship practices of heathen nations, we find amazing similarities embraced over wide areas and through long periods of time.

For instance, in Egypt, the mother and child are known as Isis and Horus; in India, Isi and Iswara; in Asia, Cybele and Deoius; in pagan Rome, Fortuna and Jupiter-puer; and in Greece, Ceres with Plutus in arms. In isolated Tibet and in China and Japan, early Roman Catholic missionaries were stunned to find counterparts of the Madonna (the Italian name for the Virgin Mary) and her child being worshipped as devotedly as in Rome itself. Shing Moo (the *"Mother of China"*) is represented with child in arms and with a halo around her head — exactly as if she had been painted by a Roman Catholic painter.

These nations all trace their common worship from Babylon — before its dispersion in the days of Nimrod. Thus, worship of Mary is Babylonian in origin. There is absolutely no suggestion of such worship in Scripture.

MARY AS THE MEDIATOR BETWEEN JESUS AND MAN

Mary is looked upon by the Catholic church as an intercessor, a mediator, and a redemptress. Some Catholics say this is not a *"defined article of the faith."* Others say it is. In any case, in practice, it is part and parcel as what is known as the *"Ordinary Teaching Authority"* of the church.

These titles signify that Mary is a universal intercessor — that is, she seeks God's Favors for all mankind. They clearly imply that Mary is so intimately associated with our Redemption that she may be considered a co-Saviour with Christ, although subordinate to Him. Church doctrine further alleges that Mary *"mediates Grace universally."*

What does this mean in plain language? Incredibly, the Catholic position is that no Grace flows from God to any person without passing through the good offices of Mary!

Some church leaders state that doctrines concerning Mary were modified and tempered by the Second Vatican Council of 1962-1965. However, this is what Catholic priest Anthony Wilhelm stated in his book, "Christ Among Us: A Modern Presentation of the Catholic Faith for Adults":

EXAMPLES

On page 90:
"God the Son became a Man through Mary, His human mother, whom we call the Mother of God. We can say that God has relatives, that God has a Mother."
Page 91:
"The 'Hail, Mary' is one of the most ancient prayers of the Church . . . 'Hail Mary, full of Grace.'
"By these privileges, which God gave to Mary, we

can see that He always prepares people for their roles in His Plan."

On page 367:

"We particularly honor Mary the Mother of Christ, because of her great role in God's Plan of Salvation. She was closer to Christ than anyone else."

On page 368:

"Mary is God's masterpiece. To honor her is to honor God, Who made her what she is.

"Because of Mary's great role she was conceived without sin, remained sinless throughout life, and was perpetually a virgin.

"We believe in Mary's Assumption, that she was taken into Heaven, body and soul, at the end of her earthly life."

On page 369:

"We give special place to Mary's intercession and sometimes consider her to be 'spiritual mother.'"

On page 370:

"Mary is the model Christian, the preeminent member of the Church."

On page 371:

"Mary is particularly the model of our worship.

"The devotion of the rosary has been a tremendous influence in helping hundreds of millions to pray."

MARY AND SALVATION?

The Roman cult of Mary erects a barrier between the individual and the Lord. It confuses the Catholic believer's perception of the Work and Functions of the individual members of the Godhead. It robs Christ of His Unique Creatorship.

Rome's theologians insist that Mary's role and function is to lead souls to Christ; however, Jesus said:

"... That which is born of the Spirit is spirit ... so is everyone who is born of the Spirit" (Jn. 3:6-8).

He further stated:

"... No man can come to Me, except the Father which has sent Me draw him ..." (Jn. 6:44).

So, according to the Bible, Mary has no role to play in the Salvation of a soul.

I go back once again to our quote from a former Catholic priest:

"The Jesus I once knew was a wafer of bread and a cup of wine; He had a Mother called Mary who stood between Him and me ..."

Does his statement sound like he was *"led to Christ by Mary"?*

DO CATHOLICS WORSHIP MARY?

In scores of letters we have received, Catholics maintain that they do not worship Mary, that she only aids them in their worship of God.

However, when the Catholic attributes the Immaculate Conception to Mary, they are conferring Divinity upon her by this claim. The term, *"Worship,"* as defined by Webster's New Collegiate Dictionary, is *"reverence paid to a Divine Being and extravagant respect or admiration for, or devotion to, an object of esteem."* In ascribing the Immaculate Conception to Mary, the Catholic church has, in effect, declared her Divine and thus renders her worship that should be reserved only to Deity. By their constant reference to her, worship is afforded.

Yes, Catholics do worship Mary. To be tragically concise, most Catholics do not understand the worship of God the Father, or of His Son, Jesus Christ.

The real focus and conception of their worship is directed to Mary. Of course, their perception of worshipping God is the worship of God through Mary. Everything must go through Mary to God — and everything must come from God through Mary.

MARY AS THE BIBLE DESCRIBES HER

To be brutally frank, considering the Catholic position, there is very little mention of Mary within the Word of God, at least, as the Catholics have given her place and position not really afforded in the Word.

MATTHEW

In Matthew, Chapter 2, we read of Mary's witnessing the adoration of the wise men.

This Chapter also recounts the events leading to the trip to Egypt.

Then, it gives the account of an experience from the Childhood of Jesus and describes Mary's concern.

MARK

Mary is mentioned only briefly in this Gospel.

She is mentioned once as simply the Mother of the Carpenter Jesus (Mk. 6:3), and again, as a family member (Mk. 3:32).

LUKE

Luke, Chapter 1, describes the visit of the Angel Gabriel to Mary. The same Chapter tells of Mary's visit to Elisabeth.

We can conclude from the statements made by Mary that she had wide-ranging knowledge of the Old Testament — which is a commentary on her spiritual perceptions.

Luke, Chapter 2, describes Mary as giving birth to the Lord Jesus Christ in a stable. She also pondered here the words of the shepherds, as well as the incident when Jesus was 12.

JOHN

In John, Chapter 2, Mary asked Jesus to perform His First Public Miracle at Cana. (Obviously, because of the confidence with which she approached the situation, she knew, or at least suspicioned, something of His Place and Position.) Oddly enough, in Mark, Chapter 3, Matthew, Chapter 12, and Luke, Chapter 8, it seems that she, however, may have harbored some confusion about His Mission.

John, Chapter 19, talks about how Mary stood at the foot of the Cross and observed with great sorrow the Death of her Son — her Saviour and our Saviour — the Lord Jesus Christ.

ACTS

According to Acts 1:14, Mary was numbered among the 120 who tarried in the Upper Room, waiting for the enduement of Power, which would come on the Day of Pentecost. She, like other Believers, needed the infilling of the Holy Spirit as Power for service.

This is all the Bible reveals about Mary. Incidentally, in the Gospels, Jesus never did call her *"mother."* He addressed her as *"woman."* However, going back to the ancient Hebrew, this was not an expression of disrespect as we might think of such presently.

WHAT THE BIBLE ACTUALLY SAYS

When the Angel Gabriel appeared to Mary, as described in Luke, Chapter 1, he used the word, *"Hail."* This simply means, *"Hello,"* or *"All joy,"* a salutation used to get a person's attention. He also used the phrase, *"Highly favored,"* which means, *"Blessed,"* or, *"Endued with Grace."* As discussed earlier, these terms do not imply anything other than the person has received an unmerited favor.

Mary was highly favored.

No doubt, hundreds of thousands (or even millions) of pious, young Israelite maidens had aspired to be the one so highly favored. They had known from ancient Prophecies that the *"Seed,"* the *"Redeemer,"* would be born to a Hebrew maiden.

From Isaiah's Prophecy, they further knew that she had to be a virgin.

"Therefore the Lord Himself shall give you a sign; Behold, a virgin shall conceive, and bear a Son, and shall call His Name Immanuel" (Isa. 7:14).

More importantly, the lineage had to come from the Tribe of Judah and through David. Matthew gave the genealogy in the royal line through Solomon.

In Luke, the royal line was given through Nathan, another son, through Heli, the father of Mary. Both lines were necessary in fulfilling Prophecy.

God had cursed Jeconiah of the royal line and had sworn that no seed of his should ever sit on the throne of David and reign in Jerusalem (Jer. 22:24-30).

DAVID THROUGH SOLOMON

God had also sworn to David that his line (through Solomon) would forever sit on his throne (II Sam., Chpt. 7). The only way this could be fulfilled was for Jesus, the Son of David (through Nathan and Mary), to become Legal Heir to the throne of David through His Stepfather, Joseph, of the kingly line (Lk. 1:32-33).

Jesus, as the Foster Son of Joseph and the Firstborn of His Family, became the Legal Heir to David's throne through Joseph.

However, it must be remembered, the royal line in Matthew was given through Solomon, which culminated in Joseph. The royal line in Luke was given through Nathan, culminating in the father of Mary, who was Heli.

So, Mary, in the royal lineage through Nathan, David's son, became the Mother of the Lord Jesus Christ.

Yes, Mary was highly favored!

Certainly, it could be said that the Lord was with her and she would be blessed among many.

HANDMAIDEN OF THE LORD

Mary called herself *"... the Handmaid of the Lord"* (Lk. 1:38).

This shows the beautiful humility characterized by Mary and is a statement that might well be studied by Catholic theologians.

However, there is a tremendous difference between *"the Handmaid of the Lord"* and *"Mother of God."*

By her own words, Mary refuted the Catholic doctrine of the Immaculate Conception:

She said, *"And my spirit has rejoiced in God my Saviour"* (Lk. 1:47).

This statement totally discounts the theory of an Immaculate Conception and the Catholic contention that Mary was ever without sin.

If God was her Saviour, which she readily admits, then she must have needed Salvation, which presupposes some history of normal human sin. No Scripture even hints that Mary was sinless.

This false cult of Mary-worship is another effort by Satan, who knows that one cannot completely accept Christ as long as one retains a radical concept of Mary.

Incidentally, Luke's statement in 1:28 quotes Gabriel's words as being, *"Blessed are you among women."* It does not say, *"Blessed are you above women."*

ACCORDING TO THE BIBLE, IS MARY AN
INTERCESSOR AND A MEDIATRIX?

No!

Jesus Alone fits that role.

"Wherefore He is able also to save them to the uttermost who come unto God by Him, seeing He ever lives to make Intercession for them" (Heb. 7:25).

Jesus Christ is our Only Intercessor, at least, in this manner. There is no hint or suggestion in the Word of God that Mary should or would occupy such a role.

Whenever Mary is inserted into the role of intercessor, as she is by the Catholic church, to intercede with her son, Jesus Christ, on behalf of individuals on Earth, this, in effect, robs Christ of the rightful position He earned through His Tremendous Sacrifice at Calvary. He paid the full price on the Cross with the shedding of His Precious Blood. It is precious because it was sinless.

Christ Alone is worthy to make Intercession for us. Christ Alone paid the price. Mary did not suffer and die on the Cross. She did not shed her blood. Neither does Christ need an assistant to motivate Him to intercede for the Saints. He is perfectly capable of performing this duty Himself, as He ever sits at the Right Hand of God making Intercession for us.

HOW IS THIS INTERCESSION BY CHRIST MADE?

In fact, Christ has to do nothing in order for Intercession to be made. His being seated by the Right Hand of the Father states that His Sacrifice has been accepted. Now, without Him saying or doing anything, His very Presence guarantees Intercession on behalf of the Saints.

"... It is Christ Who died, yea rather, Who is risen

again, Who is even at the Right Hand of God, Who also makes Intercession for us" (Rom. 8:34).

We blaspheme when we imply that Jesus Christ would not satisfactorily accomplish His Eternal Work without permission from His Earthly Mother.

We blaspheme when we add to the Word of God.

"For there is one God, and one Mediator between God and men, the Man Christ Jesus;

"Who gave Himself a ransom for all ..." (I Tim. 2:5-6).

This states boldly that there is One God. We then are told further, in equally clear terms, that there is one Mediator between God and man.

Please note that fact well.

There are not two mediators, not three or four, just One! Then, if there is any confusion, the identity of the One Mediator is revealed:

"For there is one God, and one Mediator between God and men, the Man Christ Jesus; Who gave Himself a ransom for all ..." (I Tim. 2:5-6).

Obviously, we blaspheme when we intrude Mary (or anyone else) into a mediatory role that is distinctively that of the Lord Jesus Christ Alone. Once again, there is no hint or suggestion in Scripture that any such role has ever been considered for her by God.

THE ROMAN CATHOLIC POSITION

The Roman Catholic position is that God the Father and His Son, Jesus Christ, are unreachable through normal human efforts.

By extension, they then propose that since Christ's Mother is available, petitions delivered by her will not be ignored.

Who would turn away his own mother if she came seeking a minor favor?

Thus, in Catholic tradition, when a person goes

through the mother, he gets through more quickly and more surely.

No doubt, Jesus will look with more favor on her request than on any delivered directly, hence, these bumper stickers, *"Can't find Jesus? Look for His Mother!"*

Such statements totally misinterpret the Person of God and the Incarnation, Redemption, and Plan of God for the human race.

The Apostle Paul said it well:

"Now the Spirit speaks expressly, that in the latter times some shall depart from the Faith, giving heed to seducing spirits, and doctrines of devils;

"Speaking lies in hypocrisy; having their conscience seared with a hot iron;

"Forbidding to marry, and commanding to abstain from meats, which God has created to be received with thanksgiving of them which believe and know the Truth" (I Tim. 4:1-3).

In all the Early Church, no statement is reported of an Apostle referring to Mary as the *"Mother of God."* There is no hint of prayers being offered to her or admonitions given to the Saints to honor her beyond what the Bible suggests as normal deference.

Surely, if this great fabrication were valid, we would have at least a word from the Early Church concerning Mary.

The silence is deafening!

THE ANGEL

"And the Angel came in unto her, and said, Hail, you who are highly favored, the Lord is with you: blessed are you among women" (Lk. 1:28).

The phrase, *"And the Angel came in unto her, and said,"* presents to date the greatest moment in human history, the announcement of the coming Birth of the Lord of Glory in the Incarnation.

The phrase, *"Hail, you who are highly favored,"* means, *"Much engraced,"* which signals what God freely does for an individual, in this case, Mary (Eph. 1:6).

It is not *"full of Grace,"* as so fitted to bestow it upon others, as the Catholic church teaches, but one who, herself meritless, had received signal Grace from God.

The phrase, *"The Lord is with you,"* signals her position of humility.

The phrase, *"Blessed are you among women,"* as stated, did not say, *"Above women."* Out of the countless women born into the world, she was chosen to be the Mother of the Lord.

God, not Mary, was full of Grace.

WHAT IS THIS?

"And when she saw him, she was troubled at his saying, and cast in her mind what manner of salutation this should be" (Lk. 1:29).

The phrase, *"And when she saw him, she was troubled at his saying,"* means it was a total disturbance and not a partial or light agitation.

The indication is twofold in that his glorious appearance and, as well, the manner in which he addressed her startled her.

"And cast in her mind what manner of salutation this should be," means that she in no way understood the reason that he addressed her as he did!

It seems that her reaction to the actual announcement, which was unique in the annals of human history, was of far less degree even than her reaction to the *"salutation."*

Such, I think, shows tremendous consecration and Faith in God.

FAVOR WITH GOD

"And the Angel said unto her, Fear not, Mary: for you have found favor with God" (Lk. 1:30).

The phrase, *"And the Angel said unto her, Fear not, Mary,"* proclaims basically the same words said to Zechariah.

"For you have found favor with God," should have been translated, *"You have received Grace from God."* The sweetness and plentitude of the Grace was not in Mary but in God. She was the unworthy object of that Grace.

Grace is simply the Goodness of God which translates into favor to the unworthy; patience is favor to the obstinate; Mercy is favor to the miserable; and pity is favor to the poor.

CALL HIS NAME JESUS

"And, behold, you shall conceive in your womb, and bring forth a Son, and shall call His Name JESUS" (Lk. 1:31).

According to the Greek tense, the phrase, *"And, behold, you shall conceive in your womb,"* should have been translated, *"You shall forthwith conceive in your womb,"* meaning immediately!

There is a tradition that says this announcement was made to Mary on December 25th, and on that day, the Lord was conceived (not born). The same tradition says that He was born on September 29th; however, such is speculation!

Nevertheless, it is almost certain that December 25th was not the Day of His Birth, due to the fact that when

He was actually born, shepherds were in the field with their sheep overnight, which probably would not have been the case on December 25th (Lk. 2:8).

"And bring forth a Son," proclaimed the Incarnation, *"God manifest in the flesh, God with us, Immanuel."*

Approximately 800 years before, Isaiah had prophesied, *"For unto us a Child is born, unto us a Son is given ..."* (Isa. 9:6).

"And shall call His Name JESUS," portrays the Greek version of the Hebrew *"Johoshua,"* or the shortened *"Joshua."* It means *"Saviour,"* or, *"The Salvation of Jehovah."*

So, as the Angel Gabriel told Zechariah to name his son John, which means, *"God gives Grace,"* now the same Angel tells Mary what to name her Son. In effect, He is the Promised Grace (Jn. 1:17).

THE THRONE OF DAVID

"He shall be great, and shall be called the Son of the Highest: and the Lord God shall give unto Him the throne of His Father David" (Lk. 1:32).

Jesus being called the Son of the Highest actually means, *"The Most High,"* and refers to *"Jehovah!"*

It is ironic that this title given by the Angel to the yet unborn Child was the same title given to the Redeemer by the evil spirit in the case of the maniac of Gadara (Mk. 5:7). He was the Son of God, and, consequently, demons knew Him, but the religious leaders of Israel did not know Him.

"And the Lord God shall give unto Him the throne of His Father David," places Mary in the royal lineage as suggested in Luke 3:23.

This would be the fulfillment of that which was given to David by the Lord in II Samuel, Chapter 7. The Holy Spirit would refer to Jesus through the Apostle Paul as *"the Last Adam"* (I Cor. 15:45).

OF HIS KINGDOM THERE SHALL BE NO END

"And He shall reign over the house of Jacob forever; and of His Kingdom there shall be no end" (Lk. 1:33).

"And He shall reign over the house of Jacob forever," speaks of Israel. As of yet, this has not come to pass but most surely shall! This *"reign"* will begin at the Second Coming and will continue not only throughout the Kingdom Age but, as well, as the Scripture says, *"Forever."* At His First Advent, they would not own Him, but at His Second Advent, Israel will gladly own Him because He will then be their Only Hope, as He has always been their Only Hope.

"And of His Kingdom there shall be no end," speaks of His Rule and Reign.

Man has ever attempted to rebuild the Garden of Eden without the Tree of Life, i.e., the Lord Jesus Christ. Man has ever failed, as fail he must! Only when Jesus rules and reigns will the terrible problems which beset humanity be solved and eliminated. When the *"Prince of Peace"* comes back, all war will forever end (Isa. 2:4). This *"Kingdom"* will be of *"Judgment and with justice,"* which the world has never had before (Isa. 9:7).

When He *"reigns,"* which He will do Personally, there will never be the danger of this government being overthrown. It will be, as stated, *"forever."*

Even though Gabriel was speaking primarily of the fulfillment and totality of that Kingdom, which will be spiritual, physical, and material, still, the Spiritual Kingdom has already come to the hearts and lives of millions. It is the *"Kingdom of God,"* and it is centered in Jesus, this *"Son of the Highest."*

Four angelic statements about the Wondrous Child are made in Verses 32 and 33 in the First Chapter of

Luke, and correspond to the Four Gospels.

HOW SHALL THIS BE?

"Then said Mary unto the Angel, How shall this be, seeing I know not a man?" (Lk. 1:34)

Mary exhibited far more incredulity over the salutation than she did the actual announcement. There seems to be no unbelief whatsoever. She seems to ask the question, *"How shall this be, seeing I know not a man?"* only to inquire about the method. I think the conclusion must be reached that this young lady, who was probably only about 16 or 17 years old at the time, was greatly consecrated to the Lord. Beginning with Luke 1:46, the worship exhibited portrays a spiritual depth far beyond her years.

I realize that many would argue that the worship portrayed in Verses 46 through 55 pertain to inspiration and, therefore, are not indicative of spiritual depth; however, that is only partly true.

In an expression of this nature, the Holy Spirit seldom takes one beyond one's spiritual maturity. So, even though her words were definitely inspired, still, they portray an excellence in the knowledge of the Word which is extremely rare.

Considering the statement made in these Verses, it is almost certain that Mary was very much aware of the Prophecy of Isaiah, *"Therefore the Lord Himself shall give you a sign; Behold a virgin shall conceive, and bear a Son, and shall call His Name Immanuel"* (Isa. 7:14).

THE KINGLY LINE OF DAVID

Mary knew she was of the kingly line of David through his son Nathan and that her betrothed, Joseph, was in the kingly line through Solomon.

Actually, most every person in Israel knew their lineage all the way back to the sons of Jacob and, consequently, to Abraham.

As well, all knew from the Prophecies (Gen. 49:10; II Sam., Chpt. 7), that it was through the Tribe of Judah that the Messiah would come.

So, when the Angel Gabriel made this great announcement, I personally do not think it was a great surprise to Mary.

The religious leaders of Israel had all this information, even the approximate time the Messiah was to come, according to the Prophecies of Daniel (Dan. 9:25-26). Consequently, they should have been ready and waiting for His Appearance.

However, they were not ready primarily because of their acute self-righteousness.

Likewise, the modern church should not be asleep concerning the near future. The Bible is very clear as to what is going to happen. And yet, the church, with some little exception, meanders in every direction, almost without purpose. The reason then is the reason now. There was very little true consecration to God then, as there is very little true consecration now!

Consequently, there was very little study of the Word then, and very little now.

Many, if not most, study the Word of God only to promote some erroneous doctrine.

Again, we say it, *"The religious leaders of Israel did not know, but this little teenage girl by the name of Mary knew!"*

THE HOLY SPIRIT

"And the Angel answered and said unto her, The Holy Spirit shall come upon you, and the Power of the Highest shall overshadow you: therefore also that Holy

Thing which shall be born of you shall be called the Son of God" (Lk. 1:35).

The phrase, *"And the Angel answered and said unto her,"* pertains to her question, as is obvious.

"The Holy Spirit shall come upon you," has the same connotation as Genesis 1:2, *"... And the Spirit of God moved upon the face of the waters."*

"And the Power of the Highest shall overshadow you," has the same reference as, *"And God said, Let there be light: and there was light"* (Gen. 1:3).

In other words, God simply spoke the Word, and it was done.

He spoke the conception into existence exactly as He spoke light into existence. It very well could have happened, and, no doubt, did, even as the Angel was speaking to her.

THE SON OF GOD

The phrase, *"Therefore also that Holy Thing which shall be born of you shall be called the Son of God,"* constitutes the Incarnation, *"God becoming Man."* Consequently, He would be Very God and Very Man. In other words, he was Fully God and Fully Man.

Many people misunderstand the Incarnation, thinking that Jesus was half God and half Man, etc.

The manner in which this was carried out portrays Him laying aside the expression of His Deity while never losing possession of His Deity. It is called the *"kenosis"* or *"self-emptying of Christ"* (Phil. 2:5-11).

The loss of the expression of His Deity was so complete, with His Humanity so obvious, that His Fellow Townspeople in Nazareth simply thought it absurd that He could be the Messiah (Mk. 6:1-5). They called Him the *"Carpenter, the Son of Mary,"* while the Angel Gabriel called Him, *"The Son of God!"*

ELISABETH

"And, behold, your cousin Elisabeth, she has also conceived a son in her old age: and this is the sixth month with her, who was called barren" (Lk. 1:36).

The phrase, *"And, behold, your cousin Elisabeth,"* concerned her Miracle, which it seems that Mary fully knew about.

However, the word, *"Cousin,"* in the Greek Text, is *"suggenes,"* which means, *"Countrymen,"* and not necessarily a cousin in the sense of a blood relative. Elisabeth was of the Tribe of Levi, which is clear from Verse 5, while both Joseph and Mary were from the Tribe of Judah through David (Lk. 1:27). However, it is certainly not impossible that Elisabeth was literally the *"blood cousin"* of Mary in that intermarriage between individuals of particular Tribes was done at times, if not common. As well, it is highly doubtful that she would have gone to the house of Elisabeth and stayed the period of time which she did unless she was very close to Elisabeth. This probably meant that she was her literal cousin.

The phrase, *"She has also conceived a son in her old age: and this is the sixth month with her, who was called barren,"* no doubt, encourages the Faith of Mary, that is, if such needed encouraging.

It is interesting that Gabriel mentions the fact that Elisabeth had been *"barren."* According to the next Verse, it was said in order to proclaim the Power of God, which knows no limitations.

FOR WITH GOD NOTHING SHALL BE IMPOSSIBLE

This great word given by the Angel Gabriel, *"For with God nothing shall be impossible,"* was given for many and varied reasons but, most of all, that Mary would know what is impossible with man is very much possible with God. In fact, God being Almighty, this means that there is nothing that is impossible with Him. What a Mighty God we serve!

The word, *"Impossible,"* in this instance, means that which is weak and unable to carry out that which is known to be right. God is not limited by such weakness. He is Omnipotent, that is, all-powerful, and, consequently, able to do anything He says He will do.

Unfortunately, modern religious man has limited God through unbelief to such an extent that most of that which is referred to as *"Christianity"* is little more than an empty philosophy; *"The days of Miracles are over," "It passed away with the Apostles," "It is not for this Dispensation,"* ad infinitum.

There is not one hint in the Bible that God would cease the activity of Miracles. He is a Miracle-working God, has always been, and always shall be!

However, I feel that many honest hearts have been turned off by modern claims of miracles, which have not, in fact, happened! To be sure, the Lord does not need, want, or desire false glory. Claiming He has done something when, in reality, nothing has been done is just as bad, if not worse, than the denial of His Power. Much of that which claims to be miracles presently but, in reality, aren't, are only an effort to boost self in order to make people believe that certain individuals have great power with God, etc. These false claims, which seem to be abundant in certain circles, must be extremely grievous to the Lord.

However, despite false claims or denial of His Power, *"He abides faithful"* (II Tim. 2:13).

THE HANDMAID OF THE LORD

"And Mary said, Behold the Handmaid of the Lord;

be it unto me according to your word. And the Angel departed from her" (Lk. 1:38).

The phrase, *"And Mary said, Behold the Handmaid of the Lord,"* beautifully portrays the humility of this young lady. Having referred to herself in such a manner, I think she would be greatly grieved at the unscriptural manner in which Catholicism has elevated her — even to the place of Deity.

"Be it unto me according to your word," constitutes an amazing statement. She did not question the Angel, and neither did she register unbelief in any manner. Spence said, *"She gives this consent in a word that was simple and sublime, which involved the most extraordinary act of Faith that a woman ever consented to accomplish."*

As I have previously stated, I personally feel this did not come entirely as a shock to her. And yet, she stands almost alone in her Faith — a Faith, we might quickly add, which will soon be severely tested.

THE ANGEL

"And the Angel departed from her," constitutes the conclusion, at least, to date, of the greatest event in human history, the announcement of the coming Birth of the Redeemer.

And yet, mighty Rome, which ruled the world at that time, would have given this announcement no credence at all, or, if they had known it, they would not even have believed it. The world at present has little or no record of what was taking place at that particular time regarding Rome and its vast worldwide interests, but it knows word for word what the Angel Gabriel spoke to Mary. Within itself, this should be a lesson to all. Even though certain things of this world are necessary, still, it is the things of the Lord which are eternal, and nothing else!

THE ENGAGEMENT TO JOSEPH

"Now the Birth of Jesus Christ was on this wise: When as His Mother Mary was espoused to Joseph, before they came together, she was found with Child of the Holy Spirit" (Mat. 1:18).

The word, *"Now,"* would have probably been better translated, *"But,"* in order to mark the contrast between His Birth and every other birth down through time, for they were by natural procreation, but His, by spiritual procuration.

The phrase, *"Now the Birth of Jesus Christ was on this wise,"* expresses the Incarnation, for God had to become Man, as here described, in order to redeem fallen man.

"When as His Mother Mary was espoused to Joseph," was actually an engagement, signified by a legal document, which specified a particular period of time between the espousal and actual marriage relationship (Gen. 29:18; Deut., Chpt. 20).

Consequently, Mary and Joseph were only engaged and had not yet come together as man and wife, i.e., no sexual relations.

"Before they came together," has to do with Joseph and Mary consummating the marriage, which included sexual relations, which, as stated, they had not done at this time. Mary was probably about 16 or 17 years old at the time and, as prophesied by Isaiah, was a *"virgin"* (Isa. 7:14).

WHO WAS FOUND WITH CHILD OF THE HOLY SPIRIT

The statement, *"She was found with Child of the Holy Spirit,"* merely refers to the truth that the Child was by Divine origin.

The phrase does not refer to any type of physical act,

but rather a spiritual act. It has the same connotation as Genesis 1:2, *"And the Spirit of God moved upon the face of the waters."* This, as the conception of Mary, was a spiritual act with a physical result.

The word, *"Virgin,"* as given by Isaiah, and to which we have already addressed ourselves, is in the Hebrew, *"Ha-alma,"* and means, *"The virgin — the only one who ever was, or ever will be a mother in this way."*

Some would attempt to argue that the word, *"Alma,"* could mean a young married woman, but this is not supported in any Scripture. Mary was a pure virgin who had not known man and who conceived by the Holy Spirit.

In view of the plain record of this, it only shows unbelief and rebellion against God's Word and the Perfect Plan of Redemption through a Virgin-Born Man — God manifest in the flesh — if we accept anything but what is plainly declared in Scripture (Lk. 1:30-38; Jn. 1:1-14; Rom. 8:3; Gal. 4:4; I Tim. 3:16; Heb. 1:5-7; 2:6-18).

ORIGINAL SIN

If Jesus had been conceived by the normal manner of husband and wife coming together, He would have been born in sin just as all the sons of Adam had been born in sin. As a consequence, He would have needed Redemption, as all others, and could in no way have served as the Perfect Sacrifice, which, in truth, He was. Due to the Fall, the seed of man was corrupted and, therefore, could not bring any *"sons of God"* into the world, as the Lord originally intended, but only *"sons of Adam,"* i.e., *"in the likeness of Adam"* (Gen. 5:3).

However, as Mary was not impregnated by man, but rather by the Holy Spirit as He decreed her conception, the terrible taint of sin did not pass on to Christ.

Mary's conception was much the same, at least,

as far as the act was concerned, as the account in Genesis, *"And God said, Let there be light: and there was light."* As it regards Mary, the Holy Spirit simply said, *"Let there be ... and there was ..."* (Gen. 1:3).

All serious Bible students read these words, *"Before they came together, she was found with Child of the Holy Spirit,"* with wonder, awe, and tremendous reverence. However, this was a stigma that Mary would live with all of her life in that the Enemies of Christ would ever claim that Jesus was conceived out of wedlock, and by a drunken Roman soldier, at that, and, consequently, was a *"bastard."*

John records the words that His Enemies threw at Him, *"Then said they to Him, We be not born of fornication ..."* (Jn. 8:41).

Among other things, they were implying that He was born of fornication and, as such, was illegitimate! In truth, His Birth was the only legitimate birth that ever was.

Immediately after the Fall in the Garden of Eden, the Lord said to Satan, *"And I will put enmity between you and the woman, and between your seed and her Seed; it shall bruise your head, and you shall bruise His Heel"* (Gen. 3:15).

If one is to notice, the Lord referred to *"the Seed of the woman,"* and not the seed of man. In effect, the woman has no *"seed,"* except in this one case, where it refers to the Birth of the Messiah, the Son of God.

JOSEPH

"Then Joseph her husband, being a just man, not willing to make her a public example, was minded to put her away privily" (Mat. 1:19).

The phrase, *"Then Joseph her husband, being a just man,"* is a statement by the Holy Spirit that refers to the consecration of Joseph by referring to him as a *"just man,"* i.e., *"a righteous man."* This implies that *"Joseph"* was a true son of David and desired in every respect to obey the Law.

In these words, *"Then Joseph her husband,"* we find that the engagement to be married in those times was of far greater weight than the present. Even though the actual wedding had not yet taken place, and they had not come together, still, because of the engagement, they were looked at as *"man and wife."* That's the way it was in those days.

Even though it is unsaid, one can well imagine the heartache that Joseph went through when Mary informed him of her condition.

To be frank, unless the Lord had appeared to him in a dream, as the next Verse proclaims, Joseph would not have believed Mary's story. Would you?

Before we criticize him for such an action, we must realize that Mary was relating something to him that had never happened in human history. To be sure, he had known her all her life and, no doubt, had observed a flawless, spotless life, at least, in these matters; therefore, he must have been totally without understanding. Knowing her, he could not conceive that she had been unfaithful.

But yet, he could not, as well, believe the story of her pregnancy as she related how the Angel *"Gabriel"* came to her and said, *"And, behold, you shall conceive in your womb, and bring forth a Son, and shall call His Name JESUS.*

"He shall be great, and shall be called the Son of the Highest: and the Lord God shall give unto Him the throne of His Father David:

"And He shall reign over the house of Jacob forever;

and of His Kingdom there shall be no end" (Lk. 1:32-33).

THE REACTION OF JOSEPH

Then, no doubt, Mary told Joseph that she answered the Angel by saying, *"How shall this be, seeing I know not a man?"*

She then further related to Joseph, *"And the Angel answered and said unto me, The Holy Spirit shall come upon you, and the Power of the Highest shall overshadow you: therefore also that Holy Thing which shall be born of you shall be called the Son of God"* (Lk. 1:31-35).

In truth, such an explanation would have been virtually impossible for any man, no matter how *"righteous,"* to comprehend and believe unless the Lord had intervened, which He did!

The phrase, *"Not willing to make her a public example,"* proclaims his love for her and his wanting to do all within his power to save her as much embarrassment as possible.

"Was minded to put her away privily," means to divorce her privately.

In truth, the Law of Moses demanded the death penalty for a woman in such cases, along with the man who had committed the deed. However, there is very little record of such action being actually carried out (Deut. 22:20-22).

In Joseph's case, after hearing Mary's explanation and, no doubt, being extremely confused, he had decided to avail himself of Deuteronomy 24:1, which meant to divorce her privately and not put her to death.

THE DREAM

"But while he thought on these things, behold, the Angel of the Lord appeared unto him in a dream, saying,

Joseph, you son of David, fear not to take unto you Mary your wife; for that which is conceived in her is of the Holy Spirit" (Mat. 1:20).

The phrase, *"But while he thought on these things,"* proclaims him carefully digesting her story, but yet, finding it so incredible that he simply could not believe it.

As stated, he had known her all her life and could not remotely conceive of her doing such a thing, but yet, according to her own words, she was pregnant.

Knowing that he had not come together with her, the only plausible explanation was that she had been unfaithful.

From the Text, it seems that he strongly desired to believe her but, logically, simply could not accept her explanation.

"Behold, the Angel of the Lord appeared unto him in a dream," proclaims the element of surprise by using the word *"behold!"* In other words, Joseph had already made up his mind to *"put her away"* when the *"Angel of the Lord"* appeared to him in a *"dream,"* confirming Mary's story. For this happening to occur, it must have been, and was, without a doubt, the greatest moment in Joseph's life.

SON OF DAVID

The phrase, *"Saying, Joseph, you son of David,"* reminds Joseph of the greatness of his ancestry, which, as well, spoke of the great Promise given to David in II Samuel 7:12-16.

Joseph was only a carpenter, which was certainly a noble trade, but, nevertheless, of far lesser station than the king of Israel.

Still, in God's Eyes, and, actually, the only Eyes that matter, Joseph was held in very high regard.

As stated, had the kingly line continued, Joseph

would now be the king of Israel. In a sense, even though there was no throne presently in Israel, in God's Mind, and that which He had originally intended, Joseph was king.

The Message of the Angel was simply, *"Fear not to take unto you Mary your wife."*

Without doubt, Joseph's fears were gone in a moment's time! Irrespective of what others might say or think, the wedding plans would continue, and Mary would become his *"wife"* in name and in fact.

The Angel then stated, *"For that which is conceived in her is of the Holy Spirit,"* thus verifying Mary's explanation and, as well, laying special stress on the Divine Origin of Jesus.

JESUS

"And she shall bring forth a Son, and you shall call His Name JESUS: for He shall save His People from their sins" (Mat. 1:21).

The Angel's announcement to Joseph concerning Jesus is very similar to what the Lord said to Sarah concerning Isaac in Genesis 17:19.

"And she shall bring forth a Son," is virtually that which was given to Isaiah, *"Behold a virgin shall conceive, and bear a Son, and shall call His Name Immanuel"* (Isa. 7:14). This *"Son"* was the fulfillment of the Prophecies, which began in the Garden of Eden (Gen. 3:15), and was taken up later with Abraham (Gen. 12:3), and then a little later to Sarah concerning Isaac (Gen. 17:19).

Then the Lord confirmed the Promise again to Jacob in the great Prophecy given to him shortly before he died, *"The scepter shall not depart from Judah, nor a Law-Giver from between His Feet, until Shiloh come; and unto Him shall the gathering of the people be"* (Gen. 49:10). (*"Shiloh"* is another Name for the Messiah.)

And then, of course, Isaiah's Prophecies were so pointed in detail, respecting the coming Messiah, that there was no reason for Israel not to know who this *"Son"* was (Isa. 7:14; 53:1-12)!

SAVIOUR

To date, this was the greatest event in human history, and yet, its announcement and action were given not to the religious leaders of Israel or to its nobility, but to a little teenage girl and her carpenter husband. Jesus would later say, *"... O Father, Lord of Heaven and Earth, because You have hid these things from the wise and prudent, and have revealed them unto babes."*

Then He said, *"Even so, Father: for so it seemed good in Your Sight"* (Mat. 11:25-26).

The phrase, *"And you shall call His Name Jesus,"* is actually in the Hebrew form, *"Yehoshua"* or *"Joshua,"* and means, *"Saviour, Who is Salvation."*

Of all the Names given to God in the Old Testament, *"Jehovah-Elohim,"* *"Adonai-Jehovah,"* *"Jehovah-Jireh,"* *"Jehovah-Nissi,"* etc., the greatest Name He was ever given, in both the Old and New Testaments, is *"Jesus."*

"For He shall save His People from their sins," actually says, *"For it is He Who shall save, He and none other!"*

The Glorious Name, *"Jesus,"* answers to the fact, for He Himself, in His Own Person, by virtue of What and Who He is, shall save.

Regrettably, Israel did not want a Messiah Who would save them from their *"sin,"* but instead, from the Romans, etc.

However, Israel's problem was not Rome but herself, which spoke of her sins.

As well, *"sin"* is the cause of all the problems of the human family.

THE FULFILLMENT OF PROPHECY

"Now all of this was done, that it might be fulfilled which was spoken of the Lord by the Prophet, saying," (Mat. 1:22).

The phrase, *"Now all of this was done,"* refers to God becoming Man in order to redeem man from sin. Actually, the two words, *"All this,"* constitute a gross understatement.

What was done to redeem man, which originated with God, is of such magnitude and so far outstrips the ability of man to comprehend at all that, quite possibly, it will never be fully comprehended by the natural resources of man, other than being revealed by the Holy Spirit (I Cor. 2:9-10). In other words, the Cross of Christ is an established fact, having taken place now nearly 2,000 years ago, but will have eternal, positive results and consequences.

"That it might be fulfilled," concerns the Lord bringing to pass that which was promised. His Word cannot fail!

"Which was spoken of the Lord by the Prophet, saying," refers to these great things having already been predicted by the Prophets of old, in this case, Isaiah.

Consequently, any and all of the great happenings in the New Testament were already promised in the Old, with Isaiah being the first Prophet mentioned.

It must be remembered that the Angel is continuing to speak to Joseph in the dream and is patiently explaining what all of this means!

GOD WITH US

"Behold, a Virgin shall be with Child, and shall bring forth a Son, and they shall call His Name Emmanuel, which being interpreted is, God with us" (Mat. 1:23).

The phrase, *"Behold, a virgin shall be with child,"*

proclaims the Angel laying great stress on the word, *"Virgin."*

"And shall bring forth a Son," proclaims this *"Son"* as being of such origin that, in the highest sense, He could truly be called *"Emmanuel."*

"And they shall call His Name Emmanuel," refers to the great titles of Jehovah, Emmanuel, Messiah, God, Son of God, Son of David, and Jesus as being grouped together, and is proclaimed so by the phrase, *"Which being interpreted is, God with us."*

Consequently, the phrase, *"God with us,"* proclaims the Deity of Christ even while in human form. In other words, He was Very God as well as Very Man.

That does not mean that He was half-God and half-Man, but rather Fully God and Fully Man.

THE INCARNATION

However, in the Incarnation, which this Verse portrays (God becoming Man), Christ, while never losing His Possession of Deity, nevertheless, did lose His Expression of Deity. Irrespective, He was no less God!

This teaches that Jesus perfectly expressed the Image of God. The Greek word for image is *"eikon,"* which means, *"Representation."* In classical Greek thought, the *"eikon"* had a share in the reality it expressed.

Paul called Jesus, *"The Image of God"* (II Cor. 4:4) and, *"The Image of the Invisible God"* (Col. 1:15). The word expresses the relationship of a coin to its die, that is, there is no comparison here, but rather an exact expression of the thing from which the coin is molded.

In Hebrews 1:3, Jesus is described as the *"express Image of His Person,"* and means, *"exact representation."*

God is so perfectly expressed in Jesus that when Philip asked to be shown the Father, Jesus could say, *"He who has seen Me has seen the Father"* (Jn. 14:9).

As well as Jesus being an Exact Representation of God, which, in fact, He was God, He, as well, was an Exact Representation of man, at least, in most respects. Several times the New Testament affirms that in the Incarnation, Jesus was made *"like unto His Brethren"* (Heb. 2:17) and in the likeness of sinful man, but yet without sin (Rom. 8:3), or *"in the likeness of men"* (Phil. 2:7).

IN THE LIKENESS OF SINFUL MAN BUT YET SINLESS

Although the New Testament never speaks of Jesus as being in the image of man, as it does *"in the Image of God,"* still, we should not conclude that He simply seemed to be human; for the Scripture never says that Jesus was *"like God"* or in the *"likeness of God,"* for He was fully God.

Consequently, He was *"in the likeness of sinful man,"* but only in that He was Fully Man, but yet, without sin of any nature. In Jesus, even though His Person perfectly represented God as He truly is, still, He could not perfectly represent man as he is, for humanity is tainted and corrupted by sin. Jesus' Human Nature was untainted by sin of any nature.

Thus, Jesus is in the image of redeemed humanity as it will ultimately be renewed when the drama of Redemption is finally complete.

In respect to all of this, one must believe in the *"Virgin Birth"* in order to be Saved. To disbelieve it threatens a rebellion against God and His Word, which undermines the very fabric of one's Salvation.

Therefore, those who claim to be Saved and yet disavow the Virgin Birth are basing their claims on a lie, which cannot have any validity.

God is with us through the Virgin Birth and in the form of Christ, or else, He is not with us at all!

TOOK MARY AS HIS WIFE

"Then Joseph being raised from sleep did as the Angel of the Lord had bidden him, and took unto him his wife" (Mat. 1:24).

This Passage proclaims the fact that the dream of the Angel and what was said, as given by the Lord, satisfied every question that Joseph had.

The phrase, *"Then Joseph being raised from sleep,"* means that, upon awakening, he had a full assurance in his heart of what Mary had said, and that this *"Son"* would, in fact, be the Messiah. There is no way that Joseph could not come to this conclusion after the statements made by the Angel.

The phrase, *"Did as the Angel of the Lord had bidden him,"* refers to obedience to the Heavenly Vision and an immediate setting forth to carry out the course of action.

The phrase, *"And took unto him his wife,"* tells us what that course of action was. Being fully satisfied in his heart, the original plans made in their engagement would now be carried out, and Mary would be *"his wife."*

HER FIRSTBORN

"And knew her not till she had brought forth her Firstborn Son: and he called His Name JESUS" (Mat. 1:25).

"And knew her not till she had brought forth her Firstborn Son," proved that after the Birth of the Divine Child, Mary physically became Joseph's wife; for *"He took unto him his wife, and knew her not until"* (imperfect tense in the Greek Text), that is, *"was not accustomed to cohabit with her as his wife until."*

Four sons and at least two daughters were the fruit of this marriage, as appears from Matthew, Chapter 13:55-56.

These facts destroy the Roman Catholic doctrine of the Perpetual Virginity of Mary of Nazareth.

The phrase, *"And he called His Name JESUS"* confirms what Gabriel had told Mary and, as well, the Name that the Angel had confirmed to Joseph (Lk. 1:26-31).

MARY

"And Mary arose in those days, and went into the hill country with haste, into a city of Judah" (Lk. 1:39).

The account of Joseph, the betrothed of Mary, severely doubting her account of what the Angel Gabriel had told her and the subsequent dream which cleared her, no doubt, took place immediately before the events of these in Luke, Chapter 1, Verses 39 through 56.

"And Mary arose in those days," concerned the time immediately after the appearance of the Angel Gabriel. These were momentous times, and she would seek the company of those who would have understanding regarding her experience. To be sure, that would be precious few! The value of Christian fellowship is learned from Luke, Chapter 1, Verses 39 through 56.

"And went into the hill country with haste, into a city of Judah," no doubt, refers to the area of Judaea. Tradition places the residence of Zechariah at Hebron. If so, this was a distance of approximately 100 miles or more. Exactly how Mary got there is not known. Quite possibly, friends were going there, and Joseph entrusted her to them. She would not have made the trip alone.

THE HOUSE OF ZECHARIAH AND ELISABETH

"And entered into the house of Zacharias, and saluted Elisabeth" (Lk. 1:40).

No doubt, Mary made this journey and entered into the house of Zechariah according to the Leading of the Holy Spirit. Inasmuch as Gabriel had mentioned Elisabeth to Mary and the Miracle afforded her, this most likely created a desire on the part of Mary to be with Elisabeth.

There is no evidence that Mary related her situation to anyone other than Joseph, Zechariah, and Elisabeth. If, in fact, that is correct, it is wise that she did not. Unless directed otherwise by the Holy Spirit, at times, things given to us by the Lord should be related to no one else, or only to those of like Faith. The Holy Spirit through Paul said, *"Have you Faith? Have it to yourself..."* (Rom. 14:22).

Mary needed this companionship and encouragement, and the Lord provided it in Zechariah and Elisabeth.

"And entered into the house of Zacharias," means that she was welcomed wholeheartedly!

"And saluted Elisabeth," means that she told this dear lady all the things that the Angel Gabriel had spoken unto her.

ELISABETH AND THE HOLY SPIRIT

"And it came to pass, that, when Elisabeth heard the salutation of Mary, the babe leaped in her womb; and Elisabeth was filled with the Holy Spirit" (Lk. 1:41).

"And it came to pass, that, when Elisabeth heard the salutation of Mary, the babe leaped in her womb," concerned the child, who was John the Baptist, being carried in the womb of Elisabeth, even now, six months.

This does not mean that the unborn child, John the Baptist, at this stage, had the power of comprehension, etc. It simply means that at the mention of Jesus, the Holy Spirit moved upon this unborn child, and he reacted spontaneously to the Moving and Operation of the Holy Spirit. John the Baptist was actually Called of God to serve as the introduction of Christ.

"And Elisabeth was filled with the Holy Spirit," records this event taking place at the same time that the Spirit of God moved upon the child. It was a simultaneous action.

The word, *"Filled,"* in the Greek Text is *"pletho,"* and means to *"imbue, influence, or supply."* It does not have the meaning as that which happened on the Day of Pentecost, referring to Acts 2:4.

THE DIFFERENCE

Actually, at that time, no one could be baptized with the Holy Spirit as they were on the Day of Pentecost and thereafter. John said, referring to Jesus, and concerning the coming of the Holy Spirit in this realm, *"But this spoke He of the Spirit, which they who believe on Him should receive: for the Holy Spirit was not yet given; because that Jesus was not yet glorified"* (Jn. 7:39).

Elisabeth and her unborn son, John the Baptist, were *"filled"* with the Holy Spirit, i.e., imbued with the Holy Spirit for a particular purpose and mission. In Elisabeth's case, it concerned her being the bearer of this child. In John's case, his mission was as the Prophet who would preach Repentance to Israel and, above all, introduce Christ to the world as the Son of God. Actually, the Spirit of God came upon many in Old Testament times, empowering them for a special service because they had been Called by God. David is a perfect example!

DAVID

When Samuel anointed David according to direction from the Lord, the Scripture says, *"... and the Spirit of*

the LORD came upon David from that day forward ..."
(I Sam. 16:13). However, this still was not in the same
capacity as the Acts 2:4 experience.

Actually, Jesus proclaimed John the Baptist as the
greatest man born of the woman, up to that particular
time, because of his unique position of being Called of
God to introduce Christ (Mat. 11:11). However, almost
in the same sentence, He further said, *"Notwithstanding
he who is least in the Kingdom of Heaven is greater
than he."*

By this, Jesus was referring to position and privileges
in the fullness of the Gospel, which all presently have,
but those in John's position under the Law did not and,
in fact, could not have. John could only have a measure
of the Spirit (Mat. 3:14; Jn. 1:15-17), but now, the least
Believer can have the fullness (Lk. 24:49; Jn. 7:37-39;
14:12-15; Acts 1:4-8; 2:38-39; 5:32; Eph. 3:19).

In Old Testament times, only those men with special
Callings could have certain Gifts of the Spirit, but now,
the least Believer may have any, or even all, of them
(Mk. 16:15-20; Jn. 14:12-15; I Cor., Chpt. 12).

THE HOLY SPIRIT

Actually, there are many other Blessings, which the
Gospel presently promises under this Dispensation of
Grace, that were not available under the Dispensation
of Law (II Cor. 3:6-15; Heb. 8:6; I Pet. 4:10-12).

In fact, John had much to do with the Holy Spirit,
and the Holy Spirit had much to do with him. He was
"filled" or furnished with the Holy Spirit even before he
was born, with his mother experiencing the same help.
As well, John introduced Jesus as the Baptizer *"with
the Holy Spirit, and with fire"* (Mat. 3:11).

So, even though John was not privileged to receive
this wonderful experience himself, still, he was so close

that he could introduce it in the Person and Power of the Lord Jesus Christ.

Also, if one is to notice, the Holy Spirit was totally present and working in everything that pertained to Christ; the announcement of His Birth (Lk. 1:41), the Prophecy given by Zechariah concerning the yet unborn Christ (Lk. 1:67), the Prophecy given by Simeon concerning the Baby Jesus (Lk. 2:25), the announcement of John, as stated, concerning Jesus being the Baptizer with the Holy Spirit (Mat. 3:11), and then, the Spirit of God coming upon and within Christ regarding His Ministry (Lk. 3:22).

When we observe how the Holy Spirit played such a part in everything pertaining to Christ, and then observe how He plays almost no part at all in most churches, the cause of spiritual declension becomes painfully obvious. Anywhere the Holy Spirit is present, Jesus will be glorified and lifted up. When He is not present, men's philosophies are rather encouraged.

BLESSED IS THE FRUIT OF YOUR WOMB

"And she spoke out with a loud voice and said, Blessed are you among women, and blessed is the Fruit of your womb" (Lk. 1:42).

The phrase, *"And she (Elisabeth) spoke out with a loud voice,"* concerns the Moving of the Holy Spirit on her heart, which produced this spontaneous reaction. It was *"loud"* because of the ecstasy and joy within her soul. What she would say would express the heartfelt cry of the ages respecting the Coming of the Redeemer.

If it is to be noticed, the phrase, *"And said, Blessed are you among women,"* did not say, *"Above women!"*

However, Mary truly was *"Blessed"* in that she was chosen by the Lord for this beautiful and wonderful privilege. Actually, her *"Blessing"* would be such that she is unique in this position, as should be obvious, with no other women before or since having the privilege to do this thing because such will never be needed again.

"And blessed is the Fruit of your womb," concerned Jesus Christ, for He was that *"Fruit!"*

GOD MANIFEST IN THE FLESH

The Incarnation, which means, *"God manifest in the flesh,"* or, *"God with us,"* was absolutely necessary for man's Redemption. Jesus would become the *"Last Adam"* (I Cor. 15:45).

As the first Adam was the representative man for the entirety of the human family because all, in a sense, were in his loins, his failure, which brought death, passed to all men (I Cor. 15:22).Consequently, to redeem man from this fallen position, there had to be a *"Second"* or *"Last Adam."* This was Jesus Christ and to be the *"Last Adam,"* He had to be born as a Man, but yet, not by man.

Had he been born by man, He would have been subject to the death penalty as all others because of original sin.

However, due to the fact that He was not procreated as other men, exactly as the first Adam was not procreated, He was not born with sin as all others. As the Last Adam, and there will never be a need for another one, He became, as well, the Representative Man exactly as the first Adam had been.

As the Representative Man, He acted on behalf of all. Consequently, His Victory in all respects becomes my victory, at least, to all who will exhibit Faith in His Name (Jn. 3:16). So, He truly is *"Blessed!"*

As well, the word, *"Blessed,"* should be pronounced, *"Bless-ed."* This implies a person of superior spirituality, someone who is more saintly in moral character, and, in this case, One who has Perfect Spirituality and Character.

THE MOTHER OF MY LORD

"And whence is this to me, that the mother of my Lord should come to me?" (Lk. 1:43).

The question, *"Whence is this to me ...?"* actually has a double meaning. It is as follows:

• *"Who am I that I should be privileged to associate in this glorious way with you, 'Mother of my Lord,' and, more particularly, the 'Lord Himself?'"*

• *"What does this all mean to me or to the entirety of mankind, for that matter?"*

The question, *"That the Mother of my Lord should come to me?"* presents Elisabeth calling Jesus, *"Lord,"* by the Spirit of God.

The two words, *"My Lord,"* have a wealth of meaning! Spence said, *"Not only did she bless the Mother of the coming Messiah, but the Spirit opened her eyes to see Who that coming Messiah really was."*

THE MESSIAH

The coming of the Messiah was spoken of constantly in Israel.

However, even though a few of the Prophets of the past undoubtedly had a correct view of Who and What He would be, the truth was that most people had an entirely erroneous concept. By the time Jesus made His Ministry debut, the idea that the Messiah would be a conqueror, ridding Israel of all her enemies, and restoring her place and position of supremacy, was the prevailing thought.

It was gross error and no way matched up to proper Scriptural interpretation, but, still, it was the prevailing thought. This was the bitter fruit of acute self-righteousness.

In their minds, they did not see the Messiah as God or the *"Lawful Son of the Highest!"* This is the reason the Pharisees and religious leaders of Israel bridled at the idea that Jesus claimed Deity. Their Messiah, which they imagined in their minds, could be controlled by men.

Deity could not be controlled; consequently, they rejected Him out of hand.

In the Pulpit Commentary, Dean Plumptre said: *"The contrast leaves no room for doubt. She used the word 'Lord' in its highest sense. 'Great' as her own son was to be in the sight of the Lord, here was the Mother of One yet greater, even the Lord Himself."*

THE SALUTATION

"For, lo, as soon as the voice of your salutation sounded in my ears, the babe leaped in my womb for joy" (Lk. 1:44).

The phrase, *"For, lo, as soon as the voice of your salutation sounded in my ears,"* referred to the announcement by Mary and the actual fact as to what this *"salutation"* meant. It was the Coming of the Messiah, the Lord of Glory, the Son of the Highest, even Jehovah, wrapped in the habiliment of human flesh.

The phrase, *"The babe leaped in my womb for joy,"* concerned the response of the unborn John the Baptist to this announcement.

Once again we state, it was not that the unborn child could understand or comprehend, but rather the Manifestation of the Holy Spirit which produced the response.

If this *"joy"* was expressed by an unborn child, how is it that we, who are able to understand and comprehend, should express less *"joy,"* especially considering what the Lord has done for us?

BLESSED

"And blessed is she who believed: for there shall be a performance of those things which were told her from the Lord" (Lk. 1:45).

The phrase, *"And blessed is she who believed,"* refers to Mary and her Faith in that which was told to her by the Angel Gabriel.

She did not question the Word of the Lord and is here commended by the Holy Spirit through Elisabeth concerning her Faith.

"For there shall be a performance of those things which were told her from the Lord," means that what is said shall be done. The words are, *"Shall be,"* which is certitude of action.

The Redeemer, at long last, was coming into the world, and doing so in order to redeem man, and could not be stopped by man or demon!

TO MAGNIFY THE LORD

"And Mary said, My soul does magnify the Lord" (Lk. 1:46).

As we have previously stated, one can read Luke, Chapter 1, Verses 46 through 55, which is referred to as *"The Magnificat,"* and easily determine that Mary had a tremendous knowledge of the Scripture and a spiritual depth which far surpassed most.

Even though she was a teenage girl, still, her consecration was exceptional!

It is ironic that she *"magnifies the Lord"* while the Catholic church erroneously magnifies her instead of the Lord.

The *"Magnificat"* is actually a song and is in the tradition of the *"Song of Deborah"* (Judg. 5:1-31) and the *"Prayer or Song of Hannah"* (I Sam. 2:1-10).

GOD MY SAVIOUR

"And my spirit has rejoiced in God my Saviour" (Lk. 1:47).

This statement of Mary, *"In God my Saviour,"* disproves the theory of the *"Immaculate Conception,"* or the total absence of original sin in Mary.

If God was her Saviour, then she must have been a sinner in order, therefore, to be Saved. Not one Scripture ever hints of such an idea — that Mary, or anyone else, for that matter, was sinless, except the Lord Jesus Christ. In fact, the Scripture plainly says:

"As it is written (Ps. 14:1-3), There is none righteous, no, not one" (Rom. 3:10).

So, her rejoicing was in the fact that Jesus was God and would redeem her, as well as the entirety of mankind, at least, those who will believe (Jn. 3:16). Consequently, the emphasis is placed on Jesus as *"Saviour."*

While He definitely is the Healer and the Provider of all good things, still, the emphasis must always be as Paul said it, *"Jesus Christ, and Him Crucified,"* which makes it possible for Him to redeem fallen humanity (I Cor. 2:2).

Sadly, in many Charismatic circles, the emphasis is being shifted to other things, such as prosperity, seeker sensitive, etc.

Even though the Lord is definitely a Provider, and the Greatest ever, still, such is all-dependent on Him as *"Saviour."*

As a result, the emphasis of the Church must always be on the Salvation of souls, with everything else following in that train.

THE HANDMAIDEN OF THE LORD

"For He has regarded the low estate of His Handmaiden; for, behold, from henceforth all generations shall call me blessed" (Lk. 1:48).

The phrase, *"For He has regarded the low estate of His Handmaiden,"* says several things:

• Mary's prayer or song is the highest order of worship, for it asks for nothing but only breathes out adoration and thankfulness.

• Even though she was in the royal lineage of David, still, the throne of David was no more, except in Christ. Consequently, her estate was *"low,"* meaning that she had nothing of this world's goods, and she was recognized not at all by the religious elite of Israel.

However, God recognized her in the highest possible way. Consequently, promotion does not come from man but from God.

As some have well said, *"If we look to man, we get what man can give, which is nothing.*

However, if we look to God, we get what He can give, which is everything." Mary looked to God!

"For, behold, from henceforth all generations shall call me blessed," is, in effect, a Prophecy and has been fulfilled to the letter, and I do not speak of the erroneous contention of the Catholic church.

As well, the word, *"Blessed,"* is here a single syllable and simply means a recipient of Grace.

The word *"Blessed"* in Verse 42, as stated, is a double syllable, and should be pronounced *"Bless-ed,"* which actually means the Giver of Grace here received by Mary.

HOLY IS HIS NAME

"For He Who is Mighty has done to me great things; and Holy is His Name.

"And His Mercy is on them who fear Him from generation to generation" (Lk. 1:49-50).

In these two Verses, Mary proclaims three Divine principle attributes.

They are as follows:

1. *"For He Who is mighty has done to me great things"*: this speaks of God's Attribute of Power, which alone could bring about the Virgin Birth.

2. *"And Holy is His Name"*: this proclaims His Attribute of Holiness and proclaims that it is bound up in *"His Name."* His Name is Power (Mk. 16:17), Healing (Mk. 16:18), Comfort (Song of Sol. 1:3), and, as well, is *"Holy!"*

His Name is *"Holy"* because it represents His Character and Nature. It represents the essence of His Being; consequently, He is a thrice-Holy God (Rev. 4:8).

3. *"And His Mercy is on them who fear Him"*: the attribute of *"Mercy"* is now introduced. Mary needed *"Mercy"* exactly as all others. Mercy is a product of Grace and upon introduction of Grace, it is always extended without fail!

However, *"Mercy"* is tied to the *"Fear of God."* There is no Fear of God in self-righteousness; consequently, no Mercy can be shown. The *"Fear of God"* comes from a broken and contrite spirit, realizing that we are deserving of nothing good, but, because of the Grace of God, we are given all things. Upon that realization, Mercy is always extended.

"From generation to generation," means that to those who truly fear Him, Mercy will be extended, irrespective of the generation.

The Promise is forever!

All of this is wrapped up in the Redeemer, Who Mary would have the privilege of bringing into the world. In effect, Jesus is the Mercy of God.

STRENGTH

"He has shown strength with His Arm; He has scattered the proud in the imagination of their hearts" (Lk. 1:51).

The phrase, *"He has shown strength with His Arm,"* proclaims the Power of God and the manner in which it is used. It is described in Luke, Chapter 1, Verses 51 through 53.

"He has scattered the proud in the imagination of their hearts," proclaims the Messianic reversal of man's conception of what is great and what isn't.

The idea is that the Lord ignored the proud self-exaltation of the religious elite of Israel and showered His Attention on a little *"handmaiden."*

EXALTATION

"He has put down the mighty from their seats, and exalted them of low degree" (Lk. 1:52).

It is amazing that this young lady proclaimed almost the very words of the famous Sermon her Divine Son, some 30 years later, preached in a village not far from Capernaum. He said, *"... for everyone who exalts himself shall be abased; and he who humbles himself shall be exalted"* (Lk. 18:14).

GOOD THINGS

"He has filled the hungry with good things; and the rich He has sent empty away" (Lk. 1:53).

"He has filled the hungry with good things," concerns

those who hunger and thirst for Righteousness (Mat. 5:6).

"And the rich He has sent empty away," refers to those who were *"rich and increased with goods, and thought they had need of nothing"* (Rev. 3:17).

MERCY

"He has helped His Servant Israel, in remembrance of His Mercy" (Lk. 1:54).

The phrase, *"He has helped His Servant Israel,"* concerns two things:

1. He remembered the Promises He had made to the Prophets. As such, He would bring the Messiah into the world. God keeps Covenant and keeps His Promises.

2. As promised, the Messiah would be an Israelite. This would be done despite the fact that Israel had long since ceased to serve God even though loudly proclaiming to do so. As a result, they would murder their Messiah.

"In remembrance of His Mercy," means that it was not because of their faithfulness but because of His *"Mercy."*

THE LORD SPOKE

"As He spoke to our fathers, to Abraham, and to his seed forever" (Lk. 1:55).

This proclaims the value that God places on His Promises and, as well, ends the Song of Mary. It opened with *"Magnifying the Lord"* and closed with the Promises of God being *"remembered forever."*

What a wonderful God we serve!

THREE MONTHS OF BLESSING

"And Mary abode with her about three months, and returned to her own house" (Lk. 1:56).

The phrase, *"And Mary abode with her about three*

months," means that she stayed there until John the Baptist was born, or nearly so. She had come in Elisabeth's sixth month (Lk. 1:26).

"And returned to her own house," refers to Nazareth.

It is claimed by some that Mary's condition of pregnancy was not known to Joseph at the time she went to the home of Elisabeth, consequently, with the events of Matthew 1:18 taking place after her return.

However, I do not feel that is correct, believing that she informed Joseph immediately upon the visit of the Angel Gabriel.

As well, immediately upon her telling Joseph, I believe they were married very soon thereafter.

I cannot see that it would have been any other way. If the marriage had not taken place until after her visit with Elisabeth, that would mean that she was already three months pregnant and, thereby, showing. I cannot see that the Holy Spirit would have allowed such a thing to be brought about, which would have caused untold ridicule, as would be obvious. No!

The Angel Gabriel making his appearance to her was related immediately to Joseph, as stated, with the marriage taking place very soon thereafter. Then, she would have gone to the home of Elisabeth.

ELISABETH

"Now Elisabeth's full time came that she should be delivered; and she brought forth a son" (Lk. 1:57).

Many feel that Elisabeth, at this time, could have been in her 60s or, at least, in her 50s. The Scripture uses the term *"well stricken in years"* (Lk. 1:7); however, the Lord had rejuvenated her youthfulness in that she conceived.

"And she brought forth a son," proclaims the greatest Prophet who ever lived, the one who would be the mighty forerunner of the Great King, the Lord Jesus Christ.

REJOICING

"And her neighbors and her cousins heard how the Lord had shown great Mercy upon her; and they rejoiced with her" (Lk. 1:58).

The phrase, *"And her neighbors and her cousins heard,"* refers to the knowledge of the visitation of the Angel Gabriel to Zechariah.

"How the Lord had shown great Mercy upon her," means they believed what Zechariah had said because the proof was irrefutable. They were too old to have children, but yet, her condition was beyond question. Elisabeth would not bear the stigma that Mary would bear because John's conception was by the normal manner of procreation.

"And they rejoiced with her," means the entire area was very pleased and happy that this great thing was happening in the home and lives of Zechariah and Elisabeth.

THE EIGHTH DAY

"And it came to pass, that on the eighth day they came to circumcise the child; and they called him Zacharias, after the name of his father" (Lk. 1:59).

"And it came to pass, that on the eighth day they came to circumcise the child," was according to the Command originally given to Abraham by the Lord (Gen. 17:10-12). This was a very solemn Covenant with dire penalties attached if broken. The uncircumcised Israelite was not covered by the Covenant Promise given to Abraham and was, therefore, lost.

The rite symbolized submission to God and belief in His Covenant Promise. However, God also required a *"circumcision of the heart"* (Deut. 10:16; 30:6; Jer. 4:4).

Circumcision did not bring Salvation as that came by Faith, as it always has been by Faith. It was only a result of Salvation and not the cause. The New Testament argues that Abraham was justified by Faith even while he was uncircumcised years before the rite was given. Circumcision was a sign, *"a seal of the Righteousness that he had by Faith, as stated, while he was still uncircumcised"* (Gen. 15:6; 17:10-17; Rom. 4:11).

The sign of circumcision was not carried over into the Church because that which it represented, separation respecting the Jewish people, was fulfilled in Christ. Regrettably, many Hebrew Christians struggled to impose circumcision and the Mosaic Law, as well, on Gentile Christians during the times of the Early Church (Acts 15:1). However, this was rejected at the Jerusalem Council (Acts 15:1-29).

Paul later wrote to the Corinthians, and I paraphrase, *"Was a man already circumcised when he was Called? Therefore, he could not become uncircumcised. Was a man uncircumcised when he was Called? If that is the case, he should not be circumcised, at least, on religious grounds. Circumcision is nothing, and uncircumcision is nothing. Keeping God's Commands is what counts"* (I Cor. 7:18-19).

THE SYMBOL AND REALITY

Paul's point is that God has never been concerned for the symbol as the thing in itself. God cares about reality and, consequently, to what the symbol pointed. It is our heart response to Him that counts.

Thus, looking into hearts and examining those who have responded to Christ's Gospel, the Bible says, *"It is we who are the true circumcision, we who worship by the Spirit of God, who glory in Jesus Christ, and who put no confidence in the flesh"* (Phil. 3:3).

In the Law (Lev. 12:3), the Lord ordained that the little boy be circumcised on the *"eighth day"* after he was born. This had to do with the physical properties of his blood. In other words, the coagulating agencies in the blood are not formed until the eighth day, and if the child would be circumcised before then, it could bleed to death.

Presently, the medical profession can add the agents needed, making it possible for the little boy, if so desired, to be circumcised immediately when born.

ZECHARIAH

The phrase, *"And they called him Zacharias, after the name of his father,"* presented the custom, which was to name the little boy on the day of his circumcision.

The Rabbins said this was because the names of Abram and Sarai were changed when God instituted circumcision (Gen., Chpt. 17). However, I seriously doubt that circumcision was the real reason for the name change.

However, it was very rarely that sons received the name of the father.

So, for whatever reason, the neighbors seemed to desire that the custom be changed in this case, with the child being named after his father.

As well, this denotes that Zechariah had not related to the neighbors everything the Angel Gabriel told him. They did not know the child was to be named *"John."*

JOHN

"And his mother answered and said, Not so; but he

shall be called John" (Lk. 1:60).

The phrase, *"And his mother answered and said, Not so,"* proclaimed another custom, that mothers among the Jews generally gave the children their names.

"But he shall be called John," was in obedience to what Gabriel had demanded. As stated, the name John meant, *"Jehovah shows favor,"* or, *"Jehovah gives Grace."* It was a fitting name for the one who would introduce Christ, Who, in effect, was Grace Personified. As stated, it was fitting.

LACK OF UNDERSTANDING

"And they said unto her, There is none of your kindred who is called by this name" (Lk. 1:61).

The neighbors were perplexed inasmuch as Zechariah and Elisabeth seemed to be departing from custom — the naming of the child after a relative or one of the Greats of Israel.

As well, names were chosen oftentimes to represent something good or bad which had happened in the family. Then, at times, the name was chosen by the Lord, as was the case here.

ZECHARIAH

"And they made signs to his father, how he would have him called" (Lk. 1:62).

The phrase, *"And they made signs to his father,"* lets us know that Zechariah was not only rendered speechless because of his unbelief regarding the announcement by Gabriel, but was deaf as well!

Consequently, they had to use sign language for him to understand what was being asked.

"How he would have him called," portrays that Elisabeth had deferred to Zechariah.

HIS NAME IS JOHN

"And he asked for a writing table, and wrote, saying, His name is John. And they marvelled all" (Lk. 1:63). The phrase, *"And he asked for a writing table,"* pertained to that which was common use in those days.

These *"tables"* were of ivory or wood and coated with wax, and the letters were formed by a stylus made of gold, silver, brass, iron, ivory, or bone. One end was pointed for writing while the other end was smooth and round for erasing or smoothing out the wax so it could be used again.

Edges and backs of tablets were not waxed so that when two or more were put together, they would not be marred.

Several tablets were sometimes put together at the backs by means of wire, which served as hinges. Letters, wills, and many documents of great length were written upon them. They could be bound by the outer edges with chords and fastened with a seal.

"And wrote, saying, His name is John," proclaims the obedience of Zechariah and that this child would ultimately introduce the Bearer of Grace and Truth. That Bearer was Jesus Christ (Jn. 1:17).

"And they marveled all," could possibly indicate that, at that time, Zechariah may very well have related to them the appearance of the Angel Gabriel to him some nine months earlier and all Gabriel had said.

PRAISING THE LORD

"And his mouth was opened immediately, and his tongue loosed, and he spoke, and praised God" (Lk. 1:64).

The phrase, *"And his mouth was opened immediately,"* speaks of his obedience in doing what the Angel had demanded.

"And his tongue loosed, and he spoke, and praised God," lets us know that his tongue had formerly been used at the announcement of Gabriel to register unbelief, and now does that which he should have done at that time — praised God (Lk. 1:18).

This makes it painfully obvious to all just how much stock God places in our obeying His Word. Doubt and unbelief are the bane of the modern church. Regrettably, all have been afflicted with this malady at one time or the other. The Lord desires that we believe Him and not question His Word. To do so registers doubt in His Ability to carry forth what He has promised. Considering that He is able to do all things, irrespective as to what they are or how impossible they may seem, unbelief is an insult to His Integrity.

As well, doubt and unbelief respecting God's Word go all the way back to the Garden of Eden and constitute the foundation of original sin. Adam and Eve simply did not believe what God told them. They disobeyed Him by partaking of the fruit of the tree, which they had been told not to eat (Gen. 2:15-17).

FEAR

"And fear came on all who dwelt round about them: and all these sayings were noised abroad throughout all the hill country of Judaea" (Lk. 1:65).

"And fear came on all who dwelt round about them," further proclaims the fact that Zechariah told the people of the visitation of the Angel Gabriel. They realized that a great thing was happening in their midst. While they did not understand the full portent of it all, still, they knew that God had spoken and that this child was destined for something great.

"And all these sayings were noised abroad throughout all the hill country of Judaea," meant that these things

were constantly spoken of in this area.

What Zechariah related to them was open very little to speculation. All knew that Zechariah and Elisabeth had long since passed the age of child-bearing; consequently, for her to conceive at this age was a Miracle. And then, considering that all of this had been brought about by the visitation of the Mighty Angel Gabriel, it placed a significance all out of proportion to normal thought. God was moving again in Israel! The 400-year prophetic drought was being broken. Once again, they would hear, *"Thus says the Lord ..."* Little did they realize what was actually about to happen!

CAESAR AUGUSTUS

"And it came to pass in those days, that there went out a decree from Caesar Augustus that all the world should be taxed" (Lk. 2:1).

The phrase, *"And it came to pass,"* is a term used by Luke more so than any other writer in the Bible. It is used some 55 times in the Books of Luke and Acts. It is used a number of times in the Old Testament but only 10 times elsewhere in the New Testament.

In the reckoning of time, the words, *"In those days,"* would refer to 1 A.D. (In Latin, capital A stands for *"Anno,"* meaning *"year,"* with capital D standing for *"Domini,"* meaning *"first."*) So, all time is measured in respect to Christ. (B.C. stands for *"Before Christ."*)

"That there went out a decree from Caesar Augustus," referred to Gaius Octavius, the adopted son and successor of Julius Caesar. He reigned 29 B.C. to 14 A.D.

The title, *"Caesar,"* was the actual name of an aristocratic family which established ascendancy over the Roman Republic. With the triumph of Augustus (31 B.C.), they kept it until Nero's death (68 A.D.). Its manner of government proved to be such a success that even with the elimination of the Caesarian family, their position was institutionalized and their name assumed by its incumbents.

One of the foundations of Caesar's power was his extended control of each province, embracing most of Rome's frontier forces. This would have included all of Israel, which came under the domain of Syria, as the next Verse proclaims.

TAXES

The phrase, *"That all the world should be taxed,"* is a figure of speech. The Greek word is, *"Synecdoche,"* which means, *"A whole is put for a part,"* as in Genesis 6:17; II Samuel 6:5, 15; I Kings 11:16-17; Daniel 2:37-38, etc. It was only the part of the world of which it spoke.

One tradition says that Augustus had a quarrel with Herod, who was then king of Israel. The Roman Senate, advised by Antony and Octavius, gave Herod the title *"king of the Jews."* It took him three years of fighting to make his title effective, but when he had done so, he governed Judaea for 33 years as a loyal *"friend and ally"* of Rome.

To punish Herod over whatever the argument was about, this tax was imposed. However, the Holy Spirit would use this quarrel to fulfill the Prophecy given by Micah some 700 years before. That Prophecy stated that Jesus would be born in Bethlehem (Micah 5:2). This tax would demand that each person in Israel go back to the city of his ancestry, which, in the case of Joseph and Mary, was Bethlehem.

History tells us that Herod the Great died in 4 B.C.

This was the same Herod who murdered the babies two years old and under, according to Matthew, Chapter 2. That being the case, the correct date of Herod's death should have been 1 or 2 A.D.

Some think that Jesus may have been as much as two years old when this was done, which He probably was. Actually, there is really no discrepancy with the Bible because it does not give a date.

However, to adjust the date given of Herod's death, with the knowledge that Jesus was already born when this happened, it would mean that either the date of Herod's death is wrong, or our present calendar is somewhat wrong.

There are some who claim that our calendar, which is referred to as the Gregorian calendar and was put together by Gregorian monks in the Middle Ages, is incorrect by several years.

In fact, this argument has raged for quite sometime. If that is correct, this present year (as I dictate these notes) should be about four years later than our present date.

GOVERNOR

"And this taxing was first made when Cyrenius was governor of Syria" (Lk. 2:2).

Controversy has raged over this Scripture because critics claim that *"Cyrenius"* (or called by some, *"Quirinius"*) was not made governor of Syria until 10 or 12 years after the Birth of Christ.

It is known that he was the Roman Consul in 12 B.C. and thus qualified to be a governor.

From 12 B.C. to 4 B.C., the names of governors are recorded; however, from 4 B.C. to 4 A.D., the names are not given.

It was during this time that the census took place,

and who can disprove the inspired statement here that Cyrenius was governor during this time?

As well, in the Greek Text, the word, *"First,"* in this Scripture is, *"Protos,"* and means, *"First"* or *"Before."*

So, this Verse could have been translated, *"This census was before Cyrenius was Governor of Syria"* or *"before the one made by Cyrenius."*

Also, on the question of this alleged historical inaccuracy of Luke, it should be observed that none of the early opponents of Christianity, such as Celsus or Porphyry, impugn the accuracy of this account.

Spence says, *"Surely, if there had been so marked an error on the threshold of this Gospel, these adversaries of the Faith, living comparatively soon after the events in question, would have been the first to call to attention this alleged error."*

I might quickly add, they did not do it simply because it was not error.

As well, Luke, a man of obvious education and writing skills, would not have been so specific regarding this historical statement, especially considering that it could have been so easily disproved. It was never questioned until recent years because there was no reason to question it. Luke's statement was and is absolutely correct.

Regarding *"Cyrenius,"* he is mentioned by the historians Tacitus and Suetonius. He appears to have been originally of humble birth and, like so many of the soldiers of fortune of the empire, rose through his own merits to his great position. It is said that he was a gallant and true soldier, but withal, self-seeking and harsh.

For his Sicilian victories, the Roman Senate decreed him a triumph.

As well, when he died, he received a distinguished honor of a public funeral. That was in 21 A.D.

HIS OWN CITY

"And all went to be taxed, everyone into his own city" (Lk. 2:3).

As stated, this *"tax"* was a special tax and census, which was levied on top of all the regular taxes, etc.

To ensure that all paid, one had to go back to the city of his ancestry, which, in this case of Mary and Joseph, was Bethlehem. The next Verse tells us why.

THE CITY OF DAVID

"And Joseph also went up from Galilee, out of the city of Nazareth, into Judaea, unto the City of David, which is called Bethlehem; (because he was of the house and lineage of David)" (Lk. 2:4).

As stated, Joseph traced his lineage to David through Solomon, with Mary tracing hers through Nathan, another son of David.

Solomon was in the kingly line and had the Davidic throne continued, Joseph would now be king of Judaea; however, the kingdom of David had been dismembered, conquered, and devastated.

Because of sin on the part of succeeding kings after David, the throne was no more. It was at this moment in the power of Augustus Caesar because Israel had refused to walk in the Law of the Lord. In fact, it had been in the power of Gentiles since Nebuchadnezzar nearly 600 years before. So, the one who should have been the king of Judah was but a simple village carpenter.

They were forced to go to *"Bethlehem,"* called, *"The City of David,"* because this was the birthplace of that famous king. From Nazareth, it was pretty close to 80 miles.

"Bethlehem" was a tiny village, probably only a few

hundred in population, if that, and was actually called, *"Bethlehem Ephratah,"* to distinguish it from another small village of the same name in another part of Israel.

THE PROPHET MICAH

Micah had prophesied some 700 years earlier, *"... though you be little among the thousands of Judah, yet out of you shall He come forth unto Me Who is to be Ruler in Israel; Whose goings forth have been from of old, from everlasting"* (Mic. 5:2).

How familiar Mary and Joseph were with this Prophecy is not known. However, it is almost certain that both, and especially Mary, at this time, would have been very familiar with this prediction.

If, in fact, that is the case, I wonder if Mary and Joseph ever discussed how this could be brought to pass, their being in Bethlehem at the exact time of the Birth of Jesus. In those days, travel was very difficult, especially for the poor. For a woman nine months pregnant, it was all but impossible!

ARRANGED BY THE LORD

However, little did they realize that as several months passed, a political situation was evolving, which would include Caesar and Herod. This situation would involve a tax and a census which demanded that all families go back to their ancestral homes.

In addition to all of the domain of Herod, it would involve Joseph and Mary, and would fall at the exact time that Jesus would be born.

With Micah giving this Prophecy some 700 years before, did this mean that God brought these things to pass by manipulating the wills of the individuals, whomever they may have been?

No! The Lord knew through foreknowledge that these events would take place, and through this foreknowledge, He gave the prediction through the Prophet.

And yet, at the same time, if He so desires, God is able to manipulate events wherever desired, which He does at times, without violating the free moral agency of man.

Only God could do such a thing.

MARY, READY TO BE DELIVERED

"To be taxed with Mary his espoused wife, being great with child" (Lk. 2:5).

The phrase, *"To be taxed with Mary his espoused wife,"* means that he had married Mary almost immediately after the visit to her by the Angel Gabriel, which would have been about nine months earlier (Mat. 1:18-21).

The phrase, *"Being great with child,"* means that she was about to be delivered.

The journey must have been extremely difficult for her, with her either walking or, at most, riding a donkey. Either way would have been, as is obvious, extremely strenuous.

One certainly cannot say that Joseph and Mary were shown any favoritism by the Lord even though they both were chosen by God for a unique task, especially Mary.

Their unique assignment would make possible the single most important event in human history, the Birth, Ministry, Death, and Resurrection of Jesus Christ to redeem fallen humanity.

This obviously flies in the face of modern teaching, which claims that if one has the proper confession, one can escape all the difficulties and vicissitudes of life. This example makes such false teaching seem insignificant by comparison.

IN BETHLEHEM

"And so it was, that, while they were there, the days were accomplished that she should be delivered" (Lk. 2:6).

The phrase, *"And so it was, that, while they were there,"* probably was in October, as we have previously discussed, but almost certainly not in December.

The following Verses tell us why:

"The days were accomplished that she should be delivered," concerned the most important delivery of a baby in human history.

God would become flesh and, thereby, use this flesh, His Human Body, as a Perfect Sacrifice in order to deliver humanity.

And yet, the Creator of the Ages would be born in a humble cow stable.

HER FIRSTBORN SON

"And she brought forth her Firstborn Son, and wrapped Him in swaddling clothes, and laid Him in a manger; because there was no room for them in the inn" (Lk. 2:7).

The phrase, *"And she brought forth her Firstborn Son,"* is meant to emphasize the fact that there were no other children up to this time.

As well, it refutes the error of the Catholic church, which claims that Mary had no other children, and we speak of those born after Jesus. They claim that Mary remained a virgin throughout her life.

Actually, as stated, Jesus had four half-brothers, *"James, Joseph, Simon, and Jude,"* as well as two or three half-sisters (Mat. 13:55-56).

It was predicted by God that Mary would have other children, and the Messiah would have brothers. The Scripture says:

"I have become a stranger unto My Brethren, and an alien unto My Mother's children" (Ps. 69:8-9).

As well, His Brethren are mentioned as not believing on Him until after the Resurrection (Jn. 7:3-10; Acts 1:14). Also, James is called *"the Lord's Brother"* (Gal. 1:19).

The Catholic church claims that His Brethren were cousins by another Mary and Cleophas. One of their contentions is that Joseph was too old to have children of Mary, or that he had children by a former marriage. All of this is false as nothing is mentioned in Scripture or history about these claims.

In fact, if Joseph did have children before Jesus was born, then Jesus could not be the legal Heir to David's Throne, which, by Law, went to the firstborn.

So, the Catholic claims are spurious.

SWADDLING CLOTHES

The phrase, *"And wrapped Him in swaddling clothes,"* pertains to the custom of that time.

The cloth was loosely wrapped all around the child with only its face uncovered. The cost of the material indicated the financial status and rank of the parents.

Even though the Scripture does not specifically state, still, every indication is that Joseph and Mary were very poor. As a result, this material they used would have been very inexpensive.

The phrase, *"And laid Him in a manger,"* basically spoke of a feeding place for animals.

The inn of Bethlehem was of ancient duration, actually being mentioned in Jeremiah 41:17.

This type of *"inn"* was for the poorest of the poor and

offered little more than the shelter of its walls and roof.

Either a cave or enclosure was used to stable the animals, which most every traveler had during those times.

In the case of Mary and Joseph, there are claims for both, even though the Scripture does not say. There would have been little difference in either, with a large cave affording a little more protection, but with the foul odor even worse.

Whichever it was, Joseph would have tried his best to make Mary as comfortable as possible among the animals, perhaps making her a bed of straw. Because of the many travelers coming to Bethlehem for the same reason as Joseph and Mary, the stable would have been filled with animals. The scene would not have been pretty or pleasant to behold!

In the midst of the odor of barnyard waste and by the side of donkeys and horses, Mary delivered the Baby Child Jesus, the Lord of Glory, God manifest in the flesh.

Even though it was not a pretty picture to behold, still, one can be certain that Angels were watching the move of every animal and affording minute protection for the Saviour of mankind. As well, the Glory of God must have accompanied this scene, turning the smelly stable into a place of Glory.

The Lord has turned many a hovel into a heaven! Millions have thought that a new house, a new car, or new clothes would satisfy the hunger of the heart, but they soon found that such did not and, in fact, cannot satisfy.

Only proper union with Christ can bring a peace that passes all understanding. That is at least one of the reasons Jesus said, *"A man's life consisteth not in the abundance of the things which he possesseth"* (Lk. 12:15).

NO ROOM IN THE INN

"Because there was no room for them in the inn," proclaims that God, manifest in the flesh, had come to Earth, but yet, there was no room for Him. So much the more wonderful and perfect is the love that brought Him thither. He began His Life in a manger, ended it on a Cross, and all along His Ministerial Way, He had nowhere to lay His Head!

The idea of there being no room in the inn seems to imply that Joseph dutifully inquired, with Mary's condition painfully obvious.

However, no one volunteered to give up his place in the inn even though they all, no doubt, had the opportunity to do so.

What an eternal Blessing someone would have gained had one taken this glorious privilege.

However, to the unspiritual eye, Joseph and Mary looked like just two more exhausted, poverty-stricken travelers.

Consequently, some undoubtedly heard the innkeeper dismiss them, probably gesturing toward the stables, but no one moved or spoke up to surrender his place.

Tragically, it is the same story regarding the hearts of most of mankind. There is no room for Jesus. As then, so now!

SHEPHERDS

"And there were in the same country shepherds abiding in the field, keeping watch over their flock by night" (Lk. 2:8).

"And there were in the same country," referred to the area around Bethlehem where Jesus was born.

"Shepherds abiding in the field," pertained to the

lowest cast in society at that time.

"Keeping watch over their flock by night," gives indication that December 25th was not the day on which Jesus was born.

Actually, it was very unusual for shepherds to keep their flocks in the open at night during the months of November through March. It was the custom to send flocks out after the Passover, which was in April, to stay until the first rain in October or November.

So, inasmuch as specific mention is made of the flocks being *"watched over by night,"* this pretty well tells us that December 25th would not be correct concerning the date of the Birth of Christ.

THE ANGEL OF THE LORD

"And, lo, the Angel of the Lord came upon them, and the Glory of the Lord shone round about them: and they were sore afraid" (Lk. 2:9).

"And, lo, the Angel of the Lord came upon them," proclaims the fact that the Lord's Birth was not trumpeted forth in lordly guise to priest and princes and the great ones of the Earth, but rather to obscure shepherds.

"And the Glory of the Lord shone round about them," tells of the Glory accompanying the Angel as he revealed himself to these humble shepherds.

"And they were sore afraid," proclaims this Glory known among the Jews as the Shekhinah, which was the visible token of the Presence of the Eternal. This appeared first in the bush before Moses, then in the pillar of fire and cloud which guided the desert-wanderings, and then, in the Tabernacle and the Temple.

It appeared, as well, on Jesus on the Mount of Transfiguration. It appeared on Jesus again when He was risen and when He appeared to the Pharisee Saul (Paul) outside Damascus.

Of course, it became visible on the Day of Pentecost when tongues of fire sat upon the heads of those who had gathered in obedience to the Command of Christ (Acts 1:4).

Even the slightest degree of its manifestation brings all Reverence and even fear.

GOOD TIDINGS OF GREAT JOY

"And the Angel said unto them, Fear not: for, behold, I bring you good tidings of great joy, which shall be to all people" (Lk. 2:10).

The phrase, *"And the Angel said unto them, Fear not,"* seems to be the standard statement to the reactions of those in the Presence of God, of which the Angel manifested (Lk. 1:13, 30; 2:10).

"For, behold, I bring you good tidings of great joy," proclaims that which Salvation affords upon acceptance of Christ as one's Saviour.

Actually, the Angel was proclaiming to the shepherds that with the Birth of Christ, the fulfillment of all the Prophecies was taking place. Jesus would later refer to it as *"more abundant life"* (Jn. 10:10), while Peter referred to it as *"joy unspeakable and full of glory"* (I Pet. 1:8).

"Which shall be to all people," refers to Christ being given for the entirety of the world. Consequently, there is no such thing as a *"western gospel," "eastern gospel"* etc., but there is one Gospel for the whole of mankind.

As well, *"All people,"* includes all races of *"red, yellow, brown, black, and white."* None are excluded because Jesus died for all!

However, there will be no *"good tidings of great joy"* if someone does not tell any and all. The fact of this happening is of little consequence to anyone if they have no knowledge of it.

THE SAVIOUR

"For unto you is born this day in the city of David a Saviour, Who is Christ the Lord" (Lk. 2:11).

The phrase, *"For unto you is born this day,"* proclaims the Incarnation, i.e., God manifest in the flesh, the Lord Jesus Christ. It is God becoming Man. He was born of woman, a virgin, in order that He might be the Last Adam, meaning that there will never be the need for another. He gained back by His Life, Ministry, Death, and Resurrection what the first Adam lost (I Cor. 15:45).

"In the city of David," is Bethlehem, David's birthplace. Consequently, Jesus was not only a *"Son of David"* (Mat. 1:1), but, as well, was born in the *"city of David."*

"A Saviour, Who is Christ the Lord," presents Jesus as the *"Good Tidings of Great Joy."* Consequently, this is a *"Person,"* the Lord Jesus Christ, and not some religion with its creeds, doctrines, confessions, and outward forms.

The Babe was not to become a King and a Saviour. He was born both. He was a Saviour, i.e., *"the Saviour,"* for there is no other, and He was Christ, meaning the Anointed, the Messiah of Israel. He was Jehovah.

The Name, *"Christ,"* as stated, means, *"The Anointed,"* consequently, fulfilling Luke 4:18-19.

A SIGN

"And this shall be a sign unto you; You shall find the Baby wrapped in swaddling clothes, lying in a manger" (Lk. 2:12).

The phrase, *"And this shall be a sign unto you,"* concerned where they would find this Baby, God manifest in the flesh.

The evidence is that the shepherds desired to see this *"Baby"* and evidently asked where to find Him.

"You shall find the Baby wrapped in swaddling clothes, lying in a manger," gives the description of His Whereabouts.

I wonder what came to the minds of the shepherds as they attempted to contrast the Glory of the appearance and announcement of the Angels with this lowly *"manger."* However, the Glory of Christ was not in His Surroundings, but rather His Person. Even though the Holy Spirit did not come upon Him until the beginning of His Ministry, still, that did not mean that the Holy Spirit was not there.

I personally believe that from the moment that the Holy Spirit came upon Mary, thereby, decreeing the Conception, He attended Christ from that very moment (Lk. 1:35).

PRAISING GOD

"And suddenly there was with the Angel a multitude of the Heavenly Host praising God, and saying" (Lk. 2:13).

"And suddenly," proclaims a wonder which suddenly happened.

"There was with the Angel a multitude of the Heavenly Host," does not necessarily proclaim them coming at that time, but only that the shepherds were able to see and hear them at that particular time. More than likely, they had been there all the time.

"Praising God and saying," presents sinless Angels, and not sinful men, first praising Him on coming to Earth, and yet, the Angels needed no forgiveness.

Consequently, if they praise the Lord, how much more should we who have experienced such Glorious Forgiveness and Redemption praise Him!

PEACE

*"Glory to God in the highest, and on Earth peace,
good will toward men"* (Lk. 2:14).
Three things are said here by the Angelic Host:

1. GLORY TO GOD IN THE HIGHEST

All Glory must go to God for His Great and
Marvelous Salvation Plan afforded to man. As
stated, if the Angels praise Him, how much more
should we praise Him! The sadness is, most who
call themselves Believers never praise the Lord
because they are not truly Believers. If one is truly
redeemed, one will truly praise Him.

2. AND ON EARTH PEACE

At that particular time, the Roman Empire was at
peace all over the world of that day. Consequently,
the gates of the Temple of Janus at Rome were closed,
there being no need for the presence of the war god
to guide and lead Rome's conquering armies.

Actually, there is evidence that during the entirety
of the Life of Christ, peace reigned.

However, not long after His Death and Resurrection,
the gates of Janus were only too quickly thrown open
again. War began almost immediately and little let
up until Rome finally ceased to be an empire several
hundreds of years later.

The world rejected the *"Prince of Peace,"* and,
consequently, there is no *"peace."* Men talk about
peace, even with some using great effort to bring it
about, but all to no avail.

There will be none until Christ comes again
(Rev. 19:20).

3. GOOD WILL TOWARD MEN

Never has God willed otherwise. He seeks to convince men that He desires only their good (Ps. 84:11; I Tim. 1:14; II Pet. 3:9).

God's Glory in Creation was high; in Revelation, higher; but in Redemption, highest. His Power was seen in Creation; His Righteousness, in Law; but His Highest Attribute, His Love, is seen in the Atonement.

BETHLEHEM

"And it came to pass, as the Angels were gone away from them into Heaven, the Shepherds said one to another, Let us now go even unto Bethlehem, and see this thing which is come to pass, which the Lord has made known unto us" (Lk. 2:15).

"And it came to pass, as the Angels were gone away from them into Heaven," proclaims them having visited these lowly shepherds while having ignored the High Priest as well as the religious leaders of Israel.

Why?

There are several things to be learned from this. Some are as follows:

• *"God resists the proud, but gives Grace to the humble"* (Jam. 4:6). The religious leaders of Israel were eaten up with pride and, consequently, would experience no revelation from the Lord.

• Due to their pride and self-righteousness, these leaders of Israel would not have accepted the *"Babe"* as the Messiah. The facts are, they did not accept Him, even when the evidence was irrefutable.

• Most, if not all, religion falls into the same category presently. It has no revelation from the Lord and, in fact, cannot!

THE POURING OUT OF THE SPIRIT OF GOD

At the turn of the 20th century, the Lord began to pour out His Spirit upon hungry hearts and lives even though many were uneducated. In fact, they were ridiculed and lambasted by the reigning religious order of the day.

Nevertheless, this, the mighty Baptism with the Holy Spirit with the evidence of speaking with other Tongues, has continued to fill hearts and lives until today. It has proven to be the greatest Move of God the world has known since the time of the Early Church.

As well, the vaunted Priesthood of Israel, along with its religious leaders, is gone, but the Followers of the lowly Nazarene abound until they fill the Earth.

The phrase, *"The shepherds said one to another, Let us now go even unto Bethlehem, and see this thing which is come to pass,"* represents them going to the *"House of Bread,"* for that's what the name Bethlehem means, to see the *"True Bread,"* Who has come from Heaven.

"Which the Lord has made known unto us," proclaims one of the greatest honors in the whole of human history. Out of all the people on the face of the Planet, the Lord would dispatch Angels only to these lowly shepherds in exclusion of all others.

They had experienced something glorious in the appearance and announcement of the Angels but upon seeing the Baby Christ, they would experience an even greater Revelation, actually, the greatest of all!

I have to believe that the Lord's Selection of this humble group was by no means random.

I believe they were consecrated to God, loving Him with all their hearts, and, consequently, were privileged to have this distinctive honor, and a distinctive honor it was.

THE MANGER

"And they came with haste, and found Mary, and Joseph, and the Baby lying in a manger" (Lk. 2:16).

"And they came with haste," refers to them following the directions as given to them by the Angel in Verse 12.

Even though there must have been many mangers or corrals in the Bethlehem area, still, there was probably only one *"inn"* of this nature, and so they readily knew where to go.

"And found Mary, and Joseph," was probably only hours, if that, after Jesus was born.

The accommodations were spartan, to say the least! However, this is the manner in which God the Father desired to bring the Redeemer into the world.

Why?

Due to the manner in which man fell in the Garden of Eden, pride became the crowning sin of the Universe. It characterizes all that man is and does; consequently, pomp and ceremony are the hallmarks of success, and even that of religion.

So, if Jesus had come in splendor and glory, as He certainly could have done, man may have been greatly impressed, but he would not have been redeemed. So, Jesus coming to this world as the Epitome of Humility, and surrounded by humility, portrayed the opposite of what man actually was. As one proud, man is haughty, contentious, evil, angry, conceited, and self-serving. Actually, extreme selfishness, which marks humanity, is the child of pride. Consequently, men are impressed by glitter and glamour. Therefore, to be Saved, man has to humble himself, which he does not easily do. After Conversion, the real battle begins, the subjugation of self. Jesus died on Calvary to save man from sin and self. To be truthful, sin is far more easily handled than self.

So, the Birth and Lifestyle of Jesus was such because there could be no other way, that is, if man was to be redeemed. To be sure, such a lifestyle did not save man. That could only come about by what was done at Calvary and the Resurrection.

Nevertheless, it would lay the groundwork for what Conversion would do to the heart and life of the individual — a life of humility.

"And the Baby lying in a manger," was the One, Who, some 33 years later, would die on the Cross of Calvary, thereby, delivering humanity — at least, all who will believe (Jn. 3:16).

CONCERNING THIS CHILD

"And when they had seen it, they made known abroad the saying which was told them concerning this Child" (Lk. 2:17).

The phrase, *"And when they had seen it,"* should have been translated, *"And when they had seen Him."*

Theirs were the first human eyes to see Jesus after His Birth, other than His Foster Father and His Mother.

"They made known abroad the saying which was told them concerning this Child," names them as being the first Preachers to proclaim His Birth, as Mary Magdalene was the first to proclaim His Resurrection. They related what the Angel had told them to everyone who would listen. It was a joyous Story to tell, and they told it with great joy.

WONDERED!

"And all they who heard it wondered at those things which were told them by the shepherds" (Lk. 2:18).

"And all they who heard it," means they were the very first ones to hear after the shepherds. What an honor!

"Wondered at those things which were told them by the shepherds," referred to the appearance and announcement of the Angels and, as well, their personal experience at seeing Baby Jesus. By now, Mary and Joseph had, no doubt, started back for Nazareth, with Mary well enough to make the journey.

PONDERED THEM

"But Mary kept all these things, and pondered them in her heart" (Lk. 2:19).

"But Mary kept all these things," referred to everything that had happened concerning the Birth of Jesus. This included the announcement of the Conception by the Angel Gabriel, as well as her time with Elizabeth, and even the dreams of Joseph (Mat. 1:18-21). Now, the things the shepherds had seen and heard were added to the list.

"And pondered them in her heart," means she thought about them almost constantly, and no wonder!

As she held this tiny Baby in her arms, it is obvious that she knew Who He was. Still, the magnitude, at times, may have been too much for her to comprehend, as it would have been for anyone.

THE SHEPHERDS

"And the shepherds returned, glorifying and praising God for all the things that they had heard and seen, as it was told unto them" (Lk. 2:20).

"And the shepherds returned," refers to them going back to their flock. Who attended their sheep while they were gone, the Scripture does not say. As well, seeing the Heavenly Host was a wonderful thing; however, seeing Jesus, although only a Baby at this time, would have been infinitely greater.

The phrase, *"Glorifying and praising God for all the things that they had heard and seen, as it was told unto them,"* proclaims a Pentecostal meeting, so to speak.

They had *"heard into"* something, the greatest *"Good Tidings"* that had ever fallen upon the ears of man, which was the announcement of the Birth of the Saviour. As well, they had *"seen into"* something, which, in effect, was the Heavenly Host and, above all, *"The Lord Jesus Christ."*

Actually, this is the way it always has been. When people truly seek the Lord, they will always *"hear into"* and *"see."* The Book of Acts is full of *"hearing and seeing."* The Holy Spirit means for that to continue.

JESUS

"And when eight days were accomplished for the circumcising of the Child, His Name was called JESUS, which was so named of the Angel before He was conceived in the womb" (Lk. 2:21).

The phrase, *"And when eight days were accomplished for the circumcising of the Child,"* proclaims, as previously stated, the Law as enjoined in Mosaic Commandments. Actually, Genesis, Chapter 17, gives an account of the Covenant of Circumcision as given to Abraham.

This was carried over into the Mosaic system in connection with the Passover (Ex. 12:44).

As stated here, on the eighth day after birth, the little Hebrew boy was to have the fold of skin covering the end of his penis cut off.

This was called, *"Circumcision,"* and symbolized separation from the world and submission to God, as well as belief in His Covenant Promise.

Due to the Virgin Birth, Jesus was not tainted by original sin as all others, and, consequently, these rights were not necessary, at least, as far as he was concerned.

However, the mother devoutly submitted herself and her Baby to the ancient customs, willingly obedient to that Divine Law under which she was born and hitherto had lived.

HIS NAME

The phrase, *"His Name was called JESUS,"* proclaims the way in which His Name was spelled and pronounced in the Greek, with Joshua being the correct manner in the Hebrew. The Name means, *"Saviour,"* or, *"God Who is Salvation."*

The phrase, *"Which was so named of the Angel before He was conceived in the womb,"* concerned Gabriel being sent from God to Mary. It was Gabriel who announced His Coming Birth and the manner in which He would be conceived. She was also told what He should be named (Lk. 1:26-31).

God's Delights are with the sons of men, therefore, He became a Man; and He became, and is, Their Peace. So, man could learn all of God in Man — that is, in the Man Christ Jesus (Col. 1:13-19) (Williams).

The Heavenly Father might have chosen a loftier title for Jesus, for the highest titles are His, but He passed them all by and selected a Name which speaks of Deliverance for a lost world.

Jesus was made of a woman under the Law (Gal. 4:4). This fact is emphasized by His Circumcision. The Law is mentioned five times in this Chapter, more often than in the rest of the Book, and so confirms the statement in Galatians.

To save man, who is justly doomed to death by the Law, it was necessary that Christ should be born under the Law.

THE DAYS OF PURIFICATION

"And when the days of her purification according to the Law of Moses were accomplished, they brought Him (Jesus) to Jerusalem, to present Him to the Lord" (Lk. 2:22).

The phrase, *"And when the days of her purification according to the Law of Moses were accomplished,"* speaks of 40 days after the Birth of Jesus. (It was 80 days in the case of a daughter, Lev. 12:1-6).

The birth of a child recalled the sin and disobedience of Eden and that woman was the instrument of that rebellion. Hence, after the birth of a boy, the mother was shut out of the Temple for 40 days and, in the case of a girl, as stated, for 80 days. During this time, she was not permitted to touch any hallowed thing.

"They brought Him to Jerusalem, to present Him to the Lord," fulfilled Exodus 13:12; 22:29; 34:19; and Numbers 3:12-13; 18:15.

The presentation of *"Him to the Lord"* went back to the Deliverance of the Children of Israel from Egyptian bondage. With Judgment having condemned to death all of the firstborn of the males in Egypt, including the firstborn of Israel, the latter were saved by the Blood applied to the doorposts of the houses (Ex. 12:13).

However, even though the firstborn were saved from death, they still belonged to the Lord and were to be presented to Him as a token of His Rightful Claim to them, as Mary and Joseph were doing (Num. 3:44-45; 18:15).

HOLY TO THE LORD

"As it is written in the Law of the Lord, Every male that opens the womb shall be called Holy to the Lord" (Lk. 2:23).

"As it is written in the Law of the Lord," refers to

Exodus 13:2 and Numbers 18:15.

"Every male that opens the womb shall be called Holy to the Lord," refers to the firstborn only.

Why was every firstborn *"called Holy to the Lord"?*

All firstborn males were to serve as a Type of Jesus Christ, hence, called *"Holy."* Anything that spoke of Jesus Christ, even the sacrifices, and especially the sacrifices, were referred to as *"Holy"* or *"Most Holy!"* To be sure, the *"Holiness"* was not in the person or the sacrifice, but rather in Jesus.

Jesus is called, *"The Image of the invisible God, the Firstborn of every creature"* (Col. 1:15).

It speaks of Jesus as being the Firstborn of Mary and, as well, the Creator of all things (Mat. 1:25; Lk. 2:7; Jn. 1:1-3). It must also be understood in the literal sense in connection with Jesus being the Firstborn in God's Family. However, Sonship, in this case, refers to humanity and not to Deity. It has to do with the Incarnation, God becoming Man, and, therefore, *"The Firstborn among many brethren"* (Rom. 8:29).

The word has nothing to do with Jesus dying as a sinner on the Cross, being Born-Again in Hell, etc., as some teach.

Jesus is the Firstborn in the new Creation by being raised from the dead, and is the Father of the Salvation Plan, having paid the price on the Cross, which made it all possible. He is thus the Firstborn in the entirety of the family of the Children of God, who, as we have stated, are destined to bear His Image.

THE SACRIFICE

"And to offer a sacrifice according to that which is said in the Law of the Lord, A pair of turtledoves, or two young pigeons" (Lk. 2:24).

The phrase, *"And to offer a sacrifice according to that*

which is said in the Law of the Lord," had to do with Leviticus 12:8.

This did not mean that every time a woman had a child, she had sinned and needed to make atonement for her sin of childbirth.

Her sorrow in conception simply reminded her of her original sin, a sin that deserved death, which she could not atone for, and for which a sacrifice had to be offered.

Having been saved from death in childbirth, though she deserved to die, a sacrifice was therefore commanded to be offered as soon as her days of separation were ended. The remembrance of sin was the true idea in the continued sacrifices until the Messiah should come (Heb. 10:3).

Now, if Christ is accepted as the Substitute and Saviour, there is no more such remembrance of sins (Heb. 10:1-18). All the cleansings for sin, sickness, and any part of the curse otherwise, as the sacrifices represented, were ceremonial and, as stated, served to cause men and women to remember the terrible plight they were in due to the Fall.

The real cleansing from sin had to be done, and was done, by Faith in the coming Redeemer (Rom. 4:1-25; 5:1-11; Gal. 3:8-14; Eph. 2:1-8; Heb. 4:2; 11:1-4; I Pet. 1) simply because the blood of bulls and goats could never take away sin (Heb. 10:4).

THE CROSS

When Jesus died on Calvary, He fulfilled all the types and made it unnecessary for such sacrifices to again be offered.

(And yet, they will be offered again in the coming Kingdom Age but only as a memorial of what Jesus did at Calvary and the Resurrection.)

"A pair of turtledoves, or two young pigeons," proclaimed that which could be offered in place of a *"lamb,"* providing the offerer could not afford the lamb. This tells us that Mary and Joseph were poor, at least, as far as the world's goods were concerned.

It also tells us that the Virgin Mary was not sinless, as claimed by the Catholic church. If so, she would not have had to offer the sacrifices for her impurity.

As well, even though this sacrifice caused the woman (and the man) to remember how far they had fallen, and that another fallen creature had been brought into the world (this did not apply to Jesus), still, the sacrifice of the lamb or the clean birds was, as well, a reminder that a Redeemer was coming.

I wonder if Mary and Joseph at this time fully understood that Jesus was actually that Redeemer and would fulfill all that to which the sacrifices pointed.

SIMEON

"And, behold, there was a man in Jerusalem, whose name was Simeon; and the same man was just and devout, waiting for the consolation of Israel: and the Holy Spirit was upon him" (Lk. 2:25).

"And, behold, there was a man in Jerusalem, whose name was Simeon," is proclaimed by some to be the son of the famous Hillel and the father of Gamaliel.

This Simeon, whether the same or not, became president of the Sanhedrin in 13 A.D.

Even though such is possible, it is very improbable due to the name Simeon being very common among the people. However, the Mishnah, which preserved a record of the sayings and works of the great rabbis, completely passed by this Simeon who was president of the Sanhedrin, whether the same or not! Some think, that is, if this was the same man, that he was passed over due to his belief in Jesus of Nazareth.

At any rate, whether it was that Simeon or not, the Holy Spirit honored his Faith by placing him and his experience in the Sacred Text. There could be no higher privilege!

The phrase, *"And the same man was just and devout,"* proclaims his consecration. This would have mattered little to the religious leaders of Israel, but it mattered much to the God of Heaven.

THE CONSOLATION OF ISRAEL

"Waiting for the consolation of Israel," is a term describing the Coming and Ministry of the Messiah.

There was a general feeling among the more earnest Jews at that time that the Advent of the Messiah would not be long delayed. How right they were! Actually, Daniel had pretty much pinpointed the time (Dan. 9:24-27).

The phrase, *"And the Holy Spirit was upon him,"* proclaims two things:

1. His consecration was evident by the words, *"Just and devout."* Consequently, such can only be brought about by the Holy Spirit, and, as well, the Holy Spirit always accompanies true consecration. Without the Holy Spirit, such is impossible!

2. Also, the consecration of Simeon was channeled in the right direction and, consequently, Scriptural. In other words, his every anticipation concerned the Appearance of the Messiah. As well, his hunger, which was fueled by the Holy Spirit, produced a Revelation by the Spirit, which will almost always follow such hunger.

Anything received by the Believer from the Lord

always comes by the Holy Spirit. Any consecration to the Lord will always mark a greater activity of the Holy Spirit in one's life. The person will always be drawn closer to Jesus, for that is the Business of the Spirit, and, as well, whatever the Spirit does will always be perfectly according to the Work of God.

However, many, if not most, religious denominations presently believe in the Holy Spirit very little or either ignore Him altogether. Consequently, there is almost nothing done for the Lord in these particular organizations.

As well, even in Pentecostal Denominations where the Holy Spirit is supposed to be given great latitude, He is little depended on anymore. Consequently, as the Israel of Simeon's day, precious few presently experience a genuine Move of God.

When the Pentecostal denominations in the 1950s began to accept humanistic psychology, with it presently being totally embraced, this ruled out the Holy Spirit. If one accepts humanistic psychology, one has denied the Holy Spirit and the Cross of Christ.

As stated, one cannot have the world and the Lord at the same time.

THE HOLY SPIRIT

"And it was revealed unto him by the Holy Spirit, that he should not see death, before he had seen the Lord's Christ" (Lk. 2:26).

"And it was revealed unto Him by the Holy Spirit," pertains to several things:

• As we have already stated, Simeon was extremely consecrated to the Lord, which I think is obvious.

• Anything pertaining to God or His Work that is revealed to any person is done so by the Holy Spirit. Paul said this, *"Now we have received, not the spirit of the world, but the Spirit which is of God; that we might know the things that are freely given to us of God."*

He then said, *"Which things also we speak, not in the words which man's wisdom teaches, but which the Holy Spirit teaches; comparing spiritual things with spiritual"* (I Cor. 2:12-13).

So, all Revelation comes by and through the Holy Spirit! As well, such Revelation will seldom come, if ever come, without the consecration as outlined in the first point.

• The same type of Revelation is being given presently and, actually, has always been given to honest, earnest, seeking hearts. While it is true that most of the modern church denies that such is presently done, such unbelief does not hinder the Holy Spirit from bringing Revelation to honest, seeking hearts. However, as should be obvious, all Revelation from the Holy Spirit will always coincide perfectly with the Word of God.

As well, sadly, there is much presently which claims to be a revelation of the Spirit but, in reality, is not! Just because someone says that God told them certain things, it does not necessarily mean it is so.

REVELATIONS

Many Revelations are similar to that given to Simeon of old. He proclaimed that the Lord told him he would see the Messiah before he (Simeon) died. The only way the veracity of such a statement could be made was in it coming to pass, which it did!

However, even a prediction in the Name of the Lord coming to pass does not necessarily mean that such prediction is truly of God.

If the command or prediction is unscriptural, irrespective of it coming to pass, it is not of God. Moses said, *"If there arise among you a prophet, or a dreamer of dreams, and gives you a sign or a wonder,*

"And the sign or the wonder come to pass, whereof he spoke unto you, saying, Let us go after other gods, which you have not known, and let us serve them;

"You shall not hearken unto the words of that prophet, or that dreamer of dreams: for the LORD your God proves you, to know whether you love the LORD your God with all your heart and with all your soul" (Deut. 13:1-3).

THE WORD OF GOD

The Word of God is always the criteria.

The phrase, *"That he should not see death, before he had seen the Lord's Christ,"* presents a startling Revelation.

Some claim that Simeon was very old; however, even though he may well have been, there is no proof of such.

There is an old and striking legend which speaks of this devout Jew being long puzzled and disturbed by the Messianic Prophecy (Isa. 7:14), *"A virgin shall conceive."* At length, he received a supernatural intimation that he should not see death until he had seen the fulfillment of the strange Prophecy, the meaning of which he had so long failed to see.

At any rate, the Revelation given to Simeon by the Holy Spirit was of such magnitude that it defies all description. To be able to look upon this One Who had been promised from the dawn of time was a Blessing of unimaginable proportions.

THE HOLY SPIRIT

"And He came by the Spirit into the Temple: and when the parents brought in the Child Jesus, to do for Him after the custom of the Law" (Lk. 2:27).

The phrase, *"And He came by the Spirit into the*

Temple," means that the Spirit of God impressed upon Him strongly that particular day, and even that particular time, to go to the Temple.

The *"Spirit"* gave him the Revelation and now superintends its fulfillment. One cannot help but see the constant Leading and Guidance of the Holy Spirit in all of these activities, thus proclaiming the absolute necessity of His Presence, Leading, and Guidance in the heart and life of a modern Believer (Jn., Chpt. 16).

"And when the parents brought in the Child Jesus," proclaimed Him, as predicted (Mal. 3:1), coming suddenly to His Temple. However, it was not with pomp and circumstance as the religious leaders expected, but as a Baby with working class parents, and received by an obscure company of Simeon's and Anna's — His Hidden Ones — the poor of the flock.

As well, Malachi 3:1 speaks of the triumphant entry, which took place immediately before His Crucifixion (Mat. 21:1-11).

AFTER THE CUSTOM OF THE LAW

The phrase, *"To do for Him after the custom of the Law,"* meant, as stated, that He was subject to the Law of Moses. Paul said, *"But when the fullness of the time was come, God sent forth His Son, made of a woman, made under the Law,*

"To redeem them who were under the Law, that we might receive the adoption of sons" (Gal. 4:4-5).

In effect, Christ was the only One Who actually kept the Law. All others failed, even Moses, and, therefore, came under the curse of the Law (Gal. 3:13). The curse of the Law was death.

However, upon Christ fully keeping the Law and, thereby, satisfying its demands upon simple Faith in Him, the Believer is automatically granted His Perfection as a perfect Law-keeper. In other words, upon acceptance of Christ, we are immediately transferred from the position of lawbreaker to the position of Law-keeper, all because of Christ. In other words, we are privileged and allowed to enter into His Perfection. Jesus was our Substitute and as the Representative Man, was able to do what no other man ever did. He satisfied the claims of Heavenly Justice and, as well, broke the grip of sin that Satan had on humanity.

This is the reason that God is sorely displeased with Believers who attempt to go back under Law, thereby, attaching their Salvation to their efforts.

Why should any Believer try to do such when, in effect, no one has ever succeeded in keeping the Law except Christ? Inasmuch as He has perfectly kept the Law, simple Faith in Him and what He did grants us the Victory of His Accomplishment. Consequently, for a Believer to attempt to attach Law to his walk with God, in effect, says that Jesus did not succeed, thereby, calling Him a liar. Thus, Paul said, *"... let God be true, but every man a liar ..."* (Rom. 3:4).

THE PRIVILEGE OF ETERNITY

"Then took he Him up in his arms, and blessed God, and said" (Lk. 2:28).

"Then took he Him up in his arms," proclaims Simeon as the first on record to have *"seen and handled"* the *"Word of Life,"* other than Mary and Joseph.

Quite possibly, and, no doubt, there were other parents there with their children to undergo the purification process. However, the Holy Spirit must surely have singled out Mary, Joseph, and Jesus. When this happened, Simeon, no doubt, asked Mary and Joseph if he could hold the Child!

Inasmuch as the Holy Spirit was moving in the

entirety of this situation, Mary and Joseph knew this was of the Lord and gladly consented.

What must this man have thought when he picked up Baby Jesus?

The phrase, *"And blessed God, and said,"* simply means that he had great thanksgiving in his heart for the Lord allowing him this great and glorious privilege. Consequently, he *"blessed God,"* or praised the Lord. It means his entire being was filled with peace and thanksgiving.

ACCORDING TO YOUR WORD

"Lord, now let Your Servant depart in peace, according to Your Word" (Lk. 2:29).

The phrase, *"Lord, now let Your Servant depart in peace,"* insinuates that it had been a number of years since the Lord had revealed to Simeon that he would actually, personally, see *"the Lord's Christ."* The implication is that he had tarried long for this moment.

Faith not only has to claim the Promise but, as well, has to stay the course. I am afraid the modern church, especially in the last few years, has been lead down a different path. If Faith's answer is not immediate, many soon give up, falling by the wayside. In Scriptural reality, such is not true faith. Faith to be Faith must stay the course.

As well, Simeon felt that inasmuch as he had now seen the Lord's Christ, there was nothing else in life that could really matter; therefore, he was now ready *"to depart in peace."*

"According to Your Word," means that all of this, the Promise of him actually seeing the Messiah and now the Promise becoming a reality, had all been *"according to Your Word."*

What a tremendous Blessing that this man's

experience and Testimony would be, considering it was written in the Word of God — all because of Faith in God's Word!

YOUR SALVATION

"For my eyes have seen Your Salvation" (Lk. 2:30).
Simeon did not have to ask Mary who the Child was or inquire as to the wonders of His Birth. He recognized Him at once by Inspiration as Jehovah's Anointed and said, *"My eyes have seen Your Salvation."*

He personally possessed that Salvation, for he took Jesus into his arms, and that possession conquered death and vanquished all its terror.

This Passage tells us that God's *"Salvation"* is not a philosophy, theory, formula, doctrine, or religion, but instead, a Person, the Man Christ Jesus.

Millions try to find Salvation in the Church, but it is not to be found. The Church did not die on Calvary to purchase man's Redemption. Jesus Christ did that! Consequently, He and He Alone is Salvation (Jn. 3:16).

PREPARATION

"Which You have prepared before the face of all people" (Lk. 2:31).
The phrase, *"Which You have prepared,"* means that Salvation is all of God and none of man! This is at least one of the reasons that God will not tolerate man adding his puny selfish works to the Finished Work of Jesus Christ.

"Before the face of all people," opens the door of Salvation to every human being on the face of the Earth regardless of color, nationality, or country.

Considering what God did in the sending of His Son and the great price He paid, it is our business to tell this great Story to the whole of humanity.

THE LIGHT AND THE GLORY

"A Light to lighten the Gentiles, and the Glory of Your People Israel" (Lk. 2:32).

The phrase, *"A Light to lighten the Gentiles,"* is basically a quote from Isaiah 42:6.

However, despite the fact of this Prophetic Announcement by Isaiah and Simeon further proclaiming this great truth, it was perhaps the hardest lesson the Apostles and the first teachers of the Faith had to master — this full, free admission of the vast Gentile world into the Kingdom of their God. It actually took a Divine rebuke for the Apostles to conceive such a doctrine (Acts 10:15; 11:18). It was over this that controversy raged in the Early Church (Acts, Chpt. 15; Gal., Chpt. 2).

Why was the simple Truth of the Gospel going to the Gentiles so difficult to grasp and carry out?

It is actually a spirit of self-righteousness, which desires to exclude all except for a select few. Some modern religious denominations follow suit, claiming that unless one is associated with their group, one cannot be Saved.

Sometime ago, I heard a preacher exclaim over radio that to be Saved, one must be baptized in water. However, he added that even that was not enough, as he exclaimed that a certain baptismal formula must be adhered to.

He then added the crowning clincher of all! Not only must the individual be baptized in water, and according to a particular formula, but he had to be baptized in that preacher's tank in his church.

We may possibly smile at such foolishness; however, it is actually no more foolish than claiming that one must be a Baptist, a Methodist, a Pentecostal, etc., to be Saved. And yet, the church world is full of such absurdities. Consequently, it seems that we have not progressed so very much from the days of the Early Church.

THE GLORY OF YOUR PEOPLE ISRAEL

The phrase, *"And the Glory of Your People Israel,"* nevertheless, was not recognized by Israel as such.

Israel had been raised up for the very purpose of bringing the Messiah into the world. This was their privilege and their glory. And yet, when the time came, they did not even know Who He was. Worse still, they murdered Him!

As well, Jesus Christ is the Glory of the Church. However, in too many church circles, He has been pushed aside, if recognized at all, and even denied in some cases.

The Catholic church, for instance, places Mary ahead of Jesus, the Lord of Glory! Many Methodists, Presbyterians, and Lutherans presently deny His Virgin Birth or even that He is the Son of God. As well, too often, even in Pentecostal and Charismatic circles, the Lord is little more than someone to use in order to obtain *"things."*

Whether they realize it or not, most Baptists, as well as many Holiness groups, deny Him simply because they deny the Holy Spirit with which He baptizes.

God help us!

Jesus is the only *"Light,"* and yet, the modern church holds up psychology as the answer to the ills and aberrations of man. Jesus is the only *"Glory,"* and yet, instead of lifting up Him, we parade our buildings and suchlike before the world!

JOSEPH AND MARY

"And Joseph and His Mother marveled at those things which were spoken of him" (Lk. 2:33).

Exactly how much Joseph and Mary had related to others concerning what they now knew about this Baby is not known; however, Zechariah and Elisabeth knew, as well as all those to whom the shepherds had spoken (Lk. 2:17).

Quite possibly, the information related by the shepherds had reached the ears of Simeon inasmuch as Bethlehem is only a short distance from Jerusalem and the Temple.

Irrespective, the Scriptural evidence is that he came to the Temple this day strictly by the bidding of the Holy Spirit (Lk. 2:27).

The word, *"Marveled,"* relates to their surprise at the tremendous statements made by Simeon concerning this Child. Of course, as the Holy Spirit had led him this far concerning his beholding the Messiah, the Holy Spirit would now speak through him in Prophecy concerning the Work of the Messiah.

Incidentally, if one is to notice, Luke wrote, *"Joseph and His Mother,"* and not, *"His Father and Mother."* Of course, the reason is obvious! Joseph was only His Foster Father, so to speak.

THE RISE AND THE FALL

"And Simeon blessed them, and said unto Mary His Mother, Behold, this Child is set for the fall and rising again of many in Israel; and for a sign which shall be spoken against" (Lk. 2:34).

The phrase, *"And Simeon blessed them,"* refers only to Joseph and Mary and not Jesus. While Christ blesses all, none are qualified to bless Christ! (Sometimes the word, *"Blessed,"* is used in the sense of *"praise,"* which then becomes not only acceptable but desirable.)

"And said unto Mary His Mother," refers to her only and, as stated, not Joseph. Whether Simeon, at this stage, knew about the Virgin Birth is not known. However, the Holy Spirit, Who knows all things, called Simeon to address his words exactly as they should have been.

Mary was related to Jesus while Joseph was not, at least, in a literal sense. By lineage, Joseph was related through David but not by blood.

THE FALL AND RISING OF MANY IN ISRAEL

The phrase, *"Behold, this Child is set for the fall and rising again of many in Israel,"* has come to pass in totality, and shall yet come to pass in totality!

Israel fell *"into"* because of her rejection of Jesus Christ as her Lord, Saviour, and Messiah, while a few *"rose,"* which was actually the beginning of the Early Church.

In totality, Israel suffered its most horrible *"fall"* in 70 A.D., with the destruction of Jerusalem by Titus. However, her greatest *"fall"* is yet to come when she will come close to extinction at the hands of the Antichrist, whom she, at first, will think is the Messiah. And yet, at the Second Coming when Israel will finally accept Jesus Christ as Lord and Master, then the world will witness a *"rising again of many in Israel"* almost like one from the grave.

THE SIGN

The phrase, *"And for a sign which shall be spoken against,"* as well, has been fulfilled to the letter.

For nearly 300 years, the Name of Jesus of Nazareth

and His Followers was a name of shame among both the Romans and Jews. Romans, such as Tacitus, Suetonius, and Pliny, spoke against the Name of Jesus with intense bitterness.

As well, the Jews referred to Jesus as *"The Deceiver,"* *"That Man,"* or *"The Hung."* These were common expressions used in the great rabbinical schools, which flourished in the early days of Christianity.

Even today, the Name of Jesus is referred to either with great love or hatred. Men who have agreed in nothing else have agreed in hating Christ.

Why?

Jeremiah gave us the answer. He said, *"The heart is deceitful above all things, and desperately wicked: who can know it?"* (Jer. 17:9).

The Heart of Jesus Christ was and is absolutely pure; consequently, the darkness hated and hates His Light.

Paul said, *"... There is none righteous, no, not one:*

"There is none who understands, there is none who seek after God ...."

He went on to say, *"Their throat is an open sepulchre; with their tongues they have used deceit; the poison of asps is under their lips:*

"Whose mouth is full of cursing and bitterness:

"Their feet are swift to shed blood:

"Destruction and misery are in their ways" (Rom. 3:10-16).

TOTAL DEPRAVITY

It is called the total depravity of man. Let it be known that it applies to every single person in the world, other than those who have made Jesus the Lord of their lives and, consequently, have had His Righteousness imputed unto them.

As well, education, culture, money, breeding, or power cannot change this evil, wicked condition. Men do not merely exhibit evil; they are evil.

The only Power on Earth that can change that evil is the Power of the Crucified, Resurrected Saviour. Faith in Him, and Him Alone, can set the captive free from this death of sin.

That is the reason they hated Him, and continue to hate Him!

The only thing that is keeping this world on a half-way even keel is the Saints of God who are *"the salt of the Earth"* and *"Light of the world"* (Mat. 5:13-14).

That is the reason the world is going to go downhill fast during the time of the coming Great Tribulation when the Antichrist makes his debut.

The Rapture of the Church will take every blood-bought, blood-washed Believer out of this world, leaving precious little restraint against the forces of wickedness (I Thess. 4:16-17; II Thess. 2:6-8).

OPPOSITION

In my own personal Ministry, and due to having quite a bit of experience with the media, I have noticed the manner in which the opposition works against the true Body of Christ.

The world's system, which is energized by Satan, has no love for anything that pertains to God. However, if one is to notice, if any good thing is said by the media about anything spiritual, it will, most of the time, be in favor of the Catholic church.

If any words of praise are still forthcoming at this stage, it will be reserved for the denominational churches, such as the Baptist, Methodist, etc.

For Spirit-filled Believers, the media has no good word, irrespective of what may be said or done.

In the 1980s, Jimmy Swaggart Ministries built some 40 schools in the little country of Haiti alone. Actually, we built well over a hundred in other third world countries. These were very simple affairs, which handled about 300 to 500 children each, and only went through the sixth grade. We also served a hot meal at noon each day; however, this was the only schooling that most of these children had access to. These schools cost us approximately $50,000 each to construct, plus the monthly upkeep for the teachers and hot meals each day.

A lady by the name of Judy Woodruff, who works for Public Broadcasting Service, did a television documentary on our work in Haiti.

Despite the fact that we had built some 40 schools over the island, giving an elementary education to approximately 15,000 children (schools, I might quickly add, which could be easily found), she reported that we had built only one school in Haiti. She claimed that it was built in a wealthy part of the city of Port-au-Prince, and only the children of wealthy parents were allowed to attend. If I remember correctly, this *"documentary"* was aired in 1985 or 1986.

This was portrayed over public television in Seattle, Washington, with the entire flavor of the program, as should be obvious, proclaiming us as a charlatan and cheat.

We sent the proof of the schools we had built to the manager of this respective television station, and, to his credit, he did air a retraction. However, the point is this:

This woman had no regard for the truth! She did not care that thousands of children were being educated and given at least a helpful start in life. Rather than admit that we were doing this type of work, which should have been commendable to anyone, she would do all she could to destroy us, and whatever happened to the children was of no consequence.

Reasonably, it seemed that many felt that way! That is why Paul said, *"with their tongues they have used deceit; the poison of asps is under their lips"* (Rom. 3:13).

Were one to ask these people the reason for their attitude and spirit, I am not certain they would be able to give a definitive answer. However, I know what the answer is. Their true hatred, if the truth is known, is against Jesus Christ.

THE THOUGHTS OF MANY HEARTS MAY BE REVEALED

"Yes, a sword shall pierce through your own soul also, that the thoughts of many hearts may be revealed" (Lk. 2:35).

The phrase, *"Yes, a sword shall pierce through your own soul also,"* basically pertained to the rejection of Jesus' Ministry by the religious leaders of Israel and, ultimately, His Crucifixion on the Cross.

No doubt, the time of Jesus' Childhood and His Growing into manhood were the happiest times for Mary. Especially considering that He was the Only Perfect Child who ever lived and that it exemplified itself in His Daily Demeanor and Lifestyle, this must have been a source of untold Blessing for her. However, with the Advent of His Ministry, that soon ended. The anger was so intense against Him, even in His Hometown of Nazareth, there was no way Mary could escape the brunt of this opposition.

THE PURPOSE OF THE GOSPEL

The phrase, *"That the thoughts of many hearts may be revealed,"* presents the very purpose of the Gospel of Christ. With Mary's own heart being carnal as all others, it had to come under the rays of this great Light, and her soul had to feel the piercing of the Divine Sword of the Word of God. Is it possible that she was willing to be the Honored Mother of the King of Israel (Lk. 1:32) but unwilling to be the Despised Disciple of the hated Nazarene (Mk. 3:21) Natural grief pained Mary's heart at Calvary, but this dread sword, as we have stated, had to pierce her soul also.

She was indeed blessed as the chosen vessel of the Incarnation, but women who follow Jesus are more blessed (Lk. 11:27).

The Gospel of Jesus Christ Alone penetrates the hearts of men, for this is where the true problem resides.

THE WORD OF GOD

At the dawn of time, Adam and Even fell because they did not take the Word of God seriously. The very first words that Satan said, using the faculties of the serpent, were, *"Has God said? ..."* (Gen. 3:1). He was attempting to replace the Word of God with something else, which he was successful in doing. He has been doing the same thing ever since. Consequently, the blight of the human family, even from that earliest day, has been what is referred to as *"subjective truth."* In other words, truth, according to this erroneous thinking, is whatever one wants it to be or whatever one says it is. In effect, this is the cause of all human problems.

The Bible proclaims, *"Objective Truth,"* which is Truth that does not change, either by time, race, or circumstances.

TRUTH

For instance, in the beginning of Creation, God perfected a system of Laws or Truths which are immutable. This pertains to both scientific and social. Fortunately, man cannot change the scientific Truths which are found in the Laws of mathematics as originally created by God. Man must abide by these Truths even in the total sense, or else, buildings will fall, airplanes will not fly, bridges will not hold, etc.

However, in the social sense, which Laws are just as immutable as in the scientific realm, man has changed these Laws and brought upon himself untold harm. He has inserted the drivel of evolution in place of Creationism, called abortion pro-choice instead of murder, which it rightly is, and replaced the Foundation of the Word of God, with its immutable rules for life and godliness, with humanistic psychology.

All of that is subjective truth, which means that truth has been perverted to the extent that it is whatever community standards say it is. That is the reason many marriages do not work, education little works, and wars begin. Men have taken the objective Truth of the Word of God, which never changes, and replaced it with its own and subjective truth, which, in reality, is no truth at all, and changes with the wind. The results are disaster.

The Word of God in the Person of Jesus Christ reveals the thoughts of men's hearts. In this Revelation, one of two things is brought about. Men become angrier and seek to kill the Messenger, as they did in the Crucifixion of Christ, or else, they repent. Regrettably, the latter is not usually the case.

ANNA THE PROPHETESS

"And there was one Anna, a Prophetess, the daughter of Phanuel, of the Tribe of Aser: she was of a great age,

and had lived with an husband seven years from her virginity" (Lk. 2:36).

The phrase, *"And there was one Anna, a Prophetess, the daughter of Phanuel,"* presents this dear lady as a Preacher of the Gospel.

The silly idea that God does not or cannot call women to preach has no Scriptural foundation whatsoever, as should be glaringly obvious!

In the Bible, the first woman to prophesy was Rachel (Gen. 30:24), even though she is not called a Prophetess. Actually, the Lord uses women exactly as He uses men.

In Acts 21:8-9, it is clear that Phillip's four daughters were Prophetesses, that is, they were Evangelists like their father. This is in perfect accord with Joel 2:28-29, which was carried out in the Early Church (Acts 2:16), and with Acts 2:17-18, which is being fulfilled, as well, in these last days.

In Romans, Chapter 16, we have record of a number of women Servants of the Lord in various Churches. Phebe (Vss. 1-2), Priscilla (Vss. 3-5), Mary, Tryphena, Tryphosa, Persis, and Julia (Vss. 6-15), are mentioned as laborers in the Lord.

In Philippians 4:2, Paul mentions Euodias and Syntyche as being leaders of the Church at Philippi. As well, and to which we have alluded, women were used of God in Old Testament Times as Prophetesses and Preachers (Ex. 15:20; Judg. 4:4; II Ki. 22:14; II Chron. 34:22; Neh. 6:14; Isa. 8:3).

WOMEN PREACHERS?

While it is true that all the Disciples chosen by Christ were men, still, that does not preclude God from calling women to preach. All the Disciples were men because men were created first by God and are actually under Christ, the Federal Head of the human family (Eph. 5:23).

As well, all of these men were Jews, but that did not mean that God could not call Gentile men as Preachers, which He has by the untold numbers, as should be obvious. In effect, Simeon represented men concerning the recognition and worship of Christ, even as a Baby, as Anna represented women. No favoritism or partiality was shown to either one by the Holy Spirit.

THE TRIBE OF ASHER

Most Jews, at that time, knew their tribal affiliation even though the tribal boundaries were no longer adhered to as they had been at the beginning. Rebellion against God had resulted in 10 of the Tribes (or nine) breaking off and forming the northern kingdom called Israel, Samaria, or Ephraim.

Of the Thirteen Tribes, Benjamin stayed loyal to Judah, which formed the southern kingdom called Judah. Inasmuch as Simeon was a part of Judah, they probably remained loyal to Judah as well! The Tribe of Levi, which was the Priestly Tribe, did accordingly.

During the time of Hezekiah, which was about 700 years before Christ, the northern kingdom of Israel was destroyed by the Assyrians and was never restored. Somewhat over 100 years later, at about 588 B.C., the southern kingdom of Judah was destroyed by the Babylonians. They were taken captive, as the northern kingdom had been, but were restored about 70 years later.

However, with that Restoration, many of the Tribes of the northern kingdom came back, as well, but not as a Nation. Consequently, even though all the Tribes were represented in Israel during the time of Christ, due to Roman occupation, there were no tribal boundaries as there once had been.

JUDGMENT AND RESTORATION

As is known, in 70 A.D., Jerusalem was destroyed along with the Temple, which contained all the genealogical records of all the families in Israel. As a result, Jews presently have no idea, except maybe with some small exceptions, as to their particular Tribe.

Some may ask how this would have any bearing on events at present. The answer is, *"Almost none!"* However, in the last eight Chapters of his Book, the Prophet Ezekiel predicted that the tribal boundaries, at least, after a fashion, would be restored with Israel once again being the premier Nation in the world. This will be in the coming Kingdom Age.

This is important in the sense that Israel must be restored to her rightful place and position, as previously ordained by God, before the entirety of the world can be blessed as it will be at that time period. That is at least part of the reason that David said, *"Whither the Tribes go up, the Tribes of the LORD, unto the testimony of Israel, to give thanks unto the Name of the LORD.*

"For there are set Thrones of Judgment, the Thrones of the House of David."

He then said, *"Pray for the peace of Jerusalem: they shall prosper who love you.*

"Peace be within your walls, and prosperity within your palaces" (Ps. 122:4-7).

The phrase, *"She was of a great age, and had lived with an husband seven years from her virginity,"* means that her husband died seven years after they were married.

SERVING GOD

"And she (Anna) was a widow of about fourscore

and four years (84 years), who departed not from the Temple, but served God with fastings and prayers night and day" (Lk. 2:37).

"And she was a widow of about fourscore and four years," means that it had been 84 years since her husband had died. This means she was over 100 years old, possibly between 115 and 120 years of age.

The phrase, *"Who departed not from the Temple,"* means that for some time, she had literally lived in the Temple, probably being provided a small room or chamber and being assigned some small task.

"But served God with fastings and prayers night and day," notes her wonderful consecration to the Lord. Consequently, she would be rewarded by having the privilege of seeing and recognizing the Messiah, even as a Baby. To both her and Simeon, there could have been no higher honor.

To think of coming to the end of one's life and being rewarded by the Lord in this fashion would be the absolute ultimate, to say the least.

And yet, most of the people in the world of that day would have had no interest whatsoever in such a privilege.

It is the same presently. Most of humanity has absolutely no idea of that which is of true value. Most spend their lives on *"vanity and vexation of spirit,"* which means, *"Empty nothings!"*

Most of the world does not know Jesus, consequently, has absolutely no idea as to the total satisfaction He brings to the human heart. As well, it is satisfaction and fulfillment which cannot be derived from any other source.

GIVING THANKS

"And she (Anna) coming in that instant gave thanks

likewise unto the Lord, and spoke of Him to all them who looked for Redemption in Jerusalem" (Lk. 2:38).

The phrase, *"And she coming in that instant gave thanks likewise unto the Lord,"* proclaims that the Holy Spirit revealed unto her, as well, that this Child was indeed the Messiah. Consequently, upon this Revelation, she *"gave thanks unto the Lord."*

"And spoke of Him to all them who looked for Redemption in Jerusalem," means that she related her experience at seeing Christ to all those who were truly looking for the Messiah, at least, those who were privileged to come in contact with her.

Thus, two witnesses, the one a man and the other a woman, testified to the fulfillment of Malachi 3:1. They both loved the courts of Jehovah's House, and He met them there.

WISE MEN

"Now when Jesus was born in Bethlehem of Judaea in the days of Herod the king, behold, there came wise men from the east to Jerusalem" (Mat. 2:1).

The phrase, *"Now when Jesus was born in Bethlehem of Judaea,"* proclaims this Bethlehem, for another Bethlehem was in Zebulon.

As well, Matthew gives no details on the Birth of Christ as Luke did (Lk., Chpt. 2); however, Matthew would mention the *"wise men,"* which Luke did not!

Incidentally, Jesus being born in *"Bethlehem"* was a fulfillment of Micah 5:2. This little village was then about five miles south of Jerusalem. Presently, it is basically a suburb of Jerusalem.

HEROD

The phrase, *"In the days of Herod the king,"* proclaims

this time as approximately two years after the Birth of Christ.

This was Herod the Great, son of Antipater, an Idumean, and, consequently, a descendant of Esau. So, by nature, he hated and resolved to murder the son of Jacob.

Antipater, the father of Herod the Great, was made procurator of Judaea by Julius Caesar in 47 B.C. At only 25 years old, Herod was made governor of Galilee and then, eventually, all of Judaea in 37 B.C.

He is the one who rebuilt the Jewish Temple (Jn. 2:20).

When he died in 4 B.C., his kingdom was then divided. Galilee and Perea were given to his son, Herod Antipas. He reigned from 4 B.C. to 39 A.D. (Lk. 3:1-2). This is the man who murdered John the Baptist (Mat. 14:1-11).

Judaea and Samaria were given to Archelaus, another son of Herod the Great (Mat. 2:22). He was succeeded by Herod Agrippa I in 37 A.D. He is called *"Philip"* in Matthew 14:3.

In 40 A.D., he took over all the original territory of Herod the Great. He was succeeded by Herod Agrippa II (Acts 25:13; 26:32).

Even though Herod the Great (the Herod mentioned by Matthew) expended lavish sums on the Temple, it did not endear him to his Jewish subjects.

His Edomite descent was never forgotten. If he was a Jew by religion and rebuilt the Temple of the God of Israel in Jerusalem, which he did, that still did not deter him from erecting temples to pagan deities elsewhere.

In keeping with his murderous nature, this man later executed his own sons, Alexander and Aristobulus. As well, his oldest son, Antipater, (named after his grandfather), who had poisoned

Herod's mind against his half-brothers, derived no advantage from their death.

Three years later, he too fell victim to Herod's suspicions and was executed only a few days before Herod's own death.

This suspicious, murderous nature is well illustrated by the story of the visit of the wise men and the slaughter of the infants of Bethlehem, as Matthew related.

Few men have been so ungodly!

WISE MEN FROM THE EAST

The phrase, *"Behold, there came wise men from the east to Jerusalem"* (Mat. 2:1), does not give their number, their particular country, or that they were kings. It is just known that they were from the *"east."*

Tacitus and Suetonius, both Romans, testified to the fact that in the east at that time it was believed that a king would be born in Judaea who would rule the whole world.

In fact, Daniel predicted the Coming of our Lord and His being *"cut off"* some 483 years after the Babylonian captivity commandment to restore Jerusalem (Dan. 9:24-26).

Consequently, these *"wise men"* were probably from the area that Daniel had served about 500 years before and, therefore, would be well aware of his Prophecies concerning this coming King and would be, no doubt, guided by their pronouncements.

Incidentally, the meaning of the word, *"Bethlehem,"* is, *"House of Bread."* Consequently, it was fitting that Jesus would be born here because He was *"the True Bread."*

A STAR IN THE EAST

"Saying, Where is He Who is born King of the Jews? for we have seen His Star in the east, and are come to worship Him" (Mat. 2:2).

The question, *"Saying, Where is He Who is born King of the Jews?"* proclaims the certitude of the knowledge of these *"wise men,"* and that they did not ask, *"Whether there is?"* but, *"Where is?"* They showed no sign of doubt.

The title, *"King of the Jews,"* was used first by these Gentiles and was not used again until used by another Gentile, Pontius Pilate, as well as Roman soldiers (Mat. 27:11, 37).

In actuality, the statement, *"King of the Jews,"* as used by the *"wise men,"* would have probably deeply offended the Jews as they preferred the term, *"King of Israel"* (Mat. 27:42; Mk. 15:32).

As well, the term, *"Jews,"* was not a term of endearment, at least, in the ears of Israel, while the term, *"Israel,"* reminded them of their great privileges according to the Scriptures.

WE SAW HIS STAR

"For we have seen His Star in the east," probably would have been better translated, *"We dwelling in the east saw His Star."*

This Passage, with Verses 9 and 10, seems to make it clear that the star did not precede them in their journey to Jerusalem, as is popularly supposed, but upon seeing it in the *"east,"* they knew it was *"His Star."*

Many questions beg to be asked concerning that statement, of which there are few definitive answers.

• What was this star they saw in the heavens? Astronomy can suggest nothing which satisfies all these conditions, and, therefore, the appearance must have been strictly miraculous.

About 1,600 years before, Balaam had prophesied, *"There shall come a Star out of Jacob ..."* a Prophecy with which they may well have been acquainted (Num. 24:15-19). And yet, this Prophecy alone would have given them precious little information!

• How did they know it was *"His Star"?* They were emphatic in their statement and could have only achieved this knowledge through Revelation from God, which they, no doubt, had received.

As well, they probably had hungrily studied the Prophecies of Daniel and had been convinced of this coming King.

From these brief statements, there is every evidence that they knew Who He was and What He was, at least, up to a point!

• The phrase, *"And are come to worship Him,"* does not necessarily mean the acceptance of Him as God but as Lord and King.

However, these *"wise men"* coming without delay, especially a journey of several hundreds of miles and requiring several weeks, would not have been undertaken without something powerful happening to them far greater than the ordinary.

Having tabulated Daniel's Prophecies and knowing this was the approximate time for the Birth of this King, quite possibly, they had accepted Daniel's God and had sought Him earnestly pertaining to these all-important events.

Consequently, they experienced a Revelation from the Lord of some magnitude. Little else could explain their attention, haste, and knowledge!

As well, I don't think they would have undertaken such a journey, which, in those days, was long and difficult, without something having happened to them spiritually that was far beyond the ordinary. I personally believe they had accepted Jehovah as their God and now would come to see His Son who, evidently, had recently been born.

HEROD THE KING

"When Herod the king had heard these things, he was troubled, and all Jerusalem with him" (Mat. 2:3).

The phrase, *"Herod the king,"* is in contradistinction to Jesus as *"King of the Jews."*

They are here placed side by side by the Holy Spirit in order to portray the contrast. One was notoriously wicked while the Other was Gloriously Righteous. One was a murderer while the Other was a Giver of Life. One helped drag a Nation down while the Other picked it up, at least, as much as they would allow Him!

As we have stated, had Israel not sinned terribly, bluntly refusing to repent, which necessitated their destruction by the Gentiles, Joseph would now be king and not this murderous Herod.

Consequently, it becomes obviously clear that to disobey God brings destruction and heartache while obeying Him brings joy and Abundant Life (Jn. 10:10).

However, man would disavow this, claiming that God's Restrictions hamper his lifestyle. Man also claims that the way to make a better world is to ignore God and, instead, let man himself become god, which he has with disastrous results!

THE BIBLE

Consequently, the Bible is presently held up to ridicule all over America when, in reality, every single freedom and prosperity known in America and, in fact, anywhere else in the world has its origination in the

Word of God. Sadly, blind men lead blind men, and they all fall in the ditch (Mat. 15:14).

The phrase, *"Heard these things,"* refers to the information given Herod from the *"wise men,"* who had journeyed from the east to Jerusalem.

Because the evil heart cannot understand spiritual things, little did Herod realize that he could have been one of the most blessed kings in history to have been reigning when the *"King of kings"* was born! What a privilege he would have had to have used his position to herald the Arrival of the Saviour of mankind.

"These things" were the single most important things he would ever hear in all of his life, and yet, he did the very opposite, as most!

As well, how so very important *"these things"* are to the whole of mankind, which constitutes the Word of God. And yet, most have no concern or regard but, instead, label *"these things"* as fables and, therefore, little worthy of attention!

TROUBLE

"He was troubled," has reference, at least, in a sense, to the Spirit of God dealing with him concerning what he had heard.

The Word of God never leaves one static. In other words, after hearing the Word, one is either better or worse for the hearing of it. If properly heeded, one is better, and in a way that is beyond one's imagination. If rejected, one does not remain as he was but, instead, becomes progressively worse because he has rejected Light. Therefore, the darkness becomes deeper, as it did with Herod.

The phrase, *"And all Jerusalem with him,"* was true as far as the whole was concerned. However, some two years before, some few had gathered around Elisabeth and Zechariah and Mary and Joseph, concerning the two babies.

As well, Simeon, Anna, and others were thrilled at the prospect of the Birth of Christ (Lk. 2:38).

The phrase concerning *"all Jerusalem"* must mean that the news was noised abroad in the city, but it aroused, it seems, little interest in the hearts of the religious leaders.

They were so lifted up within themselves that they could not even begin to admit that these Gentile *"wise men"* from the east could tell them anything, especially concerning the coming Messiah!

Therefore, because of hardness of heart and unbelief, they would miss the greatest event to date in human history.

WHERE CHRIST SHOULD BE BORN

"And when he had gathered all the Chief Priests and Scribes of the people together, he demanded of them where Christ should be born" (Mat. 2:4).

This Scripture says the Priests knew the Bible well; however, knowledge of the Scriptures in one's head is not the same as knowledge of the Scriptures in one's heart.

The phrase, *"And when he had gathered all the Chief Priests and Scribes of the people together,"* means that he did this forthwith and without delay.

He was gathering them together for a very negative result, which would constitute one of the most brutal acts in history.

Had he gathered them together in order to worship Christ, as the *"wise men,"* what a difference his life would have been!

However, today, Herod is in Hell, and he will be there forever and forever.

CHRIST

The phrase, *"He demanded of them where Christ should be born,"* speaks of the Jewish Sanhedrin, i.e., *"Chief Priests,"* and exactly *"where"* this act spoken of by the *"wise men"* had taken place.

The use of the title, *"Christ,"* indicates that the Priests informed him that the One he was speaking of was, in fact, the Messiah, i.e., *"the Anointed."* Consequently, he, as well as the *"Chief Priests and Scribes,"* were sinning against Light.

As stated, Christ was probably pretty close to two years old at that time, and these religious leaders of Israel had no knowledge of Him. They were so wrapped up in their own religious world that they had long since departed from the Word of God. Regrettably, it has pretty much always been that way, with the present no exception!

Most of that which God truly does is unknown completely by the religious world. Not only do they know nothing about it, but they will actively oppose it if it's called to their attention, even as these Priests and Scribes. Such characterizes all religion, which is always man-devised, and makes up the far greater part of that which calls itself *"Church!"*

BETHLEHEM OF JUDAEA

"And they said unto him, In Bethlehem of Judaea: for thus it is written by the Prophet" (Mat. 2:5).

In answering the question of the king, the *"Chief Priests and Scribes"* were speaking of the Prophecy of Micah 5:2. They knew where it was to be but had absolutely no knowledge that it had happened.

This is startling! The greatest event to date in the annals of human history had recently taken place, as well as that which the Prophets had spoken of so grandly, but these, the religious leaders of Israel, knew absolutely nothing about it. They knew the Word of God but only within their heads and not their hearts, which means they did not know its Author. They were versed in its content but were not versed in its true meaning! Such characterizes much, if not most, of modern Christendom.

TO RULE ISRAEL

"And you Bethlehem, in the land of Judah, are not the least among the princes of Judah: for out of you shall come a Governor, Who shall rule My People Israel" (Mat. 2:6).

Bethlehem of Judaea was where David was born, and now it was where the Son of David had been born.

The women who attended the birth of Obed, who was born to Ruth and Boaz, prophesied concerning Boaz, *"that his name may be famous in Israel"* (Ruth 4:14).

Even though the Holy Spirit through them was speaking of Boaz, still, Bethlehem, as a place, would gain that fame also.

In fact, at the present, Bethlehem is one of the most famous cities in the world because it was here that Christ was born.

The phrase, *"Are not the least among the princes of Judah,"* in effect, says, *"Are in no wise least among the princes of Judah."*

The idea is that Bethlehem was very small, but still, despite its smallness of size, it would gain notoriety and fame because of Who was born there, namely Christ.

"For out of you shall come a Governor, Who shall rule My People Israel," refers solely to the Messiah, i.e., Christ.

Even though Christ was denied that *"rule"* at His

First Coming, at the Second Coming, He will definitely rule all of Israel as well as all other nations of the world, and forever (Isa. 9:6-7; Dan. 2:44-45; 7:13-14, 27; Zech. 14; Lk. 1:32-33; Rev. 11:15; 20:1-15; 22:4-5).

THE STAR

"Then Herod, when he had privily called the wise men, inquired of them diligently what time the star appeared" (Mat. 2:7).

The phrase, *"Then Herod, when he had privily called the wise men,"* indicates his plot of treachery was already beginning.

"Inquired of them diligently what time the star appeared," means that he inquired *"most carefully."*

In this question, he was probably inquiring of the first appearance of the *"star"* when it appeared to the *"wise men"* in the *"east"* even before their journey began! He may have reasoned, and, no doubt, did, that the first appearance of the *"star"* sometime before signaled the Birth of the Child.

In fact, a time frame of some two years could easily have passed from its first appearance to the present and, no doubt, had. When the *"wise men"* first saw the *"star,"* a period of time probably then passed as they sought direction and possibly a Revelation from the Lord.

As well, their preparation for such a long journey could have easily taken several months. And then, adding several months that it took to make the journey of several hundreds of miles, two years could easily have passed.

THE LIES OF HEROD

"And he sent them to Bethlehem, and said, Go and

search diligently for the young Child; and when you have found Him, bring me word again, that I may come and worship Him also" (Mat. 2:8).

The phrase, *"And he sent them to Bethlehem,"* refers to what the *"Chief Priests and Scribes"* had told him concerning the place of the Birth of this Miracle Child. Of course, it was the wrong place because Joseph and Mary had long since departed from Bethlehem; however, the king would have had no knowledge of that!

The phrase, *"Go and search diligently for the young Child,"* refers to Him being older than a mere infant, i.e., *"young Child."* As stated, Jesus was probably about two years old at that time.

"And when you have found Him, bring me word again, that I may come and worship Him also," was probably spoken only to the *"wise men"* because had Jews heard him say this, they would not have believed him.

Little did he realize that if he had truly desired to *"worship Him,"* it would have been, without a doubt, the greatest moment of his life; however, he was lying. Instead, he desired to murder Him! In that, he was no different than the *"Chief Priests and Scribes,"* who, some 30 years later, would do that very thing!

So, this evil, wicked king desired to murder Jesus and so did the religious leaders of Israel! What a travesty!

THE YOUNG CHILD

"When they (the wise men) had heard the king, they departed; and, lo, the star, which they saw in the east, went before them, till it came and stood over where the young Child was" (Mat. 2:9).

The phrase, *"When they had heard the king, they departed,"* means they were proceeding on their journey, more than likely, with every thought of going toward

Bethlehem; however, something was to happen that would change their destination.

"And, lo, the star, which they saw in the east, went before them," refers to the miraculous reappearing of this *"star,"* which they had originally seen in their native country.

There is every evidence, as stated, that the star did not lead them from the east to Jerusalem, but it appeared to them sometime before in their home country.

By some type of Revelation from the Lord, they knew that it signified the Birth of the Messiah. They journeyed to Jerusalem because they knew that Daniel and his Prophecies had alluded to Jerusalem as the *"Holy City"* (Dan. 9:24-26).

As stated, as they left the palace in Jerusalem, no doubt, starting toward Bethlehem, the *"star"* reappeared.

Inasmuch as it *"went before them,"* it must have been different than any *"star"* that one could imagine! As well, it must not have been too high in the heavens for them to be able to follow it as they did.

THE STAR

The phrase, *"Till it came and stood over where the young Child was,"* actually refers to the city of Nazareth, for this is where it had led them (Lk. 2:39).

As well, if one is to notice, the phrase, *"Young Child"* is used, signifying that Jesus is no longer an infant but, as stated, actually about two years of age.

If a heart is earnest, honest, and sincere before God, that *"star,"* which is the Guiding Light of the Holy Spirit, will appear to any and all who truly seek the Lord, and they will be led to Christ. The Holy Spirit always leads people to Christ.

Herod was not led there because he had no desire

for Him. Likewise, the Chief Priests and Scribes were not led there because they had no desire for Christ either! However, if the heart truly seeks Him, the heart will truly find Him.

It is ironic that precious few in Israel knew anything about Him even though they were the very people through whom He came. But yet, several Gentile *"wise men"* would find Him. Truly, they were *"wise!"* Truly, the others were not!

GREAT JOY

"When they saw the star, they rejoiced with exceeding great joy" (Mat. 2:10).

The phrase, *"When they saw the star,"* actually refers to the *"star"* stopping over the house where Mary and Joseph lived in Nazareth with the little Boy Jesus.

"They rejoiced with exceeding great joy," is understandable. It portrays hearts hungry for God and now knowing that their long quest had finally led them to the One they sought!

It is so sad when one realizes that hundreds of millions ignore the Gospel, even though it is so near them, when these *"wise men"* would go to great expense, journeying many hundreds of miles, and enduring great hardship in order that they might find the One they eagerly sought.

Their quest was not in vain, and neither will the quest of any sincere soul who truly seeks the Lord be in vain. The Scripture says, *"And you shall seek Me, and find Me, when you shall search for Me with all your heart"* (Jer. 29:13).

It also says, *"Let all those who seek You rejoice and be glad in You ...,"* implying that those who *"seek"* will find and, consequently, will *"rejoice,"* even as these *"wise men"* (Ps. 40:16).

THE GIFTS

"And when they were come into the house, they saw the young Child with Mary His Mother, and fell down, and worshipped Him: and when they had opened their treasures, they presented unto Him gifts; gold, and frankincense, and myrrh" (Mat. 2:11).

The phrase, *"And when they were come into the house,"* further proves that it was not the stable at Bethlehem where He had been born, but rather a house in Nazareth where He had lived since being presented to the Lord 41 days after His Birth (Lk. 2:7, 21-39). As stated, He was probably about two years of age at that time.

As well, the *"house"* over which the *"star"* stopped, no doubt, was of humble design. But yet, this seemed not to hinder these *"wise men"* at all! They knew this was the place and the One they were looking for because this is where the *"star"* had led them. Consequently, they were guided by Revelation instead of appearances.

Regrettably, most of the world never finds the Lord because they look for Him in all the wrong places.

Many people attend a particular church because of the richness of its appointments and construction, or because it's the popular place to be. While the Lord may certainly be in some of these places, He is not in many of that nature, if any at all.

In fact, I think one can say without fear of contradiction that most every Move of God that has ever taken place has begun in humble surroundings and, as such, was despised by the world! Referring to the Lord, appearances can be, and usually are, deceiving!

Whatever the appearance of the humble dwelling resided in by Joseph and Mary and the little Boy Jesus, because they were peasants, this did not deter these *"wise men"* at all! They rejoiced when they arrived and, no doubt, entered into the house, continuing to rejoice.

THEY SAW JESUS

"They saw the young Child with Mary His Mother," implies that the moment they beheld Him, they knew this was the One! How did they know?

Being strangers, they had no actual knowledge of where they were or its circumstances; however, the moment they laid eyes on Jesus, something about His Countenance, even though He was only a little Boy, told them, *"This is the One!"*

As a result, they *"fell down, and worshipped Him."*

No doubt, the furnishings of the house were spartan with nothing there that spoke of royalty. But yet, they knew this was the *"King"* they had learned about by Revelation, and, in truth, they knew He was more than a King, but instead, *"The King."* Consequently, they *"worshipped Him!"* Every evidence is that they were in no way disappointed, but rather exhilarated to the point that the moment of their destination far exceeded their hopes and expectations. They had found Christ!

If one can properly see this picture in one's mind, one can see what true Christianity really is!

If one seeks religion, one will find what religion brings, which is buildings, ceremony, ritual, etc., and will find no lasting satisfaction or joy. However, when one finds Christ, regardless of the circumstances or surroundings, one has found the secret of life and the source of all fulfillment and joy, in other words, *"more Abundant Life"* (Jn. 10:10).

THE TREASURES

The phrase, *"And when they had opened their treasures,"* presents them giving to God because He had given so much to them.

What exactly had He given them?

If one truly knows the Lord, one truly knows what they received in that hour.

Were these *"wise men"* truly *"Born-Again"* at that time?

Even though the words, *"Born-Again,"* were not in use at that particular time, still, every indication is that they accepted Jesus as their Lord. This is proven by several things, I believe!

• They had had a Revelation from the Lord and, consequently, had eagerly sought the Source of that Revelation. As we have stated, every evidence in Scripture is that those who seek the Lord always find Him!

• Finding Him resulted in great *"rejoicing,"* which always follows the finding of Christ.

• They worshipped Him: Some have passed this off as merely the culture of these particular individuals. However, according to their seeking and rejoicing, every evidence is that this was more than mere culture, but instead, the worshipping of Him as the Lord of Glory.

The knowledge of these wise men had probably been learned from the writings of Daniel. While it is true that they may not have known nearly as much about the Bible as their Jewish counterparts, what little they did know, they acted on it. However, the religious leaders in Israel did not act whatsoever on what they knew.

• As the next phrase will show, they gave gifts to Him, which always follows true Conversion.

It is not that one purchases something from the Lord with such gifts, but instead, *"... to prove the sincerity of one's love"* (II Cor. 8:8).

GOLD, FRANKINCENSE, AND MYRRH

The phrase, *"They presented unto Him gifts; gold,*

and frankincense, and myrrh," implies by the word, *"Gifts,"* that they placed Him in the position of Deity with themselves placed in a subordinate position.

Why these three gifts, *"Gold, and frankincense, and myrrh?"*

Not only was their journey by Revelation but, as well, their *"gifts."*

• *"Gold":* With Joseph and Mary being poor, this was, no doubt, very much needed. As well, within days, they would have to flee to Egypt, which this *"gold,"* no doubt, financed.

Also, the *"gold"* represented Deity.

• *"Frankincense":* This is a very serious perfume of sorts and was used in the Holy Incense, which was poured on the coals of fire that were placed on the Altar of Worship in the Tabernacle and Temple (Ex. 30:34-38).

It was very valuable inasmuch as it was derived from only one type of tree.

The *"frankincense,"* along with the other spices which were poured over the coals from the Brazen Altar, spoke of worship accepted by God only as it came through Calvary, of which the Brazen Altar was a type.

Consequently, the *frankincense,"* whether the *"wise men"* understood it or not, meant that God accepted their worship of His Only Son, as He would always accept the worship of such.

• *"Myrrh":* This was a spice that came from the stem of a low, thorny, ragged tree which grew in Arabia and East Africa.

As the *"frankincense"* was used in the *"Holy Incense,"* likewise, the *"myrrh"* was used in the *"Holy Anointing Oil"* (Ex. 30:22-33).

This was used with a mixture of other spices to anoint the Priests as well as all the furniture of the Tabernacle, etc. It was a Type of the Holy Spirit.

Therefore, their *"gifts"* spoke of Deity (gold), worship (frankincense), and the Holy Spirit (myrrh).

WARNED OF GOD

"And being warned of God in a Dream that they should not return to Herod, they departed into their own country another way" (Mat. 2:12).

The phrase, *"And being warned of God in a Dream,"* means that they spent the night in Nazareth and were given further Revelation by the Lord that they should not have anything else to do with Herod but, instead, ignore his instructions for them to come back and report what they had found.

So, the Lord would lead them to what they sought and back again! What a privilege to be led by such a sure Word!

"They departed into their own country another way," was, no doubt, the way the Lord instructed them.

However, there is every evidence that the *"rejoicing"* that began upon their finding Christ continued on their journey back *"into their own country."*

What a Testimony to the faithfulness of the Lord and His Eagerness to satisfy the hunger of the searching heart. The great tragedy is that so few search for Him, and, consequently, so few actually find Him!

THE ANGEL OF THE LORD

"And when they were departed, behold, the Angel of the Lord appeared to Joseph in a Dream, saying, Arise, and take the young Child and His Mother, and flee into Egypt, and stay there until I bring you word: for Herod will seek the young Child to destroy Him" (Mat. 2:13).

With Israel, as God's Son (Ex. 4:22-23), having failed in obedience and love, it was necessary that a True

Israel should appear to vindicate God's Character and prove that He could be loved and obeyed. Hence, this was the necessity of the departure into Egypt, even over and above Herod's murderous intent.

"And when they were departed," insinuates that the action that followed was almost immediately after the departure of the *"wise men"* and could very well have taken place the next night.

THE DREAM

The phrase, *"Behold, the Angel of the Lord appeared to Joseph in a Dream,"* presents the same manner the Lord had spoken to him nearly three years earlier when Mary had informed him of her pregnancy.

"Saying, Arise, and take the young Child and His Mother, and flee into Egypt," once again proves by the phrase, *"Young Child,"* that Jesus was not now an infant.

As the Lord had told Jacob to go into Egypt (Gen. 46:1-4), He now told Jacob's son to do so as well! The insinuation was that they should go immediately!

"And stay there until I bring you word," insinuates their being led entirely by the Lord.

What a delightful way to live!

As well, this is the way the Lord desires that all His People live!

He desires to lead and guide us and will, in fact, if we will only seek His Leading (Jn. 16:13-15).

"For Herod will seek the young Child to destroy Him," implies premeditation and not momentary emotion.

Satan knew that this *"Seed of the woman"* was to crush his head and restore man's dominion (Gen. 3:15; I Jn. 3:8), so he tried many times to kill Christ even before He could get to the Cross to defeat him (Mat. 26:3-4; Col. 2:14-17; I Pet. 2:24).

EGYPT

"When he arose, he took the young Child and His Mother by night, and departed into Egypt" (Mat. 2:14).

The evidence is that Joseph awakened after the Dream and immediately *"arose,"* with Mary and him, along with Jesus, leaving for Egypt at once, even that very night.

The Message of the Angel, as is obvious, was one of urgency.

OUT OF EGYPT HAVE I CALLED MY SON

"And was there until the death of Herod: that it might be fulfilled which was spoken of the Lord by the Prophet, saying, Out of Egypt have I called My Son" (Mat. 2:15).

The phrase, *"And was there until the death of Herod,"* probably spoke of only a few months as Herod died shortly after the advent of the *"wise men."*

"That it might be fulfilled which was spoken of the Lord by the Prophet," is speaking of Hosea and his Prophecy when he said, *"When Israel was a child, then I loved him, and called My Son out of Egypt"* (Hos. 11:1).

Even though, in effect, Hosea was speaking of Israel being delivered from Egyptian bondage, as recorded in Exodus, Chapter 14, still, what was spoken of Israel was clearly true of the Greater Israel, the Lord Jesus Christ.

In effect, the crowning purpose of the Jewish Nation was to give the world the Son of God. Ideally, they were, at least, in a sense, to be the same, exactly as the Church and Christ are ideally to be the same!

Consequently, as they rejected Christ, they, as well, have been rejected by the world.

As Herod attempted to destroy Christ by murdering all the little boy babies in Bethlehem two years old and under, likewise, the Antichrist, the future Herod, will attempt to destroy Israel in the coming Great Tribulation (Mat. 24:21).

Nevertheless, as Christ was raised from the dead, in a sense, Israel, for all practical purposes, will be raised from the dead, as well, at the Second Coming.

Therefore, when Hosea spoke of Israel coming out of Egypt, likewise, he spoke of the Son of God coming out of Egypt, even as He did!

HEROD

"Then Herod, when he saw that he was mocked of the Wise men, was exceeding wroth, and sent forth, and killed all the children who were in Bethlehem, and in all the coasts thereof, from two years old and under, according to the time which he had diligently inquired of the Wise men" (Mat. 2:16).

"Then Herod, when he saw that he was mocked of the Wise men, was exceeding wroth," has reference to the fact that the *"wise men"* obeyed God rather than Herod.

While it is certainly true that according to the Bible (Rom. 13:1-7), Believers are to obey civil rulers, still, this is to be done only when the laws or instructions of such rulers do not violate the Word of God.

The Bible takes precedence over everything and is to be obeyed at all cost!

Consequently, the *"wise men"* were told by the Lord not to report to Herod as previously instructed but, instead, to go back to their land another way, which they did!

They had no intention of *"mocking"* Herod but only of obeying the Lord.

However, Herod, in his lifted up state, was exceedingly angry, as such despots are, that they did not obey his every whim. Consequently, the Scripture says, *"He was exceeding wroth!"*

MURDER

The phrase, *"And sent forth, and killed all the children who were in Bethlehem, and in all the coasts thereof, from two years old and under,"* portrays in glaring detail the murderous heart of this despot.

The idea of the Passage is that this included Bethlehem as well as the outlying countryside.

Incidentally, the phrase, *"Two years old and under,"* indicates the Age of Christ at that time. The Greek word for a child of about two years old is *"pais"* and is used in Verse 11.

The Greek word for infant is *"brephos,"* which means, *"A newly-born babe,"* and refers to what the shepherds found nearly two years before at the Birth of Christ (Lk. 2:16).

The phrase, *"According to the time which He had diligently inquired of the Wise men,"* proclaims the *"Wise men,"* no doubt, telling Herod that they had first seen the star approximately two years before. These words declare that two years, or nearly so, had elapsed since the apparition of the star in the east.

JEREMIAH

"Then was fulfilled that which was spoken by Jeremiah the Prophet, saying" (Mat. 2:17).

This pertains to Jeremiah's Prophecy given about 500 years before and recorded in his Book (Jer. 31:15).

Consequently, all the happenings to Christ, even from His Very Birth, at least, of any magnitude, had already been predicted by the Prophets. The religious leaders of Israel could have easily verified this if they had only taken the time to connect these Prophecies with Christ.

However, by the time of His Ministry, they had

already made up their minds that He was not the Messiah, and, therefore, they, as most, would not allow the Word of God to deter them. In other words, their own wicked ambitions made their decisions instead of the Bible.

WEEPING FOR THE CHILDREN

"In Rama was there a voice heard, lamentation, and weeping, and great mourning, Rachel weeping for her children, and would not be comforted, because they are not" (Mat. 2:18).

Some have claimed that inasmuch as Bethlehem was so small, only about 20 little boy babies were murdered. However, the phrase, *"In Rama was there a voice heard, lamentation, and weeping, and great mourning,"* tells us that the slaughter of the children extended at least 10 miles around Bethlehem, including Jerusalem.

"Rama" was about five miles north of Jerusalem, which was the opposite direction of Bethlehem, which was about five miles south of Jerusalem. Consequently, there could have been several hundred little boys murdered.

"Rachel weeping for her children," refers to Jacob's wife, *"Rachel,"* who was looked upon also, at least, in a sense, as the mother of the Tribes of Israel, as Sarah was looked at as the mother of Israel in general (Gen. 30:1, 22).

It was true that Rachel only bore Jacob two sons, Joseph and Benjamin, with Leah, Jacob's other wife, bearing him six.

Still, because of Rachel being Jacob's choice, she was looked upon, at least, in the titular sense, as being the mother of the Tribes.

Two servant women, according to the Blessings of both Rachel and Leah, bore two sons each to Jacob, making a total of 12. As well, Rachel was buried at Ramah (Jer. 31:15).

Regrettably, because of Israel's rejection of her Messiah, the Lord Jesus Christ, Rachel has wept almost from that time until now, and will weep even more so in the coming Great Tribulation.

WEEPING

The word, *"Weeping,"* and the fact that they cannot be *"comforted,"* adequately describes these ancient people.

As the world knows, Hitler and Nazi Germany murdered some 6 million Jews. Such horror, at least, of this magnitude, has never been seen in human history. There is no way that words could adequately describe what really took place!

Consequently, Herod's beastly action was only a prelude of what was to come!

Had Israel listened to the Pleadings of the Holy Spirit through the Prophet Jeremiah and repented, they would not have had such an animal as Herod on the throne at this time!

However, they did not repent and suffered terribly. Worst of all, they rejected their Messiah, saying, *"... We have no king but Caesar"* (Jn. 19:15). To be sure, Caesar has been a hard taskmaster!

Consequently, the phrase, *"Because they are not,"* symbolizes the many millions of Jews who have died in a most horrible manner because of their rebellion, of which the Bethlehem slaughter is only a tiny part.

THE ANGEL OF THE LORD

"But when Herod was dead, behold, an Angel of the Lord appeared in a Dream to Joseph in Egypt" (Mat. 2:19).

This is the third of four Dreams given to Joseph by the Lord.

"But when Herod was dead," portrays, as we have stated, the passing of only a few months from the time of the slaughter.

"Behold, an Angel of the Lord appeared in a Dream to Joseph in Egypt," leaves absolutely no doubt as to where Joseph and Mary, along with Jesus, were.

In the entirety of the Bible, Dreams and Visions are portrayed as a vehicle through which the Lord speaks at times (Acts 2:17).

In effect, Matthew records five Dreams in connection with the Birth and Infancy of Jesus, in three of which an Angel, as here recorded, appeared with God's Message. Later, Matthew would record the troubled Dream of Pilate's wife (Mat. 27:19).

However, one must not take any and all dreams as from the Lord. When it is from the Lord, it should be clear according to its description; nevertheless, the true meaning may need further clarification and Revelation (I Cor. 14:29).

THE YOUNG CHILD AND HIS MOTHER

"Saying, Arise, and take the young Child and His Mother, and go into the land of Israel: for they are dead which sought the young Child's Life" (Mat. 2:20).

"Saying, Arise, and take the young Child and His Mother," refers to the Lord honoring Joseph as the head of the house and not giving Mary, the Mother of Jesus, the deified position as given by the Roman Catholics!

Even though Mary was greatly loved and respected, as she certainly should have been, still, Joseph is here given the preeminence, as he should have been.

The phrase, *"And go into the land of Israel,"* does not specify which part but only back to Israel proper!

According to Luke 2:39, every evidence is that they lived in Nazareth before going to Egypt and, as well, after coming back from Egypt.

"For they are dead who sought the young Child's Life," speaks of Herod and those who were advising him.

It, as well, speaks of all despots who one day will suffer the same fate, with all rebellion against Christ ultimately being brought to an end.

THE LAND OF ISRAEL

"And, he arose, and took the young Child and His Mother, and came into the land of Israel" (Mat. 2:21).

This Passage marks Joseph's immediate obedience. The Angel said, *"Arise,"* and, therefore, *"He arose."* Such should be the obedience of all!

The phrase, *"Young Child,"* refers to Jesus being a little over two years old at that time.

Sometime back, while Frances and I were in Cairo, Egypt, we were shown the place where it is said that Joseph and Mary lived during their sojourn in this land. Whether the location is correct or not is anyone's guess.

GALILEE

"But when he heard that Archelaus did reign in Judaea in the room of his father Herod, he was afraid to go thither: notwithstanding, being warned of God in a dream, he turned aside into the parts of Galilee" (Mat. 2:22).

"But when he heard that Archelaus did reign in Judaea in the room of his father Herod," proclaims, at least, in a sense, the struggle for supremacy that took

place after the death of Herod.

It had been Herod's wish that his oldest son, Antipater, would succeed him; however, he too was murdered by his father only four days from Herod's own death. Consequently, he appointed the area spoken of to *"Archelaus."*

Nevertheless, the succession was far from certain until the consent of Caesar Augustus and was, in fact, jeopardized for awhile by certain actions of Archelaus. Eventually, however, his appointment was confirmed by Caesar, but only in a limited way, promising him that he would make him king if he *"governed virtuously."*

THE FOURTH AND FINAL DREAM

However, Archelaus did not rule virtuously and was just as guilty of cruelty and murder as his father, Herod. Consequently, a short time later, he was deposed for his cruelty and banished to Vienne in Gaul.

Nevertheless, he was reigning in Judaea when Joseph and Mary came back from Egypt.

The phrase, *"Notwithstanding, being warned of God in a Dream,"* records the fourth and final Dream of Joseph.

"He turned aside into the parts of Galilee," refers to the region north of Samaria. It was where most of Christ's Ministry would be carried out as well.

The disposition of the phrase seems to indicate that plans had originally been made by Joseph and Mary to come to another part of Israel, other than Nazareth, where they had lived after the Birth of Christ and before going into Egypt.

However, that would not be realized as Christ could not approach the throne of His Fathers, at least, at that time, and would have to take the position of a despised Nazarene.

NAZARETH

"And he came and dwelt in a city called Nazareth: that it might be fulfilled which was spoken by the Prophets, He shall be called a Nazarene" (Mat. 2:23).

Galilee was despised by Jerusalem, and the town of Nazareth was especially contemptible (Jn. 1:46). However, it was Joseph's native place, and there he plied his trade as a carpenter.

"That it might be fulfilled which was spoken by the Prophets, He shall be called a Nazarene," is not found verbatim among the Prophecies.

However, the quotation, *"He shall be called a Nazarene,"* is meant to portray the action instead of the location.

All the Prophets predicted that in His First Advent, the Messiah would be despised; that is, He would be a *"Nazarene."*

Some think that at this particular time, a Roman garrison was located near Nazareth and with all of its corrupting influence, it made Nazareth a despised place, hence, the question of Nathaniel, *"Can there any good thing come out of Nazareth?"* (Jn. 1:46).

In effect, the Jews in later years would claim that Mary was actually impregnated by a drunken Roman soldier, making Christ's Birth terribly despicable because of their lies!

THE PLAIN OF ESDRAELON

In fact, Nazareth is a beautiful place located on the northern edge of the Plain of Esdraelon.

It was said by Quaresimus, *"Nazareth is a rose, and like a rose, has the same rounded form, enclosed by mountains as the flower by its leaves."*

Sometime back, I was in Nazareth, along with

Frances and members of our television team. I asked to be taken to the brow of the hill where it is reputed that the town fathers attempted to kill Christ after He preached in their synagogue (Lk. 4:18-30).

I was taken to the place and stood in the exact area that had been quoted in Scripture. From its high point, I was able to see a panoramic view of Nazareth as well as all surrounding areas.

Nazareth is situated in the cove of a horseshoe-type hill. Part of the hill has been divided with the mining of bauxite in the area, but, of course, in Jesus' Day, it was intact.

Standing on the extreme northwest part of the hill, most of Nazareth was to my back. Immediately in front was the Plain of Esdraelon or, as it is sometimes called, Megiddo.

At about 11 o'clock, according to direction, if I remember correctly, I could see Mount Gilboa where Saul and Jonathan were killed by the Philistines.

At about 10 o'clock, further in the distance, I could see Mount Carmel, situated on the Mediterranean, where Elijah called fire from Heaven.

Immediately to my back at about 8 o'clock was the mountain where some think the Transfiguration took place. Immediately to my right at about 2 o'clock was a range of hills that separates this area from the Sea of Galilee and Capernaum where Jesus eventually made His Headquarters.

As I stood there that day, I realized that because of its solitude, many times, Christ, no doubt, stood in this exact spot, meditating on the Prophecies and seeking the Face of His Heavenly Father.

A NAZARENE

However, despite its beauty, it was then looked at

as a place of ill-fame, and Jesus would consequently be called a *"Nazarene,"* which was then a statement of derision!

Why would the Holy Spirit desire that the Son of God be raised in a place of this nature, if, in fact, it really was a place of ill-repute?

The Lord's Ways are not our ways. He seldom, if ever, goes by appearances, as most do, even Christians! He has little interest in what people think or say, at least, in respect to what He does.

It is the Will of God that all His People, even at the present, view things as He does and not as the world does. We are not to judge from appearances, but sadly, most Christians do just that!

To hypothetically state the case: if Christ were born now instead of 2,000 years ago, sadly and regrettably, most modern Christians would little think of Him as the Messiah, mostly because of His Surrounding Circumstances, as even this place where He was brought up.

How so much have all of us fallen into this trap of judging by appearances, which is almost never according to the Word of God or according to the way things really are.

We should pray that all of us would allow even this small example of where Christ was brought up to be an example to us.

JESUS AT TWELVE YEARS OLD

"And when He was twelve years old, they went up to Jerusalem after the custom of the Feast" (Lk. 2:42).

The phrase, *"And when He was twelve years old,"* refers to the age at which time every Jewish boy became, *"A son of the Law."* At this time, Joseph would have fulfilled the Law by paying five shekels in Redemption or money (Num. 3:47; 18:16), which gave him the legal right of *"father,"* claiming the obedience of Verses 48 through 51 in the Second Chapter of Luke. When a Jewish boy was three years old, he was given the tasseled garment directed by the Law (Num. 15:38-41; Deut. 22:12).

At five, he usually began to learn portions of the Law under his mother's direction. This was begun by her and continued in the synagogue under other teachers.

When the boy was 13 years old, he wore for the first time the phylacteries, which the Jews always put on at the recital of the daily prayer. The phylacteries were small containers in which were placed four Passages, Exodus 13:1-10, 11-16; Deuteronomy 6:4-9; 11:13-21, which were written by hand on small pieces of parchment.

The phylacteries were attached to leather straps by which they were fastened to the left hand and the center of the forehead by the men before morning prayers, whether in the home or the synagogue.

The Holy Spirit gives us only one glimpse of Christ between birth and manhood, which is recorded in these Verses. At the age of 12, the Jewish boy, in effect, was looked at as a man. Consequently, this will explain some of the Actions of Jesus at this age, and some of the statements made about Him.

"They went up to Jerusalem after the custom of the Feast," means that Jerusalem was where the Feast was held and, in fact, must be held. This was where the Temple was located, and these Feasts could not be properly celebrated without some things done at that Structure.

THE ACTIONS OF JESUS

"And when they had fulfilled the days, as they returned, the Child Jesus tarried behind in Jerusalem;

and Joseph and His Mother knew not of it" (Lk. 2:43).

The phrase, *"And when they had fulfilled the days,"* pertained to seven days, which actually incorporated three Feasts: the Feast of Unleavened Bread, the Feast of Passover, and the Feast of Firstfruits.

The *"Feast of Unleavened Bread"* was meant to serve as a symbol or Type of the Unblemished, Spotless Life of the Lord Jesus Christ. In other words, during this particular seven days, all bread was to be without *"leaven,"* which is a form of corruption or rot. As well, it typified His Perfect Body as a Sacrifice offered at Calvary.

The *"Passover"* symbolized His Death on Calvary.

The *"Feast of Firstfruits"* symbolized His Resurrection. So, as Mary and Joseph celebrated this week of Feasts, I wonder if they realized that Jesus, then 12 years old, was, in reality, the fulfillment of this which had been done for nearly 1,600 years.

The phrase, *"As they returned, the Child Jesus tarried behind in Jerusalem,"* presents a scene that is immensely interesting, to say the least!

The word, *"Child,"* in the Greek Text is *"Pais,"* and means, *"A servant."* Inasmuch as Jesus was now a *"Son of the Law,"* He was, as well, old enough to be the *"Servant of Jehovah,"* which He was!

This was probably the first time Jesus had been to Jerusalem and, consequently, the first time He had seen the Temple.

JOSEPH AND MARY

The phrase, *"And Joseph and His Mother knew not of it,"* presents something understandable only to the Jewish mind.

Inasmuch as He was now *"twelve years old"* and looked at as an adult, He would have been treated accordingly; consequently, He probably was pretty much left to Himself during the days of the Feasts. As He had now come of age, His Mother and Joseph would have trusted Him to have conducted Himself responsibly, which He did. This was the custom in those days because of the strict upbringing of the Child. So, when Mary and Joseph left with other friends on the trip back to Nazareth, the fact that Jesus was not with them at the moment aroused no concern. They thought He was with another group which would all join together after leaving Jerusalem.

A DAY'S JOURNEY

"But they, supposing Him to have been in the company, went a day's journey; and they sought Him among their kinsfolk and acquaintance" (Lk. 2:44).

The phrase, *"But they, supposing Him to have been in the company,"* referred to the several groups which had come from Nazareth to the Feasts. They were not concerned, thinking Jesus was with one of the groups.

"Went a day's journey," refers to the custom at that time.

An ordinary day's journey was 18 to 30 miles, but it was the custom with all caravans to travel only three to eight miles the first day, so if anything was forgotten or left behind by mistake, one could return quickly to get it in time to rejoin the company the next day.

The first stopping place of most travelers going north was at Beeroth, now El-Bireh, about six miles north of Jerusalem.

"And they sought Him among their kinsfolk and acquaintance," refers to this stopping place where all the groups returning to Nazareth were to join.

When He did not show up at this designated meeting area, they began to quickly inquire among the groups if Jesus had been seen. He was nowhere to be found!

BACK TO JERUSALEM

"And when they found Him not, they turned back again to Jerusalem, seeking Him" (Lk. 2:45).

The phrase, *"And when they found Him not,"* refers to a diligent search. It also speaks of concern and anxiety.

The phrase, *"They turned back again to Jerusalem, seeking Him,"* speaks of both Joseph and Mary.

THE TEMPLE

"And it came to pass, that after three days they found Him in the Temple, sitting in the midst of the doctors, both hearing them, and asking them questions" (Lk. 2:46).

The phrase, *"And it came to pass, that after three days they found Him in the Temple,"* probably refers to the third day after originally leaving Jerusalem. They spent the first day traveling from Jerusalem to the designated meeting point.

Upon not finding Jesus, they then journeyed back to Jerusalem the next day. That probably took a great part of the morning, with the rest of the day being used to search for Him, but to no avail. Finally, on the third day, they found Him *"in the Temple."* They should have known to have looked there first but thinking that a 12-year-old boy would have little interest in the Temple, they looked there last. Had they been thinking correctly, they would have known this was the place where He would have been.

Actually, everything in the Temple had been designed by Him before the Incarnation, with the plans faithfully delivered by the Holy Spirit to David (I Chron. 28:11-12). Solomon would carry out the actual work of constructing the Temple, which would be the most expensive building ever constructed. It would be destroyed by the Babylonians about 600 years before Christ.

After the dispersion, Zerubbabel built another edifice to take its place, but a far simpler design. Herod's Temple, which Jesus was now in, was magnificent, to say the least! It was built on the same spot as the other two had been.

The Scripture gives us very little indication as to how much Jesus knew at this particular time concerning His Role as Messiah. However, He definitely knew some things, as this account reveals.

THE DOCTORS OF THE LAW

The phrase, *"Sitting in the midst of the doctors,"* could well have included, and, no doubt, did, the most famous scholars of that day.

Among the famous doctors, or rabbis, then living and teaching in Jerusalem was the famous Hillel, then very aged, verging, we are told, on his hundredth year; and his almost equally illustrious rival, Gamaliel, the teacher of Saul of Tarsus.

As well, Simeon, the son and successor of the vaunted Hillel, would have been present also. Among others, these may well have been some of the men whom the Boy questioned at this Passover Feast.

The Lord as a Youth did not dispute with the doctors but asked questions of them and listened to their answers.

Verse 47 implies they also asked him questions.

"Both hearing them, and asking them questions," was probably carried out in one of the three synagogues located in the Temple enclosure. There the great doctors of the Law would meet and discuss this all-important subject.

Most always, a crowd would gather, listening intently to the discussion.

Jesus had probably spent much of His Time while in Jerusalem in the Temple. He would have probably been there some 10 days by now. As well, His Participation in this discussion could have very well gone on for several days.

More than likely, He had come upon the group in His Investigation of the Temple and had, no doubt, listened for quite some time.

Edging to the front of the crowd, at some point, He must have ventured a question that was so deep in its searching penetration that it immediately aroused the attention of the famous doctors of the Law. Soon, they drew Him into their very midst, with Him actually becoming a part of the proceedings.

What a sight that must have been, these most famous doctors of the Mosaic Law with this 12-year-old boy sitting in their midst, and with most of the attention directed toward Him. Did they even have an inkling as to Who He was? Did they even briefly realize that the Lord of Glory, the Creator of all things, was sitting in their very midst?

Some even think that Nicodemus, who, years later, would come to Jesus by night, may have been in this meeting.

If so, he was to never forget this moment and would later accept Christ as his Lord and Saviour.

HIS UNDERSTANDING AND ANSWERS

"And all who heard Him were astonished at His Understanding and Answers" (Lk. 2:47).

This would have referred not only to the great doctors of the Law but, as well, to the audience which stood nearby.

The word, *"Astonished,"* in the Greek Text, refers to amazement to such an extent that one is beside oneself. It means, *"Out of wits,"* or, *"Beyond comprehension."* In truth, His *"Understanding and Answers"* were far beyond that of these learned doctors.

In other words, neither the people nor the learned teachers could believe their ears at such Wisdom coming from a child.

However, what they did not know or realize was that God, His Father, had been His Personal Instructor (Isa. 50:4). As well, the indication from Isaiah is that God literally whispered into the Ear of Jesus, even at that young age, His Word and its understanding.

Jesus had earthly teachers, but He was always far ahead of them (Ps. 119:97-104).

AMAZEMENT

"And when they saw Him, they were amazed: and His Mother said unto Him, Son, why have You thus dealt with us? behold, Your Father and I have sought You sorrowing" (Lk. 2:48).

The phrase, *"And when they saw Him, they were amazed,"* means that before speaking to Him, they undoubtedly heard the exchange of questions and answers between Him and the doctors of the Law. His answers amazed them as well!

It would seem from this statement that He had not exhibited such knowledge at home but had purposely held Himself in reserve.

The question, *"And His Mother said unto Him, Son, why have You thus dealt with us?"* presents a question that should not have been asked!

She, of all people, knew Him and should have known all the time that He was in the Temple. Little else would have held interest for Him.

IT WAS DONE PURPOSELY

Of course, we have no way of knowing, but the possibility does exist that Jesus did this purposely, and was led by the Holy Spirit to do so in order to awaken Mary and Joseph to His True Mission and Purpose, even though it would not truly begin until He was 30 years of age.

The phrase, *"Behold, Your Father and I have sought You sorrowing,"* will enjoin a gentle rebuke from Jesus. Mary used the phrase, *"Your Father,"* and Jesus gently reminded her in the next Verse as to Who His Father actually was. Legally, Joseph was His Father, but only in the foster sense.

While it was true that they had been very concerned about Jesus' Whereabouts, this entire scenario portrays, as stated, that they should not have been. They should have instantly known where His Interest was at all times. However, they too often thought carnally first rather than spiritually, as we do at times, whereas He always thought spiritually. As such carnal thinking brought *"sorrow"* then, it brings *"sorrow"* now!

MY FATHER'S BUSINESS

"And He said unto them, How is it that you sought Me? wist you not that I must be about My Father's business?" (Lk. 2:49).

The question, *"And He said unto them, How is it that you sought Me?"* is actually a very gentle rebuke within itself!

He is gently reminding them that they should have known Who He was and His Mission. Regrettably, they seemed to have forgotten it. Most probably, this entire scenario was engineered by the Holy Spirit for that very reason.

The question, *"Wist you not that I must be about My Father's business?"* is another gentle rebuke, as stated, concerning Who His Father really was!

It was not in any way meant to demean Joseph, who seems to have conducted himself with dignity and aplomb, but to once again bring to the fore that which had been slowly covered, the true identity of His Person.

It is beautiful that this, *"I must be about My Father's business,"* was His First Recorded Utterance, with the words, *"It is finished,"* His Last before His Crucifixion (Jn. 19:30).

What was His Father's business?

John answered that question by saying, *"... For this purpose the Son of God was manifested, that He might destroy the works of the Devil"* (I Jn. 3:8).

The *"works of the Devil"* are to *"steal, and to kill, and to destroy"* (Jn. 10:10).

The Father's business is to destroy these works, which Jesus did at Calvary and the Resurrection. He broke the bondage of sin and darkness in which Satan had held men captive.

As well, He satisfied the Heavenly Courts of Justice in paying the price that was owed with His Own Precious Blood (I Pet. 1:19).

A LACK OF UNDERSTANDING

"And they understood not the saying which He spoke unto them" (Lk. 2:50).

How is it that they did not understand?

They should have understood, for they had had seven Testimonies as to Who He was. These were: Matthew 1:20; 2:1; Luke 1:26; 1:43; 2:9; 2:29; 2:38. He was their God and Creator, and so Mary should not have spoken to Him as she did.

IN NAZARETH

"And He went down with them, and came to Nazareth, and was subject unto them: but His Mother kept all these sayings in her heart" (Lk. 2:51).

The phrase, *"And He went down with them, and came to Nazareth,"* refers to this city being about 1,500 feet lower than Jerusalem respecting altitude.

"And was subject unto them," concerns the next 18 years.

He was conscious of Who He was; and just as that consciousness caused Him in John 13:5 to wash the feet of the Disciples, so it here caused Him to return with His Reputed Parents to Nazareth and to become subject to them.

Joseph was legally His Father according to Hebrew Law (Lk. 3:23), but only in the sense of being a foster father.

The question has been asked as to why this scene with the doctors of the Law was not repeated in the next 18 years since He may have returned to Jerusalem to keep the many Feasts.

The only answer is, it was not repeated because the Holy Spirit did not desire such.

For the 18 years between His Twelfth Birthday and the Advent of His Ministry at 30 years of age, He appears to have lived and toiled as a carpenter in Nazareth. Actually, it seems that inasmuch as Joseph was not mentioned again, the possibility exists that he died sometime during these 18 years.

As a result, Jesus, as the Eldest, would have taken responsibility for the family.

HIS MOTHER REMEMBERED ALL THESE SAYINGS

Justin Martyr, who lived about 150 years after

Christ, spoke of the ploughs and yokes that Jesus made and fashioned with His Own Hands during this particular time.

In this atmosphere at Nazareth, the Holy Spirit could teach and instruct more so than in the ritualism and rabbinical discussions at Jerusalem. This we do know, everything He did was planned and designed by the Holy Spirit, and He was quick to follow.

"But His Mother kept all these sayings in her heart," refers to all that pertained to Jesus.

Even though the Angel Gabriel had not used the word, *"Messiah,"* still, he had said enough that she should have known exactly Who and What He was (Lk. 1:32).

However, despite these wondrous things, Jesus was totally human, so much so that Mary seemed to forget at times exactly Who He was, despite His being without flaw or failure.

WISDOM AND STATURE

"And Jesus increased in wisdom and stature, and in favor with God and man" (Lk. 2:52).

The phrase, *"And Jesus increased in wisdom and stature,"* refers to His Instruction from the Holy Spirit continuing, even above and beyond that exhibited to the doctors of the Law.

"And in favor with God and man," means that He perfectly kept the Law of God and did perfectly the Will of God. As a result, the people of Nazareth thought highly of Him and continued to do so until He made His Ministry debut in this city.

Then, the *"favor"* turned to hate.

While they thought very highly of Him as a local young man because of His Godly Lifestyle, still, they were not willing at all to accept Him as the Messiah.

This was a different story entirely! In their minds, the Messiah would be One of splendor and glory and not a mere carpenter as Jesus was.

As the city fathers of Nazareth misunderstood Jesus, many do the same presently. They did not understand the Incarnation, and many little understand it now.

THE SELF-EMPTYING OF CHRIST

However, such is no longer a mystery when we understand the true *"Kenosis"* or self-emptying of Christ. He retained His Divine Nature but limited Himself to human attributes and powers during the days of His Flesh. This was so that He could be a true example of a sinless human being overcoming sin and being anointed with the Spirit to defeat Satan (Phil. 2:5-11; Heb. 2:10-18; 4:14-16; I Pet. 2:21; 4:1).

That His Power came by the Spirit Baptism and not by natural attributes and powers is one of the clearest Doctrines of Scriptures (Isa. 11:1-2; 42:1-5; 61:1-2; Mat. 3:16-17; 12:28; Lk. 4:16-21; Acts 10:38). He proved to men that by the same Spirit Anointing, they could do His Works, as He Promised (Mat. 18:18; Mk. 16:15-20; Jn. 14:12).

Jesus repeatedly said He could do nothing of Himself (Jn. 8:28).

What do all these Scriptures mean if they do not mean what they say? Could not the Gifts of the Holy Spirit accomplish through Christ all that He did? As God, with Divine Powers and Attributes, would He need an Anointing of the Spirit to do these works? If He did them because He was God, then how does He expect Believers to do them?

If He did works by the Spirit which He has also promised to all Believers, then He has a right to expect His Followers to carry on His Work the way He did

(Mat. 17:20-21; 21:22; Mk. 9:23; 11:22-24; 16:17-20; Lk. 24:49; Jn. 7:37-39; 14:12; 17:18; Acts 1:1-8).

THE MARRIAGE AT CANA OF GALILEE

"And the third day there was a marriage in Cana of Galilee; and the Mother of Jesus was there" (Jn. 2:1).

The phrase, *"And the third day,"* speaks of the amount of time which had lapsed since Jesus left the Wilderness of Temptation to begin His Public Ministry. However, as stated, His Ministry began with the Incoming of the Holy Spirit upon His Person, which took place when He was baptized of John in the Jordan. This would have been approximately 43 days earlier.

"There was a marriage in Cana of Galilee," occasions the sight of His Very First Miracle.

On this day, the poor water of man's efforts would be changed into the rich wine of God's Provision.

This tells us that the Millennial Kingdom will be the Father's House of Wine, as one might say; and the joy of that house will be the joy and love of an eternal marriage feast.

Cana, in that day, was a small town, probably about the size of Nazareth, and was situated about seven miles north of that city. It was called Cana of Galilee to distinguish it from Cana of Asher.

"And the mother of Jesus was there," indicates that she was already there and maybe had been for several hours, or even a day or two, before Jesus came with His Disciples.

Actually, marriage feasts in those days lasted a week or more.

JESUS AND HIS DISCIPLES

"And both Jesus was called, and His Disciples, to the marriage" (Jn. 2:2).

There is some indication in the Greek tense that Jesus and His Disciples were invited at the last moment. At any rate, to be invited to such a feast and not attend was an insult to the host.

Religion and asceticism, which refers to the practicing of strict self-denial as a measure of personal spiritual discipline, are often associated in the carnal mind.

Such has been popular down through the centuries, and has even been an earmark of particular religious denominations in the not too distant past. However, we see that Jesus had no sympathy with isolation, unsociableness, and austerity.

It must ever be remembered that the Biblical demand for separation from the world is not isolation from the world.

Actually, Jesus frequented all kinds of human society. He dined with the Pharisees and with Publicans, with these two being a world apart, with an impartial sociability.

He does not seem to have refused many invitations, if any, to partake of hospitality, from whatever quarter it might come.

Actually, it was a complaint brought against Him by the formalists, that He was *"gluttonous, a winebibber, and a friend of Publicans and sinners."* This was grossly untrue, but it points to a truth that our Lord had no aversion to social gatherings.

WINE

"And when they wanted wine, the mother of Jesus said unto Him, They have no wine" (Jn. 2:3).

The phrase, *"And when they wanted wine,"* means they had run out of wine.

The question has raged from then until now as to whether this was the kind of wine that makes one drunk.

No, it wasn't!

In our Commentary on St. John, the Second Chapter, we give a long dissertation that I believe conclusively proves that the water that Jesus turned to wine, and the wine they had been using up to this moment, were not alcoholic.

I would strongly advise the reader to secure for yourself this particular Commentary.

THE FATHER'S WILL

"Jesus said unto her, Woman, what have I to do with you? My hour is not yet come" (Jn. 2:4).

The phrase, *"Jesus said unto her,"* constitutes the answer to which the Catholic church should take heed.

The question, *"Woman, what have I to do with you?"* does not pose a question of disrespect, nor is it meant to do so. *"Woman,"* as then used, was basically the same as our present use of *"madam,"* or some suchlike (Mat. 15:28; Jn. 4:21; 19:26; 20:15).

However, while there is no disrespect regarding Jesus' Answer to Mary, still, there was definitely a line drawn, so to speak, as to whom He obeyed, and it was not her, but rather His Heavenly Father (Jn. 5:19-20).

The language implies that the period of subjection to Joseph and Mary was now at an end. He is now *"The Servant of Jehovah,"* and His Work as the Messiah has at last begun.

Once again, the answer as given by Jesus completely destroys the Roman Catholic myth of Mary as mediator between Christ and man.

PRAYER

In truth, the Believer is not really supposed to even pray to Jesus, but rather to the Heavenly Father, even as Jesus Himself demonstrated. By using the Name of Jesus in this respect, our petition will be granted by our Father in Heaven (Jn. 16:23-24). In fact and truth, Jesus is the Mediator and Intercessor to the Heavenly Father on our behalf, and that means Mary isn't, or anyone else, for that matter (Jn. 16:26; I Tim. 2:5).

The phrase, *"My hour is not yet come,"* refers to when and what He will do, according to directions from His Father. Only God gave Him directions, and only from God, His Father, did He take direction.

If one is to notice throughout the four Gospels, with some few exceptions, about everything said to Him by other men and women was contrary to the Will of God. Regrettably, that ratio, for all practical purposes, still holds!

Jesus came to do the Will of the Father and nothing else, which is evident in everything He did. It is proclaimed strongly, even at the outset of His Ministry. That must be the criteria of the Believer as well!

WHATEVER HE SAYS, DO IT!

"His mother said unto the servants, Whatsoever He says unto you, do it" (Jn. 2:5).

The phrase, *"His mother said unto the servants,"* may imply, as thought by some, that Mary had something to do with the responsibilities of this marriage feast, hence, her coming to Jesus.

The phrase, *"Whatsoever He says unto you, do it,"* represents the last recorded words of Mary. As stated, with this word, she stepped aside, in effect, telling the servants to turn from her to Him. When leaving the error of the Catholic church regarding Mary, the Gospels tell us very little about her. It seems that she never really identified herself with Jesus and His Disciples until Acts 1:14. Especially considering that Jesus' Half-brothers were opposed to Him (Jn. 7:5), this placed Mary in a very awkward position. However, is it not possible that everyone is placed in an awkward position regarding Christ?

And yet, the advice she gave to the servants concerning the obeying of Jesus was exactly that which should have been.

In effect, she was saying that they should not try to understand His Commands, at least, should He give any, but just do what He said!

THE WATERPOTS OF STONE

"And there were set there six waterpots of stone, after the manner of the purifying of the Jews, containing two or three firkins apiece" (Jn. 2:6).

The phrase, *"And there were set there six waterpots of stone,"* represents Jesus using these vessels for a purpose.

The number *"six"* represents the number of man and always falls short of perfection, represented by the number *"seven,"* called *"God's Number."* As well, the material of *"stone"* represented the Law (Ex. 34:1).

"After the manner of the purifying of the Jews," had to do mostly with oral laws, which were not originally given by God and were, therefore, man-devised. There were many washings of the *"hands, cups, copper vessels, and tables"* (Mat. 15:2). Sadly, all of this ritual purified nothing!

"Containing two or three firkins apiece," referred to 18 to 27 gallons, depending on the size; consequently, these waterpots were quite large.

When man begins to devise religion, he ultimately thinks that more is better. That's the reason that in some churches rules abound!

So, this Miracle would portray the difference in man's religion and Christ's Redemption! Even the Law of Moses, as given to Moses by God, could not save. Actually, it could only curse, for there was no Salvation in its commands. Salvation came then and comes now by the Believing sinner trusting in Who Jesus was and is, *"The Son of the Living God,"* and what He did, which was to go to the Cross in order that the terrible sin debt might be paid. It was paid by Jesus giving Himself as a Sacrifice, which satisfied the Righteousness of God (Heb. 7:27; 9:28).

Incidentally, before the Cross, Salvation came by trusting in Who and What the sacrifices represented, namely, Jesus and what He would do at the Cross of Calvary.

So, if the true Law of Moses could not save, where did that leave these little, insignificant, man-devised, religious laws, symbolized by the waterpots?

FILL THE WATERPOTS WITH WATER

"Jesus said unto them, Fill the waterpots with water. And they filled them up to the brim" (Jn. 2:7).

The phrase, *"Jesus said unto them, Fill the waterpots with water,"* simply means that His Hour had come, and He had been given instructions from His Heavenly Father as to what He should do.

About 450 years had now elapsed since the last public Miracle of the Old Testament. It was that of Daniel, Chapter 6.

The phrase, *"And they filled them up to the brim,"* presented all that man could do. The balance was left up to Jesus.

This is a source of tremendous encouragement to those who work for the Lord. He is able to do great and mighty things. The key is in listening for His Voice and then doing what He says do, believing that He will perform the necessary Miracle, irrespective of what it takes. Even though I have related the following in another Volume, I think it would be profitable to recount it again.

Some months back, while writing commentary on one of the four Gospels, the Lord, I believe, gave me a greater insight into this subject of *"Miracles."* Of course, most of the church world doesn't even believe in Miracles anymore, claiming they passed away with the Ministry of Christ, or stopped with the deaths of the original Apostles, or stopped when John finished the Canon of Scripture in the writing of the Book of Revelation. As well, many Pentecostals and Charismatics have been subtly led away from the God of the Bible, Who is a God of Miracles, to the psychological way, which is the way of man. I think one would have to admit that Faith in God for great things to happen in whatever capacity is not as strong as it ought to be.

As I pushed my chair back from the desk, briefly asking the Lord to give me greater insight regarding this most important subject, in a moment's time, the Presence of God came over me. The following is what I believe the Lord spoke to my heart:

A WORD FROM THE LORD

He said, *"You have not been looking at this subject as you should. In truth, I am performing Miracles constantly for those who believe Me."*

He then went on to say, *"Anytime a Believer asks Me to do something, and asks in Faith believing, and it constitutes My Will, at that moment, I begin to perform*

Miracles. While it is true that most of these Miracles cannot be seen, still, that makes them no less real."

The Lord then finished by saying, *"The moment I begin to intervene in answer to prayer, Miracles begin to happen. At that time, I cause events, or persons, or things to do what is needed in one way or the other in order to bring to pass that which is desired."*

Even though what I have just said may not seem to be a great Revelation, still, knowing and understanding the magnitude of what the Lord actually does on behalf of His Children in answering prayer and meeting needs, such will help the Believer to place such acts in their proper perspective.

As stated, the Lord always has to perform one or more Miracles, although unseen, in the carrying out of His Divine Intervention. So, one could say and not be exaggerating that the Lord is performing Miracles every day for those who truly believe Him and are asking Him to direct their lives and work. The terrible truth is that most of the church does not even believe that God answers prayer anymore, much less performs Miracles. However, despite the unbelief of most, *"... the people that do know their God shall be strong, and do exploits"* (Dan. 11:32).

DRAW OUT NOW

"And He said unto them, Draw out now, and bear unto the Governor of the feast. And they bear it" (Jn. 2:8).

The Command, *"And He said unto them, Draw out now, and bear unto the Governor of the feast,"* presents all that was done. Jesus said nothing and did nothing, at least, that which was visible or obvious.

I wonder what went through the minds of these individuals upon hearing the Command. At the moment Jesus gave the Command, had the water already been turned into wine, or did it do so as they took it to the governor?

Whichever does not really matter inasmuch as it took Faith on the part of these people to obey.

The phrase, *"And they bear it,"* proclaims their obedience. In a sense of the word, this action of the servants is a portrayal of all who labor for the Lord in any manner.

The *"water"* was all these people had; however, with Jesus on the scene, and that is the key, great and mighty things happen. He can take whatever we have and if we do what He says to do, He will turn it into whatever is needed. Again, the secret is Jesus.

The water is like the Gospel. As the Preacher prepares to deliver it to thirsty souls, it seems at first to be so little and, furthermore, to be woefully inadequate for the gargantuan task ahead. However, once the Anointing of the Holy Spirit comes upon it, it is changed into the *"wine"* of the Joy of the Lord.

MARY

First of all, we should commend Mary for going to Jesus concerning this need. We should allow her to be an example to all of us to take whatever need we have to the Lord. It doesn't matter how large or little it may seem to be, He is able to do whatever is needed.

No great thing was at stake regarding this young wedding couple running out of wine. The worst that could happen to them would be a little embarrassment. However, what Jesus did shows us that He is concerned about our small needs, as well, and that we should take everything to Him.

Secondly, whatever He tells us to do in these situations, this we must do. In the natural sense, this requires much prayer and consecration to the Lord.

We have to live close enough to Him in order to constantly hear that *"still, small Voice."* Beyond the shadow of a doubt, I know that we can receive untold benefits and Blessings from the Lord if we only will have a proper relationship with Him, which requires two things:

1. That our Faith be anchored completely in Christ and the Cross, and maintained in Christ and the Cross. This means that there can be no divided faith, meaning that everything else must go in favor of Christ and the Cross.

2. We must have a relationship with Him, as well, which can only be done through prayer and the study of the Word. This is a must for every Believer. With that being done, the Holy Spirit will lead us, guide us, help us, strengthen us, and perform in our lives what only He can do.

And finally, from this beautiful example given by John of Jesus changing the water to wine, among other things, it lets us know how much He actually desires to be a part of our everyday lives, even those things that we may think are not spiritual, such as this incident. Serving Jesus is 24 hours a day, with Him wanting total involvement in everything we do. Actually, the crowning sin of man is what he thinks he can do without the Lord. The truth is, we need the Lord, and desperately so, in every function of our lives. He Who notes the sparrow's fall and even numbers the very hairs of our heads strongly desires that He be allowed this latitude. If allowed, the Believer will find *"more Abundant Life"* (Jn. 10:10).

HE TASTED THE WATER THAT HAD BEEN
TURNED INTO WINE

"When the Ruler of the feast had tasted the water that

was made wine, and knew not from whence it was: (but the servants which drew the water knew;) the Governor of the feast called the bridegroom" (Jn. 2:9).

The phrase, *"When the ruler of the feast had tasted the water that was made wine, and knew not from whence it was,"* proclaims that he had no idea as to what had been done. Evidently, this scenario had taken place only in the presence of a few people.

This can be representative of the Gospel of Jesus Christ which goes to the sinner. They partake but have little understanding as to its origination and, above all, the Miracle which had to take place for them to partake of the Wine of Salvation. In fact, every Salvation experience is a Miracle and, undoubtedly, the greatest Miracle of all.

"But the servants which drew the water knew," speaks of Gospel workers who know and understand the Miracle of Redemption. These men had seen Jesus do this thing. They did not understand it, and neither can anyone understand the Miracle of the New Birth, at least, in the natural sense. Jesus said when He explained it to Nicodemus, *"The wind blows where it listeth, and you hear the sound thereof, but cannot tell from where it comes, and whither it goes: so is everyone who is born of the Spirit"* (Jn. 3:8).

A short time ago over our daily radio program, "A Study in the Word," I attempted to explain this very thing. Paul was dealing with the Corinthian Church, telling them what they once had been, and now what Christ had done for them.

After listing a description of some of the worst types of sin, the Lord then said, *"... And such were some of you: but you are washed, but you are sanctified, but you are justified in the Name of the Lord Jesus, and by the Spirit of our God"* (I Cor. 6:11).

We know these things are done upon confession of

Christ by the believing sinner even though we do not know exactly how it is done!

THE GOVERNOR OF THE FEAST

The phrase, *"The Governor of the feast called the bridegroom,"* indicates his surprise at the turn of events.

As governor of the feast, he was responsible for everything which took place. So, in effect, people were looking to him respecting this lack. As such, the bridegroom stood to be embarrassed because of what looked like improper planning.

Almost immediately after he had been given the news of this problem and was instantly concerned as to how it could be rectified, the servants came to him with containers of wine. He immediately tasted, thinking surely that this was a very poor product, hence, used only in an emergency. He would taste it to see if it was fit to give to the guests.

He could hardly believe what he was tasting and would exclaim such to the bridegroom immediately.

David had written so long before, *"O taste and see that the LORD is good ..."* (Ps. 34:8).

TASTE AND SEE THAT THE LORD IS GOOD

It is sad, but most of the world looks at the *"Wine of Salvation"* offered to them and never bothers to taste its flavor. They have formed an opinion based on ignorance or, else, a desire to continue in their sin, not realizing that its wages are death. However, for the few who do taste this grand elixir of life, they will always find, and without exception, exactly as David said, *"Taste and see that the LORD is good."*

Worse yet are the hundreds of millions who have no opportunity to taste. The servants (workers for the

Lord) never bothered to bring it to them.

What would have happened that day had Jesus performed this great Miracle with the servants not bothering to dispense this product?

Should that have happened, which, of course, it did not, I think these servants would have been in terrible trouble. I wonder now if many of the so-called Servants of the Lord are, in fact, in great trouble due to this very thing.

Jesus can perform the Miracle of changing men's lives. It is up to us to take this *"Wine of Salvation"* to a lost world.

THE GOOD HAS BEEN KEPT UNTIL NOW

"And said unto him, Every man at the beginning does set forth good wine; and when men have well drunk, then that which is worse: but you have kept the good wine until now" (Jn. 2:10).

Verse 10 proclaims the surprise of the governor at the quality of this newly-made wine, although he did not know it was newly-made.

Actually, as stated, he had no knowledge of what had taken place regarding Jesus performing this Miracle, which meant that his Testimony was completely unbiased.

Incidentally, the words, *"Well drunk,"* simply mean they had *"drunk freely,"* not that all were drunk, as some suppose.

It certainly would be natural to understand that the very best of anything, especially in a situation of this nature, is always given first. If more is needed, the second best will be provided, that is, if available. The governor was amazed because this rule did not seem to have been followed. But, of course, he was wrong; it was followed.

Jesus had stepped in and had created wine, and, of course, whatever He creates is the absolute best.

THE BEST FOR THE LAST

The phrase, *"But you have kept the good wine until now,"* in effect, says that the *"best was saved until the last."*

I personally believe that this has a wide spiritual application as well. It is twofold:

1. With the world, all good things come during the time of youth, with the old age generally bringing the very opposite.

However, with the Believer serving Jesus, it just gets better and better as we get older. Consequently, the best is saved for the last.

2. As well, I believe the Spirit of God during these last days is going to be poured out even to a greater degree than ever before. In Joel, Chapter 2, the Prophet speaks of a former and latter rain. The insinuation is that the *"latter rain"* will have a greater visitation even than the former (Joel 2:21-32).

The Early Church, as is recorded in the Book of Acts, constitutes the *"former rain."* The *"latter rain"* has to do with these last days and actually began, I believe, at about the turn of the 20th century. Since that time, multiple millions have been Saved and baptized with the Holy Spirit. All of this is the *"latter rain"*; however, at the very end of the *"latter rain,"* I believe that God is going to do something special. As the good wine was saved until the last, I believe the same holds true prophetically speaking.

Even though the Bible predicts a great *"falling away"* from the Faith in these last days, it also predicts, I believe, a great outpouring of the Holy Spirit at the same time.

In other words, it's like two rivers flowing side by side but in opposite directions (Acts 2:17-21; II Thess. 2:3).

THE FIRST MIRACLE

"This beginning of Miracles did Jesus in Cana of Galilee, and manifested forth His Glory; and His Disciples believed on Him" (Jn. 2:11).

The phrase, *"This beginning of Miracles did Jesus in Cana of Galilee,"* means that this was the first Miracle He performed. Consequently, this tells us that all the so-called miracles that He performed in His Childhood, as reported in the apocryphal books, are false.

For instance, these accounts claim that He stretched lumber to the desired lengths; made one grain of wheat grow 800 bushels; made birds and animals of clay and gave life to them, etc.

Actually, as here stated, Jesus did no miracle until after His Anointing with the Spirit.

So, Cana had the distinction of being the location for the beginning of the Ministry of the Son of God and the Redemption of mankind, which was the greatest event in human history.

WHAT WAS THE PURPOSE OF THIS MIRACLE
OF CHANGING THE WATER INTO WINE?

It should be obvious that by doing this, Jesus placed the highest seal of approval upon the institution of marriage. Of course, this had already been done, even from the very beginning (Gen. 2:24); nevertheless, this action by Christ placed even greater emphasis on this all-important social fabric.

As well, I think it should be very obvious as to the abomination carried out respecting so-called same-sex marriages. As is obvious, the homosexual lobby is working day and night that Congress would legitimize such action; however, Congress is one thing while God Almighty is Something else altogether. It really doesn't matter if Congress does approve of such, God never will, and it's to God that man will ultimately have to answer.

The fabric of a nation is the home. If that is destroyed, the sinew of the nation is destroyed. It is the nuclear family, which consists of a husband, wife, and children, that the Lord has designed and consequently blesses.

As the late Sen. Robert Byrd of Virginia said, concerning this proposal of congressional legitimacy, *"Regarding this issue of same-sex marriages, America is being weighed in the balances."* He then went on to say, *"Irrespective of whether we legitimize it, God will not, and we will be 'found wanting.'"*

That such would even be considered by the legislative branch of our government only shows us to what depths this nation has fallen.

JESUS CAN CHANGE THINGS

As previously stated, among other reasons, this Miracle was performed by Christ to proclaim His Power to change things, whether man's situations or events. Much of the world desires a change in their lifestyles simply because of the bondage which has been brought about by sin.

The smoker wants to quit cigarettes. The drinker wants to quit drinking. The drug addict desires to stop. Many other situations fall into the same category. However, the tragedy is that many desire to rid themselves of the penalty of sin while keeping the sin. Such is not done!

Only Jesus can change humanity. The world of psychology, as touted by the world and much of the church, can change nothing.

EVEN THE SMALL THINGS

This Miracle in what might be concluded a mundane matter shows us that the Lord is desirous of being a part of everything we do as His Children, even the small mundane matters. This Miracle portrays that.

A MIRACLE-WORKING GOD

This which Jesus did is a great encouragement to those who work for Him. We serve a Miracle-working God. He can take nothing and beautifully make something glorious of it.

A MANIFESTATION OF THE GLORY OF GOD

The phrase, *"And manifested forth His Glory,"* proclaims to us several great Truths:

• If one is to notice, it says, *"His Glory,"* instead of His Power! While it certainly took Power to do this, it was Power used in a way that is totally opposite from most of the world. When men gain power, they usually use it for themselves. Jesus used it for others, hence, *"His Glory."*

• The Greek word for *"Glory"* is *"Doxa,"* and means, *"The nature and acts of God in self-manifestation, i.e., what He essentially is and does as exhibited in whatever way He reveals Himself in the respects, and particularly in the Person of Christ, in Whom essentially His Glory has ever shown forth and ever will do."*

In this particular, it has to do exclusively with the positive. In other words, Jesus did not make anyone to be blind but made many to see. He did not cause anyone with this great Power to have leprosy, but rather healed them of their leprosy. At this time, He did not use His Power to judge mankind or to bring Judgment,

but rather the very opposite. Therefore, it was *"Glory."*
• The word, *"Manifested,"* means, at least, in this case, to manifest or proclaim something openly in that there be no doubt as to its origin. Such was this Miracle at Cana, and such were all His Miracles. This was done, at least, in part, that His Detractors might not be able to accuse Him of trickery; consequently, everything was done openly.

FAITH

"And His Disciples believed on Him," does not mean that they had formerly disbelieved Him, but that their Faith was increased due to the manifestation of His Glory in the changing of the water to wine.

For those who are truly God-Called and have a particular Mission to perform, at least one of their greatest needs is to have people around them who truly and sincerely believe in them.

If one is to notice, the Apostle Paul surrounded himself with such individuals. They believed that God had called him for world Evangelism. They believed also in the Message he preached, which was the great Gospel of Grace, i.e., *"the Message of the Cross."* This was especially significant considering that many, even some of the Believers in Jerusalem, held his views suspect or, at the least, gave him little, if any, support. Of course, it was not very difficult for the Disciples of Christ to believe on Him, especially considering that the Miracles He performed were constant and obvious.

Actually, that should have been the case with all, including the religious leaders of Israel; however, seemingly, it was not enough. Actually, willful blindness cannot see because it does not desire to see.

At the same time, a Divine Faith must be based on the Scriptures and not things which can be observed alone. In other words, all of it must match up with the Word.

CAPERNAUM

"After this He went down to Capernaum, He, and His Mother, and His Brethren, and His Disciples: and they continued there not many days" (Jn. 2:12).

The phrase, *"After this He went down to Capernaum,"* has to do with this city being of lower elevation than Cana, which, in fact, was approximately 700 feet higher in altitude.

"Capernaum" would become His Headquarters in His three and one-half years of Public Ministry. It was a very energetic trading center, quite large in size, and prospering greatly from the fishing business on the Sea of Galilee, and the great trade routes, which ran near from the north, east, and south. Actually, it was probably one of, if not the, most prosperous area in the whole of Israel.

As well, it seems that Peter had by now made this city his place of abode rather than Bethsaida (Jn. 1:44).

JESUS AND THOSE WITH HIM

The phrase, *"He, and His Mother, and His Brethren, and His Disciples,"* provides a most interesting Text.

No mention is made of Joseph, so it must be assumed that he has died. As well, no mention is made of the Half-sisters of Jesus inasmuch as they possibly were married and living in Nazareth.

The Catholic church claims that *"His Brethren,"* mentioned here, are actually His Cousins.

They also claim that Mary remained a perpetual virgin.

However, such is totally unscriptural. Mary did not remain a virgin nor were these mentioned as the cousins of Jesus, but rather His Half-brothers, one might say.

It is plainly stated in Scripture that Jesus had four brothers (half-brothers): James, Joseph, Simon, and Jude. He had at least two or three half-sisters, even though the exact number is not stated, using only the words, *"Are not His Sisters here with us?"* These are referred to as *"His Own Kin"* and *"His Own House."*

As well, Jesus is called Mary's *"Firstborn"* (Mat. 1:25; Lk. 2:7), and the natural inference is that she had other children. The Greek *"prototokos"* is used in Romans 8:29; Colossians 1:15-18; Hebrews 1:6; 11:28; 12:23; and Revelation 1:5, and means, *"The first of others."* Had Jesus been her only son, the word would have been, *"Monogenes,"* which occurs in Luke 7:12; 8:42; and 9:38.

It was also predicted by God that Mary would have other children, and the Messiah would have brothers. *"I am become a Stranger unto My Brethren, and an alien unto My Mother's children"* (Ps. 69:8).

As well, in this Text, it tells us of Mary going with Jesus to Capernaum, and it also speaks of *"His Brethren."* The children of some other woman would not be following Mary as *"His Brethren."*

FALSE!

The natural meaning of *"His Brethren"* would never have been questioned but for the fact of pagan corruption in the church — in seeking to raise Mary from a mere *"Handmaid of the Lord"* (Lk. 1:38) to that of Mother of God, and to invest her with Divine powers as a goddess. So, it is said that Mary had no other children and that His Brethren were cousins by another Mary and Cleophas, that Joseph was too old to have children of Mary, or that he had children by a former marriage.

All of this is false as nothing is mentioned in Scripture or history about these claims. If Joseph did have children before Jesus was born, then Jesus could not be the legal heir to David's throne, which, by Law, went to the firstborn.

HIS BROTHERS

Concerning *"His Brethren"* going with Him to Capernaum, the evidence is that they had not yet taken the stand against Christ, which they would later take. While we do not have information on all the half-brothers, we do know that James and Jude became great pillars in the Early Church. They even wrote two short Epistles, which bear their names, and are included in the Canon of Scripture. However, it seems they did not come to Faith until after the Resurrection. John will later record the sad statement, *"For neither did His Brethren believe in Him"* (Jn. 7:5).

Why?

Of course, the complete answer to that question could only be given by the Lord; however, some things are obvious.

They probably had great difficulty in believing that Jesus was the Son of God, the Messiah of Israel, especially considering that they had been raised with Him. During the formative years, they saw no sign of such, even though they would be forced to admit that His Life was impeccable.

As well, a little later in the Ministry of Christ, the Pharisees and religious leaders of Israel would become more and more openly hostile toward Jesus.

What type of effect this had on His Immediate Family is not known. However, considering that the townspeople of Nazareth had rejected Jesus out of hand, it probably caused some hardship on His Family.

Also, there may have been some envy or jealousy present in that He did not choose any of them to be His Closest Disciples.

SELF-WILL

Irrespective as to excuse, self-will was the mitigating factor, which cheated them out of the greatest Blessing they could ever have. To have had the privilege of being the Half-brothers of Jesus and, as well, to be a part of His Ministry, which they certainly could have been, would be the greatest thing that could ever happen to anyone. However, these four brothers missed this glorious opportunity, which they would ever regret.

Some have said that this was the reason that James, at the beginning of his Epistle, did not call himself an Apostle, but rather a *"Servant of God."* Jude, as well, addressed himself accordingly as the *"Servant of Christ, and brother of James."* Due to their rejection of Him during His Earthly Ministry, they felt they were not worthy to claim more.

The phrase, *"And they continued there not many days,"* has reference to the *"Passover,"* which was to commence shortly. As was their custom, they would attend this Passover in Jerusalem, which would be the first since Jesus had begun His Public Ministry. To be sure, as we shall see, He would stir up quite a bit of controversy.

NAZARETH

"And He went out from thence, and came into His

Own Country; and His Disciples followed Him" (Mk. 6:1).

The phrase, *"And He went out from thence, and came into His Own Country,"* refers to Nazareth. Even though He was born in Bethlehem, still, Nazareth had been His Home from the time that Joseph, His Foster Father, had been warned by the Lord in a Dream concerning where he should live. Consequently the Scripture says, *"And He came and dwelt in a city called Nazareth"* (Mat. 2:23). Nazareth was about a day's journey from Capernaum.

There is debate over whether this is the same journey recorded in Luke, Chapter 4, or another. Most think that Luke, Chapter 4, was His First, with this being His Second. And yet, the terminology is such that the possibility definitely exists that Luke, Chapter 4, and Mark, Chapter 6, are one and the same. Luke, Chapter 4, could well be given out of chronological order, as some of the experiences often are.

The phrase, *"And His Disciples followed Him,"* speaks of the entirety of the Twelve.

WHO IS THIS MAN?

"And when the Sabbath Day was come, He began to teach in the synagogue: and many hearing Him were astonished, saying, From whence has this Man these things? and what wisdom is this which is given unto Him, that even such mighty works are wrought by His Hands?" (Mk. 6:2).

They did not question the wisdom or the works, but rather His Right to do such things. In their thoughts, He wasn't worthy!

The phrase, *"And when the Sabbath Day was come,"* lends credence to the thought that He arrived in Nazareth several days before the Sabbath. The phrase, *"He began to teach in the synagogue,"* records the practice of most synagogues.

If a speaker of note came by, the ruler of the synagogue could, if he so desired, request that he speak. Having heard many wonderful things about Jesus, especially considering that He was raised in their midst, they, no doubt, eagerly requested that He teach them. The method varied in different synagogues. Sometimes a Text was appointed, and sometimes the speaker was allowed to choose that which he desired.

The question, *"Saying, From whence has this Man these things?"* is asked in contempt. The word, *"Man,"* was inserted by the translators, meaning it was not in the original Text, with them actually saying, *"From whence has 'this' these things?"* They were overly contemptuous in their question.

The question, *"And what wisdom is this which is given unto Him, that even such mighty works are wrought by His Hands?"* proclaims them addressing both that which He taught and the *"mighty works"* which He performed.

They did not deny the *"wisdom"* or the *"mighty works,"* or the fact that they were *"wrought by His Hands."* Their complaint was actually that He had no right to do such things. This has ever been the criticism of those who do not desire God's Choice. They could not attack what He said or did; consequently, they would attack Him.

He wasn't worthy! He wasn't qualified! He did not pass their test, whatever that test was! It has little changed up to the present. Those who pass God's Test will not pass man's; those who pass man's will not pass God's.

THE CARPENTER

"Is not this the Carpenter, the Son of Mary, the Brother of James, and Joseph, and of Juda, and Simon? and are

not His Sisters here with us? And they were offended at Him" (Mk. 6:3).

St. John Chrysostom said that Jesus made plows and yokes for oxen. In the minds of His Critics, this disqualified Him as a Great Teacher.

The beginning of the question, *"Is not this the Carpenter. . . ?"* no doubt, actually meant that He worked at the trade of a carpenter and continued to do so until He entered Public Ministry. So, their complaint was that He was a Carpenter and, consequently, ill-prepared to be a Great Teacher. For His Townspeople, the contrast was too great between the Peasant of Galilee, who had earned His Daily Bread by the sweat of His Brow for the first 30 years of His Life, and the Person Who delivered those wonderful discourses and performed these Miracles. They could not see past His Role and Position as a Carpenter. This was lowly in their estimation and certainly offered no preparation for a position as one of the great Teachers of Israel.

OFFENSE

The phrase, *"And they were offended at Him,"* means that He did not meet with their approval; consequently, they were scandalized that He was able to do these great things. In some weird way, they felt He brought reproach on their town of Nazareth. They were fearful they would become a laughingstock over Israel.

The very idea that this Peasant, or this *"Oaf,"* as they would have put it, would aspire to be one of the great Teachers of Israel is what was beyond their comprehension. It didn't matter that His Words were given with more wisdom than any they had ever heard before, and that *"mighty works"* were constantly performed by His Hands. Still, they could not or, in truth, would not accept Him irrespective of the great things He did! As stated, they could not explain Him, so they rejected Him.

The saddest part of all was that His Own Half-brothers and Half-sisters, sons and daughters of Mary and Joseph, disbelieved His Messianic claims. They had lived in the same home with Jesus for many years, and had been the recipients of the financial support He brought into the family by His Carpentry Work. However, His Singularly Beautiful Life had made no effective impression upon their dull, cold hearts.

MARY

And yet, I cannot believe that Mary shared the unbelief of her other sons and daughters.

From what little description we have, it seems that she was not a forceful woman; consequently, she said very little at these times although she was hurting deeply in her heart. She knew what the Angel Gabriel had said unto her, and she also remembered the Spirit of Prophecy that came on her at this occasion (Lk. 1:26-38, 46-56).

So, I think we must confine the unbelief to the half-brothers and half-sisters! As stated, it seems that Joseph had passed on by this time.

The rejection suffered here by Christ, and we speak of the city of Nazareth, had to be the *"unkindest"* cut of all. These people knew Him, especially His Own and Loved Ones.

They knew of His Impeccable Life and Perfect Character. They knew He was the Personification of Kindness.

There was, therefore, no reason for their actions. It could only be summed up as the result of cold, calculating, hardened hearts, which were so removed from God that even though they constantly spoke of

Him, in reality, they did not know Him at all! Had they known God the Father, they would have known God the Son!

HIS MOTHER

"While He yet talked to the people, behold, His Mother and His Brethren stood without, desiring to speak with Him" (Mat. 12:46).

The phrase, *"While He yet talked to the people,"* concerns the terrible Word He had just delivered concerning Israel's present and future state.

The phrase, *"Behold, His Mother and His Brethren stood without,"* refers to the probability that He was in a particular house with His Disciples and many others to whom He was speaking. As well, there must have been a sizable crowd outside, which *"His Mother and His Brethren"* had joined due to there being no more room in the house.

"Desiring to speak with Him," proclaims, according to the following statements, that their desire to speak with Him was not in a positive sense. Actually, they came to capture and confine Him — thus, in spirit, uniting with the Pharisees who planned to destroy Him. Such is man, and such is the flesh!

The Scripture says plainly that they did not at this time believe in Him (Jn. 7:5). Someone has said that Mary was willing to be the honored Mother of the King of Israel but unwilling to be the despised Disciple of the hated Nazarene (Mk. 3:21-31). However, I think that may be a little strong. We must remember at all times what Gabriel had said to her at the very beginning. I don't believe that Mary was opposed to Jesus in any fashion. Whatever it was at this time that she did, I think it was from a mother's natural instinct to protect her Son. I do not believe in any fashion that she joined in with the unbelief of the Brothers and Sisters of Jesus. Thankfully, at least James and Jude would ultimately change.

YOUR MOTHER AND YOUR BRETHREN STANDING WITHOUT

"Then one said unto Him, Behold, Your Mother and Your Brethren stand without, desiring to speak with You" (Mat. 12:47).

The phrase, *"Your Mother and Your Brethren stand without,"* implies that they were tired of waiting, especially since they were family relations and felt they deserved better treatment. Once again, I do not think that Mary would have joined in with this impatience.

DESIRING TO SPEAK WITH YOU

The phrase, *"Desiring to speak with You,"* emphasizes that they had things to say to Him, whatever they were. However, they little desired to hear what He had to say to them inasmuch as it seems that His Great Discourses, such as the *"Sermon on the Mount,"* etc., were all ignored by them. Such is difficult to understand and must have been a delight to the Pharisees, who, no doubt, exclaimed that even His Own Family did not believe in Him!

WHO IS MY MOTHER?

"But He answered and said unto him who told Him, Who is My Mother? and who are My Brethren?" (Mat. 12:48).

The question, *"Who is My Mother?"* was said for a purpose. It would totally refute the claims later made by the Catholic church. To be sure, the question is not asked with unkindness but only intending to set the record straight.

The question, *"And who are My Brethren?"* as well, is in the same vein. Jesus knew the purpose of His Relatives, which, at least, at that time, was not according to the Will of God. Whatever they wanted or desired, which His Answer proves, was not what the Father wanted and desired! How subject He was to the Will of God and how little His Followers are!

He had previously stated that *"He who loves father or mother more than Me is not worthy of Me . . ."* (Mat. 10:37). And now, that which He demanded of His Followers, He demonstrated by His Allegiance to the Heavenly Father.

The question, *"Who is My Mother?"* as stated, completely refutes the fallacious doctrine of the Catholic church that Mary is the Mother of God.

THERE STOOD BY THE CROSS OF JESUS HIS MOTHER

"Now there stood by the Cross of Jesus His Mother, and His Mother's sister, Mary the wife of Cleophas, and Mary Magdalene" (Jn. 19:25).

The phrase, *"Now there stood by the Cross of Jesus His Mother,"* spoke of Mary. (It was actually pronounced *"Miriam."*)

The suffering that Mary must have endured as she watched this spectacle is, no doubt, beyond comprehension! And yet, I know she would be very grieved if she knew the manner in which the Catholic church addresses her as the Mother of God and as an intercessor between Jesus and man.

As well, I think the Scriptural indication is that Believers, upon dying and going to be with Jesus, are at that time shut off regarding knowledge of happenings on Earth. Were this not so, great sorrow would plague many, if not all, concerning loved ones back on Earth who are going astray, or other particulars which bring grief. We know there is no sorrow or grief in Heaven; therefore, that, of necessity, demands that particular barriers be placed, the one in Heaven and those on Earth.

The phrase, *"And His Mother's sister, Mary the wife of Cleophas, and Mary Magdalene,"* perhaps was speaking of that particular moment because Matthew says that many women stood afar off beholding these things, which included Salome, John's mother (Mat. 27:55; Mk. 15:40-41).

As well, we learn that *"Mary the wife of Cleophas,"* was the sister of Mary the Mother of Jesus; however, this Mary and Mary Magdalene were actually pronounced *"Maria."* So, Mary the Mother of Jesus was actually named *"Miriam,"* and her sister, *"Maria."*

Also, this means that James the Less and Joseph were cousins of the Lord.

It is believed by many that Salome was also a sister of Mary the Mother of Jesus, which would have made James and John cousins also of our Lord.

James, the brother of John, is different than the other Disciple, *"James the son of Alphaeus"* (Mat. 10:3), whom Mark called *"James the Less"* (Mk. 15:40).

"Mary Magdalene" seems to have not been a relative of the others, but she had been delivered by Jesus from the possession of seven demons (Mk. 16:9). Consequently, she would be the very first person to herald the Resurrection of Christ (Mk. 16:10).

JOHN THE BELOVED AND THE MOTHER OF JESUS

"When Jesus therefore saw His Mother, and the Disciple standing by, whom He loved, He said unto His Mother, Woman, behold your son!" (Jn. 19:26).

This was *"John the Beloved,"* of whom Jesus spoke. It seems as if John was standing near the Mother of Jesus, attempting to console her in every way he could.

The phrase, *"He said unto His Mother, Woman, behold your son!"* was addressed to Mary and to John the Beloved.

The term, *"Woman,"* as it was used then, was not an expression of coldness, but rather an honorific title of endearment. Joseph, the Foster Father of Jesus, was now dead, and as stated in John 7:5, it seems that His Own Half-brothers did not believe in Him.

Due to this fact and of coming events, Jesus would place the care of Mary into the hands of John the Beloved.

And yet, very shortly after the Resurrection, He would appear to His Half-brother James, who would then accept Him and actually become the leader of the Church in Jerusalem (Gal. 1:19). Jude, another half-brother, would also accept the Lord as the Saviour of mankind, with both of these men writing the short Epistles, which bear their names, in the New Testament.

So, whatever problem there had been in the family caused by unbelief, it would be corrected very shortly after the Resurrection of Christ.

BEHOLD YOUR MOTHER

"Then said He to the Disciple, Behold your mother! And from that hour that Disciple took her unto his own home" (Jn. 19:27).

The phrase, *"Then said He to the Disciple, Behold your Mother!"* told John that from that moment on, he was to look at Mary exactly as his own mother.

"And from that hour that Disciple took her unto his own home," proclaims John speaking of himself in the third person. There are some who think that Zebedee

and his wife Salome and John also had homes both in Jerusalem and Capernaum, which seems to have been the case. We do know that Zebedee, the father of James and John, was not a poor man but, in fact, possessed boats and fishing tackle, and had day laborers working for him (Mk. 1:20). As well, it seems that Salome traveled extensively with Jesus' Party and ministered to Him and to the Twelve of her substance (Mat. 27:55; Lk. 8:3).

It is known that Jerusalem at that time contained a large fish market in order to supply the many thousands who came in for the great Feast Days. So, being in the fishing business, it stands to reason that they well could have had a domicile there also. Even though James and Jude, the Lord's Half-brothers, soon became Followers of Christ, still, from this one Passage it seems that John, and possibly his mother Salome, carried out the Master's Command in totality.

It is possible that the other half-brothers became Followers of Christ also. If so, this would have changed the situation of animosity in the home that had been against Jesus. Reynolds said, *"We must ever think of John and his mother Salome ever by the Mother of the Lord, whether at Jerusalem, Capernaum, or Ephesus."* And then he said, *"The few words given here by John speak volumes, and his reticence, as elsewhere, gives an unutterable grandeur to his words."*

MARY THE MOTHER OF JESUS

"These all continued with one accord in prayer and supplication, with the women, and Mary the Mother of Jesus, and with His Brethren" (Acts 1:14).

The phrase, *"With the women, and Mary the Mother of Jesus,"* concerns the women who followed Christ from Galilee (Mat. 27:55-56). As well, it should be noticed that Mary the Mother of Jesus appears here not as an object of worship, but as humbly joining in with the others in seeking the Lord.

The phrase, *"And with His Brethren,"* concerns His Half-brothers, who were *"James, Joses, Simon, and Judas"* (Mat. 13:55; Mk. 6:3).

Whether all four were present or not, we are not told. However, due to Jesus having appeared to James after the Resurrection, there is definitely a possibility that all four were there.

In fact, this statement concerning Mary and His Brethren, as given by the Holy Spirit, brings deep and sweet relief to the Christian heart.

At last, Mary and the Brothers of Jesus took their place publicly among the Disciples. Had they made this great decision at the beginning, how much happier they should have been!

It is humbling to religious self-esteem to learn that the Lord's Daily Intimate Family Life of Perfect Love and exquisite immortal beauty for many years in the home, as in Nazareth, and later, His Miracles and Teaching failed to win His Brothers and Sisters to believe on Him. Their unbelief makes more convincing the truth of the incurable corruption of the natural heart (Jer. 17:9). John recorded their attitude by saying, *"But they did not believe on Him"* (Jn. 7:5).

As it regards Mary, the Mother of our Lord, actually, the terrible sword of Luke 2:34-35, symbolically speaking, revealed the thoughts of many hearts and of her heart as well (Heb. 4:12). The pain she felt when viewing the Crucifixion belonged to the realm of nature, but the double prediction of Luke, Chapter 2, belonged to the realm of Judgment. She herself illustrated Luke 2:34.

Corrupt Christianity has composed a different history of Mary — and the natural heart prefers such — but the true Christian believes only what the infallible Spirit of God records.

Great Women of the Bible

OF THE
BIBLE

Chapter Two

THE CERTAIN
POOR WIDOW

THE CERTAIN POOR WIDOW

THE RICH MEN

"And He looked up, and saw the rich men casting their gifts into the treasury" (Lk. 21:1).

The phrase, *"And He looked up,"* could well mean that He was sitting, even resting, after the clash with the Scribes and Sadducees.

He was in the covered colonnade of that part of the Temple which was open to the Jewish women. Here was the treasury with its 13 boxes on the wall where the people could give offerings.

These boxes were called, *"Shopheroth,"* or trumpets, because they were shaped like trumpets. It is said that some of these were marked with special inscriptions, denoting the destination of the gifts. Only Mark and Luke mentioned this.

"And saw the rich men casting their gifts into the treasury," implies that they were making a show of their gifts, desiring to impress the people by the amount, etc. It seems that almost all of Israel had become one big show of religion with almost no substance in fact.

A CERTAIN POOR WIDOW

"And He saw also a certain poor widow casting in thither two mites" (Lk. 21:2).

As this woman would never have made a show out of putting in such a small amount, evidently the Holy Spirit informed Jesus of all these proceedings, her poverty, the amount given, and that she had nothing left.

The *"two mites"* were probably worth something less than a dollar and possibly much less.

In this scenario, the Lord will make abundantly clear the motive of the heart respecting giving.

He will tell us, as well, how God looks at what we give, and, to be sure, that is the only thing that is really important.

As a result, this illustration has been a tremendous comfort to millions down through the centuries who long to give to God but have precious little to give. The Lord shows here that He judges the amount given by many and different factors.

Hopefully, we will look at some of these factors.

MORE THAN THEY ALL

"And He said, Of a truth I say unto you, that this poor widow has cast in more than they all" (Lk. 21:3).

The phrase, *"And He said, Of a truth I say unto you,"* presents a new concept of giving. As will be obvious, giving had degenerated into a "show" to impress people, which, of course, eliminated most people who had no such large gifts to give.

The Lord will teach that whatever is done is judged rather by the motives than by other particulars, such as the amount, etc.

"That this poor widow has cast in more than they all," no doubt, came as a shock to the listeners as well as the Disciples of our Lord.

The words, *"Poor widow,"* mean that she worked hard for what little bit she did have.

Israel had deteriorated into this *"showy"* religion because of her *"why"* thinking, which resulted from a wrong interpretation of the Scripture or the ignoring of it all together.

POVERTY AND WEALTH

The Jews in Jesus' Day had long since come to the conclusion that wealth equated to the Blessings of

God, with poverty the very opposite.

Consequently, the richer one was, the closer to God one was, at least, in their thinking.

If that is so, then the showy method of giving followed suit. It probably was carried out under the auspices that God had blessed them abundantly, and, consequently, they were giving abundantly. All was done with great show and under a great panoply of religion, with maybe even praises to God, etc. However, it was not God Who had blessed these individuals who were rich, but rather their own cunning, etc. That is not to mean that all who are rich fall into this category, for some few did not then and do not now.

Of course, Jesus blew this thinking out of the water by stating, *"... How hardly shall they who have riches enter into the Kingdom of God!"* (Lk. 18:24). He didn't say it couldn't be done but that it was seldom done.

The moral of this is that false doctrine does not have a stopping place. Instead, it continues to go more and more astray if not corrected. In other words, a small amount of leaven ultimately corrupts the whole, and such was Israel.

In the Eyes of God, this woman had given more, not only than the giver of the richest gift, but actually all combined. At least, this is what the Lord said, which is the only conclusion that matters.

ALL THE LIVING THAT SHE HAD

"For all these have of their abundance cast in unto the Offerings of God: but she of her penury has cast in all the living that she had" (Lk. 21:4).

The phrase, *"For all these have of their abundance cast in unto the Offerings of God,"* means that they have much left, constituting very little given, at least, in the Eyes of God.

"But she of her penury (poverty) has cast in all the living that she had," spoke of her gift, as small as it was, being larger than all others combined because she gave all.

What do we learn from this?

• God doesn't judge the quality of the gift by its size but by the motivation of the heart.

• Her consecration was such that she longed to give to God even though it was such a small amount, and above all that, it was all that she had. This shows that she put God first in all things.

• Many others may get the credit here because of large gifts, while many, like this dear lady, will get the credit there. Actually, Jesus was giving us a portrayal of how God keeps score. We should heed it carefully!

• If we take the attitude that our gift is small and, consequently, of no use, we have completely misunderstood the reason for giving. We learn that the Lord delighted in what this woman did and made such obvious to all.

• The large gifts, just because they were large, did not bring about censure from Christ, but only the showy method by which they were given. It is obvious that $50,000 will do much more for the Work of the Lord than $20.

God has so blessed some individuals that they can give large amounts. However, it must be given with the thought and motivation that God, Who knows all as well as sees all, will bless us accordingly, at least, in respect to our motives.

Not too many people giving small amounts will be lifted up in pride with such, but large gifts can cause pride to be generated if we are not careful and properly motivated by Christ.

Actually, the Lord judges all things according to our motives.

THE POOR WIDOW

Despite the smallness of her gift, this *"poor widow"* was motivated to give to God because she loved Him. The rich men (at least these) were motivated to give to God in order that they might make a big show and impress others. Such does not always hold true in these situations and categories, but it does many times.

As far as we know, that which Jesus said about the widow's alms was the last word of public teaching. If, in fact, that is the case, it is significant that this last word would be on the subject of money!

Great Women of the Bible

NEW TESTAMENT

Chapter Three

MARY MAGDALENE

MARY MAGDALENE

"The first day of the week comes Mary Magdalene early, when it was yet dark, unto the Sepulchre, and sees the stone taken away from the Sepulchre" (Jn. 20:1).

The phrase, *"The first day of the week,"* was the Day of Christ's Resurrection. Actually, it had begun at sundown the day before, which was Saturday, according to the manner in which Jews then reckoned time. So, Jesus was, no doubt, raised from the dead very shortly after the sun had set and night had settled in. The Father would not leave His Son in the Tomb one minute longer than was necessary.

While Calvary was the greatest event in the history of the world, still, it was the Resurrection of Jesus Christ from the dead that ratified everything that had been done at the Cross. Of course, without the Resurrection, Calvary would have been in vain.

Heathen and foes admit the fact of the Death of Jesus; the evidence is overwhelming, multiform, and sufficient to establish itself to the ordinary reason of mankind.

It is a matter of indisputable history. The proof was given to the entire world; however, many, if not most, doubt the Resurrection.

Some would claim that the four accounts of the Resurrection do not correspond. As such, they claim a discrepancy in the Sacred Text. However, the four different accounts prove the authenticity of the Text rather than the opposite. Had the Text been *"doctored"* or *"edited,"* they would have all read the same. So, the differences, but we might quickly add, not discrepancies, only verify the Inspiration.

The four different accounts only portray what the eyewitnesses saw or what the writer heard, as in the case of Luke.

They are not contradictions, only different accounts.

Any four people could witness a graphic situation, and, upon investigation, four different accounts would be given.

For whatever reason, one or two would add things the others did not say; however, such does not mean a contradiction, as stated, only a different account.

THE FIRST DAY OF THE WEEK

As well, if one is to notice, inasmuch as Jesus rose from the dead on *"the first day of the week,"* this day was ever after celebrated as a day of worship, consequently, taking the place of the old Jewish Sabbath (Jn. 20:1, 19, 26-29; Acts 20:6-12; I Cor. 16:1-2).

The outpouring of the Holy Spirit was on the first day of the week, the day after seven Jewish Sabbaths (Acts 2:1). After Christ's Ascension, the first Gospel Sermon was preached on the first day; and the first Conversions (about 3,000) took place on the first day (Acts 2:1-42).

Also, it must be understood that no recognition was given by Christ or any Apostle to the old Jewish Seventh-Day Sabbath after the Resurrection. In fact, Sunday, the first day became known as *"the Lord's Day"* (Rev. 1:10).

MARY MAGDALENE

The phrase, *"Comes Mary Magdalene early, when it was yet dark, unto the Sepulchre,"* probably referred to about 5 o'clock in the morning.

John only mentioned Mary Magdalene, but Matthew, Mark, and Luke all spoke of other women being with her. However, John did not say the others were not present; he just failed to mention them at all.

The reason was probably because Mary Magdalene seemed to have been the first one to tell Peter and John that the stone had been rolled away from the mouth of the Sepulchre and that the Body of Jesus was missing. It seems the other women also said the same thing to Peter and John, but with Mary Magdalene possibly arriving first (Lk. 24:9-10).

As well, Luke stated that the women, plus Mary Magdalene, had seen two Angels at the Tomb, who had even spoken to them (Lk. 24:1-8); however, John did not mention this either.

It seems that all the women were thrown somewhat into a state of shock upon meeting with these events, with all running to tell the Disciples, and Mary Magdalene, as stated, possibly arriving first.

THE STONE WAS ROLLED AWAY

Even though John does not mention the fact, the women had come early that morning bringing more spices to complete the embalming process. Many have scoffed at this, claiming that Joseph and Nicodemus had already placed about 100 pounds of spices on His Body when He was placed in the Tomb three days before (Jn. 19:39). However, the skeptics err because they do not understand that these women desired to place spices on the Body of Jesus, not so much that they were needed, but because they loved Him. Consequently, they wanted to do something, and this was all they could do.

As well, this tells us that not a single one of His Followers, even those who were the closest to Him, believed that He would rise from the dead.

But, He did!

The phrase, *"And sees the stone taken away from the Sepulchre,"* proclaims something these women did not expect to find. Actually, the detailed accounts of all the circumstances surrounding the Resurrection of Christ, which registered shock and surprise regarding all parties, preclude the hypothesis that these people stole the Body of Jesus away, as circulated by the Jews of that day. To be sure, if such a thing had happened, the stories would have been told in an entirely different way, as should be obvious!

MARY MAGDALENE RUNNING TO TELL THE DISCIPLES

"Then she ran, and came to Simon Peter, and to the other Disciple, whom Jesus loved, and said unto them, They have taken away the Lord out of the Sepulchre, and we know not where they have laid Him" (Jn. 20:2).

This Passage speaks of John, for he referred to himself several times as the *"other Disciple whom Jesus loved"* (Jn. 13:23; 19:26; 20:2; 21:7, 20-25).

As well, with him relating that she was running, this probably explains her arriving a little sooner than the others.

Also, it should be noted that John, who wrote this account over 50 years after the event, it is believed, gives Simon Peter first place in recognition.

The phrase, *"And said unto them, They have taken away the Lord out of the Sepulchre,"* proclaims her still thinking of the Lord as dead, despite the fact that two Angels had plainly said to them, *"He is not here, but is risen: remember how He spoke unto you when He was yet in Galilee,*

"Saying, The Son of Man must be delivered into the hands of sinful men, and be crucified, and the third day rise again" (Lk. 24:6-7).

Quite possibly she and the others did not recognize them as Angels and, therefore, did not quite believe or, most likely, did not really understand what the

Angels had said.

"And we know not where they have laid Him," probably referred to her thinking that Joseph and Nicodemus had moved the Body of Jesus to some other place. As is obvious, she is not thinking of Resurrection.

SIMON PETER

"Peter therefore went forth, and that other Disciple, and came to the Sepulchre" (Jn. 20:3).

Exactly where Peter and John were staying in Jerusalem at this time of the Passover is not known. As we have suggested, there is a possibility that Zebedee owned a second home in Jerusalem; however, that is only conjecture.

Irrespective, whether Peter and John were staying together with all the other Disciples, or whether they were apart, Mary Magdalene brought the news of the empty Tomb first to Peter and John.

The phrase, *"Peter therefore went forth,"* refers to him going speedily because the story had seemed incredulous to him.

"And that other Disciple, and came to the Sepulchre," refers to John, as stated!

Had they believed the Lord concerning His Resurrection, they would, no doubt, have been at the Tomb when the three days and nights expired. They were not there because of unbelief; consequently, they missed being personal witnesses of the greatest Miracle ever recorded in the annals of human history.

FIRST TO THE SEPULCHRE

"So they ran both together: and the other Disciple did outrun Peter, and came first to the Sepulchre" (Jn. 20:4).

The phrase, *"So they ran both together,"* seems to

indicate that the other Disciples were not with them at this particular time. As well, this portrays the desire to examine that which Mary Magdalene had portrayed. Also, wherever they were staying in Jerusalem must not have been very far from the Tomb.

"And the other Disciple did outrun Peter, and came first to the Sepulchre," speaks of John who wrote this account. Even though it does not say so in these Passages, from Verse 11, we know that Mary followed them back to the Tomb but lagged somewhat behind due to their running.

Some have assumed from this that Peter was an old man; however, there is nothing in Scripture to verify such or even hint accordingly.

Others have suggested, as well, that Peter's heart and conscience were weighted down because of his denial of Christ some three days before. This well could have been and, no doubt, continued to rest heavily upon Peter's heart.

However, at the same time, some people just run faster than others, which is probably the case in this instance.

THE LINEN CLOTHES

"And he stooping down, and looking in, saw the linen clothes lying; yet went he not in" (Jn. 20:5).

The phrase, *"And he stooping down, and looking in,"* refers to John, who arrived there a few moments before Peter.

"Saw the linen clothes lying," referred to the *"linen cloth"* of John 19:40, which had been used by Joseph and Nicodemus to wrap the Body of Jesus with the spices.

The word, *"Lying,"* in this instance, refers to something neatly folded and orderly arranged. Of course, if someone had stolen the Body of Jesus, such would not have been done. They would not have taken the time to remove the cloth.

"Yet went he not in," refers to John, for whatever reason, not going into the Tomb but standing in the doorway where the huge stone covering had sat and looking in.

Respecting the Death and Resurrection of Christ, the following might prove helpful:

THE THREE DAYS AND NIGHTS OF JESUS IN THE TOMB

The moment Jesus died, which was on the Cross, His Soul and Spirit left His Body and went down into the nether regions for particular purposes.

During those three days and nights, He did the following:

• He preached to the spirits in prison, which referred to fallen Angels; however, the preaching was not Good News, but rather an Announcement. It is not revealed to us simply because it evidently had to do only with Angels and not men.

All the time His Spirit and Soul were doing this, His Body was in the Tomb (I Pet. 3:19).

Incidentally, the word, *"spirits,"* as here used, never refers to human beings but always to Angels, in this case, fallen Angels. These were probably the fallen Angels who tried to corrupt the human race by cohabiting with women (II Pet. 2:4; Jude, Vss. 6-7). These fallen Angels are still locked up in this underworld prison and will be there until they are cast into the Lake of Fire (Rev. 20:10).

• Jesus also delivered every single soul that was in Paradise, which accounted for every Believer since Abel, the son of Adam and Eve. There is no record that Adam and Eve ever came back to God.

While all in Paradise were comforted, still, due to the fact that animal blood could not take away sins, they actually were captives of Satan.

That's the reason that Paul wrote, *"... He (meaning Jesus) led captivity captive, and gave Gifts unto men"* (Eph. 4:8).

When Jesus died on the Cross, the sin debt was forever paid, at least, for all who will believe.

Then, Satan had no more legal right over all of these individuals because all sin had been atoned at the Cross.

So, the strange statement, *"He led captivity captive,"* means that all of these, who had been captives of Satan, now became the captives of Jesus Christ. They were taken home to Glory.

Now, and I refer to the time since the Cross, when Believers die, their soul and spirit instantly go to be with the Lord Jesus Christ, in Heaven, we might quickly add (Phil. 1:21-24).

THE GLORIFIED BODY

However, when Jesus was resurrected three days and nights after His Death, His Soul and Spirit were reunited with His Body, which was now Glorified. Consequently, in that Glorified State, He came out of the Tomb. He has remained in that state ever since and, in fact, will ever remain in the Glorified State.

His Resurrection was the Foundation and prelude for the coming Resurrection of every Saint of God who has ever lived.

One of the reasons that John may not have gone into the Tomb is because of the prohibition by the Law of Moses of touching a dead human body. If this was done, the *"man shall be unclean seven days."* He would then have to go through a purification process, which was quite extensive (Num., Chpt. 19).

This Law was enacted in order that Israel would understand the terrible consequences of sin, which is death.

However, these prohibitions were forever ended when Jesus died on Calvary, which cleansed from all sin, at least, for all who will believe.

Therefore, His Death destroyed the effect of sin's wages, which is death, which means eternal separation from God. So, there would be no defilement by going into the Tomb of Jesus.

As well, there would be no such defilement anymore in any place, at least in this fashion, because Jesus has conquered death.

PETER OBSERVING THE LINEN CLOTHES

"Then came Simon Peter following him, and went into the Sepulchre, and saw the linen clothes lie" (Jn. 20:6).

The phrase, *"Then came Simon Peter following him,"* is due to the obvious fact that John simply outran him.

However, something must have been on Peter's mind far different than that of John. The last time Peter had seen Jesus, at least, close enough to where he could see His Face, was when Jesus looked at him right after the denial (Lk. 22:61).

(Peter, no doubt, saw Jesus hanging on the Cross, but that was at a distance and, therefore, not much discernible [Lk. 23:49].)

Of course, to know exactly what Peter was thinking at this time, only God knows! However, the denial had been so traumatic!

I cannot believe that he came to this Tomb without it weighing heavily upon his mind. Will he get to look upon that Face one more time?

To end Peter's three and one-half years of public

association with Jesus and knowing that the last time he saw Him, and that Jesus looked intently at him — at the time of gross failure — is a burden not easily borne.

However, this would be rectified very shortly, but Peter, at the time, was not aware of that.

THE SEPULCHRE

The phrase, *"And went into the Sepulchre,"* proclaims that which John did not do. Whatever defilement the Law of Moses addressed concerning the dead was not on Peter's mind at present.

Did he think that Jesus was possibly risen from the dead?

Every evidence, as we shall see, seems to indicate that at this time, none thought of Resurrection but only that something had happened which they did not now understand.

Maybe someone had stolen the Body of Jesus, but whom, especially considering that this Tomb was supposed to be guarded by four Roman soldiers and, in fact, was for the last 72 hours (Mat. 27:62-66). However, there were now no soldiers in sight!

The phrase, *"And saw the linen clothes lie,"* is once again brought out by the Holy Spirit in order for us to realize its significance.

If Joseph or Nicodemus had moved His Body, as possibly Mary and others suspected, they would not have taken the linen cloth from His Body.

As well, if the soldiers, or anyone, for that matter, had moved Him somewhere else, they would not have removed this material, for such would not have been plausible.

No! Those linen items neatly folded and lying on the place where Jesus had lain in death represented His Resurrection.

Either they were removed by the Angels at the Resurrection, or they simply fell off His Glorified Body at that moment, which is probably what happened.

Either Jesus or the Angels then neatly folded these items and laid them on the burial slab.

THE NAPKIN OVER HIS HEAD AND FACE

"And the napkin, that was about His Head, not lying with the linen clothes, but wrapped together in a place by itself" (Jn. 20:7).

"And the napkin, that was about His Head, not lying with the linen clothes," presents that which is extremely interesting simply because Jesus' Head and Face had been so maltreated that it was hardly recognizable, if at all!

"But wrapped together in a place by itself," speaks of something which had fallen off by itself or had been removed. At any rate, it was neatly folded and probably laid where His Head had been.

Once again we state, in the stealing of a body, such would not have been done. None of these actions spoke of haste, which would have accompanied the moving or stealing of a body, but rather something done deliberately and with precision.

These items neatly folded and placed conspicuously shouted, *"Resurrection!"* The items themselves, plus the way they were handled, proclaim Victory over sin and death.

As well, the manner in which these things were done proclaims to all that the Resurrected Jesus was not a Spirit but capable of activity and physical exertion. In other words, He is a Living Person, not an abstract principle, an apparition, or vague force.

These are evident proofs that however great the change which had passed over Him, the Living One was the same Man that He had ever been, but yet, in a greatly expanded way.

JOHN THE BELOVED

"Then went in also that other Disciple, which came first to the Sepulchre, and he saw, and believed" (Jn. 20:8).

"Then went in also that other Disciple, which came first to the Sepulchre," speaks of John the Beloved also now entering the Tomb with Peter.

The phrase, *"And he saw, and believed,"* refers to what Mary reported and not that Jesus had risen from the dead, as the next Scripture reveals. In their minds, Jesus was still dead even though His Body had been moved elsewhere.

How they accounted for the linen wrapping is anyone's guess!

THE SCRIPTURE

"For as yet they knew not the Scripture, that He must rise again from the dead" (Jn. 20:9).

This is evidently speaking of Psalms 16:10-11, *"For You will not leave My Soul in Hell; neither will You suffer Your Holy One to see corruption.*

"You will show Me the path of Life: in Your Presence is fullness of joy; at Your Right Hand there are pleasures forevermore."

The entire region of the underworld, including not only the burning side of Hell but Paradise, as well, were all spoken of as *"Hell"* (Lk. 16:19-31).

THE DISCIPLES OF CHRIST

"Then the Disciples went away again unto their own home" (Jn. 20:10).

This simply refers to the place where they were temporarily residing in Jerusalem, respecting their being there to keep the Passover.

The idea is, it seems, they simply did not know what to do. Strange things were happening, but they really could not account for the meaning of any one of these things.

WEEPING MARY MAGDALENE

"But Mary stood without at the Sepulchre weeping: and as she wept, she stooped down, and looked into the Sepulchre" (Jn. 20:11).

The phrase, *"But Mary stood without at the Sepulchre weeping,"* presents her staying after Peter and John had gone.

Mary did not know where Jesus was, and still believing that someone had taken His Body but not knowing where, she remained near the only place she could identify with Him. Although very little is known about Mary Magdalene before this time, Mark tells us that Jesus had delivered her of *"seven demons"* (Mk. 16:9).

Even though no information is given other than that, one can well imagine the suffering she endured before she met Jesus. How she came to be demon possessed, we are not told! Neither are we told what type of woman she was which would have brought about this terrible bondage. We are actually given no account at all of how she met Jesus and experienced this great Deliverance. This we do know:

Jesus gave her back her life and for that, she would love Him in such a way that it makes understandable her actions respecting these events. She would rather be close to where His Body had been than to go anywhere else. She knew how her life had changed.

How the religious hierarchy of Israel, who professed to know God, would murder Him was beyond her comprehension or understanding. She stood there *"weeping"* with a broken heart!

Jesus was her life, and without Him, life would lose its meaning and purpose. So it is with all who truly know Him and His Power to save!

The phrase, *"And as she wept, she stooped down, and looked into the Sepulchre,"* evidently represents the second time she had done this (Mat. 28:1-7; Mk. 16:1-7; Lk. 24:1-11).

TWO ANGELS

"And saw two Angels in white sitting, the one at the head, and the other at the feet, where the Body of Jesus had lain" (Jn. 20:12).

The phrase, *"And saw two Angels in white sitting,"* apparently represents the second appearance of Angels.

It seems that she did not really understand at the time that these were Angels.

Actually, regarding the first appearance, Luke called them *"two men."* However, the Scripture often interchanges the two descriptions because Angels look very much like men.

One must understand that all of these people, especially Mary Magdalene, were grief-stricken, somewhat in a state of shock, and, therefore, probably did not evaluate things quite as they should, as anyone would do under such circumstances.

Mary Magdalene knew that the religious hierarchy of Israel had masterminded the murder of Jesus, and that the Roman governor had carried out their request of performing the foul deed. She knew, as well, that Joseph and Nicodemus, two powerful men in Israel, had prepared Him for the burial. Mary did not know what was happening. I doubt very seriously that she knew, as stated, at least at that time, that these Beings were Angels.

"The one at the head, and the other at the feet, where the Body of Jesus had lain," in a sense of the word, represents the true Mercy Seat, with the Angels representing the Cherubim. The Angels sat, but the Cherubim had stood, for expiation was now accomplished (Ex. 25:19).

Williams said, *"Most probably these Angels were Princes; for the dignity and importance of the Resurrection demanded the Ministry of the highest ranked Angels* (Dan. 9:21; 10:21; 12:1; Lk. 1:19, 26)."

WOMAN, WHY DO YOU WEEP?

"And they say unto her, Woman, why do you weep? She said unto them, Because they have taken away my Lord, and I know not where they have laid Him" (Jn. 20:13).

The question, *"And they say unto her, Woman, why do you weep?"* is somewhat more personal than the statement the Angels had made upon the first appearance.

Then they said, *"Do not fear: for I know that you seek Jesus, which was crucified. He is not here: for He is risen, as He said. Come, see the place where the Lord lay"* (Mat. 28:5-6).

The other three accounts of this first appearance are each a little different in wording but with the same meaning.

Quite possibly, the Angels said other things which were not reported at all!

In this second appearance to Mary Magdalene, they spoke directly to her as to why she was weeping. Actually, their question was a mild rebuke.

None had believed Jesus when He spoke of being crucified and then rising from the dead.

Now, no one believed the Angels; however, all of this was about to change.

He is alive, even as the Angels were proclaiming, which should be an occasion for great joy.

However, unbelief hinders the reception of this Message, actually, the greatest in human history: Jesus is not dead; He is alive!

The phrase, *"She said unto them, Because they have taken away my Lord,"* proclaims, in a sense, the heart of Mary. Jesus is *"My Lord,"* which speaks volumes. He had changed her life, and she had given Him her heart. In her mind, there would never be another because of what He did for her and, in fact, so many others as well.

"And I know not where they have laid Him," in essence says, *"Wherever He is, even though it is only a dead Body, there I want to be."*

Inasmuch as she and other of the women had come earlier in order to bring spices to add to that which had already been done by Joseph and Nicodemus, such action only portrays their desire to do something, as little as it may be. In other words, love had to express itself in some way.

JESUS

"And when she had thus said, she turned herself back, and saw Jesus standing, and knew not that it was Jesus" (Jn. 20:14).

"And when she had thus said, she turned herself back," would have been better translated, *"She was caused to turn back."*

There is no record that the Angels said anything else to her. Perhaps she noticed the Angels looking behind her, and it was that which caused her to turn around.

To a wounded heart seeking Christ Himself, Angels, however glorious, hold no interest.

This fact demonstrates the idolatry and the folly of modern Angel adoration.

The phrase, *"And saw Jesus standing, and knew not that it was Jesus,"* portrays Him in His Glorified Form but, yet, looking little different than any other man. He could have appeared in Transfiguration Glory as He had done some time past, but this was not to be.

In fact, there is no record that anyone recognized Jesus, at least not immediately, after He had risen from the dead! (Lk. 24:16; Jn. 21:4).

Why?

Concerning His Walk with the two Disciples on the road to Emmaus, which took place on the day of His Resurrection, the Scripture says, *"But their eyes were holden (blinded) that they should not know Him"* (Lk. 24:16).

The idea is that He purposely caused them to not recognize Him, at least until He was ready for them to do so!

Even though we are not specifically told, their lack of recognition seemed to have something to do with their lack of faith. He would ultimately reveal Himself to all who were His Closer Followers, but the evidence is that a test of Faith was enjoined upon all of them in one way or the other.

FAITH

He wanted them to know and understand that He had risen from the dead, and that was easy enough to prove. However, He wanted their Faith and Confidence to rest more so on the Word of God than what merely their eyes could see.

While it certainly was important that they see Him

after the Resurrection, which they did, it was even more important that they know this was in fulfillment of the Word of God (Ps. 16:10-11).

As well, the cleansing of the leper in the Law of Moses was a portrayal of the Death and Resurrection of Christ, which they should have known!

THE CLEANSING OF THE LEPER

Two birds were chosen, with one being sacrificed, representing the Crucifixion of Christ. The other was turned loose, representing the Resurrection of Christ through which sin, sickness, and the entire curse would be removed from mankind (Lev., Chpt. 14).

If Christ had died and remained dead, His Atoning Work would have been in vain. It was the Resurrection which ratified, one might say, what He had already done at Calvary (Rom. 4:25; I Cor. 15:1-23; Col. 3:1; Heb. 4:14-16; 6:20; 7:11, 17, 25; 9:24-28; I Pet. 1:3; 3:21-22).

If the Apostles and Mary Magdalene, along with others, had known the Bible as they should, His Death and Resurrection would not have been a shock or surprise. But yet, in their defense, the Holy Spirit had not yet been given, at least, in the capacity He would come on the Day of Pentecost. After this Advent, which was made possible by the Death and Resurrection of Christ, understanding these things became much easier (Jn. 7:37-39).

WOMAN WHY DO YOU WEEP?

"Jesus said unto her, Woman, why do you weep? Whom do you seek? She, supposing Him to be the gardener, said unto Him, Sir, if you have borne Him hence, tell me where you have laid Him, and I will take Him away" (Jn. 20:15).

The question, *"Jesus said unto her, Woman, why do you weep?"* is identical to that asked by the Angels.

Of course, Jesus knew the answers to all of these questions, but I think He was testing her Faith.

If we look at these incidents in the realm of one passing or failing these tests of Faith, I think we will misunderstand what Jesus was doing.

While it was a test of Faith, even in every occurrence, it was tendered in order to teach them, rather than whether they would pass or fail. Were it judged on the latter basis, all failed; however, Jesus wanted this to be a lesson. So, it was a test of Faith. However, it was tendered in order that they may understand that all things pertaining to God must be anchored on the principle of Faith, which stands on the Foundation of the Word of God and, in reality, Christ and the Cross (Rom. 6:1-14; 8:1-11; 10:17).

FOR WHOM DO YOU SEEK?

The question, *"Whom do you seek?"* presents the second question asked by Jesus and really gets to the heart of the matter.

So, that which was first said by Jesus to His Followers after the Resurrection was in the form of two questions. They are very significant and, consequently, hold much greater meaning than something merely said to Mary Magdalene.

1. *Woman, why do you weep?"*

In effect, by virtue of His Death and Resurrection, Jesus has taken away the cause of weeping relative to the great difficulties and unknowns of life. He will be with us in all trials and difficulties and, as well, has defeated sin, death, and the grave. Therefore, man can be free and not have any fear of death, but only in Christ.

So, in respect to these great problems which have plagued humanity from the very beginning, they were addressed and answered, victoriously so, I might quickly add, at a Hill called Calvary.

2. *"Whom do you seek?"*

To know that these grand and glorious things have been done presents a Truth of monumental proportions.

However, that they were done is one thing, but the main thing is the One Who did it all, i.e., *"the Lord Jesus Christ,"* and He did such by the Means of the Cross.

Many want the solution without the Saviour! Such is not to be!

A SIMPLISTIC FORM

The following, as brief as we can lay it down, presents God's Manner and Way of life and living. It is:

• The Lord Jesus Christ is the Source of all Blessings we receive from God (Jn. 1:1-3, 14, 29; Col. 2:10-15).

• The Cross of Christ is the Means by which all of these Blessings are given to us, and this means every Blessing of any and every type (Rom. 6:1-14; Col. 2:10-15).

• With Jesus as the Source and the Cross as the Means, the Object of our Faith must always be the Cross of Christ. This speaks of Who He is, the Son of the Living God, and what He did, which refers to the Cross where total and complete Redemption was furnished. There Jesus atoned for all sin — past, present, and future — at least for all who will believe (I Cor. 1:17, 18, 23; 2:2; Gal. 6:14).

• With Jesus as the Source and the Cross as the Means, and the Cross of Christ as the Object of our Faith, then the Holy Spirit, Who always works within the parameters of the Finished Work of Christ, will work mightily on our behalf (Rom. 8:1-11; Eph. 2:13-18).

If one wants the tears wiped from his eyes, he will have to embrace not only Bible Christianity but, as well, the *"Author and Finisher"* of what Christianity really is. To divorce Jesus from the Cross is for the individual to serve *"another Jesus"* (II Cor. 11:1-4). To divorce Christianity from Christ and the Cross is to leave Christianity as little more than hollow mockery, a philosophy if you please, which makes it no better than the other philosophies of the world. And yet, tens of millions attempt to do this very thing.

Tens of millions have embraced the church, which contains no Salvation. As such, Jesus is just a part of the mix, and an elementary part at that! Then the individual only has religion.

However, Bible Christianity is not a religion but a relationship. That relationship is with Jesus Christ. He is All in All!

"Whom do you seek?"

IDENTIFICATION?

The phrase, *"She, supposing Him to be the gardener,"* evidently means that she thought this man worked for Joseph of Arimathaea who owned this garden. Still, there is no thought of Resurrection!

How many times do we as Believers fail to recognize Jesus, thinking Him to be someone else? As this was because of unbelief in Mary, it is because of unbelief in all the rest of us as well!

As a Believer and having Faith in God and His Word, we must understand that, in one way or another, Jesus is literally in everything that happens to us. Of course, He is not in sin or failure in any way, but He is definitely there to bring us out of that dilemma should such occur.

Look for Jesus! Look for Him in our trials. Look for Him in the Blessings and in that which seems not to be Blessings. Look for Him in our adversities, even in that which looks like reverses. In fact, every single thing that happens to the Child of God is either caused by the Lord or allowed by Him. So, if we understand that, we will not mistake Him for the *"gardener."*

WHERE IS HE?

The question, *"Said unto Him, Sir, if you have borne Him hence, tell me where you have laid Him,"* proclaims again that she had absolutely no notion at this time of Resurrection.

She was utterly overwhelmed with one bitter, cruel thought. The Sacred Body was to be embalmed with the precious spices, which, quite possibly, she had spent all she had in order to purchase.

She probably knew that the Jews wanted to take His Body and place it in the valley of Hinnom, which, in actuality, was a garbage dump, and she may have feared this is what had happened.

The phrase, *"And I will take Him away,"* simply means that if they would allow her, she would give Him a proper burial.

The beautiful thing about this entire scenario is that Jesus appeared first to a woman, which carries deep significance (Mk. 16:9).

Due to Eve being the first to fall in the Garden of Eden, from that moment, women were treated somewhat with disdain. A woman had few, if any, rights whatsoever. Most of the time, her husband was chosen for her by her parents, with her wishes being entertained not at all. As well, all the mundane labor and chores of the household were her responsibilities in every manner, even to the point of negating all common courtesy. In other words, if something had to be carried from one place to another, and the man was standing there unencumbered, it would not even enter his mind to perform this task himself. His wife would be expected to do such.

Because of the Fall the Lord had said to her: *"I will greatly multiply your sorrow and your conception; in sorrow you shall bring forth children; and your desire shall be to your husband, and he shall rule over you"* (Gen. 3:16).

Thereafter the idea seemed to be, at least as man considered the situation, that he would make certain that the curse upon the female gender was carried out to its utter conclusion and harm.

No! The fault was not that of God for leveling such a curse, for, in reality, He had no choice. The fault was in man because of his ungodly attitude.

Sin always wreaks its deadly toll, as in the case of Eve, and Adam, as well, who actually received the greatest curse of all (Gen. 3:17-19)!

However, Adam and most all men who followed him took it upon themselves to add to the sorrow which had come to woman.

Considering how Jesus conducted Himself toward women, and especially the equality He gave them with men, we learn that it is never pleasing to God, and actually downright wicked, for any Believer in any capacity to take it upon himself to punish another. Such lies in the Domain of God altogether and never in the realm of man (Rom. 12:19).

Actually, James, in effect, said, *"Who do you think you are, thinking you are qualified to judge another?"* (James 4:12).

THE PENALTY FOR THE CURSE IS PAID

By the example of Christ, we find that the Lord paid the penalty of the curse which had been placed on woman, thereby restoring her, at least, all who will believe. Naturally, the curse was lifted on Adam, as well, and once again, to those who believe.

While it is true that man does not yet have all the benefits of what Jesus did at Calvary, at least in reality, in spirit he does!

Not only was it vastly significant that Jesus appeared first of all to a woman, the reason, as well, is of vast significance. That reason is *"Faith!"*

This tells all and sundry that God honors Faith on the part of women the same as He does men. In other words, everything is based solely upon the principle of Faith and not because of gender, wealth, education, position, race, etc.

So, it was not because that Jesus arbitrarily showed deference to Mary Magdalene by appearing to her first of all, but simply because she evidenced more Faith than anyone else.

THE FAITH OF MARY MAGDALENE

THE APPEARANCE OF JESUS
TO MARY MAGDALENE

So, it was not because Jesus arbitrarily showed deference to Mary Magdalene by appearing to her first of all, but simply because she evidenced more Faith than anyone else.

As well, we must learn that even though this was true on her part, still, as is glaringly obvious, her Faith, in fact, was extremely weak.

But yet, Jesus honored her Faith where it was, even as weak as it was, and built thereon. There is a great principle here which we should learn.

In fact, no one has perfect Faith. To be frank, even though the Faith of some is much greater than others, if we are to be honest, all of us would probably fall into the category of the man who brought his demon possessed son to Jesus and then was told by the Lord, *"If you can believe, all things are possible to him who believes."*

The man answered and said, *"Lord, I believe; please help my unbelief"* (Mk. 9:23-24).

Exactly as with that man, Jesus will always reward our Faith and will, as well, help us in our unbelief, which seems to reside in all, at least in some measure.

Last of all, Jesus appeared first to this woman even though she had formerly been possessed by *"seven demons"* (Mk. 16:9).

Of course, He delivered her. However, the moral and great Truth found in this speaks of *"Justification by Faith."* In other words, her past was not her present, with the past, in fact, having been totally wiped away by Christ.

It is sad, but many, if not most, Believers do not really understand *"Justification by Faith,"* which means they really do not understand the Grace of God.

When Jesus forgives someone, it is totally forgiven and forgotten. It is never to be brought up again, at least by those who would accuse. To do such a thing is an abomination in the Eyes of God, which, in effect, actually insults and does despite to the Spirit of Grace (Heb. 10:29).

"Justification by Faith" simply means that the believing sinner places his or her Faith exclusively in Christ and what Christ has done for us at the Cross. He or she may not understand much about it, but this is what they must believe.

This being done, the Lord will instantly impute to

such a person a perfect, spotless Righteousness.

Such declares one to be *"not guilty"*; even greater than that, *"innocent"*; and even greater than that, *"perfect."*

In fact, God cannot accept anything less than perfection. Of course, there is no perfection in any human being; it is all in Christ.

However, when our Faith is placed in Him, His Perfection is instantly and immediately given to us.

MASTER

"Jesus said unto her, Mary. She turned herself, and said unto Him, Rabboni; which is to say, Master" (Jn. 20:16).

The phrase, *"Jesus said unto her, Mary,"* proclaims the individual response which the Lord always gives to Faith.

• The first expression of *"Woman"* makes her the representative of the whole of suffering humanity.

• The second expression of *"Mary"* proclaims the individuality of the Gospel and the manner in which Jesus deals with all who come to Him.

In other words, Followers of Christ are not nameless, faceless statistics, but rather personal recipients of His Grace.

This is extremely important in that the Salvation of each Believer is a personal Salvation, rendered Personally by Jesus, and received personally by the sinner.

Psalm 147:4 says: *"He tells the number of the stars; He calls them all by their names."*

Even though, in a direct sense, this speaks of the planetary bodies, it speaks of each individual Believer as well.

John said in Revelation 1:16, *"And He had in His*

Right Hand seven stars ..." which refers to the Pastors of the seven Churches of Asia and, in reality, all Pastors and all Churches.

So, He calls every Believer by name.

AND SAID UNTO HIM, RABBONI

The phrase, *"She turned herself,"* refers to her recognizing His Voice.

"And said unto Him, Rabboni; which is to say, Master," in the Greek Text says, *"My Master!"*

However, the manner in which she addressed Jesus tells us that she still did not have the full picture as to Who He really is, *"the Messiah, the Son of God, the Lord of Glory!"*

Reynolds said: *"Her joy knew no bounds, but her conception of the reality of that which was revealed to her was most imperfect. It was the realization of Love rather than the perception afforded only by Revelation."*

In this Fourth Gospel, the Holy Spirit records four Appearings of the Lord after He rose from the dead, and these Appearings banish four great enemies of the human heart. They are:

1. Sorrow
2. Fear
3. Doubt
4. Care

Mary was weeping (Vs. 11); the Disciples were trembling, as we shall see (Vs. 19); Thomas was doubting (Vs. 25); and the Apostles were despairing (Jn. 21:3). So, the dread darkness of *"sorrow"* was addressed here by Jesus not only for Mary but for all others as well!

However, in each case, the Appearing of Jesus sufficed to dismiss the enemy and to fill his place with joy, courage, Faith, and contentment.

Many other priceless effects were resulted from these Appearings — for these were not the only ones — but, with design, the Spirit mentions no others.

TO MY GOD AND YOUR GOD

"Jesus said unto her, Touch Me not; for I am not yet ascended to My Father: but go to My Brethren, and say unto them, I ascend unto My Father, and your Father; and to My God, and your God" (Jn. 20:17).

In a sense, Mary Magdalene represents the people of Israel.

Cleansed from the evil spirit of idolatry, Israel returned from Babylon swept and garnished, but empty. Seven of the spirits more wicked took possession of her, typified by the seven demons which were cast out of Mary by Jesus.

As well, on that coming Glad Day, Jesus will rid Israel of all evil spirits, which will take place at the Second Coming as described in Zechariah 13:2.

The phrase, *"Jesus said unto her, Touch Me not,"* in effect says, *"Do not hold onto Me; do not try to detain Me."*

Evidently Mary was so literally overwrought with gladness of heart that Jesus was really alive that she clutched Him in such a way that speaks of her fear that He might be lost to her again.

The phrase, *"For I am not yet ascended to My Father,"* is believed by many that Jesus meant that He was about to go to the Father where His Shed Blood would be applied to the Mercy Seat in Heaven. I personally do not think this is the case.

The entirety of the Work of Redemption was finished at Calvary. At the moment that Jesus said, *"It is finished, Father into Your Hands I commend My Spirit,"* the giant Veil in the Temple was rent from the top to the bottom, in effect saying, *"Whosoever will may come and take the water of life freely"* (Mat. 27:51; Rev. 22:17). This could not have happened had Redemption been incomplete.

MY FATHER

As well, if one is to notice, Jesus did not say, *"Our Father,"* but rather, *"My Father."*

Reynolds said, *"He Who is Father of Christ and Father of men, is so in different ways. He is Father of Christ by nature and of men by Grace."*

His *"Father"* was in Heaven, which has every indication of being a Planet but outside of this Universe. From the description given in Revelation, Chapters 21 and 22, no other conclusion can be drawn than Heaven is a real and tangible place.

The phrase, *"But go to My Brethren,"* speaks not of those who were His Half-brothers in the flesh, but rather His Chosen Disciples (minus Judas, who was now dead).

The phrase, *"And say unto them, I ascend unto My Father, and your Father; and to My God, and your God,"* once again emphasizes the fact of the unique personal relationship between Christ and the Father, which no Believer has, at least to that degree!

However, this statement as given by Christ definitely does portray a relationship, and a great one at that, between the Believer and the Heavenly Father.

Actually, the very purpose of Calvary and the Resurrection was to establish this Relationship through Redemption, which it did!

I HAVE SEEN THE LORD

"Mary Magdalene came and told the Disciples that she had seen the Lord, and that He had spoken these things unto her" (Jn. 20:18).

Regrettably, Mary telling the Disciples that she had seen the Lord presents her account as being met with unbelief (Mk. 16:9-11).

Unbelief is a deadly thing, keeping all of us from so much which the Lord desires to do. As we have stated, this is one of the very reasons that the Disciples did not recognize Jesus when He appeared after the Resurrection.

Even His Closest Ones had misinterpreted His Mission on Earth, despite His telling them several times exactly what He was to do. In their minds, He was going to use His Great Power to overthrow Rome, once again making Israel the premier Nation in the world. Of course, the Disciples would have powerful positions in this Kingdom.

Believing this error, they believed nothing else! Consequently, they could not recognize Him, and neither can anyone who is so saddled with unbelief.

This is the reason that the Spirit of God can move mightily at times and some Believers will register unbelief right in the middle of this Move. They do not see or understand what is going on.

There is no Faith, so they do not see! Unbelief blinds, while Faith enlightens!

The phrase, *"And that He had spoken these things unto her,"* portrays her telling them exactly what Jesus had said.

They probably would not have accused her of lying but obviously did believe that, in her grief, she was hallucinating.

However, as it would prove, this was no hallucination. Mary had seen the Lord and talked with Him. As well, she had the distinct privilege of being the first person to herald the Resurrection of our Lord.

What an honor!

Great Women OF THE BIBLE

Chapter Four

MARY AND MARTHA

MARY AND MARTHA

"Now it came to pass, as they went, that He entered into a certain village: and a certain woman named Martha received Him into her house" (Lk. 10:38).

The certain village addressed in Verse 38 is *"Bethany,"* a suburb of Jerusalem (Jn. 11:1; 12:1-3).

The home referred to is that of Mary, her sister Martha, and their brother Lazarus.

This section opens with the action of one woman (Mary), and closes with the exclamation of another (Martha).

Thus, the lesson is taught that the closest physical relationship to Jesus, although it is that even of a mother, does not and cannot secure Spiritual Life. Martha had a physical relationship with Christ in serving Him, while Mary had a Spiritual relationship by hearing and worshipping Him.

The word, *"Received,"* has the idea of Martha having planned and, consequently, preparing a meal for Christ and possibly some of His Disciples. This was probably about four months before the Crucifixion.

MARY

"And she had a sister called Mary, who also sat at Jesus' Feet, and heard His Word" (Lk. 10:39).

In the Christian life, the daily study of the Word of God must have first place. All other duties must give way to it. These Passages proclaim that to us.

Sitting at Jesus' Feet is a safe refuge from assaults upon the authority and Inspiration of the Scriptures. As well, one must have his or her Faith anchored securely in Christ and the Cross, realizing that Jesus is the Source of all things we receive from God, and the Cross is the Means.

The word, *"Also,"* shows that Mary took a fitting share in the household duties.

However, inasmuch as Jesus was Personally present, she felt she must glean from Him all that was humanly possible. Consequently, in this scenario, we will learn a valuable lesson.

MARTHA

"But Martha was cumbered about much serving, and came to Him, and said, Lord, do You not care that my sister has left me to serve alone? bid her therefore that she help me" (Lk. 10:40).

The phrase, *"But Martha was cumbered about much serving,"* tells us several things:

• Martha was doing a good thing, but it was not the best thing. Basically, the great choice with the Child of God is the choice between the good and the best. Satan would desire that one do nothing; however, if he cannot succeed in that fashion, he will attempt to keep us from the best, as he here did Martha.

• In this scenario, we will learn God's Priorities in these matters. We should learn them well!

• We learn that one can be very much involved in the Work of the Lord and little involved in Worship of the Lord. However, the Lord is much more concerned about the Worker than the Work. If the Worker is right, the Work will be right as well!

DO YOU NOT CARE?

The question, *"And said, Lord, do You not care that my sister has left me to serve alone?"* tells us that Martha did not fully realize that Jesus was Jehovah, else she never would have spoken so petulantly to Him.

"Bid her therefore that she help me," proclaims her

telling the Lord what He should do, which characterizes so many Believers.

Evidently, the Lord was teaching, with Mary and others eagerly listening. Quite possibly, she had previously been helping her sister but had stopped due to listening to what Jesus had to say and, consequently, was being greatly blessed. Martha, who desired to prepare a good meal for the Master, which is certainly commendable, had become somewhat exasperated that Mary had ceased to help. However, while certainly to be commended for her concern and industry, Martha still failed in the most important part of all. While bread was important, it alone would not suffice. The Word of God, which Jesus is giving here, is even more important.

From these Passages we learn that the Church world is, by and large, divided respecting two directions:

1. Those who are working in some capacity for the Lord but have little, if any, relationship with Him.

2. Those who work for the Lord but, as well, like Mary, have a deep relationship. It is only this group who will accomplish anything for Jesus even though they are little regarded by the world or even by much of the church.

TROUBLED ABOUT MANY THINGS?

"And Jesus answered and said unto her, Martha, Martha, you are careful and troubled about many things" (Lk. 10:41).

Jesus addressing Martha is said in pitying love. The same type of love was evidenced toward Peter when Jesus said to him, *"Simon, Simon,"* (Lk. 22:31), and *"Saul, Saul,"* speaking to Paul in Acts 9:4.

The phrase, *"You are careful and troubled about many things,"* concerned things which were important but not the most important!

This is the Message conveyed by Jesus.

As stated, if Satan can maneuver a Believer into this position, sooner or later he will effect *"burn-out"* on that person, hence, the great number of nervous breakdowns among Preachers, etc.

The church has, by and large, attempted to use secular psychology to address this problem (burn-out), when the reason is found in these very Passages and was placed there accordingly by the Holy Spirit.

CLOSE RELATIONSHIP WITH CHRIST

Irrespective as to who the person may be and how involved he is in the Work of God, and no matter how important that Work is, personal and close relationship with Christ must have preeminence at all times, or else, anxiety and agitation will become more and more pronounced, resulting in an emotional runaway engine.

Most of this is caused by the Believer trying to live for God by the means of law and/or the flesh. This will effect *"burn-out"* very quickly.

In fact, the Believer cannot really have a proper relationship with the Lord without his Faith being exclusively in Christ and the Cross. This being done, Grace will then be evidenced toward such a Believer, which means the Holy Spirit will do great things in our hearts and lives.

On a personal basis, I know what it is to try to live by law and the flesh. To be sure, at that time, I did not know or understand that's what I was doing, but I was, and it almost destroyed me.

I look now at what the Lord has done for us in portraying to us that which had originally been given to the Apostle Paul as it regards the Cross of Christ. To learn that every Blessing comes through Christ but by the Means of the Cross is perhaps the greatest lesson that any Believer can ever learn. Then such a person is living by Faith. Otherwise, it is works, law, and the flesh, which will ultimately destroy a person.

Regrettably, not knowing or understanding the Cross of Christ respecting Sanctification, virtually the entirety of the church world, even those who truly love God, is functioning under the realm of works, law, and the flesh. To be sure, it's a miserable way to try to live.

THE GOOD PART

"But one thing is needful: and Mary has chosen that good part, which shall not be taken away from her" (Lk. 10:42).

The phrase, *"But one thing is needful,"* proclaims to us the Mind of God and tells us exactly where all Victory is. What is that *"one thing?"*

It is that which Mary was doing, sitting at the Feet of Jesus and hearing Him speak. This can only be done presently by the method of prayer, study of His Word, and placing our Faith exclusively in Christ and the Cross. Tragically, much, if not most, of the church world specializes in and makes other things priority which are not *"needful."* Notice, He did not say, *"Two, four, or ten,"* but only, *"One!"* Therefore, He makes it very easy for the Christian to understand and leaves no excuse for us failing in this area.

"And Mary has chosen that good part," means that this is a *"choice,"* a choice, incidentally, which every Believer must make. Regrettably, most choose that which Martha chose, hence, the spiritual leanness.

The phrase, *"Which shall not be taken away from her,"* proclaims that if the Believer will choose this *"good part,"* the Holy Spirit will guard this sacred choice. This is the very place to which the Holy Spirit desires to bring the Child of God. This is the "Holy of Holies!"

These are the people who touched the world.

It would have been far better that day for cold leftovers to have been placed on the table, with everyone hearing eagerly the Words of Jesus, rather than a nicely prepared hot meal and then not being able to hear His Words.

Many pastors erroneously think that if they can build a new church building, etc., things will greatly improve. They find to their dismay that there is no improvement, for those things cannot bring the Child of God to the place of worship which the Holy Spirit desires.

Consequently, our real need is not buildings, money, place, or position, but rather Communion with Christ.

LAZARUS

"Now a certain man was sick, named Lazarus, of Bethany, the town of Mary and her sister Martha" (Jn. 11:1).

The *"Lazarus"* spoken of in this Verse is not the Lazarus of Luke, Chapter 16, who had died sometime before now.

This Lazarus was the brother of the two sisters, Mary and Martha. All that we know of him is given in Chapters 11 and 12 of this Book. And yet, one of the greatest Miracles ever recorded in the annals of human history was preformed on Lazarus. He was raised from the dead even after four days of being in the tomb. John, no doubt, was an eyewitness of these events and in his usual style goes into detail respecting this momentous happening.

Strangely enough, despite the great Miracle here recorded, not a single word of Lazarus is recorded.

As well, nothing is told us about his experiences during *"those four days"* when he was in the tomb, and no Revelation is made concerning the conditions of life in the Paradise of that time.

BETHANY

The phrase, *"Of Bethany, the town of Mary and her sister Martha,"* speaks of the small village, which was about two miles from Jerusalem, situated on the eastern slope of the Mount of Olives.

The account seems to imply that when Jesus was in Jerusalem, He often resorted to this little village at night, even to the home of this brother and his two sisters.

There is some indication that they may have been people of means due to the fact that Mary anointed Jesus with a very costly ointment. Because of their hospitality to Jesus, they were privileged to experience three things:

1. To sit at His Feet and hear Words of Life unparalleled in human history.

2. Lazarus would be raised from the dead.

3. Mary would have the privilege of anointing the Feet of Jesus with ointment, which was a prelude to His Burial.

Such is the wonder of anyone who is privileged to have Jesus as his Lord. The things He will do in every capacity literally defy description. If that is not the case, such can only point to an extremely tepid relationship and total lack of consecration.

However, the sadness is that the majority of those who claim to follow Christ little take advantage of Who He actually is and what He can actually do! To describe such a loss, one cannot!

To be sure, as He did wondrous things for this family, He will do for any and all who will dare to believe Him.

I think that if any one word could explain the *"why"* and *"how"* of these things, that word would be, *"Relationship."* This trio had an excellent relationship with Jesus, which anyone can have if he so desires. Who He is, which can only be learned by relationship, is the key to what He does.

ANOINTING THE FEET OF CHRIST WITH OINTMENT

"It was that Mary which anointed the Lord with ointment, and wiped His Feet with her hair, whose brother Lazarus was sick" (Jn. 11:2).

"It was that Mary which anointed the Lord with ointment," is the manner in which John identifies Mary and, as well, proclaims the significance of this act. The *"anointing"* took place very shortly before the Crucifixion and after the event of Lazarus being raised from the dead.

The phrase, *"And wiped His Feet with her hair,"* proclaims Mary, I think, anointing this portion of His Body because she believed that One Who could raise her brother from the dead could, as well, overcome death Himself and walk out of that tomb, which He did! Incidentally, this occasion, no doubt, occurred after Jesus had raised Lazarus from the dead.

This one thing is sure: Mary was not at the tomb on that glorious morning of His Resurrection. I think she knew He would not be there.

The phrase, *"Whose brother Lazarus was sick,"* tells us the following:

• Even though great Blessings come to this house as a result of the association with Jesus, still, this did not mean that they were immune from the trials and vicissitudes of life, even as this sickness proclaims.

• The error that proclaims that upon a proper confession of Faith, one can avoid all unpleasant circumstances, is error indeed!

• *"Many are the afflictions of the Righteous: but the LORD,"* as here stated, *"delivers him out of them all"* (Ps. 34:19).

SICKNESS

"Therefore his sisters sent unto Him, saying, Lord, behold, he whom You love is sick" (Jn. 11:3).

"Therefore his sisters sent unto Him," presents that which has been done countless times since.

At all times, but especially in times of crisis, we send for *"Him,"* the Only One, in fact, Who can really help, for He has the Power of life and death in His Hands.

The phrase, *"Saying, Lord, behold, he whom You love is sick,"* refers to something more than just a mere malady, but rather a life-threatening affliction, which, in fact, did take his life, at least, at the time.

The word, *"Love,"* as used here, has to do with relationship. The implication is that Jesus and Lazarus, as well as the sisters, were very close friends. And yet, from the study of this relationship, we know that this friendship with Jesus was different, as it had to be, than it would be with other men and women. The best way for it to be explained would probably be in the realm of the shepherd and the sheep.

I do not personally feel that during the time of the Life of Christ anyone was ever buddy-buddy with Jesus. It certainly was not that He was aloof, for He was not. The idea has more to do with the sheep than the Shepherd. All who were close to Jesus immediately found, as the Text suggests, that even though a great nearness and friendliness were possible, no doubt, more so than with any other person, still, there was something about Him that placed Him in an altogether different position than other human beings.

His Demeanor inspired worship rather than comradeship.

As well, do you realize that no one, not even His Closest Disciples, referred to Jesus by His Name, but rather by using terms such as *"Master"* or *"Lord"?*

TO GLORIFY THE SON OF GOD

"When Jesus heard that, He said, This sickness is not unto death, but for the Glory of God, that the Son of God might be glorified thereby" (Jn. 11:4).

The phrase, *"When Jesus heard that, He said,"* presents the messenger, having been sent by the sisters, now arriving and giving Jesus the message.

At this time, Jesus was *"beyond Jordan, at the place where John had first baptized,"* a distance of approximately 25 to 30 miles (Jn. 10:40).

The Text seems to imply that Jesus was not aware of the situation until informed by the messenger. However, immediately, it seems, the Holy Spirit gave Him instructions respecting what should be done.

THIS SICKNESS IS NOT UNTO DEATH

The phrase, *"This sickness is not unto death,"* seems to be contradicted by the facts. However, the Greek Text actually proclaims Jesus saying, *"He shall not fall a prey to death,"* which is the way it should have been translated.

The phrase, *"But for the Glory of God, that the Son of God might be glorified thereby,"* gives us in the word, *"Glorified,"* a greater insight into what is happening.

In the Greek Text, the word, *"Glorified,"* as it is used elsewhere, means, *"Sacrifice on behalf of."* So here, the very suffering of Lazarus and of the sisters, and the tears of Jesus over the grave, are part of the Sacrificial

Ministry by which the Glory of God, as it pertains to the Son of God, may be advanced.

This tells us that even though the Lord does not receive glory from sickness, He definitely does receive glory from the healing of sickness.

The same can be said for sin. He gets no glory out of sin, but He does get great glory out of one obtaining Victory over sin.

In no way can God be blamed for the maladies and depravity of the human family, for He is neither the author nor instigator of such, but rather Satan himself. In other words, sin, sickness, poverty, ignorance, and death are all *"the works of the Devil"* (I Jn. 3:8). Jesus came to destroy those works!

ISRAEL

As well, as is the case with most, if not all, the Miracles of Jesus, a far broader picture is presented here. The impotent man (Jn., Chpt. 5), the blind man (Jn., Chpt. 9), and Lazarus picture Israel as morally impotent, blind, and dead. Of these three demonstrations of Christ's Deity, the last was the greatest.

The sick may be healed, but there is no remedy for death. Death convicts man as being a sinner and conducts him to Judgment, for because of sin, it is appointed unto man once to die, and after this, the Judgment.

So, Jesus waited for sin to do its utmost to the body of Lazarus, and we speak of original sin, not some sin that Lazarus then committed. Then He went to manifest His Divine Glory in raising him to life, although already corrupt from being dead four days.

Such is His Present Action in respect to Israel. The Nation, spiritually speaking, is dead: however, He loves it, even as the sisters suggested in Verse 3.

At the Second Coming, He will raise the Nation into Millennial Life (Hos. 6:2).

Also, in a sense, this demonstration, as here recorded, represents not only Israel but every individual who has ever lived. The Born-Again experience is the spiritual application of Resurrection. The sinner is raised from the death of sin to the Life of God, a work only Jesus could bring about by His Death and Resurrection.

SACRIFICIAL MINISTRY

Even though we have already touched on the subject, due to its weight, please allow me the privilege of addressing myself to the *"Sacrificial Ministry"* in which every Believer, in some sense, must be engaged. As we have stated, the cause of these things, in whatever capacity they may be, is not to be laid at the Feet of the Lord.

Nevertheless, He is glorified in overcoming sin, sickness, and death.

Therefore, in one way or the other, all Believers are to be a part of *"Sacrificial Ministry,"* that is, if they allow the Lord to handle the situation, whatever it may be. Regrettably, many, if not most, Believers resort to other means, which effect little or no help, and robs Christ of the glory which He could derive from effecting Deliverance.

A PERSONAL EXPERIENCE

This Fourth Verse is very dear to me personally. At a very critical time in this Ministry, something happened, which has proven to be exactly as the Lord said.

It was Sunday morning. It was in November, 1991, if I remember correctly. Service that Sunday morning was ending. I was seated in the last chair next to the railing which separates the platform from the audience. All were standing and worshipping, and I was worshipping as well.

All of a sudden, the Presence of God came over me, and the Lord spoke this very Verse to my heart: *"This sickness is not unto death, but for the Glory of God, that the Son of God might be glorified thereby."*

Even though I had read this Text many times in the past, I had not read it lately, and it had not even been on my mind. I am saying that it was not the product of wishful thinking. Beyond the shadow of a doubt, especially considering the manner in which it was given, I knew it was from the Lord.

As I have stated, the Lord receives no glory out of sin or failure of any nature; however, He does receive great glory out of Victory over sin and failure. And now, over 20 years later, I am beginning to see that which will bring great glory to the Lord. Let me say it again:

While the Lord never gets glory out of sin, as ought to be obvious, most definitely, however, He does get glory out of Victory over sin.

LOVE

"Now Jesus loved Martha, and her sister, and Lazarus" (Jn. 11:5).

Normally, the man would be placed first; however, *"Martha"* is placed first here because, in all probability, she was head of the household.

The manner in which this is stated, and especially the way the word, *"Loved,"* is used, tells us that this is the result of a long acquaintance. Actually, of all the families in Israel at that time, it seems that Jesus may have spent more time at this home than any other. What a Blessing it was to have the Holy Spirit say of these three how much they were loved by Jesus.

No greater honor could be bestowed on anyone than to have such forever inscribed in the Word of God.

JESUS TARRIES FOR A SHORT WHILE

"When He had heard therefore that he (Lazarus) was sick, He abode two days still in the same place where He was" (Jn. 11:6).

Hearing that Lazarus was sick seems to indicate that a messenger was sent before Lazarus died.

Consequently, when the message was delivered, Lazarus had already died, probably expiring a short time after the messenger had left.

However, there was no way that he could be apprehended in order that the correct message be given to Jesus, but, nevertheless, the Holy Spirit would reveal to Him that Lazarus had died.

The phrase, *"He abode two days still in the same place where He was,"* proclaims that He did so on instructions from the Holy Spirit. Evidently, it took a day for the messenger to arrive to where Jesus was located. Jesus then waited two more days, with the journey to the home of Lazarus taking another day, making four in all, even as the Scripture said (Jn. 11:17).

JUDAEA

"Then after that said He to His Disciples, Let us go into Judaea again" (Jn. 11:7)

His action in waiting seemed to contradict His Profession of affection; and His Statement that the sickness was not unto death, or rather that *"Lazarus would not fall a prey to death,"* seems to be a contradiction by death actually occurring. However, Resurrection resolved this difficulty. The purpose of the sickness was not to demonstrate the power of sin and death, as it normally would do, but to furnish an occasion for the Glory of God, i.e., a Manifestation of His Glorious Power in Resurrection, and that the Son of God might be glorified thereby, i.e., through it.

"Then after that said He to His Disciples," portrays to us the exact Timing of the Holy Spirit. Everything Jesus did was according to instructions given Him by the Spirit of God. He was totally led and directed by the Spirit, which should be an example to us.

PRAYER

For example, Jesus prayed all night long before the choosing of His Disciples, portraying to us the absolute necessity of a very strong prayer life (Lk. 6:12-13).

If Jesus as the Son of God had to seek the Face of the Father to such an extent in order to find the Direct Will of God, how much more is it incumbent upon us to do the same! Tragically, most Christians, even Preachers, pray little at all. This is the reason so much is done that is not of God; it simply being that He has not been sought for Leading and Guidance. The results of such actions are always detrimental to the true Work of God.

"Let us go into Judaea again," was for the purpose of raising Lazarus from the dead.

Reynolds said, "The use of the word 'again' points forcibly back to the last visit, when He told both friends and foes that the Good Shepherd would snatch His sheep from the jaws of death, even though He laid down His Own Life in the doing of it."

THE DISCIPLES

"His Disciples said unto Him, Master, the Jews of late sought to stone You; and You are going there again?" (Jn. 11:8).

The phrase, *"His Disciples said unto Him,"* presents a true and sincere concern for His Welfare.

The word, *"Master,"* is actually the word, *"Rabbi,"* and is frequently used by John as the term of respect applied to both the Baptist and our Lord. This title, incidentally, was one of extraordinary dignity as it was then used by the Jews.

The question, *"The Jews of late sought to stone You; and You are going there again?"* refers to His Last Visit to Jerusalem in the account as given in Verse 31 of the previous Chapter. As stated, they had great concern for Him.

How different this language is from that of His Own Brothers (Jn. 7:3-5)!

THE LIGHT OF THIS WORLD

"Jesus answered, Are there not twelve hours in the day? If any man walk in the day, he stumbles not, because he sees the light of this world" (Jn. 11:9).

The question, *"Jesus answered, Are there not twelve hours in the day?"* proclaims the Lord balancing the length of the days, which were about 14 hours at their longest during the summer and about 10 hours at their shortest in the winter. He is using this terminology as an analogy.

"If any man walk in the day, he stumbles not, because he sees the light of this world," refers to the sun shining on the world according to the rotation of the Earth and, consequently, providing light. Most work was done during the day at that time because there was very little artificial light, only candles or torches.

The idea of the statement, however, pertains to the Believer understanding that the only *"Light"* is from the Lord Jesus Christ, which comes through the Holy Spirit, as well, regarding Direction, Guidance, Leading, and opportunity. All else is darkness. So, inasmuch as most work is done during the day respecting natural light, therefore, the Believer must look at the Holy Spirit as the Giver of *"Light,"* and that all must be done in that *"Light."*

The reason that much of the church world *"stumbles"* so much is because it does not have the *"Light"* of the Spirit for instruction and guidance.

Jesus was telling His Disciples two things:

1. Despite the animosity of the Jews against Him, He was going back into Judaea because the Holy Spirit had given Him instructions to do so. As stated, He likens it as *"Light."*

2. The absolute necessity of all Believers being led by the Spirit is portrayed in this statement as well.

STUMBLES

"But if a man walk in the night, he stumbles, because there is no light in him" (Jn. 11:10).

By using the phrase, *"But if a man walk in the night, he stumbles,"* Jesus presents Him using a natural expression to express a Spiritual Truth.

All Believers must have the Leading and Guidance of the Holy Spirit in all that we do, which can only be brought about by a strong prayer life and a constant study of the Word of God. Sadly, both of these absolutely indispensable traits are in short supply in the lives of most Believers.

In the fall of 1991, the Lord instructed me to conduct two prayer meetings a day (minus Saturday morning and Service times). This we did for over 10 years. In fact, I still do the same thing but actually going before the Lord three times a day, which I have felt led to do.

I had some people mention, *"Nothing is happening in these prayer meetings,"* thinking that their purpose was for Prophecies, prayer for the sick, etc.

While those things may definitely happen at times, that is not the purpose of prayer meetings.

We are there to seek God, not necessarily to minister to each other, even though, as stated, those things will take place at times. However, most modern Believers, even Pentecostals and Charismatics, have totally forgotten, that is, if they ever knew, what true prayer meetings are all about. They are simply meant to be times of us speaking to the Lord and, more importantly, the Lord speaking to us. These are the times that the Spirit of God gives enlightenment.

As well, and I think I can say without exaggeration, He does so most of the time through the Word of God. However, as stated, irrespective of His Manner, it will never contradict the Word. If so, it is not the Spirit of God but another spirit entirely.

NO LIGHT

The phrase, *"Because there is no light in Him,"* destroys the doctrine of the *"inner light"* as claimed by man in natural birth. In truth, man within himself has no light. He is totally estranged from God, Who is the Source of all Light because He is Light. As such, man *"stumbles"* respecting any and everything he does, irrespective of what direction it takes.

I have always maintained, and continue to do so, that every single freedom in this world, as well as all prosperity, has come about as a result of the *"Light"* of the Gospel of Jesus Christ.

Sometime back, a billionaire from Texas gave several millions of dollars to Yale University in order that they might establish a *"chair"* respecting "the origin of Western civilization." In other words, what was Western civilization, and how did it come about?

After several years, Yale University returned the money to the benefactor, stating, *"We do not know how to address ourselves to such a subject!"*

They were exactly right; they did not have a clue!

The idea that the greatest freedoms and prosperity the world has ever known has come about because of the *"Light"* of the Gospel of Jesus Christ, which has resulted in Western civilization, is lost completely upon these professors of education. It is lost upon them because they have no *"light."* However, those who have this *"Light"* know!

Tragically, almost all the world *"walks in the night"* and, consequently, *"stumbles"* because they have had no opportunity to have this *"Light,"* or else, have rejected it.

These Words as given by Jesus proclaim the Source of all intelligence, understanding, and knowledge, at least, about things as they really are.

SLEEP?

"These things said He: and after that He said unto them, Our friend Lazarus sleeps; but I go, that I may awake him out of sleep" (Jn. 11:11).

The phrase, *"These things said He,"* refers to the fact that the Disciples did not quite understand why Jesus wanted to go back into Judaea, especially considering that the animosity there was so great against Him that His Very Life would be in danger.

As well, if He was going to return, why would He wait two whole days before leaving?

The Truth given in John 11:9-10 proclaims that Jesus did what He did because that is what the Holy Spirit had instructed Him to do. As stated, this is to be the criteria for all Saints — to be led by the Spirit of God in all things.

"And after that He said unto them, Our friend Lazarus

sleeps," presents further information given to Him by the Holy Spirit in that Lazarus had died.

It is interesting that Jesus used the word, *"Asleep,"* respecting death. Actually, the Holy Spirit uses the term frequently concerning other Saints regarding death (Acts 7:60; I Cor. 11:30; 15:18-20; I Thess. 4:13-17). Jesus also used this term respecting the death of Jairus' daughter (Mat. 9:24; Mk. 5:39; Lk. 8:52).

FALSE DOCTRINE

Some have derived a false doctrine from this statement by Christ, and others similar, claiming that when the Believer dies, his spirit, soul, and body sleep until the Resurrection. It is called, *"Soul sleep."* However, this is totally incorrect.

In the Greek Text, we know that the object of this metaphor is to suggest that as the sleeper does not cease to exist while his body sleeps, so the dead person continues to exist, despite his absence from the region in which those who remain can communicate with him. Also, as sleep is known to be temporary, so the death of the body will be found to be temporary as well.

In other words, it is only the body of the Believer that sleeps and not the soul and the spirit, which immediately go to be with Christ.

Actually, the soul and spirit of Lazarus went down into Paradise at this time because Jesus had not yet been glorified.

Since the Believer is in that state in which he is absent from the body but is at home with the Lord, Paul describes this state in Philippians 1:23 as being *"far better."*

Of course, he is speaking of the state of the deceased Believer and not for the loved ones left on Earth, and even for the Work of God, for that matter.

That is why Paul also said, respecting his continuing to live instead of going to be with the Lord, *"Nevertheless to abide in the flesh is more needful for you"* (Phil. 1:24).

The phrase, *"But I go, that I may awake him out of sleep,"* refers to the fact that the Holy Spirit had told Jesus to raise this man from the dead. That which He would do respecting Lazarus was an *"earnest"* of what He will do in the coming Resurrection when all the Sainted Dead will be raised (I Thess. 4:16-17).

The Greek word for *"earnest"* is, *"Arrabon."* It means *"a pledge or first-payment."* In other words, the raising of Lazarus from the dead was a Resurrection but not the Resurrection.

THE DISCIPLES

"Then said His Disciples, Lord, if he sleep, he shall do well" (Jn. 11:12).

Their answer proclaims that they did not know what Jesus was saying.

If one is to notice, the understanding of the Disciples concerning spiritual things was woefully inadequate at this time even though they definitely were Saved men. The reason for this spiritual dullness was the absence of the Holy Spirit, at least, as He would come on and after the Day of Pentecost.

The difference in these men after Pentecost, in every way, is astounding, to say the least! That is remarkable considering that they were walking shoulder to shoulder with Jesus for some three and one half years. However, the infilling of the Holy Spirit, as it would be given on the Day of Pentecost because Jesus had been glorified, would prove, in a sense, to be even greater, at least regarding their spiritual growth, even than their personal walk with our Lord.

That is why Jesus said, *"... It is expedient for you that*

I go away: for if I go not away, the Comforter (Helper)
will not come unto you; but if I depart, I will send Him
unto you" (Jn. 16:7).

Of course, Jesus was speaking of the Coming of the
Holy Spirit.

THE HOLY SPIRIT

How could this be better for the Disciples even than
His Personal Presence with them?

The answer is found even in the question. Jesus
was only with them, but the Holy Spirit would literally
be in them and, consequently, able to give them the
Power and capability of understanding the Things of
God. Also, Jesus, in His Physical Body, could only be
in one place at a time while the Holy Spirit can be in
all, at all times, and everywhere. If one looks at this
scenario, one can easily see the difference in Spirit-filled
Believers and those who are not Spirit-filled.

Sadly, the far greater majority of Spirit-filled Believers
little allow the Holy Spirit to have proper latitude within
their lives, therefore, greatly hindering what He desires
to do within them.

DEATH

"Howbeit Jesus spoke of his death: but they thought
that He had spoken of taking of rest in sleep" (Jn. 11:13).

The phrase, *"Howbeit Jesus spoke of his death,"*
portrays John, who wrote this account, as outlining
in detail the exact moment of this particular time. He
does not hide the fact of their spiritual dullness.

"But they thought that He had spoken of taking of rest
in sleep," proclaims them putting a carnal interpretation
on His Statements.

I wonder how many of us presently tend to misread

that which the Holy Spirit gives unto us.

Paul said:

"That the God of our Lord Jesus Christ, the Father of Glory, may give unto you the Spirit (*Holy Spirit*) **of Wisdom and Revelation in the Knowledge of Him."**

He then said:

"The eyes of your understanding being enlightened; that you may know ..." **(Eph. 1:17-18)**.

LAZARUS IS DEAD

"Then said Jesus unto them plainly, Lazarus is dead" (Jn. 11:14).

There is no contradiction with Verse 4, where Jesus said, *"This sickness is not unto death."* As we have stated, the actual meaning was that Lazarus *"shall not fall a prey to death,"* at least at this time.

While, in fact, death would attempt to claim him, Jesus would nullify the efforts of the grim reaper, showing that His Power to give Life, as He has been constantly stating, also means the Power to overcome death. In other words, the two go hand in hand. To have the Power to give Life is, at the same time, to have Power to overcome death.

A GREATER MIRACLE

"And I am glad for your sakes that I was not there, to the intent you may believe; nevertheless let us go unto him" (Jn. 11:15).

The phrase, *"And I am glad for your sakes that I*

was not there," portrays the fact that if Jesus had been there, Lazarus would not have died. Jesus would have healed Him. However, a greater Miracle would now be performed in the raising of Lazarus from the dead, which is what Jesus meant.

Actually, we never read of anyone dying in the Presence of the Prince of Life. Also, there is some indication that He broke up every funeral to which He came in contact.

Augustine, who lived a little over 300 years after Christ, stated that Jesus raised many from the dead, even other than the accounts given in the Gospels. No doubt, that is true!

The phrase, *"To the intent you may believe,"* has reference to the fact that the Holy Spirit instructed Jesus to perform this Miracle for a variety of reasons, among them, to teach the Disciples the fact of the coming Resurrection.

To be sure, Jesus had raised others from the dead but none who had been dead four days as Lazarus, signifying what the coming Resurrection will be like.

A DESIGN OF THE LORD

As we have repeatedly stated, everything Jesus did was not only for the sake of the person or persons involved but, as well, to proclaim a much grander lesson.

As well, everything Jesus did was designed to increase the Faith of His Followers. It continues in this vein presently.

The Lord designs every happening and every act to be a lesson in Faith. Even our failures, which He certainly does not orchestrate or cause, are meant to serve as an instructor in this all-important aspect of our Christian experience.

As well, every attack by Satan against the Believer,

irrespective of the nature of that attack, whether it be physical, domestic, financial, or spiritual, is designed by the Evil One for one purpose and one purpose alone. That purpose is to destroy or at least to seriously weaken our Faith.

Actually, the only fight in which the Believer is to engage is *"the good fight of Faith"* (I Tim. 6:12).

It is a *"good fight"* because it is the *"right fight."*

The phrase, *"Nevertheless let us go unto him,"* has a double meaning:

1. All Believers will ultimately go the way of death, even as Lazarus, except those who are alive at the time of the Rapture (I Thess. 4:17).

2. All Believers will experience a Resurrection, whether dead or alive, even as Lazarus.

THOMAS

"Then said Thomas, which is called Didymus, unto his fellow-Disciples, Let us also go, that we may die with Him" (Jn. 11:16).

Thomas is perhaps branded unfairly as a doubter, etc. However, if one closely analyzes his statements, a far different portrayal begins to appear. He did have a problem being convinced.

However, concerning the Resurrection of Christ, the record portrays, I think, that once he was convinced, his Faith flowered. It is said that he ministered greatly in Parthia and India in his future ministry and there suffered martyrdom.

Incidentally, other than the Prophets who predicted these events, Thomas was the very first one to give the Title of God to Jesus.

This happened after the Resurrection of Jesus, with him exclaiming after observing the prints of the nails, *"My Lord, and my God!"* (Jn. 20:26-28).

TO DIE WITH JESUS?

The phrase, *"Let us also go, that we may die with Him,"* tells us several things:
• Thomas realized the tremendous animosity of the Jews against Jesus. By this time, he was not in doubt as to their hatred or the reason for that hatred.
• This shows that the body of the Disciples was being more and more blended into a unity.
• In seeing the danger to the Lord, with the spirit of self-surrender, Thomas is ready to share His Fate.

By this statement, it seems that Thomas has pretty much given up hope of a Messianic Kingdom, which the Disciples had thought Jesus would introduce immediately.

As a footnote, tradition has associated Thomas with Jude, the Lord's Half-brother, the writer of the short Epistle which bears his name.

MARY AND MARTHA

"Then Martha, as soon as she heard that Jesus was coming, went and met Him: but Mary sat still in the house" (Jn. 11:20).

Verse 20 implies that upon coming close to Bethany, Jesus stopped short of coming into the town and, above all, of going to the house of the two sisters.

Knowing the tremendous animosity against Him, He did not desire to attract any undue disturbance, especially at this time. Evidently, He had sent someone to their home to inform them that He had arrived, with information as to where He was. Martha immediately went to meet Him.

It is inconceivable that the anger and hostility of the religious leaders against Jesus had become so acute that it was dangerous for the two sisters to even be seen in His Presence. However, that was the state of affairs at that time.

Of course, such attitude and position always brings spiritual declension because the Spirit of God can never sanction such attitudes. In the case of Christ, it meant the destruction of Israel simply because most people would not buck the system.

It is the same presently and, in fact, always has been. That is why it was said of Jesus concerning Israel, *". . . He was moved with compassion on them, because they fainted, and were scattered abroad, as sheep having no shepherd"* (Mat. 9:36).

HIRELINGS

Israel had scores of religious leaders in her day who called themselves shepherds but, in reality, were *"hirelings."*

To be frank, Satan's greatest efforts against the Work of God do not come from the world's system, but rather that which calls itself *"Church."* The more of Christ that something is, the more it will be opposed. This is the reason it is absolutely imperative that each and every Believer know and understand the Word of God for themselves. As well, they must be prepared to obey what it says and be willing to pay whatever price is demanded. That may seem stringent, but all must understand that we are speaking of the souls of men. In other words, there is far more at stake than meets the eye. The very soul of each individual is hanging in the balance.

Actually, during the time of Christ, the Pharisees had impeccable reputations over Israel. They were looked at as the spiritual guides of the people and, in fact, were extremely religious. As a result, it would have been very difficult to have persuaded the majority in Israel that these men were murderers at heart. However, that is exactly what they were, as is now grossly obvious. The same is true presently.

At this present time, most Christians think and believe that all who call themselves religious leaders are, in fact, godly people. It doesn't matter the position they hold, whether they are denominational heads or otherwise.

While that certainly is true of some few, it is definitely not true of most. Most have the same murderous intent in their hearts as the Pharisees of old. The only reason they do not carry out these intents is simply because the law of the land prohibits such.

I realize that most would think that I am extreme in my statements, but I am not extreme at all.

The truth is, while there are some few good Churches with godly Pastors who truly love the Lord and are attempting to preach the Gospel without compromise, the far greater majority are in the opposite camp, despite their claims, and are actually furthering the cause of Satan.

In fact, it was that way with Israel of old. In a sense, there were always two Israels, those who truly loved God, which were always in the minority, and the others who served Him in name only.

THE GOSPEL

What I am saying represents Satan's greatest efforts to destroy the Work of God. He always brings about greater damage from within than he does without. I do so only because this is what is borne out in the Scriptures and represents Satan's greatest efforts to steal, kill, and destroy.

Consequently, every Believer must take serious inventory as to where he or she attends church, and what is taught and preached from behind the pulpit. They must forget about particular denominational names, irrespective if their families have attended particular churches for several generations. Those things do not count!

The only thing that counts is the Gospel that is preached behind the pulpit, and the layman in the pew knowing enough about the Word of God to properly ascertain the Scripturality of what is being preached. Multiple hundreds of millions are in Hell right now simply because they failed to do what I am saying, blindly following so-called religious leaders into spiritual oblivion.

The phrase, *"But Mary sat still in the house,"* seems to proclaim this done with purpose because friends of the family were constantly coming by to pay their respects, and someone had to be there to receive them.

MARY'S QUESTION

"Then said Martha unto Jesus, Lord, if You had been here, my brother had not died" (Jn. 11:21).

The phrase, *"Then said Martha unto Jesus,"* as is obvious, refers to her finding Jesus wherever He had been waiting.

The phrase, *"Lord, if You had been here, my brother had not died,"* places Martha in the position of limiting Jesus.

Evidently, it does not seem that she thinks of Jesus being able to raise the dead, or else, she reasoned in her mind that inasmuch as her brother had been dead for four days, such a Miracle could not be.

Surely she had knowledge of Jesus having raised others from the dead, but it does not seem to enter her mind that He would do such for her brother because of the problems mentioned.

MARTHA'S UNDERSTANDING

"But I know, that even now, whatsoever You will ask of God, God will give it to You" (Jn. 11:22).

Martha's terminology shows that she had not risen to the highest Light on the Lord's Mysterious Relation to the Father. She speaks of Him and to Him as a strangely-gifted human friend, but to the full understanding of Who Jesus exactly was is not completely clear to her. However, she will learn from this exchange things about Jesus she had not previously known.

Due to His Humanity, in other words, being totally human while never ceasing to be God, it seems that such was so overwhelming that all, even His Most Ardent Followers, had difficulty in understanding that He was also Deity, in other words, the Jehovah of the Old Testament.

Considering the human equation, and then on top of that, adding that He was but a Peasant and not at all of the aristocracy of Israel, it greatly exacerbated this difficulty. However, on the other hand, His Miracles were so astounding that it was impossible for such to be done other than by the Power of God.

As well, more than one time, He explained fully as to Who He was and exactly as to What His Mission entailed. But, due to the fact that His Humanity was so overwhelming, it was, it seems, very difficult to see past that.

Even though Martha used the word, *"Whatsoever,"* regarding what Jesus could ask of the Father, still, it seems that she limited such in her own mind.

THE RESURRECTION?

"Jesus said unto her, Your brother shall rise again.
"Martha said unto Him, I know that he shall rise

again in the Resurrection at the last day" (Jn. 11:23-24).

Very plainly Jesus tells her what is about to happen, but in her doubt, she misunderstands.

The phrase, *"Martha said unto Him,"* proclaims her answer regarding the Resurrection and her understanding of this great Doctrine to be far in advance of most in Israel.

Her statement about the Resurrection portrays that she had probably learned such at the Feet of Jesus, for He had said much about the Resurrection (Dan. 12:2, 13; Jn. 6:39-40, 44, 54; 12:48).

I AM THE RESURRECTION, AND THE LIFE

"Jesus said unto her, I am the Resurrection, and the Life: he who believes in Me, though he were dead, yet shall he live" (Jn. 11:25).

The phrase, *"Jesus said unto her, I am the Resurrection, and the Life,"* puts an entirely different perspective on this Doctrine.

In other words, He was saying to Martha, *"Martha, look at Me. You are looking at the Resurrection and the Life. I am the Resurrection and the Life."* This means that Jesus was not merely a Teacher of this Doctrine, or even a part of such, but, in reality, the actual *"Resurrection"* because He is the actual *"Life."*

This also means that Jesus does not merely contain Salvation but, in fact, is *"Salvation!"* He does not merely contain *"Life"* but, in fact, is *"Life!"* He does not merely know the *"Word"* but, in fact, is the *"Word!"* As well, He does not merely know the *"New Covenant"* but, in fact, is the *"New Covenant."*

This places Him in an entirely different perspective than anything or anyone else. Others show the way, while He is the *"Way!"* Others have *"truth,"* while He is *"Truth!"* Others have *"love,"* while He is *"Love!"*

This means that He is the Reservoir of all these things. He is the *"Resurrection and the Life"* simply because He has overcome death and paid the price for man's Redemption. These things He did in His Perfect Humanity; however, these resident forces within Him and the ultimate Power to carry them out pertain to His Deity.

So, we have the joining of the two, His Humanity and His Deity, so closely intertwined that He has only one Personality and one Nature.

As someone said, *"While He laid aside the expression of His Deity in the Incarnation, He never for a moment lost possession of His Deity."*

SPIRITUAL LIFE

The phrase, *"He who believes in Me, though he were dead, yet shall he live,"* says two things:

1. It speaks of the Spiritual Life that is imparted to the believing sinner, which brings him from spiritual death to Spiritual Life.

When man fell in the Garden of Eden, he died spiritually, which means separation from God, Who is the Life Source.

Consequently, unregenerate man is *"dead in trespasses and sins"* (Eph. 2:1).Upon Faith in Christ, Saving Grace is imparted to the believing sinner. He is then restored to God, now having *"Life,"* and is no more *"dead,"* i.e., *"separated from God."*

2. The statement pertains to the coming Resurrection of the dead (those in Christ). This is the moment that the soul and the spirit are reunited with a new Glorified Body, which can never again suffer physical death, etc.

This is what is referred to as the *"Out Resurrection from the dead,"* when the Sainted Dead will be resurrected from among the wicked dead, who will not be resurrected until 1,000 years later, and then only to be placed in the Lake of Fire (I Cor. 15:51-57; I Thess. 4:16-17; Rev. 20:5-6).

SHALL NEVER DIE

"And whosoever lives and believes in Me shall never die. Do you believe this?" (Jn. 11:26).

The phrase, "And whosoever lives and believes in Me shall never die," in effect, says, *"Whoever believes in Me in this life will live eternally"* (Jn. 6:27). This is, without a doubt, one of the greatest promises found in the entirety of the Word of God.

The key is *"believing,"* and more perfectly, believing in Jesus.

What does that mean?

In its most simplistic form, it means that the believing sinner must believe that Jesus Christ is God, and that He came down to this world, took upon Himself a Human Body, and offered it up on Calvary's Cross as a Sin-Offering in order to pay man's terrible sin debt. The sinner must believe that this Sacrifice of Christ paid it all, and that whosoever believes in Him and what He did will have Eternal Life imparted unto them.

To be sure, the believing sinner may only have a partial grasp of the few things I have said, but God looks far more at the heart than He does the actual words expressed, or even our total understanding (I Sam. 16:7). Of course, many other things are a part of Salvation, such as the Resurrection, which the Believer will ultimately come to know and understand.

THE CONDITION

The question, *"Do you believe this?"* states the condition.

Martha believed that Jesus could heal the sick and that there would be a future Resurrection; however, these facts were valueless in the presence of death. But Jesus was there, and He was not only the Resurrection but also the Life.

Lazarus being dead, Resurrection had to come first, which it did. By His Death, Christ abolished sin, death, Judgment, and all that belonged to the life that man had lost respecting the Fall in the Garden of Eden.

At Calvary, Jesus went under all the power of the enemy in all its totality and came up from it in the Power of a New Life in Resurrection, which was done exclusively for sinners.

In respect to that Life He purchased at Calvary, He becomes Life to the Redeemed, for He communicates it to them. As a result of this impartation, the Believer is in a wholly new state with the old life, and also the wrath attached to it, being behind him forever.

All this Power of Resurrection and of Life is lodged in the Person of Christ, and the Resurrection of Lazarus demonstrated that fact. He would raise Himself from the dead (Jn. 2:19), and God, as well, would raise Him from the dead (Acts 3:15). Hence, He raised Lazarus, for He is God; but this Resurrection was exercised in obedience to and dependence on the Father.

Resurrection is the end of death; consequently, death has no more to do with the Redeemed. It has done all it can do. It is finished! The Redeemed live in the imparted Life that put an end to it. For us, the old life and its death and Judgment no longer exist.

LORD, I BELIEVE!

"She said unto Him, Yes, Lord: I believe that You are the Christ, the Son of God, Who had come into the world" (Jn. 11:27).

The phrase, *"She said unto Him, Yes, Lord,"* proclaims her affirmation of Faith, which now takes her to a Spiritual height to which she had not known previously. So, this which Satan attempted to do, the killing of Lazarus, would instead serve as a greater opportunity that *"the Son of God might be glorified thereby."*

To be frank, most of the great Spiritual victories are won at times when it seems like there is great defeat.

The phrase, *"I believe that You are the Christ, the Son of God,"* proclaims her belief in the Lord in a different light than she had known Him previously.

Whatever she had once known now came into full flower. He was no longer merely a Man with extraordinary Power. He was *"Christ,"* i.e., *"the Anointed,"* i.e., *"the Messiah,"* *"the Hope of Israel,"* and *"the Hope of the World."*

As well, she now knew that He is *"the Son of God,"* not merely one of the Prophets of old, as some believed the Messiah was to be.

She now believed that Jesus is God!

The phrase, *"Who had come into the world,"* refers to Jesus being the fulfillment of all the Prophecies (Gen. 3:15; 12:3; 22:14; 49:10; Isa. 7:14; Isa., Chpt. 53).

THE MASTER IS COME, AND CALLS FOR YOU

"And when she had so said, she went her way, and called Mary her sister secretly, saying, The Master is come, and calls for you" (Jn. 11:28).

The phrase, *"And when she had so said, she went her way,"* portrays undoubtedly a springing well of hope and joy that must have filled her heart.

A few minutes before, all was darkness, but now, all is Light. From the statements given by Jesus, I believe that she now knew that He was going to raise Lazarus from the dead.

To be frank, no one has ever left the Presence of Jesus without being blessed in such a way that it defies all description, that is, if they believe on Him.

While it may not be as dramatic as it was with Lazarus being raised from the dead, still, this encounter has been even greater with untold millions who have come to a Saving Knowledge of Jesus Christ. Their *"way"* is made immeasurably easier by this glorious and wonderful encounter.

"And called Mary her sister secretly," proclaims Martha making her way to the side of Mary even while many others were, no doubt, in the house at that time. How much she secretly revealed to her sister at that time concerning what Jesus had said, we cannot now know. However, I do believe that when Mary looked at Martha's face, she knew that something wonderful had happened.

The phrase, *"Saying, The Master is come, and calls for you,"* has to be one of the most beautiful statements found in the entirety of the Word of God.

Jesus had evidently requested Mary to be present so she could witness the Resurrection of her brother. Jesus waited for her to come before proceeding to the tomb.

COMING TO JESUS

"As soon as she heard that, she arose quickly, and came unto Him" (Jn. 11:29).

The phrase, *"As soon as she heard that,"* proclaims the greatest Message that she or anyone, for that matter, could ever hear.

As stated, it is not known exactly as to what Martha related to Mary, but there is an excellent possibility that she told her all, especially on the short journey to where Jesus was outside of the small town.

"She arose quickly, and came unto Him" proclaims that she did such with a great spirit of anticipation.

What would Jesus do?

Whatever it was, it would be wonderful. Could it be that He would really raise her brother from the dead?

WHERE JESUS WAS

"Now Jesus was not yet come into the town, but was in that place where Martha met Him.

"The Jews then which were with her in the house, and comforted her, when they saw Mary, that she rose up hastily and went out, followed her, saying, She goes unto the grave to weep there" (Jn. 11:30-31).

"The Jews then which were with her in the house, and comforted her," seems to be a different set than those mentioned in Verse 19. Actually, this was the custom, with some coming to weep and mourn, etc.

"When they saw Mary, that she rose up hastily and went out, followed her," presents them observing what had happened respecting the coming of Martha and Mary leaving with her, but with no knowledge as to what had transpired between them.

"Saying, She goes unto the grave to weep there," was their assumption. Little did they know or realize what was about to happen, actually, not even knowing that Jesus had come.

WORD FOR WORD

"Then when Mary was come where Jesus was, and saw Him, she fell down at His Feet, saying unto Him, Lord, if You had been here, my brother had not died" (Jn. 11:32).

Mary's action in falling at the Feet of Jesus represents, in a sense, her anticipation.

The phrase, *"Saying unto Him, Lord, if You had been here, my brother had not died,"* is word for word what her sister had said to Jesus a short time earlier.

Even though her words seem to indicate that she was not expecting the Resurrection of her brother, still, I think that was not the case.

As stated, it is almost positive that her sister related to her what Jesus had said concerning Lazarus being raised from the dead. However, in view of the preponderance of this situation, I am sure that both Mary and Martha did not want to be shown as assuming more than they should.

In human history, such had never been done, the raising of one who had been dead for four days. As well, it was very difficult for one to even think of the actual happening of such an event. So, I think we should not jump to the conclusion that Mary was registering unbelief. I think it is not so much unbelief as it is the difficulty of coming to *"belief,"* or Faith, as the record, I think, will show.

JESUS GROANED IN THE SPIRIT, AND WAS TROUBLED

"When Jesus therefore saw her weeping, and the Jews also weeping which came with her, He groaned in the Spirit, and was troubled" (Jn. 11:33).

Verse 33 proclaims these mourners following Mary to the Side of Jesus. He did not seem to mind their presence or their going with Him and the sisters to the tomb.

"He groaned in the spirit, and was troubled," portrays His Response to death and all that Satan had done to humanity. The Greek word for *"groaned"* is, *"Embrimaomai,"* and means, *"To be very angry, and moved with indignation."* What He was moved against here was, no doubt, the satanic powers that had

Lazarus in their grip (Heb. 2:14-15). Of this moment, Reynolds said, *"Jesus saw the long procession of all mourners from the first to the last, all the agony, all the hopelessness which sin had brought into the world, in thousands of millions of instances. There flashed upon His Spirit all the terrible moral consequences of which death was the ghastly symbol."*

In a short time, He would take upon Himself the sin penalty of man and would, as well, take upon Himself man's death.

The words, *"In the Spirit,"* refer to the Holy Spirit and presents the entirety of the Godhead in opposition to the terrible results of the Fall, for both Jesus and the Holy Spirit were sent by the Father and came from the Father.

THE TOMB

"And said, Where have you laid him? They said unto Him, Lord, come and see" (Jn. 11:34).

The question, *"And said, Where have you laid him?"* presents the beginning of this momentous occasion.

The skeptics, completely misunderstanding the Person of Christ, would scoff at Jesus not knowing the location of the tomb. However, they fail to understand that Jesus was God and, in fact, never ceased to be God, and that He, in fact, did lay aside voluntarily the expression of His Deity, while never losing the possession of His Deity.

Consequently, all that He did was done as a Man empowered by the Holy Spirit. So, the Holy Spirit told Him some things, and other things were not related to Him. In that case, He found out things as all other men come to information.

The phrase, *"They said unto Him, Lord, come and see,"* proclaims the Jews who followed Mary answering

Him. In other words, they would lead Him to the tomb!

"Jesus wept" (Jn. 11:35).

Reynolds said, *"This is the shortest Verse in the Bible, but one of the most suggestive in the entirety of Scripture."*

Some claim that Jesus was weeping for sorrow regarding Lazarus; however, this is not true, for He would raise Lazarus from the dead in a matter of minutes.

His weeping was caused by His Fellow-feeling with human misery in all its forms then imaged before Him in the grave of Lazarus.

Other than the Person of Jesus, neither mankind nor the world has ever been viewed as they were originally made. Both man and the world are under a curse because of the Fall in the Garden of Eden, which has brought untold misery and heartache. This will only be assuaged when Jesus comes back to reign supremely, which He will do at the Second Coming. Then the world will know peace and prosperity as it has not known previously.

However, until then, the tears that Jesus shed are but symbolic of an ocean of tears shed by all of humanity.

MISUNDERSTANDING JESUS

"Then said the Jews, Behold how He loved him!

"And some of them said, Could not this Man, which opened the eyes of the blind, have caused that even this man should not have died?" (Jn. 11:36-37).

These people were right in that Jesus did love Lazarus very much and, in fact, the entirety of the world, for that matter.

However, His Tears had to do with a far greater degree of misery than was evident here.

The beginning of the question, *"And some of them said, Could not this Man, which opened the eyes of the blind ...?"* suggests in the original Greek that the cure of the blind man by Jesus, which had taken place not so long before, had created a great commotion, with some saying it was only a delusion.

It is difficult to believe that they had not heard of the raising of the daughter of Jairus or the widow's son of Nain, for almost all of what He did was spread far and wide. However, it seems that the dreaded virus of unbelief had wreaked its terrible toll on these, who seemed to have been somewhat different than those of Verse 36.

RELIGIOUS EVIL

The conclusion of the question, *"Have caused that even this man should not have died?"* as stated, seems to be said with some sarcasm!

The hearts of men, and especially religious men, are evil beyond compare. No hatred was manifested toward Jesus by those who made little or no claim of religion even though they were obviously wicked.

It remained for the religious crowd to express their hatred, which they would do in a very bloody way in a very short time.

While all unsaved people are greatly deceived, still, religious deception is the worst of all! It not only conjures up its own salvation but, as well, bitterly opposes that which is truly of God.

THE CONSTERNATION OF JESUS

"Jesus therefore again groaning in Himself comes to the grave. It was a cave, and a stone lay upon it" (Jn. 11:38).

Verse 38 seems to portray once again the Lord being seized by this terrible sorrow, which resulted in what seems to be overwhelming indignation.

If there is anything which symbolizes all the pain and hurt resulting from the fall of man, the *"grave"* or *"tomb"* is that example. Death in all of its forms is a result of the Fall. In death is sickness, and in sickness is the germ of man's inability to save himself. Despite all the vaunted medical technology, sickness is just as rampant at present as it ever was.

We must realize that God created man to live forever, and that in actuality the physical body is so wondrously made that medical science is not sure as to why it ages and ultimately dies. They tell us that it somewhat rejuvenates itself every seven years, and that there is no reason the organs, such as the heart, lungs, etc., should not last forever.

Of course, we know the reason is original sin. Death always follows sin in some fashion.

Respecting both the Old and New Testaments, the Bible traces the entry of sin into the world back to Adam.

Looking at the Fall, Paul explains that:

"Just as sin entered the world through one man (*Adam*), **and death through sin, and in this way death came to all men, because** (*in Adam*) **all sinned" (Rom. 5:12)**.

Adam's sin was not his alone. He sinned for the entirety of the human race. The death that struck him, and was expressed not only physically but in every relationship, has been passed on to every succeeding generation. Paul states that even those who, before Moses, did not sin by breaking a particular Commandment (Rom. 5:14), still found themselves in the grip of death. Death then is not natural.

It is not rooted in the nature of the Universe; it is not simply an expression of the way things are.

Death is unnatural, brought on mankind by a shattering event that shook the material Universe (Rom. 8:19-22), and so warped human nature as to affect the experience of every person ever born.

The only way out of death is through the Lord Jesus Christ, Who defeated death at Calvary's Cross. That's the reason that He told Martha, *"And whosoever lives and believes in Me shall never die"* (Jn. 11:26).

Of course, more than all, He was speaking of spiritual death, which means eternal separation from God; however, death in all of its forms will be eradicated when Jesus comes back.

TAKE AWAY THE STONE

"Jesus said, Take ye away the stone. Martha, the sister of him who was dead, said unto Him, Lord, by this time he stinks: for he has been dead four days" (Jn. 11:39).

When Jesus said, *"Take ye away the stone,"* this presents itself as one of the most poignant moments in human history.

As someone has well said, the Believer can *"throw stones"* or *"roll away the stone."* In fact, the entirety of Christianity is on one side or the other. It is throwing stones or removing stones.

On which side are you?

Martha, complaining about the disposition of her brother's body, inasmuch as he had been dead for some four days, now seems to be vacillating regarding the Instructions of Christ.

Had she really believed that Jesus was going to raise Lazarus from the dead even as He had said?

Did she properly understand His Explanation of Himself as the *"Resurrection and the Life"*?

Or, was it that her Faith began to wane and weaken when she stood before the cold reality of this tomb?

The idea seems to be that she had originally believed, but now the magnitude of what Jesus had stated descended upon her. Not only was her brother dead, but corruption had already set in on the body.

The phrase, *"For he has been dead four days,"* seems to express the idea that irrespective of what Jesus had said, her Faith simply could not reach to these outer limits.

I seriously doubt if any of us would have done any better.

DO YOU BELIEVE?

"Jesus said unto her, Said I not unto you, that, if you would believe, you should see the Glory of God?" (Jn. 11:40).

The beginning of the question, "Jesus said unto her, Said I not unto you ...?" presents Him reminding her as to what He had said that He would do.

Corruption, whether physical or moral, is no obstacle to Him Who is the Resurrection and the Life.

The continuing of the question, *"That, if you would believe ...?"* does not mean that her Faith or the lack of it had any bearing whatsoever on what Jesus would do. It merely referred to the fact that if she had enough Faith to stand there and observe, she would see this great Miracle.

FAITH

As well, this tells me that Martha had believed when Jesus said what He would do respecting the

Resurrection of her brother. It seems that she took this Faith and His Promise with great joy to her sister.

However, now the cold reality of death, even to the condition of the corpse, is staring her in the face.

Lest we criticize her too severely, we need to remind ourselves of the times we have allowed circumstances to weaken or even rob us of Faith. As well, I must remind the reader that whatever the circumstances were that caused us difficulties, they were insignificant to this which faced Martha and her sister Mary.

Thankfully, the Lord does not require perfect Faith, only perfect obedience. How many times have we obeyed, even as Martha will here do in allowing the rolling away of the stone, when actually we have little capacity left to believe!

The conclusion of the question, *"You should see the Glory of God?"* presents Jesus proving to Faith that He could and would destroy the power of death, rob it of its sting, swallow up the grave in victory, and proclaim the everlasting curse of this mysterious flesh of ours to be a vanquished foe.

The *"Glory of God"* refers to God's Glorious Power manifested in Resurrection.

THE PRAYER OF CHRIST

"Then they took away the stone from the place where the dead was laid. And Jesus lifted up His Eyes, and said, Father, I thank You that You have heard me" (Jn. 11:41).

Verse 41 portrays several people evidently removing this huge slab from the tomb.

At this point, it was very simple for the onlookers to see the body of Lazarus lying on the shelf provided for the corpse, wrapped in its mummy-like burial shroud. This was done to hold the spices next to the body, which would tend to lessen the odor of the corruption.

The phrase, *"And Jesus lifted up His Eyes, and said, Father, I thank You that You have heard me,"* proclaims this as a thanksgiving for that which had already been prayed and heard.

Evidently, the Holy Spirit had already informed Christ of what was here to be done, which probably was revealed some three days before.

It seems that Jesus had sought His Heavenly Father after this information was imparted unto Him as to exactly what steps He was to take in carrying out this Miracle.

THE FATHER HEARS JESUS ALWAYS

"And I knew that You hear Me always: but because of the people which stand by I said it, that they may believe that You have sent Me" (Jn. 11:42).

The phrase, *"And I knew that You hear Me always,"* presents a powerful statement:

• This that Jesus said speaks of relationship. It is not a prayer of petition, but rather thanksgiving, as we have already stated.

The relationship between Christ and His Father was meant, among other things, to serve as an example for all Believers.

What type of relationship do you have as a Believer with your Heavenly Father?

I do not mean to imply that any Believer can have the exact type of relationship that Jesus had with the Father. However, I am greatly persuaded that such a relationship can be grandly improved in the hearts and lives of all Believers, that is, if we diligently seek for it to be improved.

To be sure, such improvement can only come about with a proper prayer life and a proper regimen of the study of the Word of God.

However, the greatest factor is that we place our Faith exclusively in Christ and what He did for us at the Cross. This is absolutely imperative.

To ignore the Greatest Act of God in human history is a slap, so to speak, in the Face of God.

It is not that these things earn us anything before God, for they do not.

It simply means that it's impossible to have proper communion and fellowship without our Faith being exclusively in Christ and the Cross, along with prayer and a proper understanding of the Word.

• Because of this relationship, every single thing that Jesus asked of the Father, it was instantly granted. Jesus said that the Father heard Him "*always.*" John also said, "*. . . if we ask anything according to His Will, He hears us.*"

He then said, "*And if we know that He hears us, whatsoever we ask, we know that we have the petitions that we desired of Him*" (I Jn. 5:14-15).

• If our relationship is as it ought to be with the Lord, we will never ask anything that is not of His Will. Actually, the primary concern of a true relationship is not that the Lord answers our prayers, but that, above all, the Will of God be done.

So, faith that does nothing but claim answers, with little concern as to the Will of God, is, in truth, no faith at all!

THE REASONS AS GIVEN BY CHRIST

The phrase, "*But because of the people who stand by I said it, that they may believe that You have sent Me,*" is uttered in this fashion for several reasons:

• Jesus wanted the people to understand the link between Him and the Father.

He is praying to the Father, and now the dead will be raised. Above all, this should lay to rest the idea that He is performing these Miracles by the power of Satan, as the religious leaders have claimed.

• If this conclusion is drawn, which it must be if a person is honest, then the people must also admit that God has sent Him and that He truly is the Messiah.

• Even though He does not refuse praise Himself, and rightly so, still, He desires the people to praise the Father instead of Him, at least, in this setting.

Actually, at the earlier part of His Ministry, He had refused to accept the praise of the people simply because their motivation was improper (Jn. 2:23-25).

That which He now does will cause some to *"believe on Him"* (Vs. 45).

LAZARUS, COME FORTH

"And when He thus had spoken, He cried with a loud voice, Lazarus, come forth" (Jn. 11:43).

The phrase, *"And when He thus had spoken,"* proclaims the conclusion of His Prayer.

Jesus seldom prayed long prayers in public, but in privacy, at least one time, He prayed all night long (Lk. 6:12).

The phrase, *"He cried with a loud voice,"* has been explained in many and varied ways as to the reason for the loudness; however, I think this explanation is probably closer to the exact reason.

He spoke loud enough that all standing could hear the command and see that even the dead were subject to Him.

The phrase, *"Lazarus, come forth,"* constitutes a command, and by the Creator of the ages.

Someone has suggested that Jesus called the name of Lazarus in order that only he would come forth. The implication being that inasmuch as Jesus is the Lord of Glory, the Resurrection and the Life, He had to be specific, considering He was addressing the dead, or all the Sainted Dead at that moment would have come forth. That is, no doubt, true!

Paul said, when speaking of the Resurrection, *"For the Lord Himself shall descend from Heaven with a shout,"* which could well be the words, *"Come forth"* (I Thess. 4:16). We do know this: whatever that shout will be will cause all the Sainted Dead to *"rise first!"*

THE RESURRECTION

"And he who was dead came forth, bound hand and foot with graveclothes: and his face was bound about with a napkin. Jesus said unto them, Loose him, and let him go" (Jn. 11:44).

The phrase, *"And he who was dead came forth,"* had to be, due to the circumstances, the greatest Miracle performed by Christ and, consequently, the greatest in human history.

What must have been the reaction of the people as they saw Lazarus rise up from the place where they had laid him and then walk out of that tomb? How could one describe such a scene? What did the two sisters think at that time?

The phrase, *"Bound hand and foot with graveclothes,"* has been the cause of some discussion.

Some claim that the burial wrappings had been wound tightly about him, which would have made it impossible to walk, therefore, constituting another Miracle when he *"came forth."* However, that seems to be unlikely.

Most likely his legs were bound separately, which would have made it difficult to walk but not impossible, hence, the latter Command of Christ.

LOOSE HIM, AND LET HIM GO

The phrase, *"And his face was bound about with a napkin,"* concerns a cloth which had been tied over his face, but which he had partially removed.

The phrase, *"Jesus said unto them, Loose him, and let him go,"* refers, as is obvious, to this burial shroud being taken off his body.

As well, it refers, I think, to the idea that his legs were wrapped separately, etc.

Lazarus was called up from Paradise where he had been for the past four days. One can only surmise as to what happened when the Voice of Jesus rang out in that place concerning Lazarus.

However, I think that during the three and one half years of Jesus' Public Ministry, Paradise had become quite accustomed to hearing that Voice in one way or the other. As I have stated, even though the Gospel only gives us the account of three people being raised from the dead by Christ, no doubt, He raised many more as well!

Actually, from this moment, it would only be about two months until the whole of Paradise would be emptied. All of the Sainted Dead who had been placed here, even held captive by Satan, which included all the Old Testament Greats, along with John the Baptist and others, would be liberated by Jesus Christ and taken to Heaven itself (Mat. 27:52-53; Eph. 4:8-10).

PARADISE

Before Jesus died on Calvary, thereby, satisfying the claims of Heavenly Justice and, as well, destroying the power of Satan and death, all the Sainted Dead went to Paradise, which was separated from the burning side of Hell only by a great gulf (Lk. 16:19-31).

While these people were definitely Saved by Faith in Christ exactly as all are Saved, still, their sins were not taken away but only covered because the blood of bulls and goats could never take away sins (Heb. 10:4).

However, when Jesus came, paying the price at Calvary, then Satan had no more claim because sins were no longer held against anyone who expressed Faith in Christ because they had been taken away (Jn. 1:29). Consequently, Satan had to let them go. Now, every Believer who dies instantly goes to be with the Lord Jesus Christ (Phil. 1:23).

MANY BELIEVED

"Then many of the Jews which came to Mary, and had seen the things which Jesus did, believed on Him" (Jn. 11:45).

The phrase, *"Then many of the Jews which came to Mary,"* probably refers back to Verse 20, when Mary remained in the house to accept the condolences of those who came to pay their respects while her sister Martha went to meet Jesus.

The phrase, *"And had seen the things which Jesus did, believed on Him,"* should certainly have garnered their response. However, Jesus would later say, *"... blessed are they who have not seen, and yet have believed"* (Jn. 20:29).

THE PHARISEES

"But some of them went their ways to the Pharisees, and told them what things Jesus had done" (Jn. 11:46).

The information contained in Verse 46 proclaims something extremely hard to believe.

How is it that individuals could observe the type of Miracle just witnessed and still oppose Christ?

Christ's Miracles and Words produced a twofold effect and made a frequent division among the Jews, thus, bringing to light who were and who were not His True Disciples. The same facts excited Faith in some and roused animosity in others. The Great Sign has been dividing men into hostile camps ever since.

The phrase, *"And told them what things Jesus had done,"* constitutes such being done not with joy, but with skepticism and sarcasm. Consequently, they were rejecting God with cold calculation and in the face of incontrovertible proof. One must remember, this was the church of Jesus' Day!

JESUS

"Then Jesus six days before the Passover came to Bethany, where Lazarus was which had been dead, whom He raised from the dead" (Jn. 12:1).

Verse 1 represents the closing days of the Master's Ministry and Work. This which had been planned from before the foundation of the world (I Pet. 1:19-20) was now about to be brought to pass.

It is ironic! The greatest event in the history of mankind was about to be carried out, and Rome, which ruled the world of that day and boasted itself of its knowledge respecting its far-flung empire, in fact, had absolutely no knowledge whatsoever of this event, the greatest of all! Sadder still, the church of that day, i.e., Israel, did not know either, or else, some of them did know but refused to believe. In fact, only a handful of people had any knowledge of this event, and even their knowledge was fragmentary.

Such portrays the utter depravity of the human family. Man is created a tripartite being, composed of spirit, soul, and body. The physical body relates to the world while the soul relates to self. The spirit relates to God, or at least it does if it is regenerated by the Power of the Holy Spirit. To make it a little easier to understand, one could say that the body is world-conscious while the soul is self-conscious, and the Spirit is God-conscious, or at least it is supposed to be. This tells us that during Jesus' Day, precious few people were conscious of God and His Ways, or they would have known Who Jesus was and for what He had come. Regrettably, even the few who knew Him, and as stated, only had a very fragmentary knowledge of Him, showed that their God-consciousness was very weak.

Thankfully, it is some better at present due to the Holy Spirit being poured out for nearly 2,000 years, and especially since the turn of the 20th century.

LAZARUS

The phrase, *"Where Lazarus was which had been dead, whom He raised from the dead,"* proclaims Jesus going to where He was welcome.

He was not welcome in the Temple even though it was His House, so His Presence there, in a short time, would be looked at as an intrusion, as it is in most churches presently. Likewise, He was not welcome where the High Priest was carrying out his duties, even though He was supposed to be a Type of Christ, exactly as He is not welcome in the lives and ministries of most modern preachers and priests. So, that of which we witness here is somewhat similar to what would be witnessed now were Jesus to appear.

The Holy Spirit here proclaims the notable Miracle of the raising of Lazarus from the dead for several reasons:

• Lazarus is a type of all Believers who have died in Christ and will be raised at the Resurrection of Life.

• Speaking in a spiritual sense, he is a symbol of one who had been dead in trespasses and sins but has been *"raised from the dead,"* i.e., *"Born-Again."*

• Not only was he raised from the dead, but the sickness which had brought on the death to start with had been totally healed, symbolizing the washing of sins by the Blood of Jesus. Sin is what causes spiritual death in all men to begin with.

THE SUPPER

"There they made Him a supper; and Martha served: but Lazarus was one of them who sat at the table with Him" (Jn. 12:2).

The phrase, *"There they made Him a supper,"* does not tell us exactly where it was, but it was probably in the house of Simon the Leper (Mat. 26:6; Mk. 14:3). Some have suggested that Simon was the husband of Martha, which may well have been, but the Scripture gives no proof.

As well, some contend that there were two anointings at this time, one in the house of Simon and the other in the house of Lazarus.

However, there is no proof of that, and I think there was only one anointing.

As well, even though Jesus did come to Bethany six days before the Passover, as outlined in Verse 1, that does not mean that the supper was then made.

Actually, the mention of *"two days"* by both Matthew and Mark does not within itself necessitate that the supper took place at that time either. Without violating Scripture, the supper could have taken place anytime during the six days Jesus was in Bethany before the Passover.

MARTHA

The phrase, *"And Martha served,"* seemed to have

been her manner (Lk. 10:38-42); however, she would have served Jesus and the others at this time with a far greater joy than anytime previously.

The reason is that not only Lazarus her brother had been raised from the dead, but even more so, she, along with the others, saw Jesus in an entirely different Light than before. They now know Him as *"the Resurrection and the Life!"*

The phrase, *"But Lazarus was one of them who sat at the table with Him,"* in effect, I think, tells us that there were more at the table even than Mary and Jesus' Disciples. As stated, I believe Simon the Leper was at the table as well.

If, in fact, Simon was there at that table, there would be seated two transcendent proofs of the Power of Jesus to save, not only from the semblance of death, as was Simon the Leper, but from the reality of death by the Resurrection of Lazarus.

THE ANOINTING

"Then took Mary a pound of ointment of spikenard, very costly, and anointed the Feet of Jesus, and wiped His Feet with her hair: and the house was filled with the odour of the ointment" (Jn. 12:3).

It is very difficult to translate into the proper worth respecting the money of our day. However, according to what Judas said that it might be worth (300 pence), it would probably translate into a year's wages at modern minimum wage, which would be approximately between $10,000 and $15,000.

Some have even suggested, without proof, that this *"alabaster box,"* as recorded by Matthew, could have been brought out of Egypt some 1,600 years earlier, thereby, being in the family all this time. If, in fact, this could possibly be true, then the phrase, *"Very costly,"* becomes even more apropos.

"*And anointed the Feet of Jesus,*" is specified particularly by John while Matthew and Mark mentioned that Mary anointed His Head (Mat. 26:7; Mk. 14:3).

Jesus simply used the term, "*She is come aforehand to anoint My Body to the burying*" (Mk. 14:8). There is no contradiction, as we shall see!

WIPING HIS FEET WITH HER HAIR

The phrase, "*And wiped His Feet with her hair,*" gives us the reason, I think, that John the Beloved only spoke of anointing His Feet.

Harmonious with the purpose of this Gospel setting forth the Deity of the Lord Jesus, only the anointing of His Feet is recorded.

By the performing of this act, Mary of Bethany proclaimed that Jesus had a value transcending all else. Thus, the Faith that regards Him and knows His Love, which passes knowledge, is a sweet odor, and it fills all the house.

Man misjudged her, as we shall see; He vindicated her and understood her.

That was all she wanted. She unconsciously erected to herself an eternal monument as lasting as the Gospel, and linked with it. Thus, the facts of His Earthly History constitute the substance of the Gospel; and His Prediction of the enduring remembrance of Mary's action demonstrates His Judicial Supremacy in the government of the world.

At His Feet, she probably learned that on the third day, He would rise again, and so, the spikenard she had prepared for His Dead Body, she now poured "*beforehand*" on His Living Body.

It was a Testimony to His Resurrection, and she knew she would have no other opportunity. Incidentally,

Mary was not found at the empty Sepulchre. She was too spiritually intelligent to be there.

By Mary anointing His Feet and wiping them with her hair, she testified to His Coming Resurrection, which she seems to be the only one who believed this great Truth. While Jesus would be carried into the Tomb, He would walk out under His Own Power, hence, the emphasis on His Feet.

HUMILITY AND SUPREMACY

As well, by emphasizing the anointing of His Feet, John testified to His Humility while Matthew and Mark, speaking only of the anointing of His Head, testified to His Supremacy. I think one could say without fear of contradiction that such is unique in Christ, *"Humility joined with Supremacy."*

As most Bible students know, John portrayed Jesus as *"God,"* while Matthew portrayed Him as *"King,"* Mark as *"Servant,"* and Luke as *"Man."*

How wonderful that the Holy Spirit links humility with Deity when the thoughts of men would be otherwise.

THE OINTMENT

The phrase, *"And the house was filled with the odour of the ointment,"* speaks of the Preciousness of Jesus to His Father and should speak accordingly to the world, as well, but seldom does. To the Church, His True Body, *"Your Name is as ointment poured forth"* (Song of Sol. 1:3). As the *"ointment"* was poured forth, so was His Life.

The type of *"ointment"* used by Mary contained *"spikenard,"* which was an herb related to valerian and was imported from North India, and was, as the Scripture said, *"Very costly."*

Likewise, such typified, as stated, the Preciousness of the Life of Christ.

The type of ointment used by Mary was almost exclusively a perfume, while the type spoken of in the Song of Solomon mostly had a soothing, healing effect.

So, we learn from this that His Name is not only symbolic of great Power but, as well, is a healing medicine.

This is the type made of olive oil and used by shepherds to soothe the bruised foreheads of sheep having scraped themselves in foraging for food.

In our everyday walk before God, we become bruised at times and need the healing ointment, which only His Name can provide.

Consequently, when a person has been with Jesus, the "*odour of the ointment*" fills the house, i.e., the heart and life of the Believer.

As that which Mary's act symbolizes, wherever Jesus is found, this wonderful fragrance will fill the place.

JUDAS ISCARIOT

"*Then said one of His Disciples, Judas Iscariot, Simon's son, which should betray Him*" (Jn. 12:4).

This "*Simon*" mentioned here was not "*Simon the Leper*" in whose house this supper was prepared, as should be obvious.

Judas is spoken of accordingly in order to distinguish him from the other Disciple named Judas, who was also called Lebbaeus or Thaddaeus (Lk. 6:16; Mat. 10:3).

The phrase, "*Which should betray Him,*" was written by John about 50 years after the actual happening of the event.

Unfortunately, Judas is not the only one who has betrayed Christ.

Actually, every preacher who fails to preach the

Word of God, but rather proclaims *"another gospel,"* is betraying Christ.

Likewise, every Believer who does not follow Him with all of their hearts, in some way, betrays Him.

While it may not be as serious as that of Judas, still, it is betrayal.

The word, *"Betray,"* in the Greek is, *"Paradidomi,"* and means, *"To deliver over treacherously by way of betrayal to an enemy."* Consequently, when preachers do not preach the Word, they are delivering over to Satan the True Word, i.e., *"Christ,"* and doing so treacherously. They have betrayed their Calling and their Christ.

THIS OINTMENT

"Why was not this ointment sold for three hundred pence, and given to the poor?" (Jn. 12:5)

Reynolds said, *"Sinful motive often hides itself under the mask of reverence for another virtue."*

In fact, what should be the priority of the Church?

While to help the unfortunate in whatever capacity is definitely a part of Christianity, even as is borne out in the Book of Acts and elsewhere, still, that is not priority for the Church.

The business of the Church, actually, the main business, the priority, must always be the spread of the Gospel of Jesus Christ (Mk. 16:15).

There are several reasons for that, which should be obvious:

• The Salvation of the soul is the single most important thing there could ever be. Even though the *"poor"* are definitely in need of many things, still, a person can be right with God although poor, but an individual cannot be right with God if he does not hear the Gospel and have an opportunity to accept Jesus.

• While it is true that the world, at least at this

present time, will always have its complements of the *"poor,"* still, when the Gospel is presented to the poor, with its acceptance, a way out of poverty is given. In other words, the old adage is apropos, that if you give a man a bushel of corn, you have provided food for him for several meals; however, if you teach man how to plant corn and cultivate it, you have shown him a way out of hunger.

The Gospel of Jesus Christ does exactly that! It proclaims to any and all, along with the great Plan of Salvation, the way even to economic prosperity.

• The moment the person comes into the Family of God, irrespective of his economic poverty, the Blessings of God automatically begin to come to him, thereby, lifting him out of this state of privation and want.

Actually, Jesus told us to *"take no thought"* regarding these things (Mat. 6:25-34). Once an individual enters into Salvation, he then comes under the Care, Guidance, Leading, Protection, and Blessings of God, actually under God's Economy, hence, Jesus saying, *"But seek you first the Kingdom of God, and His Righteousness; and all these things shall be added unto you"* (Mat. 6:33).

PREACH JESUS

In the 1980s, we were conducting city-wide Crusades in some of the largest stadiums in the world and various countries. The crowds were enormous, up to 100,000 people per night.

The Lord specifically told me to preach *"Jesus"* to these people. He told me to proclaim in no uncertain terms that Jesus was their Answer, not government, not America, or anyone or anything else.

The reason is obvious. Once the person accepts Jesus, he has entered into the Kingdom of God, and if he will believe God, great and glorious things are always brought unto him. As well, it covers every facet of one's life, be it domestical, physical, economical, or spiritual.

So, by this act, Judas was casting an aspersion upon Christ, Who Alone could alleviate the problems of the poor, or anyone else, for that matter.

While Judas seemed to have been the ringleader in this dissension, Matthew stated that some, if not all, of the other Disciples chimed in with their protests as well (Mat. 26:8).

Of course, Judas, as the next Verse portrays, had little, if any, regard for the poor. And yet, this tells us how that such negativism and skepticism once presented can easily be picked up even by good people, such as the other Disciples.

HE WAS A THIEF

"This he said, not that he cared for the poor; but because he was a thief, and had the bag, and bear what was put therein" (Jn. 12:6).

The phrase, *"This he said, not that he cared for the poor,"* means that this was not his real reason.

Verse 6 proclaims the fact that Judas desired that this expensive ointment be sold, with the money being placed in the common treasury of the group, with him as the dispenser of such. Then he would have the opportunity to steal at least a part, if not all, the proceeds. Several questions arise out of this:

• How long had he been stealing? Of course, that is anyone's guess. However, he probably had begun only a short time before when he came to the realization that Jesus was not going to set up an earthly kingdom. With that door of advancement closing, the next step was to pilfer the funds, which evidently he began doing.

Even though I believe the Scripture plainly proclaims that Judas was right with God at the beginning, self-will slowly but surely began to gain the upper hand. Now, his service for Christ was in the realm, "*What's in it for me?*" Regrettably, the modern greed gospel fosters the same attitude and spirit in its followers.

• Why was Judas appointed to serve as the treasurer? As stated, I think the record is clear that Judas was not a thief at the beginning but only became such after a period of time. Inasmuch as Jesus allowed it, one has to conclude that his appointment was the Will of God. He, no doubt, showed great diligence at the beginning and probably served in an admirable way in this capacity.

LARGE SUMS OF MONEY?

During the first two years of Jesus' Ministry, especially considering the tremendous number of people being healed, and considering the size of the crowds, there were probably great sums of money given to the Lord respecting gratitude on the part of those who had experienced His Miracle-working Touch.

Considering that He had not too much short of 100 people traveling with Him much of the time, the care and upkeep of such a group would have required quite large sums, as should be obvious.

• Did Jesus know when the stealing began on the part of Judas? He undoubtedly did! Saying nothing of the situation does not speak of ignorance, but rather Grace. I think the Scripture is replete with every effort being made by Christ, attempting to turn this man from the awful course on which he had placed himself.

Actually, there are thousands of people presently in high positions in the realm of the Gospel who are, in one way or another, doing the same as Judas.

For long periods of time, the Lord will show Mercy and Grace, but His Seeming Silence does not indicate ignorance and certainly not approval.

As stated, it only portrays His Love and Grace. Ultimately, that is if no repentance is forthcoming, therein will be the same as Judas, at least as far as the loss of the soul is concerned.

THE BURIAL

"Then said Jesus, Let her alone: against the day of My Burying has she kept this" (Jn. 12:7).

The phrase, *"Then said Jesus, Let her alone,"* is proclaimed in this manner for two reasons:

1. Jesus placed His Seal of Approval on that which she was doing and, in effect, demanded that any activity against this act be stopped.

2. Her act also proclaims that she knew and understood that He was soon to die, even though none of the Disciples seemed to have any comprehension, despite all the things Jesus had said about this very event. In effect, it seems her spiritual intelligence far exceeded anyone else at that particular time.

The phrase, *"Against the day of My Burying has she kept this,"* seems to indicate that Mary had had this expensive *"nard"* in her possession for quite some time.

Perhaps she had had many opportunities to sell it for a considerable sum but, for whatever the reason, had not done so.

Now she knows why she has kept this expensive perfume. It is for the Burial of Christ, the single most important thing in human history.

Why is it that Mary seemed to have a far greater understanding of the Mission of Christ even than His Chosen Disciples?

PRIDE AND HUMILITY

I personally think it goes back to self-will. As

someone has said, *"Pride has its own agenda, while humility has the agenda of Christ."*

The Disciples pictured Jesus as a Conquering Messiah, Who would overthrow Rome and make Israel once again the premier Nation in the world.

Of course, they would be His Chief Lieutenants, occupying positions of power and honor in this Kingdom; however, that was not the Mission of Christ, even though the Disciples kept trying to force the issue.

Mary evidently saw the situation as it actually was. While her understanding at this time would have probably been limited, still, she believed what Jesus said about His Death and Resurrection.

None of the others did.

THE SACRIFICIAL OFFERING

As well, this act of Mary anointing the Head and Feet of Jesus with this expensive ointment, even with its wonderful fragrance filling the house, portrays to us what God thought of the Sacrificial Offering of His Only Son.

It was to be a beautiful and wonderful thing in the Sight of God, even though it would be at such price, simply because it would redeem with love mankind, God's Greatest Creation.

This is evident even in the sacrifices of old. It was said of Noah's sacrifice after the flood, *"And the LORD smelled a sweet savor ..."* (Gen. 8:21).

Concerning the Peace Offering as outlined in the Book of Exodus, it says, *"And you shall burn the whole ram upon the Altar: it is a Burnt Offering unto the LORD: it is a sweet savor ..."* (Ex. 29:18).

Actually, the entirety of the Pentateuch is filled with this statement, *"A sweet savor unto the LORD,"* speaking of sacrifice (Lev. 1:9; 2:2, 9, 12; 3:5; Num. 15:3, 7, 10,

14, etc.). All of this represented the Offering up of
Christ at Calvary.

THE POOR

*"For the poor always you have with you; but Me you
have not always"* (Jn. 12:8).

The phrase, *"For the poor always you have with you,"*
presents that which is regrettable but true! Sadly, it will
remain this way until the Second Coming of the Lord.

At that time, all poverty will be forever erased, along
with every other malady that besets the human family.

"But Me you have not always," refers to Jesus being
present in the Flesh. While He is with us now, and, in
fact, always has been, at least in the hearts and lives of
Believers, such is carried out through the Person and
Agency of the Holy Spirit.

It is very sad that this thing which was so dear to
the Heart of God, the Offering up of His Son for the
Redemption of humanity, was understood not at all by
even His Choice Disciples, with them construing this
"anointing" as a waste.

I have to wonder if the true Plan and Purpose of God
is too often presently treated accordingly!

"I love Thy Kingdom Lord,
"The house of Thine Abode,
"The Church our blest Redeemer Saved,
"With His Own Precious Blood.

"I love the Church, O God!
"Her walls before Thee stand,
"Dear as the apple of Thine Eye,
"And graven on Thy Hand.

"For her my tears shall fall,

"For her my prayers ascend;
"To her my cares and toils be given,
"Till toils and cares shall end.

"Beyond my highest joy,
"I prize her heavenly ways,
"Her sweet communion, solemn vows,
"Her hymns of love and praise.

"Sure as Thy Truth shall last,
"To Zion shall be given,
"The brightest glories Earth can yield,
"And brighter bliss of Heaven."

Great Women OF THE BIBLE

Chapter Five

JESUS AND THE WOMAN

JESUS AND THE WOMAN

"And one of the Pharisees desired Him that He would eat with him. And He went into the Pharisee's house, and sat down to meat" (Lk. 7:36).

Verse 36 constitutes the enemy of the *"wisdom"* mentioned in Verse 35. This incident is peculiar to Luke. Evidently, the Pharisee invited the Lord to his table in order to belittle and insult Him, for he refused Him the customary courtesies of a host to a guest, and forced Him to find a place for Himself as best He could.

The Lord did not resent this studied insult; He gently took a place, probably at the door, and waited for the honor that comes from above. It was quickly sent. The Glory of Christ's Person and the majesty of His Deity were both demonstrated, and wisdom's child — the woman — justified her Lord.

Being in the early part of Christ's Ministry, the relations between the Lord and the dominant religious parties in Israel had not yet reached a state of positive hostility. They would shortly!

Even though this very invitation was probably extended to Christ in order that He may be studied by this Pharisee, at this time, they had not yet declared Him a public enemy and blasphemer.

As well, he may well have been influenced in a positive way by Christ and would seek this opportunity to learn more about this Man, Who was different than anyone he had ever met.

JESUS ACCEPTS THE INVITATION

The phrase, *"And He went into the Pharisee's house, and sat down to meat,"* implies that Jesus was given no prominent place at the table, and, as stated, that He had to find seating for Himself.

This was a tremendous insult to Him and, evidently, was meant to be that way.

Quite possibly, Simon the Pharisee knew he was watched that day, and that among his guests were men who would report every action of his on that occasion to the leaders of his party in Jerusalem.

Consequently, his cold, almost total lack of courtesy towards the Master was probably the result of his fear of man and of man's judgment.

In those days, meals were not undertaken in the modern manner of sitting on a chair at a table. Rather, one would recline on a couch, with one's elbows on the table and the unsandaled feet stretched out on the couch behind.

It seems to us presently a difficult way to eat a meal; however, meals then were quite different than now. Then, it was a time of fellowship, enjoyment, and relaxation, which served a purpose of far greater degree than merely satisfying hunger.

So, the insult tendered toward Christ, referring to the Pharisee's neglect of his guest, was of far greater degree than mere lack of courtesy.

A WOMAN WHO WAS A SINNER

"And, behold, a woman in the city, who was a sinner, when she knew that Jesus sat at meat in the Pharisee's house, brought an alabaster box of ointment" (Lk. 7:37).

The phrase, *"And, behold, a woman in the city, who was a sinner,"* was not Mary Magdalene, as some have suggested, for this was in Nain (Lk. 7:11-35), not Magdala, the home of Mary Magdalene on the Sea of Galilee. Who the woman was, we are not told, and it really does not matter.

As well, what type of *"sinner"* she was is of no consequence either.

From the way Luke describes her, she evidently was someone known throughout the city of Nain, with her lifestyle being one of shame.

The phrase, *"When she knew that Jesus sat at meat in the Pharisee's house,"* tells us several things.

Due to the Miracles Jesus was constantly performing, His Whereabouts were always known. He had just raised the widow's son from the dead, plus healed countless other diseases. No doubt, He was the talk of all of Nain. During all of these conversations, she heard that Jesus was at this particular house.

There is even a possibility that she had heard the Words of Jesus when He pleaded with sinners, *"Come unto Me, all you who labor and are heavy laden, and I will give you rest."*

This immediately followed the discourse concerning John the Baptist and was recorded by Matthew but not by Luke (Mat. 11:28-30). Whatever the case, she now came to Jesus!

Her situation is the same the world over. They must know and hear about Jesus, especially considering that He is the Only Answer. Paul said, *". . . how shall they hear without a Preacher? And How shall they preach, except they be sent ...?"* (Rom. 10:14-15).

THE ALABASTER BOX OF OINTMENT

So, I think it would be obvious that priority with God is the taking of His Word to the entirety of the world. Nothing must stand in the way of this all-important task, and yet, I am concerned that much is standing in the way presently.

The phrase, *"Brought an alabaster box of ointment,"* is said to have been made in and named from Alabastron, Egypt, where soft marble is found. Vessels were called *"alabaster"* that were also made from other materials.

They were of various shapes and sizes; the average held about a pint.

The word translated, "*Ointment*," was used for any kind of sweet-smelling vegetable essence, especially that of the myrtle. Exactly why she brought this and what she felt she would do with it upon coming is anyone's guess. However, we shall soon see that for which it was used, and which the Holy Spirit through Luke carefully notes. It is said that this type of ointment was very expensive and much used by wealthy Roman ladies.

What the cost represented to this woman is not known; however, she would use it in the holiest of purposes.

THE WEEPING WOMAN

"*And stood at His Feet behind Him weeping, and began to wash His Feet with tears, and did wipe them with the hairs of her head, and kissed His Feet, and anointed them with the ointment*" (Lk. 7:38).

The phrase, "*And stood at His Feet behind Him weeping*," represents an act of Repentance. As we have stated, more than likely, she had heard Him in the last few hours and had been brought under great Conviction for her sinful lifestyle. Sensing that He held the answer to the craving in her heart, which her sin had never satisfied and, in fact, could not satisfy, she now sought out Jesus, seemingly determined to approach Him at any cost.

In these oriental feasts in those days, the houses were often left open and uninvited strangers frequently passed in through the open courtyard into the guest chamber and looked on.

Presently, such would be impossible and, as well, undesirable; however, in those days, there was a great class distinction in society. For certain individuals such as Simon the Pharisee, who was, no doubt, wealthy, to have the lower class stand at a respectable distance and observe the opulence and wealth, which was, at times, employed on these occasions, was a matter of pride. These onlookers would then go out and tell others how grand and glorious such an occasion was, which boosted the reputation of one such as Simon.

DESPERATION AND DETERMINATION

Consequently, for this woman to break protocol, in fact, come into the very dining hall itself and stand at the Feet of Jesus, portrayed her desperation and, therefore, determination.

What she did was unusual for the reasons stated; however, her persistence and risk would prove to be the greatest thing she ever did.

Now that she had found Jesus and had even gained His Presence, why was she weeping?

The Presence of God often elicits *"weeping"* as a response. The heart is greatly touched and moved for a variety of reasons. It is somewhat a mixture of sadness and joy — sad because of failure and joy because of the work being carried out in the heart by Christ.

I personally believe that the moment she came into His Presence, she realized that He, and He Alone, could change her life.

She sensed that which millions have sensed and which millions have received. It is called *"the Gift of God,"* which is *"Eternal Life"* (Rom. 6:23). All of this is *"through Jesus Christ our Lord."*

Accepting Christ is not a cold, intellectual decision, although it certainly does affect the intellect. It goes much deeper than merely one's mind. It goes down to the very recesses of the soul. Consequently, one believes with the heart (Rom. 10:9-10).

AND BEGAN TO WASH HIS FEET WITH HER TEARS

The phrase, *"And began to wash His Feet with tears,"* presents more than just the shedding of a few tears. The woman must have been sobbing almost, if not, uncontrollably.

The Presence of God does not affect all in this manner, but it does affect many, this Evangelist included.

I suspect that it is very difficult for anyone to properly explain what happens in the heart, in fact, in the entirety of one's being, during these times of consecration.

It is as if the Lord cleanses the soul to such an extent that a oneness with Christ is brought about, which can hardly happen any other way. This type of *"brokenness"* typifies a yielding to the Lord, which gives occasion for the Holy Spirit to perform His Invaluable Work. To be sure, this is the greatest therapy there is and, in fact, the only true therapy there is.

So, one might say and be totally correct that this is not for sinners only but for Believers as well.

Amazingly enough, when the Holy Spirit begins to move, the effect on Believers and unbelievers is generally the same, especially if all are yielding to Christ.

SHE WIPED HIS FEET WITH THE HAIRS OF HER HEAD

The phrase, *"And did wipe them with the hairs of her head, and kissed His Feet,"* constituted an act that was not as strange then as it would seem now.

It is stated that this was a custom among the Jews, Greeks, and Romans. It was a mark of affection and Reverence.

It was practiced by supplicants in making an important request and by conquered people as a token of subjection and obedience.

So, by this act, she was telling Jesus that she yielded to His Mastery, in effect, accepting Him as the Messiah. He was now her Lord and Master but in a way that she had never known before.

Slaves at times did this to their Masters, so, in effect, she was telling Jesus that because of what He had done for her, she would be His Slave from here forward. Actually, Paul, in essence, did the same thing (Eph. 3:1).

Of course, this was all done in the heart with no words having passed between Jesus and this woman as of yet.

AND ANOINTED HIS FEET WITH THE OINTMENT

In those days and at such a gathering, the duty of the host was to assign someone to wash the feet of the guests.

Most roads were unpaved and with most wearing little more than sandals, their feet became dirty. Upon coming to a gathering of this nature, immediately upon entering the house, the person assigned this task was to remove the sandals from the feet of the guest and then wash the feet of the dust and grime of the road. The insult tendered toward Christ by Simon the Pharisee ignored Jesus in this respect, with no one washing His Feet.

Consequently, the Holy Spirit would attend to this common courtesy ignored by Simon, causing Jesus' Feet to be washed with the tears of this woman and then "*anointed*."

There is evidence that the other guests were not treated so harshly by Simon. As a sinner washed and anointed His Feet, likewise, sinners gave Him the only crown He wore — a crown of thorns. As the songwriter said, "*His Kingdom was in hearts alone!*"

THIS MAN ...

"Now when the Pharisee who had bidden Him saw it, he spoke within himself, saying, This Man, if He were a Prophet, would have known who and what manner of woman this is who touches Him: for she is a sinner" (Lk. 7:39).

The phrase, *"Now when the Pharisee who had bidden Him saw it,"* refers to the action of this woman. There is evidence that her weeping had been very quietly carried out, with her being as unobtrusive as possible. However, after a period of time, the Pharisee saw her and noted carefully her actions.

The phrase, *"He spoke within himself, saying,"* means that he reasoned in his own mind and concluded that Christ did not know what kind of woman this was. In other words, he was judging both Christ and the woman, and very wrongly we might add. Judgment on appearances only is almost always wrong. And yet, so few are spiritual enough not to commit this sin, for sin it is!

A PROPHET?

The phrase, *"This Man, if He were a Prophet,"* portrays the fact that Simon the Pharisee had noted all the great Miracles performed by Christ but, yet, had not made up his mind if He was genuine or not! In no way had he even remotely come to the conclusion that Jesus might be the Messiah, only *"if He were a Prophet?"*

As we have repeatedly stated, all the things that really pointed to the Messiah, which were abundantly given in the Scriptures, were obvious in Christ but ignored by these unbelievers. The Jews had envisioned a Messiah Who would use His Power to overthrow Rome and make them the leading Nation in the world once again, as in the days of Solomon. Their view was completely unscriptural but, yet, a view held by almost all of the religious elite. So, by knowing this Man was a Peasant from the despised town of Nazareth, in Simon's mind, it meant that He could not be the Messiah. This little incident with the weeping woman only goes to prove what he had already thought.

SHE IS A SINNER

The phrase, *"Would have known who and what manner of woman this is who touches Him: for she is a sinner,"* proclaims the judgment made by this man of both Jesus and the woman.

He was wrong on both counts.

Jesus did know what manner of woman this was; however, this is the very reason He came.

Religion is untouchable. In its self-righteousness, it wants nothing which will embarrass it.

To the contrary, Jesus accepts any and all who come to Him. In reality, which speaks of the Eyes of God, Simon the Pharisee was in far worse spiritual condition than this poor woman, which the Holy Spirit is very careful to delineate.

And yet, this Pharisee had an impeccable reputation in the city while the reputation of this woman, as is obvious, was not too good, to say the least.

No! This does not mean that all who profess Salvation are like Simon the Pharisee and, therefore, worse than a woman of the streets, if, in fact, that is what she was. It does mean that many fall into that category, and, as well, God looks on the heart while men judge from appearances.

Also, whatever the woman had been, the moment she touched Jesus, her heart was totally changed, which, in effect, would change her life.

So, it was not a vile woman who touched Jesus, but rather one who had in the past been so. We must remember, Believers have no past.

This proclaims to all how quickly the Grace of God can change an individual.

However, all self-righteous Pharisees, as Simon, would, no doubt, demand a long period of penance, or some such trial period, before her Testimony could be accepted, if ever.

Jesus accepted her immediately and if the truth be known, she was probably never accepted by the religious establishment. I wish it were possible to say that the situation has presently changed; however, it is doubtful that it has changed at all.

THE WORDS OF JESUS

"And Jesus answering said unto him, Simon, I have somewhat to say unto you. And he said, Master, say on" (Lk. 7:40).

Verse 40 concerns the Answer of the Lord to this attitude and should be heeded by all because it is meant for all. The Holy Spirit told Jesus what the man was thinking.

The phrase, *"And he said, Master, say on,"* is laced with sarcasm and little expects the words of wisdom he will receive.

He has already revealed the unbelief of his heart by using the words of Verse 39, *"This Man, if He were a Prophet ...."*

TWO DEBTORS

"There was a certain creditor who had two debtors: the one owed five hundred pence, and the other fifty" (Lk. 7:41).

Verse 41 refers to a moneylender who had loaned different sums of money to two individuals. This type of business was provided by the Law but regulated strictly to assure justice (Ex. 22:25-27; Lev. 25:14-17, 35-37; Deut. 23:19-20; 24:6-17).

Actually, all debts were to be forgiven to brethren every seven years under the Mosaic Law, but not to strangers (Ex. 21:2-6; Deut. 15:1-3). Christian lending is on a different basis (Mat. 5:42; Lk. 6:34).

This illustration used by Jesus was something well-known in Jewish life and would have been readily understood by all present.

The phrase, "*The one owed five hundred pence, and the other fifty,*" would have been worth about $20,000 and $2,000 respectively in 2013 dollars.

WHO WILL LOVE HIM THE MOST?

"*And when they had nothing to pay, he frankly forgave them both. Tell me therefore, which of them will love him most?*" (Lk. 7:42).

Verse 42 pertains to the fact that when the debt was due, the two debtors, large and small, could not pay.

The phrase, "*He frankly forgave them both,*" refers to the creditor writing off the debts.

Jesus is likening the "*creditor*" to God and the "*two debtors*" as sinners in debt to God and, irrespective of the amount, owing a sum they could not even begin to hope to pay.

They were both sinners before God and both equally insolvent in His Eyes.

Whether the debt was much or little, it was to the Almighty Creditor a matter of comparative indifference — He frankly forgave them both (better, "*freely forgave of His Generous Bounty*").

The question, "*Tell me therefore, which of them will*

love him most?" now comes to the point illustrated by the Parable. In the Mind of Jesus, the larger debt pictured the terrible catalogue of sins which the penitent woman acknowledged she had committed; the smaller, the few transgressions which even the Pharisee might have confessed to having been guilty of.

It should be understood that Jesus was appealing to this man on his own level. Without a doubt, God would have judged it the other way around, with the sins of this man the blacker of the two.

So, even on the level of the Pharisee, he would be forced to admit the rightness of the Action of Christ plus the response of this dear woman.

TO WHOM HE FORGAVE MOST

"Simon answered and said, I suppose that he, to whom he forgave most. And He said unto him, You have rightly judged" (Lk. 7:43)

Simon's answer was actually the only answer which could be obviously given.

The phrase, *"And He said unto him, You have rightly judged,"* in effect, judged himself.

There is no hatred like religious hatred. In fact, it was self-righteousness which nailed Christ to the Cross. If the Believer does not place his or her faith exclusively in Christ and the Cross, self-righteousness will always be the concluding result.

Sad to say, this means that this modern church is the most self-righteous of anytime back to the Reformation.

SEE THIS WOMAN ...

"And He turned to the woman, and said unto Simon, Do you see this woman? I entered into your house, you gave Me no water for My Feet: but she has washed

My Feet with tears, and wiped them with the hairs of her head" (Lk. 7:44).

The phrase, *"And He turned to the woman,"* records the first instance of Jesus acknowledging the woman in any way.

The question, *"And said unto Simon, Do you see this woman?"* places the woman in an entirely different light than the manner in which she was spoken of by Simon. In effect, how many millions has the Lord spoken of just as this is a trophy of Grace!

The phrase, *"I entered into your house, you gave Me no water for My Feet,"* proclaims the studied insult now being noted.

The reader should take into account the entirety of this scenario as it portrays the heart action of all, whether good or bad.

As we have stated, it was the custom for a servant to wash the feet of guests upon arrival, which Simon had neglected to do with Jesus.

"But she has washed My Feet with tears, and wiped them with the hairs of her head," proclaims the Holy Spirit rebuking the insult of this man by this act of courtesy being carried out in the most beautiful and wonderful way.

Even if Simon had seen to it that a servant washed the Feet of Jesus, there would have been no kindness in the action, only courtesy. However, this Pharisee did not bother with even this most common act.

While the world, or even most of that which calls itself *"church,"* gives Jesus little honor, as here, multiple tens of millions drawn by the Holy Spirit praise and worship Him as the Lord of Glory and the Saviour of their souls.

Consequently, this scenario is a perfect picture of the church as a whole, which gives Jesus little credence, if any at all, and the true regard in worship He receives at the hands of those who have felt His Glorious Touch.

KISSING THE FEET OF JESUS

*"You gave Me no kiss: but this woman since the time
I came in has not ceased to kiss My Feet"* (Lk. 7:45).

The short phrase, *"You gave Me no kiss,"* was, as
well, a custom that men greeted each other with a kiss
on the cheek (Gen. 27:27; 29:13; 33:4; 45:15; 48:10;
Ex. 4:27; 18:7; I Sam. 20:41; Lk. 15:20; Acts 20:37).

As well, this common courtesy, no doubt, extended
to others, was not extended that day to Jesus.

As we have stated, the possibility definitely existed
that this man's actions would be reported to other
Pharisees in Jerusalem. Consequently, in front of
these eyes, he must portray a cold distance.

Unfortunately, this practice did not die with the
Pharisees of old. I have marveled as I have watched
modern preachers do the same with my own person,
concerned that someone might report to denominational
heads that they had shown me an act of kindness of
some sort.

As a result, they had to make certain that nothing
but coldness was extended because of man fear.

Such is not Christianity! Such is religion, pure and
simple. It serves men instead of God.

The phrase, *"But this woman since the time I came
in has not ceased to kiss My Feet,"* has a meaning far
greater than meets the eye.

Simon would not kiss the Face of Jesus, denoting, at
least of Christ, His Kingship. However, the Holy Spirit
had the woman to kiss the *"Feet"* of Jesus, denoting
His Authority, Power, and Rule (Lk. 10:19).

ANOINTING THE FEET OF JESUS

*"My Head with oil you did not anoint: but this woman
has anointed My Feet with ointment"* (Lk. 7:46).

The phrase, "*My Head with oil you did not anoint,*" presented another custom of that day.

Anointing with olive oil mixed with fragrant and costly spices was customary in the coronation of kings (II Kin. 11:12), installing High Priests (Ps. 133:2), and an act of courtesy and hospitality toward guests (Deut. 28:40; Ps. 23:5; 92:10; 105:15).

As well, this particular scenario had a spiritual application in that Simon, by not anointing the Head of Jesus, in effect, was saying that he did not believe that Jesus was the Messiah, i.e., The Head.

The phrase, "*But this woman has anointed My Feet with ointment,*" has the same connotation as the last phrase in the previous Verse. With the Holy Spirit having this woman anoint the Feet of Jesus, He was saying by symbolism that despite what Simon believed, or the whole of the religious elite of Israel for that matter, Jesus was anointed by the Holy Spirit as the Messiah (Lk. 4:18).

Whether Simon fully understood what Jesus was saying is anyone's guess! Actually, in his spiritual state of attempting to please man and God, he would conclude by pleasing no one.

HER SINS ARE FORGIVEN

"*Wherefore I say unto you, Her sins, which are many, are forgiven; for she loved much: but to whom little is forgiven, the same loves little*" (Lk. 7:47).

Verse 47 presents a statement of startling proportions to all who were present that day. Who is this Man Who can forgive sins?

In essence, Jesus was performing that which only the Messiah could actually do, which Simon had denied and Jesus now declared. When He said these words, what the woman had already felt now became a reality.

She was forgiven of all her sins, which only God could do.

The phrase, *"For she loved much,"* does not mean that she was forgiven because she first loved. The last Verse tells us her *"Faith"* caused her to be Saved, as it causes all to be Saved!

What is wanting in order to love much is not sin but the knowledge of it.

Salvation is a heart experience, as this example portrays. Her Salvation was probably brought about in this manner: Already sickened by her present lifestyle, she came in search of Christ, and those who truly search for Him will truly find Him.

The moment she came into His Presence, her heart reached out to Him.

This is expressed in her Repentance, which is portrayed, at least in this instance, through her emotion. She began to weep, as stated, probably for a mixture of sadness and joy. At that moment, she was Saved, and without her actually uttering a word.

To be sure, the confession, no doubt, quickly followed (Rom. 10:9-10). Jesus announcing that her sins were forgiven was the result of an act already performed.

Her *"loving much,"* which was expressed in her acts of kindness of washing His Feet with her tears and anointing His Head with ointment, was a result of what He had already done.

Consequently, she *"loved much!"*

TO WHOM LITTLE IS FORGIVEN, THE SAME LOVES LITTLE

The heading does not mean that Simon or others like him only have a few sins to be forgiven, but that they will little admit, as this woman, that their sins are many. Consequently, most of their sins, which they will not admit to because of their self-righteousness, are not forgiven.

Though this Pharisee was very religious, his life, in fact, was disfigured with censoriousness, narrowness, harshness, and pride, really the sins of self-righteousness — the many faults of his class.

As we have stated, the Lord implies in His Sad Irony that the little forgiveness which Simon had received was his own fault, for he did not think in his self-righteousness that he had any need to be forgiven. Therefore, he *"loved little,"* which is obvious in his treatment of Christ.

Regrettably, much, if not most, of the church world falls into that same category.

Religious self-righteousness, resulting from religious pride, can never admit its true state but must always hold up the façade of a proposed righteousness, which, in fact, is only self-righteousness.

Self-righteousness comes through the flesh while the Righteousness of God comes through the Cross and our Faith in that Finished Work of Christ.

YOUR SINS ARE FORGIVEN

"And He said unto her, Your sins are forgiven" (Lk. 7:48).

The phrase, *"And He said unto her,"* means that He had made the announcement of her sins being forgiven to Simon and others in the room but not directly to her. Now, He speaks directly to her!

The phrase, *"Your sins are forgiven,"* is said without any attachment. In other words, no penance was required and no religious works counseled. It was done, a Finished Work!

As well, it should be quickly added that this woman was Saved without Water Baptism.

Even though this Ordinance is important, and every true Believer will engage in such after Conversion, still, the act within itself of Water Baptism plays absolutely no part whatsoever in the Salvation process. That, as we have stated, is *"by Faith alone."*

Water Baptism is to portray the fact that one has already been Saved.

WHO IS THIS WHO FORGIVES SINS ALSO?

"And they who sat at meat with Him began to say within themselves, Who is this Who forgives sins also?" (Lk. 7:49).

Verse 49 portrays the exclamation of all the guests at His Telling the woman that her sins were forgiven.

The question, *"Who is this Who forgives sins also?"* refers to the fact that only God can forgive sins. This should have told them and, in fact, did tell them that Jesus was the Messiah.

YOUR FAITH HAS SAVED YOU

"And He said to the woman, Your Faith has saved you; go in peace" (Lk. 7:50).

The phrase, *"And He said to the woman,"* now proclaims the cause of her Salvation, which was her Faith in Christ.

As well, this was a rebuke to Simon the Pharisee and others like him who were trying to earn their Salvation by their religious works, as does much, if not most, of the modern church.

God's Will is that the guiltiest, who believe upon the Son of His Love, should enjoy assurance of Salvation and the conscious forgiveness of sin.

Jesus did not say to the woman, *"Your love has saved you,"* or *"Your tears have saved you,"* but *"Your*

Faith has saved you."

The phrase, *"Go in peace,"* should have been translated, *"Go into peace."*

The *"peace"* that one receives upon the acceptance of Christ is that which comes as a result of the enmity between God and man being taken away.

Man fell because he sinned against God. In other words, God did not wrong man; man wronged God! As a result of this wrong, an *"enmity"* developed in man's heart, which means hatred against God.

There is a perpetual war with God in the heart of the unbeliever, which necessitates the absence of peace. Never having had peace, unredeemed man does not really realize this terrible loss.

As well, the word, *"Enmity,"* which means, *"Hatred,"* refers not only to man hating God, but God hating the sin and rebellion in man, which has brought about this terrible condition.

THE CROSS

To remedy this terrible situation, at least to those who will believe, Jesus Christ, by His Death at Calvary, restored to man the peace that was lost.

Consequently, Paul said:

"For He is our Peace (*meaning Jesus*), **Who has made both one** (*made Jew and Gentile one and God and man one*), **and has broken down the middle wall of partition between us** (*the sin and its penalty which caused the rupture*)."

Paul then said:

"Having abolished in His Flesh (*Jesus' Death at Calvary*) **the enmity** (*hatred*), **even the**

Law of Commandments contained in Ordinances (*abolished the Law which pointed out man's sin*); **for to make in Himself of twain one new man** (*neither Jew nor Gentile but one in Christ*), **so making peace** (*He took away the sin and penalty which was causing the war*)" **(Eph. 2:14-17)**.

Upon acceptance of Christ, the enmity and hatred stop, which means the war has stopped, with "*peace*" being instantly given.

Without a doubt, the "*peace*," which instantly comes upon acceptance of Christ, is the greatest sign of all. This takes place in one's spirit when that person is Saved, hence, the term, "*Making peace with God.*"

The only thing that can destroy this peace or take it away is sin. Sin, which caused the offense against God to start with, continues to function in the same manner as at the beginning if it is committed after Salvation.

That is the reason a heavy weight returns to the Believer if sin is committed and not confessed with Repentance engaged (I Jn. 1:9).

However, the moment proper confession to the Lord is made, the "*peace*" returns!

This woman who came to Jesus that day had never known true "*peace*," as no unbeliever has ever known "*peace*."

However, despite her many sins and because of her Faith in Christ, she left with "*peace*" while Simon the Pharisee, although very religious, had no peace at all because he did not know God despite his claims.

"*Blest be the tie that binds*
"*Our hearts in Christian love;*
"*The fellowship of kindred minds*
"*Is like to that above.*

*"Before our Father's Throne
"We pour our ardent prayers;
"Our fears, our hopes, our aims are one,
"Our comforts and our cares.*

*"We share our mutual woes,
"Our mutual burdens bear;
"And often for each other flows
"The sympathizing tear.*

*"When we asunder part,
"It gives us inward pain;
"But we shall still be joined in heart,
"And hope to meet again."*

Great
Women
OF THE
BIBLE

NEW TESTAMENT

Chapter Six

THE WOMAN WITH
THE ISSUE OF BLOOD

THE WOMAN WITH THE ISSUE OF BLOOD

"And a woman having an issue of blood twelve years, who had spent all her living upon physicians, neither could be healed of any" (Lk. 8:43).

The phrase, *"And a woman having an issue of blood twelve years,"* probably referred to a female disorder, which seemed to rupture constantly.

Due to this sickness, this woman was ceremonially unclean according to Leviticus 15:19.

It is worthy of note that the daughter of Jairus of the previous Chapter was *"12"* years old, while the woman of our subject had been sick *"12"* years.

While the sameness of these numbers may be mere coincidence, still, *"12"* represents God's Order of Government. If His Government had been clung to instead of what man presently had, the girl would not have been at the point of death or the woman sick, for there would have been no death or sickness.

In the coming Kingdom Age and forever, God's Government will once again be supreme, guaranteeing prosperity in every capacity such as man has never known before.

NO HELP FROM THE MEDICAL PROFESSION

The phrase, *"Who had spent all her living upon physicians, neither could be healed of any,"* was recorded by Luke, a physician himself (Col. 4:14).

Mark implies that these particular *"physicians"* knew they could not help her but treated her solely for the money.

There is even the intimation that whatever type of treatment they gave her not only did not help her but made the situation worse (Mk. 5:26).

At any rate, as there was no earthly remedy for her sickness, there is no earthly remedy for sin. However, there is a remedy, as we soon shall see!

TOUCH THE BORDER OF HIS GARMENT

"Came behind Him, and touched the border of His Garment: and immediately her issue of blood stanched" (Lk. 8:44).

The phrase, *"Came behind Him,"* was probably for several reasons. The crowd was large and if she had desired to personally speak with Jesus about her sickness, this had now become virtually impossible due to the press of the people.

However, while the throng definitely was a factor, due to her being ceremonially unclean, she was not even supposed to be in this crowd, for *"Whosoever touched her, or that she touched, would be unclean until nightfall"* (Lev. 15:19). So, she was faced with a dilemma, and what was she to do?

Tradition says that she lived out of town, and this may be the last time she would have the opportunity to be in the Presence of Jesus.

So, she evidently reasoned within her mind that she must take her chances and do whatever possible to receive Healing, irrespective of the consequences. She was dying anyway, and she had nothing to lose by what she was about to do.

She had already reasoned in her heart, which was, no doubt, instigated by the Holy Spirit, that if she could but touch Him, even the end of the blue tassels which hung upon the shawl thrown over His Shoulder, she would be immediately whole.

Furthermore, if she was behind Him, quite possibly, He would not know it, and she would be healed without her infraction being noticed.

JESUS

There is also evidence from Mark 5:27-28 that she had not even heard of Jesus before this time. This seems difficult to comprehend; however, we are told that the Greek Text bears it out.

Upon her arriving in Capernaum, for whatever reason, the talk seemed to be of nothing but Jesus. Consequently, in a short time, she would have known of His Healing Power.

Therefore, the moment the news came that He was expected shortly, as quickly as possible, she went to His Expected Place of Arrival, and so did hundreds, if not thousands, of others.

Even though the Text does not bear it out, the Presence of God must have emanated from Him to such an extent that Faith instantly detected it. Quite possibly, others were being healed as well. At any rate, Faith built within her heart, and, irrespective of the difficulties, Faith will always find a way.

The phrase, "*And touched the border of His Garment,*" pertained to one of the four tassels which formed part of the Jewish mantle, one of these so arranged as to hang down over the shoulder at the back. It was this one which the sufferer's fingers grasped. The blue of the tassel, which was worn by most men, reminded Israel that their help came from above and of their duty to keep the Law (Num. 15:28-41; Deut. 22:12).

Some have claimed that she was a Gentile and lived in Caesarea Philippi and that her name was Veronica. However, every indication is that she was Jewish, especially considering that she seemed to understand the spiritual value of this blue tassel.

The phrase, "*And immediately her issue of blood stanched,*" is stated by Mark that "*she felt in her body that she was healed of that plague*" (Mk. 5:29).

Whatever it was, she knew she was healed, and beyond the shadow of a doubt. Mark also said, *"And straightway the fountain of her blood was dried up,"* meaning that the flow did not merely stop, but rather what was causing it was completely healed (Mk. 5:29). In other words, it was a permanent cure, something she would never be troubled with again.

Of all the physicians she had come to, she had now come to the right One.

WHO TOUCHED ME?

"And Jesus said, Who touched Me? When all denied, Peter and they who were with him said, Master, the multitude throng You and press You, and You say, Who touched Me?" (Lk. 8:45).

The question, *"And Jesus said, Who touched Me?"* startled Peter because many were touching Jesus; however, He was not speaking of the many but of this lone individual.

How could He distinguish her touch from all the others? As well, what was different about her touch than the others? For Him to have noticed it in particular, there had to be something different. The difference was Faith!

While there were scores touching Him out of curiosity and with others not really knowing why they touched Him, this one was different because of the Faith she exhibited.

This means that one can literally feel Faith! It also means that Faith literally pulls from God that which is needed. In fact, I think one could say without fear of contradiction that it is the only commodity to which our Lord responds.

If one cannot please Him without Faith, then everything displeases Him which is faithless (Heb. 11:6).

HEALING

As well, we learn from this that what Jesus did for the people in the realm of Healing was not without price. To fully explain it I think would be impossible; however, with each Healing, there must have been a drain on Him in the physical, emotional, and spiritual sense. We do know that at certain times He was so physically exhausted from healing the sick that He could hardly stand. The Greek Text in Mark 4:36 bears that out.

The phrase, *"When all denied,"* refers to whoever was standing close to Jesus. It seems they did not exactly know what He was talking about.

The question, *"Peter and they who were with Him said, Master, the multitude throng You and press You, and You say, Who touched Me?"* is actually as much an exclamation as it is a question.

Peter affirms that scores are *"thronging and pressing"* Jesus, with them, it seems, having difficulty keeping any semblance of order. Consequently, Jesus' question perplexed them.

VIRTUE IS GONE OUT OF ME

"And Jesus said, Somebody has touched Me: for I perceive that virtue has gone out of Me" (Lk. 8:46).

The phrase, *"And Jesus said, Somebody has touched Me,"* speaks of a distinct type of touch other than the grabbing, striking type.

The phrase, *"For I perceive that virtue has gone out of Me,"* speaks of Power.

In other words, Power went out of Him the moment the woman touched Him in Faith. Several things can be learned from this:

• It is possible for people to touch the Lord even though He has not touched them.

What do we mean by that?

Jesus did not touch this woman; she touched Him. In that, we are given a very valuable lesson.

As an example, whenever individuals go forward for prayer in Church (or wherever), if Healing comes, or whatever, that is the same as the Lord touching us. However, if we do not receive what we have gone for following that course, there remains, as this woman of old, another alternative; we can touch the Lord.

This speaks of going before Him in intercessory prayer and continuing until the need is met. Admittedly, it may take time, as it often does.

However, we have His Promise that if we truly need certain things, in whatever capacity, if we will persist, He will do it. Luke, Chapter Eleven, especially bears this out. You may check that Chapter for more extended commentary; however, in brief, it tells us to "*knock until the answer comes.*" To be sure, this takes a greater degree of Faith than the Lord touching us; however, the spiritual benefits derived from such an excursion are of inestimable value, to say the least!

FAITH IN GOD

• Jesus, in the Incarnate State as a Human Being, although never ceasing to be God, still did not know this woman was in the crowd or even that she existed. And yet, by touching Him, she received her Healing.

This tells us that Faith in God is such a powerful factor that it could effect a tremendous result even though Jesus did not even know she was there.

Many Believers do not understand exactly how God looks at Faith. Our association with Him is based entirely on Faith. One could say without fear of contradiction that no other attribute is held so highly by God. Actually, every single thing that comes into notion in our relationship with the Lord is activated by Faith.

However, when we speak of Faith, we are not speaking of presumption. Many have mistaken the two. Faith in God is not a credit card to purchase anything we so desire but, in effect, the things He desires. The idea is that our relationship with Him is to be so close that we will only desire what He desires.

• We learn from this scenario that true Faith in God, even though faced with terrible obstacles exactly as this woman of old, will not allow those circumstances or difficulties to hinder. Such Faith in God refuses to look at the obstacles, but rather keeps its eyes fastened on the Object, which should always be Jesus (Heb. 12:2).

THE WOMAN

"And when the woman saw that she was not hid, she came trembling, and falling down before Him, she declared unto Him before all the people for what cause she had touched Him and how she was healed immediately" (Lk. 8:47).

The phrase, *"And when the woman saw that she was not hid,"* means that she evidently was trying to hide.

The phrase, *"She came trembling,"* was probably for several reasons.

First of all, it must have startled her that Jesus would stop, in essence, calling for her. Mark said, *"He looked round about to see her who had done this thing,"* meaning that He knew it was a woman who touched Him (Mk. 5:32).

Consequently, I think her fear was normal and something to which any of us would have responded in a similar manner.

As well, she knew that according to Levitical Law, she was unclean and as a consequence, was not supposed to be in this crowd, much less touching Him.

She knew that the Levitical Law stated that not only was she unclean, but all who touched her were unclean. Consequently, her fear, which caused the "*trembling,*" could well have been caused by this knowledge.

SHE FELL DOWN BEFORE HIM

The phrase, "*And falling down before Him,*" proclaims her stepping out from the crowd, falling on her knees at His Feet.

The phrase, "*She declared unto Him before all the people for what cause she had touched Him,*" meant that she explained her sickness, and to the extent that all knew she had been ceremonially unclean. She withheld nothing!

The phrase, "*And how she was healed immediately,*" relates what she told Jesus, which was heard by all, how that "*she felt in her body that she was healed of that plague*" (Mk. 5:29).

She may have been greatly concerned, which she, no doubt, was, regarding her being unclean due to her sickness, but she also knew that she was healed. So, in effect, she was no longer unclean because of her contact with Jesus.

YOUR FAITH HAS MADE YOU WHOLE

"*And He said unto her, Daughter, be of good comfort: your Faith has made you whole; go in peace*" (Lk. 8:48).

The phrase, "*And He said unto her, Daughter,*" proclaims a wonderful and beautiful statement.

At first, she was referred to as "*a woman*" (Vs. 43), and now she is referred to as "*Daughter,*" drawing our attention to several things:

• He now claims her as His Own.
• He makes her a part of the Family of God.

• She is not only healed physically but spiritually as well.

As someone has said, *"Yesterday, she was one of the Devil's nobodies, and now she is one of Heaven's somebodies!"*

The phrase, *"Be of good comfort,"* addresses itself to her fear concerning her previous uncleanliness. She need have no fear that anyone would judge her unclean now because all evidence of her uncleanness was gone. This is a perfect picture of the Redemption in Christ.

The phrase, *"Your Faith has made you whole; go in peace,"* refers to the pipeline which brought her Healing from the Lord.

As well, it must be hurriedly said that if her Faith made her whole, it will do the same for all who will believe. God is no respecter of persons; what He did for her, He will do for all (Acts 10:34).

The *"peace"* here given means that not only was the woman healed, but she was Saved also! There is a beautiful spiritual application in this illustration. It is as follows:

THE WOMAN WAS CHAINED

This speaks of being chained by sickness and, from the context, sin as well! She is typical of all the world that is chained by the maladies of darkness. In effect, all unbelievers are in a spiritual prison, which spills over into every facet of their lives.

Even though these were chains on this woman which could not be seen by the physical eye, nevertheless, they were chains.

As well, the entirety of the world is chained by alcohol, drugs, jealousy, envy, immorality, sickness, disease, fear, religion, etc.

Only Jesus, as here, can break those chains.

THE WOMAN WAS CHANGED

This was done by the Miracle-working Power of God.

Regrettably, the world turns to its own sources, which, in effect, can change nothing. The church follows suit far too often. Psychology has become the great change agent at the present; however, it cannot really change anything.

Only Faith in God and the Miracle-working Power of Christ can truly change a person. It is done by the person placing his Faith entirely in Christ and the Cross, which then gives the Holy Spirit latitude to work within his life. As this woman was instantly changed by touching Jesus, so have multiple millions of others been changed.

The Testimonies we have received into our office over the years number into the hundreds of thousands, if not millions, and are so remarkable that they defy description.

That and that alone, the Gospel of Jesus Christ, is the Answer.

THE WOMAN WAS CLAIMED

She was not only changed but was claimed into the Family of God. She was given a new life and even a new status. She was now a Child of God and, consequently, a member of the greatest Family on Earth.

Incidentally, tradition says the name of this woman was Veronica.

Eusebius, who lived about 350 years after Christ, is said to have seen the house in which this woman lived.

It was at Caesarea Philippi or Paneas, as it was sometimes called, and had at its door on a stone pedestal two brazen statues. One represented a woman kneeling, and the other, a man with his cloak over his shoulder and his hand stretched out toward the kneeling woman, representing Jesus.

It is also stated that this same woman gave the handkerchief to wipe the Face of Jesus as He carried the Cross up to Calvary.

"Oh Zion, haste, your mission high fulfilling,
"To tell to all the world that God is Light;
"That He Who made all nations is not willing
"One soul should perish, lost in shades of night.

"Behold how many thousands still are lying,
"Bound in the darksome prison house of sin,
"With none to tell them of the Saviour's Dying,
"Or of the life He died for them to win.

"Proclaim to every people, tongue and nation,
"That God in Whom they live and move is Love;
"Tell how He stooped to save His Lost Creation,
"And died on Earth that man might live above.

"Give of your sons to bear the Message glorious;
"Give of your wealth to speed them on their way;
"Pour out your soul for them in prayer victorious;
"And all you spend Jesus will repay."

Great Women OF THE BIBLE

NEW TESTAMENT

Chapter Seven

THE WOMAN AT JACOB'S WELL

THE WOMAN AT JACOB'S WELL

SAMARIA

"And He must needs go through Samaria" (Jn. 4:4).

The Israel of Jesus' Day was somewhat divided into some five sections. Judaea, which included Jerusalem, was at the southern extremity. Samaria bordered Judaea on the north and Galilee on the south. In other words, Samaria was between these two areas. Northeast of Galilee was Paneas, which bordered Decapolis to its south, the area of the 10 cities. Both of these, Paneas and Decapolis, were east of the Jordan River.

Another district called *"Perea"* was also east of the Jordan and extended up into the Decapolis area. It also bordered parts of Judaea and Samaria on the west. In addition, it extended south to approximately midpoint of the Dead Sea.

The Jews did not consider the Samaritans to be true Israelites, but rather a mixture of Gentiles and Jews, which was unacceptable. Consequently, there was a tremendous animosity between these people, with the greater amount seeming to be on the part of the Jews.

THE ORIGIN OF THE SAMARITANS

The origin of the Samaritans came about after the defeat of the northern kingdom of Israel by the Assyrians (II Ki., Chpt. 17).

With these Gentiles taking many Jews captive at that time, and with many Jews having fled after this defeat, the Assyrians populated the area with people from Babylon and other places (II Ki. 17:24).

These gradually intermixed with the Jews who were already there and others who later came back and were called *"Samaritans."*

This happened about 700 years before Christ.

About 332 B.C., the governor of Samaria under the Persians went over, it is stated, to the side of Alexander the Great, who gave him permission to build a temple on Mount Gerizim like the one built by Ezra in Jerusalem.

He built it for his son-in-law and made him High Priest. The Samaritans then established rival worship in Jerusalem and accepted the Pentateuch as their Bible.

The great controversy between the Jews and Samaritans, who the Jews considered to be half-breeds, was whether to worship on Gerizim or Moriah, the latter being where the Jewish Temple stood in Jerusalem.

As stated, the rivalry was great, with most Jews so despising the Samaritans that they would take the eastern route on the other side of the Jordan when traveling between Judaea and Galilee, even though it extended the journey some three days. However, as stated, Jesus ministered to the Samaritans, treating them the same as the Jews.

Consequently, He would go through the area at this time because it was the Will of His Heavenly Father. As such, one of the greatest Conversions ever would be brought about.

The idea is that the woman of this story could not come to Jesus, but Jesus came to her. The striking similarity exists with all.

We could not go to the Lord, but He came to us, with our situation so desperate, as this dear lady at Jacob's well.

JACOB AND JOSEPH

"Then comes He to a city of Samaria, which is called Sychar, near to the parcel of ground that Jacob gave to his son Joseph" (Jn. 4:5).

The place which was then called "*Sychar*" is said by some to refer to the ancient city of Shechem, while others claim it is a different town altogether.

Irrespective, it was near Jacob's well.

The phrase, "*Near to the parcel of ground that Jacob gave to his son Joseph*," proclaims, as is obvious, this spot having a long Bible history.

The Patriarch Jacob purchased this area from the children of Hamor. For this piece of land, he paid "*an hundred pieces of money*," however much that would be (Gen. 33:19).

Genesis, Chapter 48, Verses 17 through 22, records Jacob giving this portion "*to his son Joseph.*"

In Joshua, Chapter 24, Verse 32, we find the bones of Joseph were deposited there, even at his request (Gen. 50:25-26).

This was done because Joseph knew when dying that God would surely redeem Israel out of Egypt. He knew the Promise that God had made to Abraham, to Isaac, and to his father Jacob concerning this land of Canaan.

Here his people would grow into a great Nation and would ultimately bring the Messiah into the world.

Even though he had lived many years in Egypt, even as its viceroy, his heart was still in the Promised Land. There his Faith did reside, and now the very One in Whom his Faith was held sits on the very well dug by his father Jacob.

Jesus was the Author and Finisher of that Faith.

JACOB'S WELL

"*Now Jacob's well was there. Jesus therefore, being wearied with His Journey, sat thus on the well: and it was about the sixth hour*" (Jn. 4:6).

The phrase, "*Now Jacob's well was there*," proclaims

this historical sight being preserved, even as it is unto this day, some 2,000 years after Jesus and about 3,800 years after Jacob.

I have had the privilege of visiting this spot, which, with its valleys and hills, is one of the most beautiful in Israel. Inasmuch as wells are not easily moved, it is without question that this is the exact spot where Jesus ministered to the woman of Samaria.

The phrase, "*Jesus therefore, being wearied with His Journey, sat thus on the well,*" proclaims His Humanity. Hence, John impresses upon us the full Humanity, the Definite Human Existence of Jesus, even though He was "*the Only Begotten Son of the Father.*" He was "*the Word made flesh*" (Jn. 1:14).

JESUS

The Gospel of John alone records His Presence and Miracle at Cana, His travel-worn sympathy with our weakness, His Making Clay with spittle, consequently, bringing about the Miracle of Healing of the man born blind, His Weeping over the grave of a friend, His Thirst upon the Cross, the Blood that issued from His Wounded Side, and the obvious physical reality of His Risen Body, and thus furnishes the Church with the grounds on which the Apostle maintained His Divine Humanity (Reynolds).

The phrase, "*And it was about the sixth hour,*" has been argued as to its correct computation almost from the time it was written.

If John was using Jewish time, it would have been noon. However, if he was using Roman time, which, in one sense, seems to be the case, it would have been 6 a.m.

It is possible for Him to have been weary with His Journey at this time, but more than likely if it was noon.

THE WOMAN OF SAMARIA

"There comes a woman of Samaria to draw water: Jesus said unto her, Give Me to drink" (Jn. 4:7).

For the woman who came to the well that day to draw water, and who would meet Jesus, this day would prove to be the greatest moment of her life. As well, most of the water was drawn in the early morning in order to have a supply during the day. But yet, at times, some women, for it was women who drew the water during that particular time, would come to the well at a later time because of particular reasons. This is probably what happened here.

"Jesus said unto her, Give Me to drink," presents a startling moment for this woman inasmuch as most Jews, as she knew Jesus to be, would not even speak to a Samaritan, much less ask a favor.

Thus opens the scene at Jacob's well, which will prove to be one of the most amazing in human history. The dread Judge of both the quick and the dead and one of the vilest of sinners are met together.

However, He is there not to condemn her but to seek and to save her.

The Mighty God, the Everlasting Father, the Prince of Peace, was sitting weary by a well and thirsty but had no means even to quench His Thirst. He as Man was dependent on an outcast woman for a little water. His Grace and Love, rejected by Israel, now pour out their fullness upon an impure Samaritan — for love is pained unless enabled to act.

The floodgates of Grace lifted themselves up to bless the misery which love pitied.

Man's heart withered with self-righteousness cannot understand this. Thus, sinners respond to the Grace which Pharisees proudly refuse, for Grace flows in the deep channels dug by the misery of sin (*Williams*).

THE DISCIPLES

"For His Disciples were gone away unto the city to buy meat" (Jn. 4:8).

Either this was early in the morning, which would have been the case if John was using Roman time, or else at noon, which would have been the case if reckoned by Jewish time.

Even though most of the Disciples had gone into the city to purchase food, some expositors feel that John the Beloved, in fact, had remained behind with Jesus. It was John's custom not to mention himself in relating these experiences even though he was present.

Considering the detail to which he outlined this extremely interesting episode, it gives credence to the thought that he was present.

THE JEWS AND THE SAMARITANS

"Then said the woman of Samaria unto Him, How is it that You, being a Jew, ask drink of me, who is a woman of Samaria? for the Jews have no dealings with the Samaritans" (Jn. 4:9).

Verse 9 proclaims these two isolated hearts meeting — His isolated by Holiness, for He was separate from sinners, hers by sin, for she was separate from society — and this encounter of Holiness and sinfulness resulted in the Salvation of the sinner, for Jesus is *"the Saviour."*

Jesus, as well, was the patterned soul-winner. With Divine skill He led this defiled woman by five steps into the Kingdom of God.

These steps were: contact (Vs. 7); interest (Vs. 10); conscience (Vs. 16); Holiness (Vs. 24); and Revelation (Vs. 26).

He disarmed suspicion, opposition, and hostility and won sympathy and confidence in Faith by asking for a drink of water. This was the point of contact. It touched her nature as a woman — for it was the appeal of need — and to that appeal a woman's nature responds.

The tender word, "*Woman*," occurs 13 times in this incident. The number "*13*" is a happy one for Believers. At the thirteenth circuit, the walls of Jericho fell down, and in the "*thirteenth year*," Abraham won his great victory.

THE GREAT QUESTION

The question, "*How is it that You, being a Jew, ask drink of me, who is a woman of Samaria?*" proclaims that she knew He was a Jew by His Speech, Dress, and Appearance, which was different from the Samaritans.

She was perplexed that He would address her at all, much less ask of her a favor!

"*For the Jews have no dealings with the Samaritans*," referred to hospitality, for ordinary buying and selling were, in fact, carried on. While it was true that most "*Jews*" felt this way, Jesus did not entertain such animosity at all.

Racism, bias, and prejudice characterize the whole of humanity, at least those who do not know God. It is ugly and without merit and can be cured only by Christ. He cured it by example and, above all, by the Power of the changed heart, which He Alone can do.

That's the reason Paul said, "*There is neither Jew nor Greek, there is neither bond nor free, there is neither male nor female: for you are all one in Christ Jesus*" (Gal. 3:28).

THE GIFT OF GOD

"*Jesus answered and said unto her, If you knew the Gift of God, and Who it is Who says to you, Give Me to drink; you would have asked of Him, and He would have given you Living Water"* (Jn. 4:10).

Verse 10 proclaims Jesus arousing interest in this woman's heart, which should be the object of every Preacher.

The phrase, *"If you knew the Gift of God,"* proclaims Jesus as that Gift and the Salvation He Alone affords.

The tragedy is she did not know the Gift or anything about the Gift. She had some rudimentary knowledge of God, but it was only fragmentary, as is that of most of the world. She knew nothing of His Great Plan of Salvation for the human family in the sending of His Only Son to redeem mankind. *"... People are destroyed for lack of knowledge ..."* (Hos. 4:6).

On the other side of the coin, so to speak, it is our responsibility as Believers to take the Message of the Gift of God to the entirety of the world. God's Way is to anoint Preachers of the Gospel to take the Word. The Holy Spirit through Paul asks, *"... how shall they hear without a Preacher?"*

He then asks, *"And how shall they preach, except they be sent ...?"* (Rom. 10:14-15).

This means that not only must there be Preachers who are touched by God to take the Message, but, as well, those who remain behind must support them. For those whom God calls, He also calls an appropriate number to support them prayerfully and financially.

Presently, we have two problems.

PAUL

First of all, there aren't many who are truly Called of God to take the Message. Secondly, for the few who are truly Called, some of the time, it is difficult to get support. Sadly, this is not something new as it has always plagued the Work of God.

When Paul was in prison in Rome, he had difficulty finding someone who would go to Philippi. He said, *"For I have no man like-minded, who will naturally care for your state."*

He then said, *"For all seek their own, not the things which are Jesus Christ's"* (Phil. 2:20-21).

Concerning finances, he said, *"Now you Philippians know also, that in the beginning of the Gospel, when I departed from Macedonia, no Church communicated with me as concerning giving and receiving, but you only"* (Phil. 4:15).

Verse 10 also tells us that even the Philippians had stopped for a period of time, leaving the Apostle in very short supply.

So, it is not a new problem. The tragedy is, one day all of us will stand at the Judgment Seat of Christ. We will all answer for our lives lived in Christ respecting our work for Him. Then, a lot of things we thought very important here will have no significance there. As well, the things which were so very important and which had eternal consequences, we will find that too often we did not properly understand their worth.

LIVING WATER

The phrase, *"And Who it is Who says to you, Give Me to drink,"* proclaims her so close to Eternal Life, but yet, so far!

The phrase, *"You would have asked of Him, and He would have given you Living Water,"* proclaims Him asking her for water to slake the physical thirst while, in turn, He will give her *"Living Water,"* which will forever slake her spiritual thirst.

The phrase, *"Living Water,"* expressed Salvation apart from religious ceremony, which characterizes so much of the world.

In fact, Salvation is not in a church, ceremony, ritual, Ordinance, or even that which is labeled a "*Sacrament*," but only in Jesus.

Yet, in most places, it has been reduced to formality, ceremony, creed, culture, ritual, etc.

Multiple hundreds of millions wallow in religion all their lives, even as the Samaritans, and never really know God because they do not know His Son, the Lord Jesus Christ, Who Alone is the Way to the Father (Jn. 14:6).

As well, and as here described by none other than the Lord Himself, to obtain this "*Living Water*," all one has to do is "*ask*," and it is his for the asking.

If it is so simple, why is it so hard?

Millions attempt to earn it but fail, as fail they must. Others attempt to merit it but find only an empty heart.

A PERSONAL EXPERIENCE

Sometime back, I witnessed over television a Buddhist monk who had completed a seven-year regimen of physical torture and privation. It was an extreme regimen, so severe, in fact, that only a few in history had succeeded in finishing this torturous course. He was one of that few.

Consequently, quite a number of reporters were there from Japan, as well as elsewhere around the world, to record this momentous occasion.

When he came in from his last jaunt and crossed the threshold, which marked the finish line, the television cameras began to whirl, with scores attempting to touch him because he was now pronounced, "*Holy*."

A few minutes later, they interviewed him for the press. His answers were revealing.

When asked, "*How do you feel?*" he replied, "*I don't know!*"

"*Do you feel holy?*" they asked, because this regimen was supposed to make him a holy man after a successful completion.

"*I feel no different!*" he said. Then he added, "*I think I will begin another seven-year regimen!*"

He said that because there was no satisfaction, fulfillment, or anything, for that matter, that greeted him at the end of this torturous seven-year trek.

Most of the world, in one way or the other, attempt to find God or reach some particular status or place by similar actions of one type or the other. They serve a god of their own making, and, as such, this god of necessity must be inferior to its maker.

And yet, they try to improve themselves by that which is less than they already are.

THE WELL IS DEEP

"*The woman said unto Him, Sir, You have nothing to draw with, and the well is deep: from where do You get this Living Water?*" (Jn. 4:11).

The Eleventh Verse presents this woman thinking in material terms. She doesn't quite know what He is talking about, and yet, she is suspicious, but there is far more to this than material things, as her other questions portray.

In reality, He was the Only One on the face of the Earth Who could actually draw water from this well. Others have claimed to do so, as the fake luminaries of the past and the present, but none ever has because none can!

"*The well is deep,*" she said, and of that she was right, far deeper than even she imagined! It was and is so deep, in fact, that only God has plumbed its depths and reveals it to us only through His Son, the Lord Jesus Christ.

This is why Jesus *"needs go through Samaria."* He was searching for a lost soul who was evidently hungry for God and had not been satisfied. In fact, she could not be satisfied by the false worship of her religion.

WHERE DOES THIS LIVING WATER COME FROM?

Her question, *"From where do You get this Living Water?"* portrays her being drawn out spiritually, at least to a small degree. She is puzzled by His Statement, but yet, finds the phrase, *"Living Water,"* to be intriguing!

And yet, it is intriguing not merely as a matter of curiosity but more so toward the thirst of her soul. The phrase must have been the most beautiful she had ever heard, and, likewise, has it been to millions.

Living Water! What a symbolism; what a description!

Even as I dictate these words, I sense the Presence of God. It is as if I am there with her, standing nearby, and yet, close enough to hear these Glorious Words which came from the Lips of the Master. Somehow I know they are for me as well as for her.

That day, she would drink of that Well, that Spiritual Well, and she would find it to be exactly as He had said. Since that time, other millions have come, I among them. It is just as satisfying now as it was then.

This was to be the greatest day of her life, as the Day of Salvation is the greatest for all. She would meet Jesus, Who, in reality, is the *"Living Water,"* and she would never be the same again.

ARE YOU GREATER THAN JACOB?

"Are you greater than our father Jacob, who gave us the well, and drank thereof himself, and his children, and his cattle?" (Jn. 4:12).

The question of the Twelfth Verse proclaims to us

several things, with her being closer to the truth than even she realized.

In her question concerning Jacob, we observe the claims of the Samaritans to be a descendant of Ephraim, son of Joseph, and actually of Jacob himself who dug the well.

By her use of the pronoun, "*Our,*" she lays claim to the Patriarchs exactly as the Jews. They did not recognize her claim, but Jesus did, at least, in a limited sort of way.

The conclusion of the question, "*And drank thereof himself, and his children, and his cattle?*" pulls her back to material and even carnal things, which characterized the Samaritans. Their worship of God was based on a false premise and, therefore, unacceptable, as Jesus will soon relate. So, as millions do, she tries to link the "*Living Water*" with this ancient well!

How many millions of Catholics attempt to link God with a statue, a candle, a person such as the Pope, etc.?

How many Protestants attempt to link God with a church building or a particular religious denomination when, in reality, there is no connection?

Yes! Jesus was Greater than Jacob, far Greater, in fact, even than the Temple or the Sabbath. He is Greater than anything one could ever begin to name.

THE WATER OF THE WORLD NEVER SATISFIES

"*Jesus answered and said unto her, Whosoever drinks of this water shall thirst again*" (Jn. 4:13).

Verse 13 presents Jesus slowly leading the woman to the meaning of His Great Spiritual Truth.

As with Nicodemus, so with the Samaritan; the Lord hastened to raise the question of sin in the conscience. Nicodemus was highly moral and this Samaritan grossly immoral, yet there was no difference between them — both were sinners needing cleansing and Salvation.

However, how different was the Lord's Method with each of them! The moralist was at once met with the abrupt words, "*You must be Born-Again,*" but to the sinner, He said, "*Whosoever drinks of the water that I shall give him shall never thirst.*"

The phrase, "*Whosoever drinks of this water shall thirst again,*" presents one of the simplest, and yet, at the same time, one of the most profound statements ever uttered. While Jesus certainly was speaking of the water from Jacob's well, He was also speaking of all other efforts to slake the spiritual thirst in the soul by means other than Himself. Men attempt to slake that thirst with money, power, prestige, education, culture, accomplishments, achievements, and a host of other things, all to no avail!

As someone has said, "*The soul of man is so big that only God can fill it up!*"

A WELL OF WATER SPRINGING UP INTO
EVERLASTING LIFE

"*But whosoever drinks of the water that I shall give him shall never thirst; but the water that I shall give him shall be in him a well of water springing up into Everlasting Life*" (Jn. 4:14).

This statement, as given by Jesus, is so freighted, so weighted, and so all-encompassing that its potential could never be exhausted. The following is but a few of the great Truths it contains:

BUT ...

This conjunction links the hope of this Promise to the hopelessness of the previous statement.

It is such a short distance but has the length of Eternity.

The skeptic may ask, *"If Christ satisfies to such an extent, why is it that the entirety of the world does not accept Him?"* The answer is simple!

Men do not want to give up their sins, and they are deceived into believing that by coming to Christ, they will lose their pleasure and gain nothing. They do not realize that they will lose nothing and gain everything!

WHOSOEVER

All are lost, therefore, all can be Saved. None are excluded. When Jesus died on Calvary, He died for all of mankind for all time.

The hellish doctrine proposed by some of a *"limited Atonement,"* which means that Jesus died only for a few, and is an attempt to explain their erroneous concept of predestination, is, in fact, hellish indeed!

Jesus died for every single human being who has ever lived, who is alive now, and who shall live in the future. *"Whosoever"* means exactly what it says.

DRINKS

This means there is a part for man to play. God does not give Salvation to those who refuse to receive. The *"receiving"* is the *"drinking."*

Holding a glass of water before someone will never slake his thirst. Irrespective as to how clear and cold it may be, they must drink of it. The Psalmist said, *"O taste and see that the LORD is good ..."* (Ps. 34:8).

OF THE WATER

Here Jesus uses *"water"* as a symbolism for Salvation, and an apt symbolism it is!

He has called it, *"Living Water!"*

THAT I SHALL GIVE HIM

Jesus Alone is the Purveyor of this *"Living Water!"*

As well, it is *"given"* free of charge and as the Prophet said, *"... without money and without price"* (Isa. 55:1).

In fact, if one tries to merit, earn, or purchase this *"Living Water,"* one automatically forfeits its possession. However, if one comes to Christ, knowing that he deserves nothing good, throwing himself on God's Mercy and Grace, and trusting in Jesus to save, he will be given Eternal Life because Salvation is a *"Gift."*

SHALL NEVER THIRST

This is an unconditional guarantee. It means the searching is over, and the Pearl of Great Price has been found, but yet, given free of charge. In fact, there is nothing else in the world, irrespective of its content, which can satisfy or slake the thirst of the human heart. Only that which Jesus gives satisfies; consequently, it is priceless!

BUT THE WATER THAT I SHALL GIVE HIM
SHALL BE IN HIM

This speaks of the difference in man's efforts and God's Remedy.

Man attempts to assuage his problem by external means, which are the only means he has. Consequently, he tries to rehabilitate, which is impossible!

Why?

Cancer cannot heal cancer, and weakness cannot cure weakness. Sin cannot cleanse from sin, and death cannot save from death, with but one exception.

I speak of the Death of the Lord Jesus Christ, the Lord of Glory, Who provided the Perfect Sacrifice that in His Death, we might find Life, even as He is Life. The Lord begins with a heart, consequently, *"In Him!"*

A WELL OF WATER SPRINGING UP INTO EVERLASTING LIFE

This speaks of a continuous fountain. In effect, and in a spiritual sense, Jesus is saying, *"I do not give a simple 'drink of water' but I cause a spring, a perennial fountain, a river of Divine pleasure to issue and flow from that inward satisfaction which follows a reception of My Gift; and it is so abundant that it is enough for everlasting needs. The water that I give becomes a fountain, and the fountain swells into a river, and the river expands into and loses itself in the great ocean of eternity"* (Reynolds).

However, we are never to conclude that the Divine Life, once given, becomes consciously a self-dependent force within the soul. This would not be justified by all the analogy of the Divine working in humanity, which, though abundant and satisfying, never repudiates its Divine Source, the Lord Jesus Christ, but continually proclaims Him.

In effect, Jesus is saying that this fullness of the Gift of God transcends all the needs of this life and is enough for eternity and more!

Hallelujah!

NO FULFILLMENT IN THE WORLD

The great problem with the world, which characterizes the whole of humanity, is that this Creation of God, called mankind, attempts to find fulfillment in its work, in the husband or wife, with money, or whatever, for that matter! It never works as it cannot work.

That is the reason that many marriages dissolve. The husband attempts to make his wife fulfill all his needs, and many wives attempt to make their husbands fulfill all their needs.

As always, one demands more of the other than could ever be given; consequently, the marriage breaks down.

As well, most people attempt to find fulfillment in religion. However, religion without Christ can never satisfy.

That is the reason Jesus spoke of *"thirsting again,"* as all do who attempt to fulfill themselves by means other than that which is provided by the Lord.

When one fully knows Jesus, making Him the Lord of one's life, irrespective of where one is or what one does or doesn't have, one is automatically and instantly fulfilled in every way.

While it is true that man does need bread for physical sustenance, still, he does not live by that alone, *"... but by every Word which proceeds out of the Mouth of God"* (Mat. 4:4).

Jesus can take the place of anything, but nothing can take the place of Jesus.

The world does not understand the elderly woman who lives alone with barely enough to keep body and soul together, and yet, exhibits a satisfaction and joy which are totally unexplainable to those who do not know Jesus. They brush it off as a poor individual who is simple-minded and, consequently, does not really know how bad off she is.

No! She and millions like her are not simple-minded. Actually, they have been *"transformed by the renewing of their minds, that they may now prove what is that good, and acceptable, and Perfect Will of God"* (Rom. 12:2).

GIVE ME THIS WATER ...

"The woman said unto Him, Sir, give me this water,

that I thirst not, neither come here to draw" (Jn. 4:15).

The phrase, *"The woman said unto Him, Sir, give me this water,"* proclaims that she now had some understanding, although faint, of what Jesus was speaking. She sensed that it was not literal water of which He spoke, but rather something else altogether.

The Words that Jesus gave unto her spoke of *"Living Water."* He stated that upon the reception of such Water, one would never *"thirst again"* and, as well, it would be perpetually in them, *"springing up unto Everlasting Life."*

Without a doubt, these Words were accompanied with a strong and powerful Anointing of the Holy Spirit. Jesus had already stated that He was *"anointed to preach the Gospel to the poor (meek)"* (Lk. 4:18).

Consequently, she was greatly moved by this Anointing, with the Holy Spirit thrusting the meaning of these words deep into heart. Of course, her understanding would have been shallow.

Nevertheless, considering Who spoke these words, she probably had more knowledge then, even in a moment's time, concerning true Salvation, than most others in Israel at that time.

THAT I NEVER THIRST AGAIN

The phrase, *"That I thirst not,"* which was heavily anointed by the Holy Spirit, no doubt, caused her to see, although weakly, that this pertained to spiritual thirst and had no relationship with literal water. As stated, her knowledge would have been scant; however, the Holy Spirit is able to reveal things very quickly, especially if the heart is open, as hers undoubtedly was.

Just the other day while watching one of the network news programs, the commentator was addressing himself to the inner city gangs and the terrible difficulties of trying to reach these young men and women. They portrayed one young man who had just been shot in the neck and had miraculously survived. The ugly scar was very visible and portrayed the seriousness of a close brush with death.

As they questioned this young black man, possibly about 18 years old, his answers were far beyond his years. Briefly, he began to relate how he now looked at things totally differently.

They then cut away to a shot of him praying, and the thing that amazed me was this:

THE PRAYER

I had no knowledge of his past but surmised that he probably had not had much spiritual instruction in his life since he had been raised in the inner city and ran with this gang for years. I imagine that he knew only immorality, drug-taking, violence, and bloodshed, but I was pleasantly surprised as I heard him pray for a few moments.

He began to say, *"Lord, I come to You, not with my own good works or merit, but according to Your Grace,"* or words to that effect! The point I wish to make is this:

In a very short period of time, the Holy Spirit had revealed to him that which most never learn in a lifetime.

Irrespective of his background, which certainly was not conducive to the Ways of the Lord, the Spirit of God had portrayed to him what Salvation was all about and what it meant to be truly Saved.

As stated, I was amazed at the spiritual depth he exhibited in these few words I heard him pray. He was far ahead of most church members who have been raised in church all their lives.

The reason is, the Holy Spirit had brought about this miraculous change in this young man's life as he had accepted Jesus as his Lord and Saviour.

The reason most church members have little knowledge of what I am speaking is because the Holy Spirit is not present in most churches simply because He is ignored or else downright denied.

However, where the Holy Spirit has an opportunity, irrespective as to whom that person may be or what his background, in a moment's time, as Faith acts on the Word of God, Jesus Christ comes into the heart, with the Holy Spirit revealing Him to that person's soul. Actually, this is the Miracle of the New Birth. This is the reason it is not intellectual, philosophical, or psychological. It is spiritual and, therefore, a Work carried out entirely by the Person and Office of the Holy Spirit. He Alone can reveal Jesus to the heart and life as He acts upon the Word of God.

CONVERSION

So, the Conversion of this woman is not nearly as strange as some would think, that is, if they know and understand the Moving and Operation of the Holy Spirit. In truth, all come the same way. The Spirit of God moves upon the spoken Word of God, and Jesus is made real to the heart.

All of a sudden, as Jesus spoke these Words, the Holy Spirit took them like an arrow straight to her heart. In a moment's time, He revealed to her the great need of her life and, as well, at least to a certain degree, what Jesus was actually saying.

The truth is this woman had thirsted all her life. Her immorality had not slaked that thirst, and neither did her many husbands.

As well, the religion of the Samaritans gave her no satisfaction at all.

She was a thirsty woman, but not for that which this

world gives, but that which only God can give.

The same can be said for every single person in the world who follows heathenistic religions or even the part of Christianity which is apostate.

In these religions, of whatever stripe, there is no satisfaction, no fulfillment, no development, and above all, no power to help them break the bondages of darkness and the terrible grip of sin.

Only Jesus Christ and what He did for us at the Cross can accomplish that.

A PERSONAL EXPERIENCE

Some years ago, a woman questioned me rather sarcastically as to why I did not cease my activities respecting the spreading of the Gospel to the world. She said, *"These people have their own religion, and they are happy with it. Leave them alone and quit trying to force your religion down their throats,"* or words to that effect.

The sadness of this is that this woman called herself a Christian. I'm afraid my answer to her was somewhat cryptic.

While it is true that these people do have their religions, it is also true that these religions are of the Devil and can never even think of slaking the thirst that's in the human heart. Actually, religion only makes it worse. There is only One Answer to that dilemma, and that is Jesus.

No! I will never leave them alone because in doing so, such would consign them to a Devil's Hell forever and forever. That is the reason Jesus said, *"... Go ye into all the world, and preach the Gospel to every creature"* (Mk. 16:15).

Actually, I seriously doubt this woman who made this statement to me was Saved. I cannot understand how anyone could really and truly know Jesus Christ and be so ignorant in spiritual things as to make the statements she did.

Tragically, much of Christendom falls into the same category.

Even though most do not express themselves as this poor deceived soul, still, by their actions of unconcern and apathy, they are saying the same thing that she said.

TO DRAW THE WATER?

The phrase, *"Neither come here to draw,"* proclaims that she knew He was not talking about literal water. In other words, it could not be secured from this particular well even though having once belonged to the great Patriarch, *"Jacob,"* or any other well, for that matter.

Regrettably, many in modern Christendom, that is, if one is to call them Christian, seem to not know nearly as much as this woman of so long ago. For instance, Catholicism is rife with religious *"things,"* whether real or imagined.

Martin Luther said that one of the things that turned him off so terribly to Roman Catholicism, even though he was a priest in that false religion, was the trip he took to Rome in order to visit the Vatican. He said he saw wagonload after wagonload of bones being brought to Rome, with someone claiming these were the bones of particular Saints who had long since died, etc.

In Israel presently, a Catholic church or Greek Orthodox is built over most holy sights, or at least nearby. In other words, *"Jacob's well"* is big business and always has been; however, as the true Jacob's well brought no Salvation then, neither does it bring any now. And yet, millions try to *"draw"* from these decrepit examples of the past but ever come up empty.

However, when Jesus comes to the place, or any

place for that matter, then and then alone is Salvation procured.

Jacob's well actually played no part; it just happened to be the place where this occurred.

JESUS SAID TO HER ...

"Jesus said unto her, Go, call your husband, and come here" (Jn. 4:16).

The woman's sin was now to be dealt with, hence, Jesus telling her, *"Go, call your husband."*

When you have a profession of Faith in Christ that ignores the question of sin, the Holiness of God, the spirituality of worship as distinct from sacerdotal ceremonies, the need of pardon, and the condition of trust in an Atoning and Revealed Saviour, such a profession is worthless.

The words, *"And come here,"* have a far greater meaning than geographical location or obedience to a particular request.

The idea behind the request or demand pertained to the impossibility of a mere human being resolving the terrible bondages of sin which plague the human family.

The world of psychology attempts to deal with these problems in many and varied ways. It attempts to shift blame and responsibility to sources other than the individual, such as things which happen to one as a child.

In some cases, psychology teaches that the thing is wrong only because the person thinks it's wrong.

In other words, they must feel good about themselves, irrespective of what has been done, and then the guilt will go away, etc.

This speaks of subjective truth, which, in reality, is no truth at all.

PSYCHOLOGY

There is no answer in psychology. It is a bankrupt system which was conceived in the heart of unregenerate man. It proclaims a basic turning away from the God of the Bible and ridicules Jesus Christ as the Answer and Solution to the ills and problems of mankind.

So, it is impossible for one to serve God, trust and depend on Him, and look to His Word for Leading and Guidance and, at the same time, trust the foolishness of man-derived psychology.

It is like evolution! One cannot believe in evolution and God at the same time. Some may claim they can, but they only do so out of ignorance, which results in no faith at all.

This woman could not go back and bring all her husbands to Jesus or the terrible details of a sordid misused and misspent life. However, she could bring the sin to Jesus, and this is what He really desired of her. It must be dealt with, and now would be dealt with, but not in condemnation.

A HUSBAND?

"The woman answered and said, I have no husband. Jesus said unto her, You have well said, I have no husband" (Jn. 4:17).

The phrase, *"The woman answered and said, I have no husband,"* presents a truth, but only partially so!

Undoubtedly, she suspected what was about to happen; her life of misery, immorality, and reckless living was about to be revealed.

The Gospel always exposes sin. As a result, it glaringly portrays its horror and bondage. In doing so, it reveals to the heart of man exactly what he is, a sinner, lost and undone without God.

Men do not enjoy facing up to these realities. Actually, it is something they will not do unless moved upon strongly by the Holy Spirit. Men love to blame others for their dilemma, even as Adam blamed God, and Eve blamed the serpent. The Gospel places the blame where it rightly belongs, squarely in the heart of the individual being dealt with.

This is why neither psychology nor any other philosophy of man can even hope to compare with that which is done by the Holy Spirit by the Word of God. Being human, even the best of us, whomever that may be, only sees the outward. The Lord sees the heart and judges accordingly!

NO HUSBAND?

The phrase, *"Jesus said unto her, You have well said, I have no husband,"* bores to the very heart of her problem. It speaks to her domestic and spiritual life and points out her problem and the solution.

Every problem has a solution. However, to all matters pertaining to behavior and irrespective as to direction, the solution is spiritual, and spiritual alone, i.e., Jesus and the Word of God. To address it in any other manner is doomed to failure even at the outset.

In this brief exchange, He would tell her the problem, the cause, and the solution. As it was for her, so it is with us, for this exchange was meant for us as well!

FIVE HUSBANDS?

"For you have had five husbands; and he whom you now have is not your husband: in that said you truly" (Jn. 4:18).

The phrase, *"For you have had five husbands,"* must have come as a shock to her, especially considering that she knew He did not know her. Incidentally, He knew this by the "*Word of Knowledge*" (I Cor. 12:8).

In this Revelation, one can feel the misery and heartache that must have resulted in a lifestyle that would bring about such aberration.

While it may be true that one or two of these former husbands had died, the implication is that such had not happened and, if so, had no bearing whatsoever on what brought this about.

Such activity proclaims a "*thirst*" which is not satisfied and, in fact, cannot be satisfied by these means. And yet, the world continues to clamor after another wife, another husband, more money, a different place to live, etc., ad nauseam.

However, in this Answer given to her by Jesus, we find the cause, which is far greater than her personally.

It is ironic that she had had "*five husbands*," and, as well, that this was the exact number of gods that had characterized the Samaritan religion from its inception.

THE SAMARITAN RELIGION

When the northern kingdom called Israel, sometimes called Ephraim or Samaria, was taken by Assyria, the area was left almost without population. Tens of thousands of Jews had been killed, with tens of thousands taken captive, and others fleeing to surrounding countries. As a result, the land had few inhabitants.

In view of this, as we have previously stated, Sennacherib, king of Assyria, sent people from Babylon and other places to inhabit the area formerly known as Israel.

They brought with them their gods, which were five in number, and set up worship to them in the land. This greatly influenced coming generations, of which Jesus particularly speaks.

They are as follows:

NERGAL

This was a well-known Assyrian deity. He was called *"the god of battles" and "the god of the chase,"* the last being his principle title. He was the patron of hunting and was supposed to represent the deified hero and hunter Nimrod. His symbol was a man-lion or human-headed lion with eagle wings.

ASHIMA

This was the god of Hamath, a deity worshipped under the figure of a goat without wool.

The goat is found among the sacred animals of the Babylonian monuments.

Ashima corresponds with the Egyptian Mendes, the Greek Pan, and the Phoenician Esmun.

NIBHAZ AND TARTAK

These two gods were of the Avites, with both being similar and thought to be in the form of a man with the head of a dog or in the form of an ass.

ADRAMMELECH

This was a god of the Sepharvites and was supposedly identical with Molech.

ANAMMELECH

This was also a god of the Sepharvites and was supposed to be in the form of a horse. Human sacrifices were offered to it as well!

The people of Samaria, as this region was known, and with its people hence called *"Samaritans,"* worshipped all these gods in their own way, in all high places, and in their own cities.

They feared Jehovah but served other gods (II Kin. 17:32-33), that is, they were afraid of Jehovah, but not enough to serve Him or keep His Laws.

At a point in time, the Samaritans drifted partially toward the true worship of Jehovah and ultimately forsook these idol gods; however, Judah would have nothing at all to do with them.

In 332 B.C., they built a Temple to Jehovah on Mount Gerizim. As stated, they laid aside their idols and accepted the Pentateuch as their religious Text Book and began to attempt to observe the Law of Moses.

However, they rejected all the other Books of the Bible, which, in Jesus' Day, consisted of the entire Old Testament.

Nevertheless, recognizing a part of the Bible is not enough, which Jesus will exclaim momentarily.

The *"five husbands"* had taken their terrible toll!

NOT YOUR HUSBAND

The phrase, *"And He whom you now have is not your husband: in that said you truly,"* proclaims two things as well.

1. The man she was now living with was not her husband. This proclaims that she had thrown away all convention, with her life becoming more and more sordid, even by the day. This tells us that no pretence was left, with her basically exclaiming, *"What's the use!"*

2. This false worship in which the Samaritans were presently engaged was no more God than the idols of the past had been. Spiritually speaking, the Samaritans had no *"husband,"* i.e., True God!

So, her problem paralleled the entirety of Samaria. It also parallels the entirety of the human family.

Most presently worship false gods or else have a corrupt form of Christianity exactly as the Samaritans had a corrupt form of the Law of Moses. I speak of Catholicism, Mormonism, and, in fact, any and all religious denominations and/or churches which ignore the Cross of Christ. The Cross is the signal point of the entirety of the Word of God and the entirety of Christianity. If preachers are preaching anything other than the Cross of Christ, whatever it is they are preaching is not really the Word of God. It may be about the Word of God and point toward the Word of God, but it's really not the Word if the Cross of Christ is not prominent in some way.

In other words, the Preacher has to understand the following:

• Jesus Christ is the Source of all things we receive from God (Jn. 1:1, 14, 29; 14:6; Col. 2:10-15).

• With Jesus Christ being the Source, the Cross is the Means, and the only Means by which all of these good things are given to us (Rom. 6:1-14; I Cor. 1:17).

• With Christ as the Source and the Cross as the Means, and the only Means, the Cross of Christ must be the Object of our Faith at all times. We are speaking of what Jesus there did, the Victory He there won (I Cor. 1:18, 21, 23; 2:2; Col. 2:10-15; Gal. 6:14).

• With the Cross of Christ ever as the Object of our Faith, then the Holy Spirit, Who works exclusively within the parameters, so to speak, of the Finished Work of Christ, will grandly work on our behalf (Rom. 8:1-11; Eph. 2:13-18).

In short, we have just given you the Message of the Cross, which is the Gospel of Jesus Christ. If that is not preached, whatever is being preached, as stated, is not the gospel.

A PROPHET?

"The woman said unto Him, Sir, I perceive that You are a Prophet" (Jn. 4:19).

The woman thinking Jesus was only a Prophet had to do with the beliefs of the Samaritans and their interpretation of who the Messiah would be.

Although the Samaritans accepted the Books of Moses (Genesis-Deuteronomy), they, as stated, did not accept the historical, wisdom, or Prophetic Books of the balance of the Old Testament.

They derived their interpretation of the Messiah from Deuteronomy 18:15, *"The LORD your God will raise up unto you a Prophet from the midst of you, of your brethren, like unto Me; unto Him you shall hearken."*

While this Passage definitely was referring to the Messiah, Who would be Jesus Christ, the Samaritans were misinterpreting the Promise.

THE MISTAKE OF THE SAMARITANS

The Samaritans did not understand the Incarnation, and they erroneously believed that the Messiah would be a Samaritan, i.e., *"from the midst of you."*

The Jews, as all know, were looking for a Messiah, as well, but had built up an exaggerated and carnal view of just Who He would be and What He would do. Consequently, both were wrong!

Israel was looking for a *"king,"* but the wrong type of king, while the Samaritans were looking for a *"Prophet,"* but for both the Jews and the Samaritans, the Messiah, in their thinking, would be a mere man.

Not believing the historical Books, the Samaritans did not understand that the Messiah would actually be David's Son.

Not believing Isaiah, they did not believe He would be *"Virgin Born,"* and, in effect, *"the Son of God."*

So, their thinking, as the thinking of most in this world, was skewed simply because of a lack of believing the Word and a false interpretation of what little they did know and believe. So, when this woman addressed Jesus as a *"Prophet,"* she thought in her heart that He just might be the long-awaited Messiah. And yet, He was a Jew, which was glaringly obvious. This confused her somewhat inasmuch as she believed that the Messiah would be a Samaritan.

OUR FATHERS?

"Our fathers worshipped in this mountain; and You say, that in Jerusalem is the place where men ought to worship" (Jn. 4:20).

The mountain addressed in Verse 20 was Mount Gerizim. It is about 50 miles north of Jerusalem.

As stated, rival worship in Jerusalem had been set up on this mountain with the Temple built in 332 B.C.

The *"fathers"* of whom she spoke, no doubt, went back to Abraham, Isaac, and Jacob, who worshipped and labored at Shechem, which was nearby.

As well, she used the word, *"Our,"* probably claiming that they were the *"fathers"* of both the Jews and Samaritans, which was wrong. The Patriarchs were not the fathers of the Samaritans but only the Jews. (Abraham was also the father of the Arabs.)

JERUSALEM

The phrase, *"And You say, that in Jerusalem is the place where men ought to worship,"* pertains to her believing that Jesus fit the profile of the great Prophet Who would come as Moses had predicted, but she was perplexed because He was a Jew and worshipped in Jerusalem.

The Samaritans claimed Gerizim and the Jews Moriah, with this latter as the place where Abraham offered his typical sacrifice. They both regarded the worship celebrated in each shrine — the daily Offerings, the annual Offerings (the Passover especially) — as giving worthiness to all the prayers and praises which they might be induced to offer in all places where they might sojourn.

All of this was very important, not a matter of mere semantics, because the worship was the sacrificial worship where sin, such as hers, could alone be cleansed, and where her conscience could be set free for calm and continuous communion with God.

However, she knew that her life had not been changed by the worship in which she had previously been engaged, and now she sensed that Jesus was about to give her what she had craved all along, Salvation from sin and true communion with God.

However, as stated, she was confused because Jesus did not match up to her beliefs.

How so much like the world and, at the same time, how so much unlike the world.

The similarity is in the woman needing help but looking for it in the wrong place; however, the similarity ends with her accepting Jesus while the world will not.

THE HOUR IS COMING

"Jesus said unto her, Woman, believe Me, the hour comes, when you shall neither in this mountain, nor yet at Jerusalem, worship the Father" (Jn. 4:21).

The phrase, *"Woman, believe Me,"* presents an expression which says several things:

    1. He was asking her to believe Him, and He was

answering her question regarding if He was that *"Prophet,"* fulfilling Moses' Prophecy, but, in reality, much more. He is Deity, i.e., *"God, manifest in the flesh."*

2. He was saying that He held the answer to her dilemma and rather than believing the arguing factions among the Samaritans and Jews, she was rather to *"believe Him!"*

What a lesson for us presently!

Arguments over religion rage constantly, bringing hundreds of millions into its maw exactly as it did in the Day of Jesus.

However, the One Criteria, the One Foundation, and the One Principle which must be heeded is the Lord Jesus Christ.

If the doctrine is wrong about Jesus, then whatever else it has is of no consequence.

When one stands before God, whatever their church, religious denomination, preacher, etc., said will matter little. It's what God has said and, hence, Jesus saying, *"Believe Me!"*

A NEW DAY IS COMING

The phrase, *"The hour comes, when you shall neither in this mountain, nor yet at Jerusalem, worship the Father,"* proclaims an unparalleled Truth.

Jesus was saying that the time was near, and actually would be completed very shortly, when He would die on Calvary and be raised from the dead.

The Day of Pentecost would signal the new form of worship.

In truth, all the Temple worship, sacrifices, and Feast Days were about to draw to a close. All of these were Types of Jesus Christ regarding Who He Was and/or What He did and would do.

All of these Types and Shadows would serve their

purpose until He would come and would carry out that to which they had pointed. So, the argument as to where men should worship would be moot very shortly anyway.

Actually, Jerusalem, at that time, was the correct place, even as Jesus would shortly say, but it too was about to be brought to a close, having fulfilled its purpose.

Also, by Jesus using the title, "*Father,*" He proclaimed that the coming worship would be far more intimate than the previous. God would be looked at in an entirely different light because a relationship would have been established by Believers because of what Jesus would do at Calvary.

What must this woman have thought when Jesus used the title, "*Father,*" so readily, implying a relationship of previously unknown proportions?

The very way He used the word implied that such a relationship could never be brought about by sacrifices, Feast Days, ceremonies, and rituals. This was a nearness to God that she had never known, heard of, or experienced.

As well, He was intimating that all could have this relationship! How her heart must have thrilled at this.

WORSHIP?

"*You worship you know not what: we know what we worship: for Salvation is of the Jews*" (Jn. 4:22).

The phrase, "*You worship you know not what,*" tells her, in no uncertain terms, exactly what was right and wrong.

Her Samaritan style of worship was all wrong. It was that which God would not accept and, in fact, could not accept, irrespective as to how much they used His Name.

How this should be a lesson to all of us! To be frank, the Samaritan way of worship was far closer to Scriptural Truth than Catholicism, but yet, unacceptable. The same can be said for many protestant churches and denominations. They really don't know what they worship.

A PERSONAL EXPERIENCE

Years ago, I happened to be in the presence of a businessman in Houston, Texas. I asked him where he went to church.

He told me he was *"Episcopalian!"* He then added, *"I am in charge of the worship at our church."*

I asked him what that meant.

He explained that he was not sure if he understood what it meant himself. He related how he would collect the *"holy water,"* which was used in wedding ceremonies, kept it until the next Sunday when he would walk up and down the aisle, sprinkling it on individuals sitting nearby.

He then added how he had brought in *"folk singers"* who sat on the Altar and sang folk songs. How that related to worship I have not yet understood.

In truth, he had no idea what the true worship of God actually was. To be factual, the man was not even saved, and neither was the pastor of the church. Truthfully, it is very doubtful that anyone in that church, as with most churches, was saved. No true gospel was preached there; consequently, the Holy Spirit had no opportunity to function in any capacity.

To be frank, the Holy Spirit was not in the proceedings whatsoever, as He was not in the proceedings of the Samaritans, etc.

Sadly, He was not in the proceedings of the Jews either as they had long since left the true worship of

God, with the Temple rituals having deteriorated into mere formality.

I realize that Jesus would be thought of as uncouth by many today or even argumentative by flatly stating that the Samaritan way was wrong. Such would be somewhat destructive to unity, they would say!

However, if the soul of man is important, then the lie he believes must be addressed. To call it any other way than what it actually is, is an affront to God and a terrible disservice to the individual in question.

THE CROSS

In fact, no Believer can properly worship the Lord unless he has an understanding of the Cross of Christ. In other words, he must understand, as already stated, that Jesus Christ is the Source of all things we receive from God, while the Cross of Christ is the Means, and the only Means, by which all of these things are given unto us. We must know that, believe that, and continue to believe that. In fact, the entirety of the Story of the Bible is the Story of Jesus Christ and Him Crucified. If one doesn't believe that, then one is going to have a hard time trying to comprehend the Word of God. The Scripture plainly says:

"In the beginning was the Word, and the Word was with God, and the Word was God" (Jn. 1:1). It then says that the *"Word became flesh, and dwelt among us ..."* (Jn. 1:14). He did so for one purpose, and that was to go to the Cross. When John the Baptist introduced Christ, He said:

"... Behold the Lamb of God, Who takes away the sin of the world" (Jn. 1:29).

Jesus was referred to as a *"Lamb"* because He was the Fulfillment of the millions of sacrifices of lambs which had been offered up in the past.

As well, something was said of Him that had never been said of any other and, in fact, could not be said of any other. It was said that He would *"take away the sin of the world."* Animal sacrifices could not take away sins; they were woefully insufficient. They served as a stopgap measure in order to cover sins until the Redeemer would come.

However, the Lord, by what He would do at the Cross, would do much more than cover sins. He would take that sin away, meaning that it would no longer be held against the person, at least for those who would believe (Jn. 3:16).

In the last 50 years, the Cross of Christ has been so little preached, even for Salvation, that anymore, it has deteriorated into mere sentimentality. While the term, *"Jesus died for me,"* is still looked at in the correct way by most, sadly, even that is falling by the wayside. The only answer for sin is the Cross, but the modern church is looking at other avenues of approach, which cannot address sin at all.

In other words, it refuses to admit that sin is the problem. If you admit that sin is the problem, you have to admit that the only solution for sin is the Cross of Christ. Until you know that and understand that, you cannot properly worship the Lord.

DOCTRINES!

What Jesus told the woman at the well that day, flatly stating, *"You worship you know not what,"* is that which must be addressed and proclaimed presently as well.

If it's wrong, one must say it is wrong. If it is a doctrine that is causing people to be lost because it is a lie, even as the Samaritan doctrines, it must be addressed accordingly.

It is incumbent upon every Preacher of the Gospel to tell the Catholics that the church cannot save, and, in effect, *"the Just shall live by Faith."* They must be told that praying to the Virgin Mary is wrong and actually blasphemy against God. They must be told that confessing to a priest is unscriptural and that, in reality, when doing so, their sins are unforgiven.

As well, they must be told that there is no such thing as a *"priest"* in the New Covenant, and that the establishment of a priesthood is, as well, an abomination in the Eyes of God. There is only One Priest, Who is our Great High Priest, and I speak of the Lord Jesus Christ (I Tim. 2:5; Heb. 8:6; 9:15; 12:24).

Protestants must be told, as well, even as the Catholics, that their church cannot save them and neither can Ordinances, such as *"Water Baptism"* or *"the Lord's Supper."*

Also, they must be told that denying the Baptism with the Holy Spirit with the evidence of speaking with other Tongues will, in effect, deny a great portion of the Word of God, which will leave them powerless and, for the most part, spiritually blind.

Finally, the Pentecostals must be told that they must return to the Holy Spirit, from Whom most have departed, and *". . . do the first works; or else I will come unto you quickly, and will remove your candlestick out of his place, except you repent"* (Rev. 2:5).

Overall, the entirety of the church must return to the Cross. The Cross of Christ is the Foundation of all Doctrine in the Bible.

It was the first Doctrine, one might say, that was ordained by the Godhead, which was done so even before the foundation of the world, which means even before man was created (I Pet. 1:18-20).

So, if any doctrine confuses the Cross, misinterprets the Cross, or denies the Cross, this means it is wrong.

Let us say it again: Every Bible Doctrine, irrespective as to what it is, is built squarely on the Foundation of the Cross of Christ.

So, the Preacher of the Gospel has a choice! He can compromise the Gospel and do nothing for God, or else he can preach exactly as Jesus, which will win many souls but, at the same time, will incur great opposition and even persecution.

Regrettably, most opt for the former while rejecting the latter.

WE KNOW WHAT WE WORSHIP

The phrase, "*We know what we worship*," proclaims unequivocally that there is a right way to worship. As well, I might quickly add that there is only one right way and not several. While all the spokes on a wheel may well lead to the hub, all ways do not lead to God. There is only One Way, and that One is Jesus and Him Alone!

All worship must be in accordance with the Word of God, and, if so, it will truly have the Moving and Operation of the Holy Spirit.

The man of whom I spoke a few paragraphs ago had no idea what he was worshipping. He called it "*worship of God*," but it was anything but that.

Regrettably, such will be very similar in most churches this Sunday morning.

SALVATION IS OF THE JEWS

The phrase, "*For Salvation is of the Jews*," means that it was not of the Samaritans or anyone else, for that matter.

Irrespective of Israel's present backslidden condition and her departure from the True God, and despite the continuing of the religious ceremonies and rituals, still, that which had been given to this world by God had come through the Jewish people.

It was to Abraham God first spoke and gave the Promise concerning the people who would come from his loins, and from among those people, *"the Messiah,"* Who would redeem mankind (Gen. 12:1-3).

To Abraham and Sarah was born Isaac, through whom the Seed would come, the Lord Jesus Christ, but yet, many generations removed.

From Isaac came Jacob, from whom came the 12 sons who headed up the Twelve Tribes of Israel.

To these people, the Jews, were given the Prophets and the Word of God, i.e., the Bible. As well, ultimately through them, the Tribe of Judah, the House of David, and the Virgin Mary, came the Messiah, not for the Jews only, but for the whole world (Jn. 3:16).

Consequently, the world owes an incredible debt to the Jew but has mostly paid that debt with hatred, murder, vengeance, and the threat of annihilation. Actually, they would have long since been annihilated were it not for the Hand of God.

ISRAEL

While it is true that Israel has forfeited her position by her rejection of her own Messiah, still, the Prophets have proclaimed that Israel will ultimately be restored. This actually began in 1948 with Israel, after some 1,900 years, finally once again becoming a Nation. The full Restoration will not come until the darkened days of the Great Tribulation are past, even as Jesus said (Mat. 24:21). However, they will come, and Israel will finally accept her Messiah and will be restored to her proper place and position, even as the Promises were given to the Patriarchs and Prophets of old (Ezek., Chpts. 38-48; Zech., Chpts. 13-14; Rev., Chpt. 19).

In fact, much of the progress in this world, such as technological advancement, the rapid progress of medicine, as well as other scientific achievements, has been brought about by those of Jewish descent.

Some years ago, I had the occasion to be a part of the program in which Prime Minister Yitzhak Rabin was the principle speaker. This was shortly before he became prime minister.

He said, "*How many Jonas Salks or Albert Einsteins died in the Holocaust?*" The point was well taken.

Yes, Salvation is of the Jews, "*even though the world little knows it, and to which the Jews will not admit, and because of their rejection of Jesus Christ.*"

IN SPIRIT AND IN TRUTH

"*But the hour comes, and now is, when the true worshippers shall worship the Father in spirit and in truth: for the Father seeks such to worship Him*" (Jn. 4:23).

The phrase, "*But the hour comes, and now is,*" actually says the same as Verse 21, but with added emphasis respecting the time. Jesus is not here, and the entirety of things is about to change. Every single Prophecy of the Old Testament, all of the sacrifices, along with the Feast Days, as well as what the Tabernacle and Temple stood for, all pointed to one Person, the Lord Jesus Christ. He was and is the Fulfillment of all these things. It was done so for the purpose of opening up the way that the Holy Spirit could come down and dwell in the hearts and lives of Believers in a manner which could not be done previously.

When Jesus died on Calvary, thereby, satisfying the claims of Heavenly justice and defeating Satan, as well, His Resurrection would afford a place and position with the Father for Believers heretofore unknown.

Consequently, it would be the greatest pivot point in history, with Believers becoming *"... an habitation of God through the Spirit"* (Eph. 2:22).

It is amazing that Jesus would tell these things to a poor Samaritan woman, who had been immoral, to say the least, but would not reveal such to the religious hierarchy of Israel. It has not changed presently.

Those who accept God's Way, which is the only Way of Righteousness, will receive God's Revelation, while those who do not accept it, even though professing greatly, have nothing revealed unto them.

TO WORSHIP THE FATHER IN SPIRIT AND IN TRUTH

The phrase, *"Shall worship the Father in spirit and in truth,"* refers to the spirit of man, but the Spirit of God, as well, and in the Truth of God's Word.

While all true worship of God has always been in this capacity, before Calvary, worship was far more ritualistic in regard to the sacrifices, Feast Days, etc. This was due to the Holy Spirit not being able to take up abode in the hearts and lives of men because of sins not being taken away. Animal blood was insufficient to do so; it only covered the sins.

Even though the word, *"Spirit,"* as used here by Jesus, pertains to the spirit of man, the Holy Spirit also is the very Person of the Godhead Who makes it possible for the Believer to truly worship God. In fact, without the Baptism with the Holy Spirit with the evidence of speaking with other Tongues, there isn't very much true worship that takes place.

FOR THE FATHER SEEKS SUCH TO WORSHIP HIM

The heading means that by the word, *"Seeks,"* such are not easily found.

As it is today, so it was then. The sinner tried by a proposed religious discussion about churches to put aside the matter of her shameful life.

However, Jesus gently and courteously explained to her that the true Way of Salvation had been revealed to the Jews, even though it was little heeded, and that the true place of worship was the heart, not either Gerizim or Jerusalem, for God is Spirit and Truth. Worship, therefore, must be spiritual and must be in subjection to the Word of God.

- The Holy Spirit seeks pupils (Jn. 16:13-15).
- The Father seeks holy worshippers (Jn. 4:23).
- The Son seeks sinners (Lk. 19:10).

Many in the church have concluded that God seeks holy worship. He does not! He seeks holy worshippers! There is a vast difference.

GOD IS A SPIRIT

The phrase, "*God is a Spirit*," simply means that "*God is a Spirit Being.*"

In other words, He is not the sun, moon, stars, or an image of wood, stone, or metal. As well, He is not an animal or a man. He is not the air, wind, universal mind, the force, love, or some impersonal quality.

He is a Person with a Personal Spirit Body, a Personal Soul, and a Personal Spirit like that of Angels and like that of man except His Body is of Spirit Substance instead of flesh and bones (Jn. 13:8; Heb. 1:3).

He has a Personal Spirit Body (Dan. 7:9-14; 10:5-19); Shape (Jn. 5:37); Form (Phil. 2:5-7); and Image and Likeness of a man (Gen. 1:26; 9:6; Ezek. 1:26-28; I Cor. 11:7; Jam. 3:9).

He has Bodily Parts such as back parts (Ex. 33:23), heart (Gen. 6:6; 8:21), hands and fingers (Ps. 8:3-6; Heb. 1:10; Rev. 5:1-7), mouth (Num. 12:8), lips and tongue (Isa. 30:27), feet (Ex. 24:10; Ezek. 1:27), eyes (Ps. 11:4; 18:24; 33:18), ears (Ps. 18:6), and hair, head, face, and arms (Dan. 7:9-14; 10:-19; Rev. 5:1-7; 22:4-6).

He has Bodily Presence (Gen. 3:8; 18:1-22), and goes from place to place in a Body like all other persons (Gen. 3:8; 11:5; 18:1-5, 22, 33; 19:24; 32:24-32; 35:13; Dan. 7:9-14; Zech. 14:5; Tit. 2:13).

He has a voice (Ps. 29; Rev. 10:3-4); breath (Gen. 2:7); and countenance (Ps. 11:7).

He wears clothes (Dan. 7:9-14; 10:5-19); eats (Gen. 18:1-8; Ex. 24:11); dwells in a mansion and in a city located on a material Planet called Heaven (Jn. 14:1-3; Heb. 11:10-16; 13:14; Rev., Chpt. 21); and sits on a Throne (Isa., Chpt. 6; Dan. 7:9-14; Rev. 4:1-5; 22:3-6).

He has a personal soul with feelings of grief (Gen. 6:6); anger (I Kin. 11:9); jealousy (Ex. 20:5); hate (Prov. 6:16); love (Jn. 3:16); pity (Ps. 103:13); fellowship (I Jn. 1:1-7); and other soul passions like other beings (Gal. 5:22-23).

God has been seen bodily a number of times (Gen., Chpt. 18; 32:24-30; Ex. 24:9-11; Josh. 5:13-15; Isa., Chpt. 6; Ezek., Chpt. 1; Dan. 7:9-13; Acts 7:56-59; Rev., Chpts. 4-5); and can be understood by the things that are made.

Man is the visible image and likeness making the invisible God clearly seen, as in Romans 1:20.

WORSHIP

The phrase, *"And they who worship Him must worship Him in spirit and in truth,"* constitutes the second time this statement is given, and with Divine Purpose by the Holy Spirit. When something is repeated, it is done so for emphasis.

Several things are said here:

• If the worship is not in spirit (man's spirit moved upon by the Holy Spirit), and in Truth, which refers to the Word of God, it is worship that God will not accept and, in fact, cannot accept.

On this very day, tens of millions of Muslims will pray several times a day, going through their outward circumstances and motions. It is not in spirit and in Truth and, consequently, cannot be accepted by God. Tragically, the same would pertain in one form or the other to many, if not most, Christians.

• The word, "*Must,*" tells us that this is not one of several ways accepted by God but, in fact, the only Way.

• The Holy Spirit will always abide by the Word, and that's the reason the Believer cannot properly worship the Lord except by the Revelation of the Holy Spirit.

THE WOMAN

"The woman said unto Him, I know that Messiah comes, Who is called Christ: when He is come, He will tell us all things" (Jn. 4:25).

The phrase, "*The woman said unto Him,*" proclaims the tender word, "*Woman,*" occurring some 13 times in this incident. She was speaking to the One, actually, the only One Who could satisfy the longing of her soul. How privileged she was, and how privileged we are to be able to talk to Him as we do in prayer.

CHRIST

The phrase, "*I know that Messiah comes, Who is called Christ,*" proclaims the Samaritans also looking for a Messiah Who would come as promised in Deuteronomy 18:15. So, it seems that she as well as possibly many other Samaritans had adopted the word, "*Messiah,*" which, in effect, was a Hebrew word and was common among the Jews. Of course, there was no messiah promised to the Samaritans, or anyone else for that matter, other than the Jews, and that Messiah was Jesus. However, Israel did not know or recognize Him!

In similarities at the present time, as the Samaritans and Jews of old, the modern Muslims, along with the Jews, are looking for a messiah as well! However, as there was no such thing as a Samaritan messiah, likewise, there is no such thing as a Muslim messiah.

WHEN HE IS COME

The phrase, "*When He is come, He will tell us all things,*" constituted truth, but not in the way this woman suspected. However, her statement, even though unscriptural and improper, nevertheless, contained a hunger and thirst for Righteousness.

In this statement, one senses a weariness with religion and a longing for someone to set the record straight. In other words, her heart cried out for more than the mere ceremonies in which she had been busily engaged for so long. She realized that all the ceremonies in the Samaritan religion had not changed her wasted, misused, and misspent life. Her five marriages and present situation loudly proclaimed this.

So, Jesus ignored her continued error and reached down into her heart and did something so remarkable that it absolutely defies description! The next Verse tells us what.

I AM HE

"*Jesus said unto her, I Who speak unto you am He*" (Jn. 4:26).

It is nothing short of amazing that Jesus little revealed Himself to Nicodemus, except in a veiled way, but plainly and clearly revealed Himself to this woman, and a Samaritan at that!

The woman now arrived at the point: a Redeemer was promised; everything would depend upon Him; *"He would tell us all things"*; and He would be the Saviour. Jesus said to her, *"I am He!"* and she was Saved in and by that Revelation (Mat. 11:27). For intelligence in Divine things comes by conscience and Revelation and not by intellect.

Thus, as the Living Water, the Holy Spirit quickens the moral man (Nicodemus), yet unsaved, and indwells the Believer (the Samaritan). The water that flows from the Smitten Rock becomes, when drunk, an internal Well perpetually springing up and a Life that is Everlasting. Such was the life into which Nicodemus ultimately entered, along with the Samaritan, who instantly entered. Merit in the one case did not admit into that life, and demerit did not exclude from it.

The idea that Jesus would plainly and clearly reveal Himself to a woman, and a hated Samaritan who was so grossly immoral at that, is not understood at all by the self-righteous, but yet, is the undergirding strength of Salvation.

GRACE

To be qualified for Grace is to be unqualified and know it. One has to admit he is lost before he can be Saved. This the self-righteous cannot do, but one such as the Samaritan can easily do. Hence, Jesus would later say, *"I thank You, O Father, Lord of Heaven and Earth, because You have hidden these things from the wise and prudent, and have revealed them unto babes."*

He then said, *"Even so, Father: for so it seemed good in Your Sight"* (Mat. 11:25-26).

The self-righteous always mistake Grace for a condoning of sin; therefore, they show no grace and, thereby, receive no grace. Consequently, Jesus said of them, *"... the publicans and the harlots go into the Kingdom of God before you."*

He then said, *"For John came unto you in the way of Righteousness, and you believed him not: but the publicans and the harlots believed him: and you, when you had seen it, repented not afterward, that you might believe him"* (Mat. 21:31-32).

THEY MARVELLED THAT HE TALKED WITH THE WOMAN

"And upon this came His Disciples, and marvelled that He talked with the woman: yet no man said, What do You seek? or, Why do You talk with her?" (Jn. 4:27).

The phrase, *"And upon this came His Disciples,"* refers to their coming back from the town where they had gone to purchase food. However, as stated, the possibility definitely exists that John the Beloved, who gave this account, stayed behind and witnessed the entire episode, hence, his remarkable attention to details.

The phrase, *"And marvelled that He talked with the woman,"* may seem strange to most presently. However, there were no dealings normally between Jews and Samaritans, and even above that, rabbis did not converse with women in public or instruct them in the Law. No rabbi would even converse with his wife, sister, or daughter in public or in the street. Of course, these were rulings laid down by men and not God.

Actually, this is one of the reasons that the Pharisees and ruling hierarchy of Israel hated Jesus so very much. He completely ignored their man-made rules and conducted the Will of the Father as if none of these rules existed.

Actually, one of the Miracles of the Lord's Ministry was to break down the wretched, rabbinical prejudice against the spiritual capacities of women and the oriental folly which supposed that she contaminated their sanctity. He lifted women to their true position by the side of man. Actually, women were His Most Faithful Followers.

They ministered unto Him of their substance. They shared His Miraculous Healing Power, Feeding, and Teaching. They anointed His Feet, they wept over His Agony, they followed Him to the Cross, they were early at the Sepulcher, and they greeted Him as the Risen Lord. They also received the Baptism with the Holy Spirit. Actually, in Christ, there is neither male nor female. Both are one in Him.

I would hope that the western world understands that the freedom enjoyed by women in western societies was paid for by the Lord Jesus Christ. He lifted woman from the position of condemnation and burden, and restored to her that which religion had taken away. As we have attempted to properly elucidate, the Ministry of Christ gave ample proof of that.

THE TESTIMONY OF THE WOMAN

"The woman then left her waterpot, and went her way into the city, and said to the men" (Jn. 4:28).

The action of the woman in leaving her waterpot and becoming an unconscious Preacher demonstrates the death of self and the occupation of her heart with Jesus and His Grace and Goodness.

So overwhelming was her consciousness of His Person and His Action that it, in a sense, annihilated the consciousness of her own sinfulness. Due to her acceptance of Christ, for that's what she did, Christ Himself filled all her world.

So, a woman became the first Preacher of the Gospel to the Gentile people, and so effective was her preaching that it caused a Revival. She became a vessel to receive and then to minister the Gift of Life.

The phrase, "*And went her way into the city, and said to the men,*" refers to the fact that she went directly to the leaders of the particular Samaritan religion.

COME SEE A MAN

"*Come, see a Man, Who told me all things that ever I did: is not this the Christ?*" (Jn. 4:29).

The word, "*Come,*" is the greatest evidence of all of everyone's Salvation. They hungrily desire to bring others to Jesus.

Why?

Salvation, as given by Christ, is a peculiar thing in that its Glory is not obvious until one has accepted Christ. When this happens and suddenly the Glory appears, the first desire is that others know as well!

The full phrase, "*Come, see a Man, Who told me all things that ever I did,*" is, once again, the epitome of true Bible Christianity.

Christianity is not a philosophy or a religion. It is really, as stated, "*a Man,*" the Man Christ Jesus.

Whether Jesus told her other things or not, we do not know. However, He told her enough that she was thoroughly convinced Who and What He actually was. This is what makes Christianity so different from the religions of the world.

Such religions have to do with the externals only because it is impossible for them to do otherwise; consequently, they never address the real problem, only the symptoms.

As we have stated many times, Christianity is not a philosophy even though many have made it into such. It is, in fact, a relationship, pure and simple, with Jesus. As well, as God, He is able to know all things and to do all things.

IS NOT THIS THE CHRIST?

He not only tells one what one has done but also can cure one for and from what one has done.

For Jesus to relate to this woman only what she had done would have been of little consequence, as magnificent as it would have been. As well, He had to give her the Living Water, which healed the malignancy of her actions. Love must act or its not love.

The question, *"Is not this the Christ?"* presents a very clever way of expressing herself.

Her question presupposes that her fellow Samaritans, as stated, were looking for a Messiah. Evidently, such was the topic of many conversations and seems to have been the reigning subject at this time.

How was it possible for these men, who were obviously leaders in the Samaritan religion, to be so swayed so quickly by this woman's Testimony, especially considering who she was?

Who she was and what she was may have been the very reason they did heed her words. Evidently there was a marked and obvious change in her, which could be readily observed in her spirit and which made them extremely curious.

THEY CAME TO SEE JESUS

"Then they went out of the city, and came unto Him" (Jn. 4:30).

Verse 4 says, *"And He must needs go through Samaria,"* and now we know why. The Holy Spirit knew there were hungry hearts in this place and would respond accordingly.

I wonder how many hungry hearts there are in the world at this time, but yet, there is no one to bring them the Gospel.

MANY OF THE SAMARITANS BELIEVED ON HIM

"And many of the Samaritans of that city believed on Him for the saying of the woman, who testified, He told me all that ever I did" (Jn. 4:39).

Verse 39 proclaims the information of this unique instance in the Gospels of a true moral revival on a large scale produced by preaching apart from Miracles.

The Preachers were the woman Samaritan (the Scripture does not give her name) and the Messiah.

Her Ministry was the more remarkable because she apparently was unordained. In other words, she went without being sent. She was a volunteer Preacher.

However, the Holy Spirit often ordains and equips and sends forth without outward appointment. So, her action was a beautiful instance of the Energy of the Spirit in making men and women witnesses for the Cause of Christ.

The phrase, *"He told me all that ever I did,"* in no way expresses a mere faultfinding session, but, as well, means He gave her something, *"Living Water,"* i.e., Salvation.

While Jesus did expose her sin, as the Gospel always does, it was not done in a negative, condemnatory fashion, but rather to deliver her from sin. He then gave her Eternal Life.

LORD, TARRY WITH US

"So when the Samaritans were come unto Him, they besought Him that He would tarry with them: and He abode there two days" (Jn. 4:40).

The phrase, *"So when the Samaritans were come unto Him,"* bespoke hearts ready to receive from God. As stated, this group, no doubt, included some, if not most, of the religious leaders of that region.

They had been so convinced because of the glorious change for the better of this woman, even an instant change that they had to see for themselves.

"*They besought Him that He would tarry with them,*" was a request that was not denied and, in fact, is a request that will never be denied.

This is a beautiful moment in the Ministry of the Master because much of the time, He was rejected or, at most, tolerated by the religious powers. Actually, the hostility on the part of the Jews, which had already begun, would continue to increase from this point forward until it came to a head at a white-hot pitch. How different it could have been, and how different it would have been if they had only believed Him.

The phrase, "*And He abode there two days,*" presents Him doing what the Pharisees would not do, but, of course, their hearts were ruled by hate while His was ruled by Love. This one thing is sure: this "*two days*" was the greatest time that these people had ever experienced or would ever experience.

MANY MORE BELIEVED

"*And many more believed because of His Own Word*" (Jn. 4:41).

This refers to the second group back in the city who heard Christ teach and preach during these two days, and who "*believed*" as well! It could have easily numbered into the hundreds or perhaps even several thousands. The next Verse tells us what they "*believed.*"

THE SAVIOUR OF THE WORLD

"*And said unto the woman, Now we believe, not because of your saying: for we have heard Him ourselves, and know that this is indeed the Christ, the*

Saviour of the world" (Jn. 4:42).

The phrase, *"And said unto the woman, Now we believe, not because of your saying,"* should have been translated, *"Not only because of your saying,"* because her saying was the Testimony which originally brought them to Christ.

"For we have heard Him ourselves, and know that this is indeed the Christ, the Saviour of the world," proclaims one of the most profound statements ever made and occurs only one other time in the Bible (I Jn. 4:14). It fell from the lips of Samaritans.

These Samaritans recognized in Jesus not only the Anointed of Israel but, as well, the Saviour of all mankind, i.e., *"the world."*

And so He is!

Regrettably, toward the end of His Ministry, there were other Samaritans who would not receive Him (Lk. 9:51-56).

> *"We have heard the joyful sound:*
> *"Jesus saves! Jesus saves!*
> *"Spread the tidings all around:*
> *"Jesus saves! Jesus saves!*
> *"Bear the news to every land,*
> *"Climb the steeps and cross the waves;*
> *"Onward! 'Tis our Lord's Command;*
> *"Jesus saves! Jesus saves!*
>
> *"Waft it on the rolling tide;*
> *"Jesus saves! Jesus saves!*
> *"Tell to sinners far and wide:*
> *"Jesus saves! Jesus saves!*
> *"Sing, you islands of the sea;*
> *"Echo back, ye ocean caves;*
> *"Earth shall keep her jubilee,*
> *"Jesus saves! Jesus saves!"*

Great Women OF THE BIBLE

Chapter Eight

THE WOMAN OF CANAAN

THE WOMAN OF CANAAN

THE COASTS OF TYRE AND SIDON

"Then Jesus went thence, and departed into the coasts of Tyre and Sidon" (Mat. 15:21).

The phrase, *"Then Jesus went thence,"* portrays Him leaving (probably leaving Capernaum) and going to the borders of *"Tyre and Sidon."* These two cities were located on the Mediterranean Sea north of Israel. Both are very prominent in Old Testament history.

The Scripture does not say that Jesus went into these cities but merely to the border between Israel and Lebanon where they were located.

These two areas of *"Tyre and Sidon"* were steeped in heathenistic idol-worship. Their gods were Baal and Ashtaroth, which they continued to worship in one form or the other even during the Time of Christ.

A WOMAN OF CANAAN

"And, behold, a woman of Canaan came out of the same coasts, and cried unto Him, saying, Have Mercy on me, O Lord, Thou Son of David; my daughter is grievously vexed with a demon" (Mat. 15:22).

The two words, *"And, behold,"* mark the sudden intrusion of this woman into the Mission of Christ. When Matthew wrote these words, no doubt, the Holy Spirit moved upon him to say them as he did in order to highlight this unexpected turn of events.

The phrase, *"A woman of Canaan came out of the same coasts,"* concludes her to be a Gentile. Mark called her a *"Greek"* and a *"Syrophoenician."*

At any rate, the phrase, *"A woman of Canaan,"* says it all! She was an *". . . alien from the Commonwealth of Israel, and a stranger from the Covenants of Promise, having no hope, and without God in the world"* (Eph. 2:12). As such, she was typical of all Gentiles and epitomizes all of us who are Gentile.

Her life was one of idol-worship, and a cruel worship it was, even employing human sacrifice.

(Whether human sacrifice continued unto the time of Christ is not known, but in centuries past, they had been rampant.)

How this woman heard of Jesus is not known. No doubt, His Fame had spread to this part of the world, and the stories abounded of the tremendous Miracles He was performing.

And now, He was close to her home. It would be the greatest day of her life. If He had not come to this area, she would never have had the privilege of knowing Him or experiencing the tremendous Deliverance afforded her daughter. So it is with all the places where the Gospel is taken, or withheld.

AND CRIED UNTO HIM

The phrase, *"And cried unto Him,"* constitutes a Message within itself.

This woman was desperate! She had come to receive something from Christ, and she would not leave without getting that which she asked.

Inasmuch as the word, *"Cried,"* meant to *"clamor,"* or in other words, to speak with great emotion, the Holy Spirit through Matthew gives us an idea as to her desperation and the cry of her heart. I dare say that if anyone will come to Christ in this manner, an answer will be forthcoming.

Too many people approach the Lord in a lackadaisical way, and most of the time, they receive nothing. To be sure, one is not advocating that the loudness of one's approach assures His Answer, but this we do know:

True Bible Faith will not be denied. There is always an urgency about Faith which produces an emotion in the soul of the individual who comes to God. One can see this in the lives of the Bible Greats such as Abraham. He felt the urgency so greatly to see the Promise of God carried out in his life respecting this coming Child that he would even attempt to help the Lord. This, of course, was wrong, but, nevertheless, it portrayed his feelings.

HAVE MERCY ON ME

The phrase, "*Saying, have Mercy on me, O Lord, Thou Son of David,*" presents a petition to the Lord, which was actually wrong in principle but not in Faith.

Christ, as a Minister of the Circumcision for the Truth of God to fulfill the Promises made to the Fathers, refused to answer the Gentile petition addressed to Him as "*Son of David.*" However, when the woman took the place of a "*dog,*" thus admitting she had no claim, and threw herself on His Mercy and Grace as Lord, He at once responded.

The Scripture said that He was so to act that the Gentiles might also glorify God for His Mercy (Rom. 15:8-12).

Why would she have used this phrase, "*Son of David,*" when speaking to Christ?

Living as close as she did to Israel, she was probably well acquainted with the hopes and aspirations of the Jews respecting their coming Messiah.

Hearing the conversations of His Great Miracles and the discussion as to whether He was the Messiah, she, no doubt, concluded in her heart, and irrespective of what others may have said, that Jesus was indeed the Messiah, the "*Son of David,*" and, in effect, the "*Son of God.*"

As a Gentile, she had no Scriptural right to address Christ as the "*Son of David*," but, still, she probably did not know that. Her story is an example to all of us.

If the Lord demanded that our approach to Him be totally proper in every respect, most of us would fall by the wayside.

Thankfully, He does not demand that. He only demands Faith, and this woman had Faith!

Even as I write these words, I strongly sense the Presence of God. Even with tears, I feel the emotion of the moment as she approached Christ. I see myself in her, as you should as well!

She was out of dispensation, even unscriptural, and actually had no right for what she was asking. However, her petition would not be denied, and neither will the petition of anyone else be denied if one comes in the manner in which she came — of humility and Faith.

The Holy Spirit had this glorious example portrayed to us by both Matthew and Mark that its great lesson would not be lost upon us. If she received, you can receive as well!

DEMON POSSESSION

The phrase, "*My daughter is grievously vexed with a demon,*" gives the state of her child, which was serious indeed!

The Lord did not contradict her respecting the diagnosis, so, undoubtedly, demon powers were the cause of this affliction.

This is a subject in which not many are knowledgeable, and I speak of even children being influenced or even possessed by demon spirits.

Actually, this is not the exception, especially in the world in which she lived, or even in the world in which we live today.

Tragically, most children in America, or any country in the world for that matter, are raised in homes which little know God. They are submitted to profanity, immorality, and a very atmosphere that is charged by the powers of darkness.

Consequently, even as children, they provide a fertile territory for the activity of demon spirits.

If one could look into the spirit world, one would see demon spirits graphically operating in the lives of many, if not most, teenagers and even pre-teens.

A DOCUMENTARY

In a documentary, which I saw over television in the recent past, the commentator was remarking about the callousness of some teenagers who had committed murder. *"They seemed to show no remorse whatsoever concerning the terrible thing they had done,"* she said.

"Killing a fellow human being was no more to them than a flick of the wrist," she added.

If I remember correctly, the ages of the two *"killers"* she interviewed were 12 and 14.

She was nonplussed over their attitude, as well as multiple tens of thousands of other teenagers and pre-teens exhibiting traits that are completely unexplainable to the sociologists, psychologists, etc.

The answer now is the same as it was then, *"Vexed with a demon."*

There is only One Answer to this terrible malady, and it, as well, is the same now as then, *"Jesus."* All the sociologists and psychologists in the world cannot help such a one. This is the reason that the Gospel of *"Jesus Christ and Him Crucified"* must be preached in all of its Power. It is the answer and, in fact, is the only answer.

There is no other!

THE DISCIPLES OF OUR LORD

"But He answered her not a word. And His Disciples came and besought Him, saying, Send her away; for she cries after us" (Mat. 15:23).

In the entirety of this scenario, as intended by the Holy Spirit, we are given a perfect description as to how to approach the Lord and how to receive from the Lord. It will be an invaluable lesson.

The phrase, *"But He answered her not a word,"* was by design. Everything that Jesus did, even down to the Words He spoke, was guided by the Holy Spirit. Therefore, as this scene unfolds before us, there is a carefully crafted plan engineered by the Holy Spirit in order to meet this woman's need, i.e., the Healing and Deliverance of her daughter.

So, His Failure to answer was not meant at all to put her off or to deny her request, but instead, in order that she might receive what she had asked. The Ways of God are not our ways! However, those Ways are meant for our good. The lesson here taught and to be learned is that if the Lord does not answer immediately, we are not to stop our petition.

The phrase, *"And cried unto Him,"* as given in the previous Verse, meant that she kept crying. In other words, she would not stop. It is regrettable that a great part of the church world is being taught that we are only to ask the Lord one time and that any further petitions are a sign of lack of Faith.

The Scripture abundantly proclaims that such is not true. If at first we do not receive, we are importuned to continue asking (Lk. 11:8).

DELAY?

As well, the delay, if there is delay, is not to be

antagonizing to the seeker. The Lord does all things for a purpose. Along with giving us what we request, He, as well, always teaches us lessons by the manner in which He gives them.

Regrettably, most Christians presently ask once or twice, if that, and then quickly tire, claiming that God does not answer prayer, or else give some other excuse.

The lesson taught in this experience is that if we do not at first receive, we continue to ask, and as this *"woman of Canaan,"* be sure that we continue asking in Faith. Delay does not mean denial! It only means that we are to continue asking and believing.

HIS DISCIPLES

The phrase, *"And His Disciples came and besought Him,"* proclaims them doing this after her repeated petition; however, if one is to notice, there is another powerful Truth in this phrase.

This *"Woman of Canaan"* did not come to the Disciples but directly to Jesus. It is sad when Catholicism erroneously encourages its people to pray to dead Saints or even some of these Disciples, or more particularly, Mary the Mother of Christ.

In the Four Gospels, which give the account of the Ministry of the Master, one finds precious little evidence that individuals in need came to the Disciples, but instead, directly to Christ.

It would surely seem that the Holy Spirit is telling us something in these many accounts of seekers coming to Christ.

The truth is that all petitions must be made directly to the Father in the Name of Jesus (Jn. 16:23). All other prayers and petitions are useless, with no help forthcoming whatsoever from these other sources, because to do otherwise is unscriptural.

GRANT HER REQUEST

The phrase, *"Saying, Send her away; for she cries after us,"* probably would have been better translated in another manner inasmuch as the true meaning is here obscured. It should have been translated, *"Grant her request; for she cries after us."*

It seems they were perturbed due to her petition, and a loud petition at that. In other words, she would not stop her *"crying,"* and neither should we!

Every evidence is that the Disciples grew impatient with her. To be frank, sadly, most of the hindrance of our present petitions, especially if the answer is not forthcoming immediately, comes directly from the Saints of God, even as the closest companions of Christ, His Disciples.

THE MISSION OF CHRIST WAS TOTALLY TO THE JEWS

"But He answered and said, I am not sent but unto the lost sheep of the house of Israel" (Mat. 15:24).

The phrase, *"But He answered and said,"* presents what seems like another rebuke to the woman. Her Faith would be sorely tested, which, no doubt, the Holy Spirit intended to do.

The phrase, *"I am not sent but unto the lost sheep of the house of Israel,"* proclaims His Mission, at least in His First Advent, as exclusively to the Jews although it would ultimately fall out to the entirety of the world (Jn. 3:16).

As a *"Man,"* Christ was *"sent,"* and was, therefore, a Servant, hence, the silence of Verse 23.

As God, He had liberty of action. In Grace, He could respond to the need, which He ultimately would, which Faith presented to that Grace. Otherwise, He would have denied His Own Character and Nature as God.

Due to the Prophecies and the Plan of God, Jesus had to first come to Israel. They were His People or, at least, should have been! All the great Promises had been made to them. Therefore, the Gospel should have been offered to them first before it was offered to the Gentiles.

Even from the very beginning, the Plan of God was that Israel would accept their Messiah and then take His Glorious Message to the entirety of the world. This was God's Intention from the very beginning as He told Abraham, "... *in you shall all families of the Earth be blessed*" (Gen. 12:3). However, the Jews refused to give that "*Blessing*" to the Gentiles or even accept it themselves.

LOST SHEEP!

The words, *"Lost sheep,"* respecting Israel, are interesting indeed!

Very few, if any, Jews would even think of admitting they were "*lost.*" By now, they had come to the place that they believed simply being a Jew constituted their salvation. In other words, their salvation was their nationality, and their nationality was their salvation.

It is the same presently with most so-called modern Believers! Their association with a certain church is their salvation, and their salvation is their association with a certain church.

However, there is no salvation in nationality, as there is no salvation in association with particular churches.

The words, *"Lost sheep,"* are interesting in another capacity as well!

UNCONDITIONAL ETERNAL SECURITY?

The modern teaching of Unconditional Eternal

Security claims that, "*Once a sheep, always a sheep.*" However, Christ here says the very opposite. He calls Israel, or at least the greater part of it, "*Lost sheep.*"

It meant that they were supposed to be His People, and in truth, some of them had once been His People, and some few still were. However, now, as a whole, these "*sheep*" had refused to recognize Christ as the Messiah or to accept Him as Saviour. Therefore, in their refusal to do this, they did not discontinue being "*sheep*" but were, in fact, "*lost sheep.*"

As well, a modern Believer, although at one time in Faith, can cease to believe and then becomes what one might call, "*A lost Believer.*" These individuals were once in Faith, and it certainly was God's Will that they remain in Faith. However, by their own volition, they removed themselves, and if they remain in that state, as Israel of old, they are "*lost.*"

As well, the word, "*Lost,*" in the Greek, is "*apollumi,*" and means, "*To destroy fully,*" to "*perish.*"

Consequently, it does not mean a loss merely of fellowship, as some teach!

LORD, HELP ME

"*Then came she and worshipped Him, saying, Lord, help me*" (Mat. 15:25).

According to Mark, the phrase, "*Then came she and worshipped Him,*" seems to indicate that Jesus had left the street where this "*Woman of Canaan*" first approached Him and now went into a house with her following. Once again, and even greatly so, her persistence is proclaimed. She has met two rebuffs already from Christ, or at least what probably seemed to her as such, but she was not deterred. Instead, she fell at His Feet and worshipped Him. If one is to notice, she has graduated from petition to "*worship.*"

To be sure, this entire episode is remarkable. The lessons contained therein should stand as a beacon of hope for all who believe God and are determined to receive certain things from Him.

The phrase, "*Saying, Lord, help me,*" is actually a completely different petition than her first when she addressed Christ as "*Thou Son of David.*" However, even though this plea, "*Lord, help me,*" was better than her first one, still, she did not get the Blessing until she added: "*I am a dog.*" This was the same ground the publican took when he said, "*... be merciful to me a sinner*" (Lk. 18:13).

FAITH AND HUMILITY

There are two things which stand out so dramatically about this woman, and which should be an example to us. They are as follows:

1. Faith: She would not stop her petition. She had a need and she knew that Jesus was the Only One Who could meet that need, and she was determined to get what she had come for. We are constantly admonished in the Word of God to do the same (Mat. 21:21-22; Mk. 11:24; Lk. 11:8; Jn. 15:7).

2. Humility: This trait stands out so dramatically in the action of this lady. Despite the seeming rebuffs, she would fall at His Feet and worship Him.

How many Believers presently hold a grudge against God because He did not do something they thought He should have done?

The truth is, none of us are worthy of anything from God, and until we understand that, the granted petitions are going to be few and far between.

Preachers are very fond of talking about one's "*rights*" in Christ. Despite teaching to the contrary, and even despite our having received the great Born-Again experience and becoming a Child of God, still, we have no "*rights*," only "*privileges*." Jesus said, "*For whosoever exalts himself shall be abased; and he who humbles himself shall be exalted*" (Lk. 14:11).

I wonder what the Lord must think of us demanding our "*rights*." Far too often, Healing, prosperity, and a host of other things are demanded as the "*rights*" of the Believer. No! The Only One Who has "*rights*" is Christ. He Alone is "*Worthy, to receive Glory, and Honor, and Power*" (Rev. 4:11). All of these things, even being a "*Joint Heir with Christ*," are but a "*privilege*"; but what a "*privilege*" it is!

THE CHILDREN'S BREAD?

"*But He answered and said, It is not meet to take the children's bread, and to cast it to dogs*" (Mat. 15:26).

The phrase, "*But He answered and said*," would now constitute the third rebuff to this woman (a rebuff, at least as it looked outwardly, but in actuality, was the manner in which she could receive that for which she came).

The phrase, "*It is not meet (proper) to take the children's bread, and to cast it to dogs*," is strong indeed!

In effect, He was calling her a "*dog*," which she readily understood! As well, this word, "*Dog*," meant the lowest form of the canine variety, a "*cur dog*."

So, in effect, He was speaking of her and her people as being idol-worshippers and, in fact, some of the worst kind. As stated, they were worshippers of Baal and Ashtaroth, which signaled the worst form of depravity and pollution.

The "*children's bread*" referred to Israel, who were recipients of the Promises and the Prophets and, in effect, were the only ones in the world who had any knowledge of Jehovah. Consequently, they were called "*children.*"

The word, *"Bread,"* speaks of the Word of God and all that it entails.

In truth, Jesus' Own People, the Jews, were in worse spiritual condition even than these heathen. They were worse simply because they had been given the Light, albeit rejected, while the Gentiles had been given precious little Light at all!

That is the reason Jesus placed a curse upon Israel and used the very area that this woman came from as an example by saying, *"... for if the mighty works, which were done in you (Israel), had been done in Tyre and Sidon, they would have repented long ago in sackcloth and ashes"* (Mat. 11:21).

So, if these (Tyre and Sidon) were *"dogs,"* what category must Israel fall into?

THE CRUMBS

"And she said, Truth, Lord: yet the dogs eat of the crumbs which fall from their masters' table" (Mat. 15:27).

She has suffered three rebuffs but is not deterred by any:

1. *"He answered her not a word"*: this concerns her first petition when she spoke of her daughter.

2. My Mission is only to Israel: this, in fact, excluded her, but she responded by *"worshipping Him."*

3. He called her a dog, which was the worst cut of all: by this time, most would have left, but not her. In fact, the answer that she gave Him is one of the greatest answers of Faith in recorded history.

TRUTH LORD

The phrase, *"And she said, Truth, Lord,"* proclaims her acknowledging her position as undeserving and without legal Covenant rights to the children's bread.

In other words, she was saying that she knew she had no claim on the Lord. She realized that she was but a heathen, a Gentile "*dog.*" All of this was true and she admitted to it.

What made this woman persist in her petition?

Of course, the ready answer would be that her daughter was in a terrible condition and desperately needed help. While all of that is true, still, despite His Response to her, there must have been something about Christ that caused her to press on until the victory came.

To be sure, there was something about Christ!

Even though His Statements to her were extremely negative, still, His entire manner and personality were those of pure love. This must have encouraged her to press forward.

This should be a lesson to us that even though the situation may be critical, with even our wrong or sin most terrible, which demands Judgment, still, to any and all who come to Him, they will find Him always to be loving, kind, considerate, compassionate, longsuffering, and quick to forgive.

THE DOGS

The phrase, "*Yet the dogs eat of the crumbs which fall from their masters' table,*" in effect, turns the Words of Christ back to Himself. She used His Own Words as a means to receive Healing and Deliverance for her daughter, which in no way would abrogate His Mission to Israel, but, at the same time, would grant her request.

In effect, she was saying, "*The Jews are the children, while we are dogs, but, as dogs, we claim our portion, even if only crumbs.*"

One can sense the Presence of the Lord even in the saying of these words.

This lady is an example to us all, as the Holy Spirit intended her to be.

Most Believers (I do not believe I exaggerate) try to find ways as to why God will not do certain things. To be sure, that list is endless; however, this dear lady did the very opposite. She turned every negative into a positive; every darkness into a light; every "*no*" into a "*yes!*" What she was doing was totally Scriptural. Paul would later say, "*For all the Promises of God in Him are yes, and in Him Amen, unto the Glory of God by us*" (II Cor. 1:20).

GREAT IS YOUR FAITH

"*Then Jesus answered and said unto her, O woman, great is your Faith: be it unto you even as you will. And her daughter was made whole from that very hour*" (Mat. 15:28).

The phrase, "*Then Jesus answered and said unto her,*" is emphasized by the word, "*Then!*"

All the time the Holy Spirit had been drawing her to this place, and now she would receive what she had come for. Did Jesus change His Mind?

No! He wanted her to have her petition all along but had to bring her to the place to where she could receive it.

It was true that these other situations were hurdles that had to be overcome; however, Faith can overcome any and every hurdle, as Jesus now proclaims.

The moral of the story and the lesson the Holy Spirit is teaching is the lesson of Faith. As well, it is the type of Faith that will not be denied.

The phrase, "*O woman, great is your Faith,*" proclaims His Answer to her persistence. As well, what she had was "*great Faith.*" Only two people are spoken of as having "*great Faith.*"

The first was the Gentile Centurion who came for the Healing of his servant (Mat. 8:5-10), and now this Gentile woman. What a rebuke to Israel!

The reason we have included her in "Great Women of the Bible" is because of the Great Exclamation of Christ regarding her *"great Faith."* She was the only woman, a Gentile at that, who received this accolade by Christ.

BE IT UNTO YOU

The phrase, *"Be it unto you even as you will,"* proclaims, as is obvious, her getting exactly what she wanted.

What a lesson for all others!

WHOLE

The phrase, *"And her daughter was made whole from that very hour,"* proclaims this woman receiving exactly that for which she had asked. Mark portrayed Christ saying, *". . . For this saying go your way; the demon is gone out of your daughter"* (Mk. 7:29). Consequently, this woman's diagnosis of her daughter's condition was exactly right!

Along with all the other many valuable lessons taught us in this portrayal, the tremendous lesson of intercession on behalf of another, as this mother, should not be lost upon us.

To be sure, most, if not all, who come to the Lord do so simply because someone, as this woman, interceded before the Lord for them.

Regrettably, most of the energy of the church in the last few years has been spent on trying to get *"rich"* instead of this all-important task.

Satan has successfully appealed to the covetousness in the hearts and lives of many, and successfully drawn them away from that which is all-important, the Salvation of souls.

Nevertheless, there are still many in this world who, like this Gentile lady, will press forward until they have that which the Lord Alone can give them and, in fact, that which He desires to do.

"Whosoever hears shout the sound!
"Spread the blessed tidings all the world around;
"Tell the joyful news wherever man is found.

"Whosoever comes need not delay,
"Now the door is open, enter while you may;
"Jesus is the True, the Only Living Way.

"Whosoever will, the Promise is secure;
"Whosoever will, forever must endure;
"Whosoever will, 'tis life forevermore;

"Whosoever will may come."

Great Women of the Bible

NEW TESTAMENT

Chapter Nine

LYDIA

LYDIA

COME OVER AND HELP US

"And a Vision appeared to Paul in the night; there stood a man of Macedonia, and prayed him, saying, Come over into Macedonia, and help us" (Acts 16:9).

The phrase, *"And a Vision appeared to Paul in the night,"* proclaims the Holy Spirit now telling Paul exactly where He wanted him to go.

The Leading of the Lord is generally a step at a time, even as here.

Such develops trust and causes one to continue seeking the Lord respecting what is to be done, whatever that might be.

As well, this statement portraying the *"Vision"* given to Paul by the Lord expresses another way in which the Lord communicates with His Children.

In fact, *"Visions"* and *"Dreams"* have been and continue to be used to impart information. The only difference in a Vision and a Dream is that the former is given while awake, with the latter being given while asleep (Joel 2:28; Acts 2:17).

The phrase, *"There stood a man of Macedonia,"* presents the northern part of modern Greece from the Adriatic to the Hebrus River. It is centered on the plains of the Gulf of Thessalonica, running up the great river valleys into the Balkan Mountains. It was famous for timber and precious metals.

This province included six Roman colonies, of which Philippi, Paul's first stop, was one.

Despite this area being a part of Greek culture, which actually influenced the entirety of the world even unto Paul's time, due to Roman subjugation, many of the people were in a state of privation and want. II Corinthians 8:1-5 bears this out!

THE VISION

The "*man*" who Paul saw in the Vision was a pagan who needed God. Whether he was a particular person who Paul later recognized upon going to the area or representative of all pagans is not known. At any rate, Paul now had direction.

The phrase, "*And prayed him, saying, Come over into Macedonia, and help us,*" presents the heart's cry of the lost who do not know the Way and, within themselves, cannot find the Way. Someone must help them find Jesus!

If it is to be known, how many at this very moment all over the world are crying in the very same manner?

However, sadly, there are precious few, if any, to help them!

Great segments of the church, although claiming to be Spirit-filled, are attending seminars where they will be told how to get rich. Many others, also in the Pentecostal realm, are wandering in confusion, following false shepherds and, therefore, cannot hear the Call. Countless others fall into the category of apathy. They simply have little or no concern at all for the lost. Also, I wish to emphasize the fact that only those who are baptized with the Holy Spirit according to Acts 2:4 can be used in such a fashion.

Without this Great "*Helper,*" the Believer can be little led by the Lord, if at all! So, virtually all of the true mission work which has been done in the 20th century has been done exclusively by Spirit-filled Believers (Acts 1:8).

Satan seeks to keep Believers from being baptized with the Holy Spirit. If he cannot succeed in that, he seeks to divert those who are truly Spirit-filled to other pursuits which have little meaning and, in fact, are unscriptural. For the most part, he succeeds!

WESTERN CIVILIZATION

Concerning this Macedonian Call, Hervey said: *"Thus was ushered in the most momentous event in the history of the world, the going forth of Paul to take the Gospel to the Nations of the West." In fact, this is the beginning of what is presently referred to as "Western civilization."*

Consequently, the Apostle Paul, at least as far as a Messenger is concerned, is the greatest contributor to this all-important aspect of civilization, with the Message of Jesus Christ being the actual Foundation.

However, the east was not left without a witness, with Paul going there later himself, and especially the other Apostles.

There is a strong tradition that the Apostle Thomas went to South India, had a great Ministry, and was ultimately martyred there near Madras. However, as is obvious, it would be the west which would open its heart more so to the Gospel of Jesus Christ.

Even then, Satan made great inroads in his attempt to stop the Message by the apostasy of the church, with it ultimately sinking into that which is presently known as Catholicism.

However, there was always a Remnant which held true. With the coming of the Reformation in the 16th Century, the way was ultimately prepared for the great Latter Rain Outpouring (Joel 2:28-29; Acts 2:17-18), which commenced at the turn of the 20th century and continues to this hour.

TO PREACH THE GOSPEL UNTO THEM

"And after he had seen the Vision, immediately we endeavored to go into Macedonia, assuredly gathering that the Lord had called us for to preach the Gospel unto them" (Acts 16:10).

By the use of the pronoun, "*We*," as given in this Tenth Verse, we find that Luke, the writer of the Book of Acts, was now with Paul here at Troas.

He would travel with Paul, Silas, and Timothy to Philippi, but seemingly went no further regarding the second Missionary journey. However, on the third Missionary trip, he seems to have joined Paul there again (Acts 20:5-6).

Acts 21:1 finds Luke still with Paul and going with him to Jerusalem and then to Caesarea. It seems he remained there all the time Paul was a prisoner in that city (Acts 27:1).

As well, he accompanied him on the voyage to Rome, which is the last place where we hear of him (Acts 27:2-3; 28:2, 11, 14-16).

It is believed by some that Luke wrote the Gospel which bears his name during this time of Paul's imprisonment at Caesarea, and did much work on the Book of Acts there as well.

Very little information is given about Luke or even how he came to know Paul.

It is quite characteristic of the Holy Spirit to relate things at times without any explanation. Hence, the simple pronoun, "*We*," speaks of Luke's presence.

THE THIRD GOSPEL AND ACTS

Irenaeus, who lived in the Second Century after Christ, was the first person to refer clearly to Luke and to name him as the author of the Third Gospel, which bears his name, and the Book of Acts.

Tradition also says that he came from Antioch in Syria, which, in a sense, was Paul's home Church. It is said that he was not married and, therefore, had no family. He died at the age of 84 in Boeotia; however, that cannot be proven.

Paul mentioned him in his last Epistle, saying, *"Luke alone is with me"* (II Tim. 4:11).

Consequently, this confirms the close link between the two men.

The phrase, *"Assuredly gathering that the Lord had called us for to preach the Gospel unto them,"* proclaims an instant obedience to the Macedonian Call.

So, they left Troas with a definite objective in mind, anxious to begin their work of proclaiming the Gospel in this area. They had every confidence it would be received, and gladly so!

TRAVEL

"Therefore loosing from Troas, we came with a straight course to Samothracia, and the next day to Neapolis;" (Acts 16:11).

"Samothracia" is a small island in the Aegean Sea. This sea is actually a part of the Mediterranean Sea, which separates Europe from Asia.

This island, though small, has a 5,000-foot mountain. In clear weather, it guided them on a straight course, which was a little short of being halfway to Neapolis.

"Neapolis" was actually the harbor of Philippi, which was about 10 miles away.

All of this is extremely important and for several reasons:

• They were answering the Macedonian Call, which was a Direct Admonition of the Holy Spirit.

• This would be the very first presentation of the Gospel on European soil, which would have such a bearing on what is presently referred to as *"Western civilization."*

• There would be a great harvest of souls in this area now known as Greece, resulting in the planting of several Churches.

PHILIPPI

"And from thence to Philippi, which is the chief city of that part of Macedonia, and a colony: and we were in that city abiding certain days" (Acts 16:12).

Philippi was Paul's destination.

The Scripture is not clear if the Holy Spirit directed the Apostles to Philippi, or that they went there simply because it was the chief city, which seems to have been the case. The Message and the Vision simply was, *"Come over into Macedonia, and help us."*

"And a colony," simply refers to Philippi being a colony of Rome. It had gold mines, and as a result of that, plus other things, it was now as Paul said, *"The chief city"* of the area.

It received the name of Philippi from Philip, the father of Alexander the Great, who extracted a great revenue from its gold mines. Its great historical celebrity arose from the battle in the plain of Philippi, in which Antony and Octavian fought against Brutus and Cassius, with the former winning this conflict. This was 42 B.C.

Its prominence was enhanced further when, after the battle of Actium in 31 B.C., in which Octavian defeated the forces of Antony and Cleopatra, the town received a settlement of Italian colonists, with privileges conferred upon them. This gave them the same rights as if their land were part of Italian soil.

The phrase, *"And we were in that city abiding certain days,"* represents tremendous hardships they were forced to undergo, as we shall see. However, as well, the Lord was moving mightily on their behalf, with a Church established.

A CHURCH SERVICE

"And on the Sabbath we went out of the city by a

riverside, where prayer was wont to be made; and we sat down, and spoke unto the women who resorted thither" (Acts 16:13).

Their meeting out in the open by the river evidently meant that there was no synagogue in the city.

Synagogues were generally built next to a river or a body of water of some type if such were available. Inasmuch as there evidently were not enough Jews in Philippi to have a synagogue, the few Jews, plus interested Gentiles, obviously met on the Sabbath at this particular place.

This river was probably a small stream called the Ganga or Gangites, which is crossed by the Via Egnatia, about a mile out of Philippi.

"And we sat down, and spoke unto the women who resorted thither," seems to tell us that no men were present other than Paul and his party.

Evidently there were some Jewish women present, plus proselytes to Judaism, or at least interested parties.

Obviously Paul had inquired if there was any meeting place of this type in the city, especially respecting synagogues, and was evidently informed of this meeting place. As was ever Paul's method, at least where possible, he always went to the Jews first because of his obvious burden for his own countrymen.

LYDIA

"And a certain woman named Lydia, a seller of purple, of the city of Thyatira, who worshipped God, heard us: whose heart the Lord opened, that she attended unto the things which were spoken of Paul" (Acts 16:14).

Lydia was evidently a businesswoman.

"Thyatira" was a city in what is now Asiatic Turkey, in other words, in the very area where Paul had intended

to go before being directed to Macedonia by the Holy Spirit. In fact, a Church would later be planted there, being one of the seven Churches of Asia to which Jesus directed seven letters (Rev. 2:18-29).

It was not only an important point in the Roman road system, for it lay on the road from Pergamum to Laodicea, but it was also an important center of manufacturing, with dyeing and garment making being a part of its prosperity.

"*Lydia*" was probably the overseas agent of a Thyatiran manufacturer. She may have been arranging the sale of dyed woolen goods, which were known simply by the name of the dye. This "*purple*" was obtained from the madder root and is still produced in the district under the name, "*Turkey Red.*" It was a luxurious and expensive product!

THE WORSHIP OF GOD

The phrase, "*Who worshipped God,*" proclaims her as a Gentile who had probably begun visiting a Jewish synagogue in Thyatira. Now, on being transferred to Philippi, if, in fact, that was the case, she continued her worship.

The words, "*Heard us,*" referred to the fact that Paul evidently was asked to speak to these women, thus proclaiming the Story of Jesus Christ, His Death on Calvary, and His Resurrection.

"*Whose heart the Lord opened,*" presents her hungry for God, which I think is obvious, or she would not have been at this prayer meeting.

As the Holy Spirit anointed Paul to speak, the Lord, at the same time, began to deal with the heart of this wealthy businesswoman.

Actually, this is the method of the Holy Spirit in reaching souls. The Gospel is presented, with the

Holy Spirit anointing its presentation by anointing the Preacher and, at the same time, convicting the individual for whom the Gospel is intended. However, the structure of the Text implies that the Holy Spirit moved upon "*Lydia*" to a greater degree than normal. This, as well, shows the state of her heart. She, as stated, was hungry for God.

However, the heart of the person is not arbitrarily opened by the Lord but is done so only if the person freely yields. Otherwise, it is hardened! The Gospel always has that type of effect. It either softens the heart or hardens the heart, with it all dependent upon the person's free moral agency. It is like the sun which softens wax and hardens clay. The result is in the material, not the sun.

THAT WHICH PAUL PREACHED

The phrase, "*That she attended unto the things which were spoken of Paul,*" refers to her eagerly grasping the Great and Grand Story of Jesus Christ. The word, "*Attended,*" in the Greek Text is "*prosccho.*" It means, "*To hold the mind, or to have regard.*"

One can only imagine the thoughts of her heart, the feelings of her soul, and the grasping of her very being upon hearing the grandest Story ever told, especially considering that she had never heard it before! It was like water for a thirsty soul or bread for a hungry heart.

Why is it that some few respond in this manner, with most refusing and rebelling?

I suppose God Alone would know the answer to that question. Once again, even though the Holy Spirit moves upon and convicts the sinner, still, the person's free moral agency, in other words, his free will, is never violated. The decision to accept Christ or reject Him is always the decision of the individual.

LYDIA GAVE HER HEART TO CHRIST

"And when she was baptized, and her household, she besought us, saying, If you have judged me to be faithful to the Lord, come into my house, and abide there. And she constrained us" (Acts 16:15).

"And when she was baptized, and her household," seems to imply a particular period of time. In other words, it seems that all of this did not take place immediately upon Lydia hearing the Message the first time.

At some point, she was baptized in water, as well as the entirety of her household, which, no doubt, included servants and associates, who had evidently come to Christ as a result of Paul's Ministry and Lydia's Testimony. Consequently, the very first Convert in Europe was a woman, and the very first Church established was in this woman's house. Once again, we see the tremendous part played by women in the realm of the Gospel.

The phrase, *"She besought us, saying, If you have judged me to be faithful to the Lord, come into my house, and abide there,"* seems to have a twofold application.

This tells us that she must have had quite a large residence, which evidently speaks of her station in life. In other words, she was a successful businesswoman.

She wanted Paul and his party to make her house their headquarters while they were in Philippi and, as well, to establish the Church in her house.

SHE CONSTRAINED PAUL AND LUKE

The phrase, *"And she constrained us,"* means at first, they did not acquiesce, feeling perhaps that it may be an imposition on her. However, her continued assurance to them otherwise brought about their acquiescence.

This, no doubt, was a great help to Paul respecting not only very suitable accommodations but, as well, a place to establish the Church.

However, this woman's generosity and kindness were of far greater import than she could ever begin to imagine. Little did she realize at the time that this noble deed would be remembered forever. How could she know that what she did would become a part of the Word of God, and would be read by literally tens of millions of people down through the centuries!

Of course, those things were not in her mind and, in fact, could not be; however, that was not the point anyway. She was obeying God in what she did and would have the privilege of helping to establish the very first Church in Europe.

What an honor that was bestowed upon "*Lydia, the seller of purple!*" And yet, the idea is that every Believer should conduct himself or herself accordingly. To be sure, exactly as the record was kept of this noted lady, likewise, it is kept of all that is done for Christ, which will have eternal consequences.

Incidentally, according to the Fortieth Verse, men were soon added to the Church.

Great Women OF THE BIBLE

NEW TESTAMENT

Chapter Ten

AQUILA AND PRISCILLA

AQUILA AND PRISCILLA

THE APOSTLE PAUL

"After these things Paul departed from Athens, and came to Corinth" (Acts 18:1).

Verse 1 seems to imply that Paul departed alone, with Silas and Timothy joining him later at Corinth.

How long Paul stayed at Athens we are not told; however, joining together the things which were done, it seems he must have stayed there at least a month or maybe longer!

The phrase, *"And came to Corinth,"* presents a distance of about 50 miles.

Corinth was now a Roman colony and, as well, the capital of the province of Achaia and the residence of the Roman proconsul.

It was also a great commercial city, the center of the trade of the Levant, and, consequently, a great resort of the Jews. It also had a very large Greek population. Ancient Corinth had been destroyed by Mummius, surnamed Achaicus, in 146 B.C., and remained waste for many years.

Julius Caesar founded a Roman colony on the old sight, which consisted principally of freed men, among whom were great numbers of the Jewish people.

CORINTH

Corinth was also a center of idolatry and licentiousness. It is said that no city in Greece or in the Roman Empire, for that matter, was more corrupt. It was filled with Greek adventurers, Roman merchants, lustful Phoenicians, sharp-eyed Jews, ex-soldiers, near-philosophers, sailors, slaves, and agents of every kind of vice (Horton).

The town was dominated by the Acrocorinth, a steep, flat-topped rock, surrounded by the Acropolis, which in ancient times contained a temple of Aphrodite, goddess of love, whose service gave rise to the city's proverbial immorality.

Actually, the vice and immorality at Corinth were of such magnitude, and so much known far and wide, that the term, *"To be corinthianized,"* became a byword concerning those who dipped deep into the swill of immorality.

The city was also famous for the Corinthian order of architecture, which continues even unto this day. According to the testimony of Chrysostomus, in the Second Century of our era, Corinth had become the richest city in Greece and was well on its way at the time of Paul. Its monuments, public buildings, and art treasures are described in detail by historians.

It seems that Paul at first had no intention of making this city a base of operations, for it seems that he wished to return to Thessalonica.

However, his plans were changed by a Revelation, which we will see in this Chapter, with the Lord commanding him to speak boldly and remain in the city some 18 months. Consequently, a great Church was founded, which occasioned Paul to later write two Epistles regarding particular problems in the Church. As well, he almost certainly wrote a third Epistle, and even maybe a Fourth, of which we have no record of the latter two.

AQUILA AND PRISCILLA

"And found a certain Jew named Aquila, born in Pontus, lately come from Italy, with his wife Priscilla; (because that Claudius had commanded all Jews to depart from Rome:) and came unto them" (Acts 18:2).

Verse 2 pertains to a husband and wife team who became very close friends to Paul.

Aquila was a Jew from a family of the Roman province of Pontus, located in northern Asia Minor east of Bithynia on the Black Sea (Horton).

It seems that when the Romans took Pontus, his family was captured and sold as slaves in Rome.

Priscilla was not Jewish and seems to have been a Roman lady of one of the upper classes of society. It is even thought that she may have been the daughter of Aquila's former master. Whatever the case, it seems likely that Aquila may have helped her to believe in the One True God, the God of Israel. When he was set free, they then married, or so it may have been!

ROMAN WAYS

It is believed that the incident regarding the phrase, *"Because that Claudius had commanded all Jews to depart from Rome,"* probably occurred in about 49 A.D. or 50 A.D. That would have meant that Paul arrived in Corinth in 50 A.D.

Suetonius mentions the expelling of the Jews from Rome by the Emperor Claudius but, unfortunately, does not say in what year of Claudius' reign it took place.

It seems that the cause of this expulsion was the disturbances among the Jews, which by and large consisted of unbelieving Jews attacking Christian Jews, similar to that which had happened in Jerusalem and elsewhere! However, the Romans did not discriminate between Jews and Christian Jews and so expelled all of them. Therefore, Aquila and Priscilla, victims of this expulsion, found themselves now at Corinth.

However, as is obvious, the Holy Spirit was directing things in totality even though at first, possibly not recognized as such!

There is every indication that both Aquila and Priscilla were already Christians upon meeting Paul in Corinth. When Paul finally left, as we shall see, they accompanied him as far as Ephesus where they received and assisted to a fuller Faith the very influential Apollos. Actually, they were still at Ephesus, and a Church was meeting in their house when the Epistle of I Corinthians was written.

PAUL MEETS AQUILA AND PRISCILLA

However, it seems that at some point, perhaps taking advantage of relaxations toward Jews after the death of Claudius, Aquila and Priscilla went back to Rome (Rom. 16:3). Furthermore, this Passage in Romans shows how widely this ever hospitable couple was known and loved in the Gentile Churches.

The phrase, *"And came unto them,"* pertains, at first at least, to their tent-making craft, as explained in the next Verse. However, it was definitely no chance meeting but was orchestrated totally and completely by the Holy Spirit.

In most places, Paul had no means of support, with the exception of plying his tentmaking, which he was now compelled to do.

We learn elsewhere in Paul's writings that Churches at times supported him, but that seems to have been at a later date. At this particular time, he seemed not to have had any support at all from the Church at Antioch or even those he had recently planted.

TENTMAKERS

"And because he was of the same craft, he abode with them, and wrought: for by their occupation they were tentmakers" (Acts 18:3).

Verse 3 means that Paul had inquired concerning those involved in this occupation, and upon coming to them, seems to find that they were working out of their home.

Evidently, they invited him to take up residence with them, joining his hands with theirs respecting their craft. This must have been a delightful time for Paul, especially having the company of those who were as congenial as these two, and above all, considering their consecration to the Lord.

Some commentators have ventured that this pair were not Believers at this particular time but were quickly won to the Lord by Paul.

While that is certainly possible, from the manner in which Luke treats this subject, it is my thought that they already were Believers in Christ. I believe the evidence leans in that direction totally.

THEIR OCCUPATION

The phrase, *"For by their occupation they were tentmakers,"* presents that which was common with the Jewish people.

Every Jewish boy was compelled to learn a trade. This was their culture and custom. For parents to fail to teach their son or sons a trade was considered disreputable.

The rabbis said, *"Whosoever does not teach his son a trade is as if he brought him up to be a robber."*

The word, *"Tentmaker,"* as it was used of Paul, was perhaps not exactly the best translation. Actually, most of Paul's labor in this capacity involved the repairing of tents.

Quite possibly the Apostle had the knowledge and understanding of how to make tents, but in reality, as he attempted to support himself in various places, he rather repaired tents instead of the wholesale manufacture of these items (Acts 20:34; I Cor. 4:12; II Cor. 9:8-9; II Thess. 3:8).

In the midst of all of this, it is very obvious that the Apostle did not consider himself to be above menial labor, in which category the craft of tentmaking surely belonged.

Paul stayed in Corinth about 18 months and established a thriving Church (Acts 18:11). However, now he would leave, with Priscilla and Aquila with him, and go into Syria.

The Scripture says concerning this:

"And Paul after this tarried there yet a good while, and then took his leave of the brethren, and sailed thence into Syria, and with him Priscilla and Aquila; having shorn his head in Cenchrea: for he had a vow" (Acts 18:18).

THE WILL OF GOD

Some contend that this particular period of time, ever how long it was, was in addition to the 18 months of Verse 11. However, I do not think there is any credence for that, with the situation with Gallio taking place sometime during the 18 months and not after! This much is sure, after the decision by the Roman proconsul, Paul would then have had little opposition at all from the Jewish quarter in Corinth.

The phrase, *"And then took his leave of the brethren,"* pertained to Corinth and was done strictly according to the Timing of the Lord.

Paul ever sought the Will of God in all that he did, which should be obvious!

That referred not only to where he would go but, as well, what and how he would do after arriving, and then staying and leaving according to the Lord's Timetable. This is where most Christians fall down.

SEEKING THE LORD

Most do not seek God's Face respecting His Will for their lives, and I speak of totality.

Many Believers take the position somewhat like the Stoics of old, which is a fatalist's view, in other words, "*What will be, will be!*" Nothing could be further from the truth!

The Believer must seek the Lord constantly respecting leading, guidance, and direction. As well, a person merely saying that is what they want is not enough. I suppose that most, if not all, would fall into that category.

Knowing that it is Satan's business to confuse the issue and that he works tirelessly to this end, every Believer must have a strong prayer life and a strong habitual study of the Word of God.

Above all, every Believer must have his or her Faith centered in Christ and the Cross.

We must always understand that while Christ is the Source of all things we receive from God, the Cross of Christ is the Means by which all of these good things are given to us.

If anything other than the Cross of Christ is the object of the Believer's faith, this constitutes confusion, which pertains to a divided faith, which God can never bless. It is Christ and the Cross, or it is nothing.

The truth is, because of falling down regarding this of which we have stated respecting the Cross, most Believers only partially realize the Will of God in their lives, which causes them to forfeit untold Blessings.

One's personal relationship with Christ, and I speak of one really knowing Who Jesus is, is far beyond "*things*" He gives us.

We shortchange ourselves terribly so if the Lord is reduced to the level of a glorified bellhop!

WITH HIM PRISCILLA AND AQUILA

The phrase, *"And sailed thence into Syria, and with him Priscilla and Aquila,"* presents Luke placing Priscilla first, even as he usually did concerning this couple. This probably means that she was the stronger of the two relative to the Work of God.

However, in no way is this meant to take away from Aquila because there is not the slightest indication in the Text that he was weak or of little consecration, but rather the very opposite.

One need only notice Paul's statement about this couple in Romans 16:3-4 in order to understand their worth to the Kingdom of God.

THE WOMAN

The idea of the woman taking the lead in spiritual matters, as is obvious here, in fact, is the case many times. To be sure, the husband should take the lead in spiritual matters and, in fact, is ordained by God to do so.

However, if, for whatever reason, that is not the case, no violence is done to Scripture whatsoever for the wife to stand in that place, as is here evidenced by Priscilla and Aquila.

Having said that, every woman who finds herself in the place of Priscilla should take extra care that her husband, as the head, be recognized as such in every way possible (I Cor. 11:3).

Syria mentioned here was not Paul's first stop, that being Ephesus, at least after leaving Greece. He would ultimately go to Jerusalem, with Israel then looked at as a part of Syria.

In other words, this was his ultimate destination respecting this trip.

APOLLOS

"And a certain Jew named Apollos, born at Alexandria, an eloquent man, and mighty in the Scriptures, came to Ephesus" (Acts 18:24).

The phrase, *"And a certain Jew named Apollos,"* introduces a man whom Paul came to hold in high esteem. Other than this Passage, he is mentioned in Acts 19:1; I Corinthians 1:12; 3:4-6, 22; 4:6; 16:12; Titus 3:13, all in a positive sense.

From these incidents in the Book of Acts, even as of Apollos, we learn certain things:

Even though the Twelve Apostles, plus others, were doing great things for the Lord at this particular time elsewhere in the Roman Empire, still, the major thrust of the Holy Spirit was with Paul. The reasons are obvious.

Paul as no other man held up the True Gospel of Jesus Christ, which meant that it was distinct and apart from the Law. He, as well, was attempting to take this great Message to the furthermost frontiers. Consequently, anyone who became part of this in any way was honored greatly by the Lord, even as Apollos.

HELPERS TO PAUL

This is certainly not to say that other things which were happening at the time, even to which we have alluded, were not important. In fact, they were, extensively so! However, beginning with the Thirteenth Chapter of Acts, the emphasis is with Paul.

I think we should learn from this that those who helped Paul in this greatest of all endeavors would be greatly honored and blessed by the Lord. That should be obvious! As well, it should be obvious that those who attempted to hinder Paul would not be looked at favorably at all by the Lord!

The moral is that the Believer must make an effort to find out exactly what the Lord is doing around the world. To be sure, that will not be difficult if one will only seek the Lord and inspect the fruit (Mat. 7:15-23).

When that direction is ascertained, the Believer in the Will of God should support it financially, prayerfully, and personally wherever possible!

The tragedy is, even as with Paul, the detractors abound, or those who help are in short supply.

Regrettably, many, if not most, Believers follow or support certain things simply because it is the policy of their particular religious denomination. Others follow or support someone simply because of circumstances, whatever they may be.

All of these reasons are wrong simply because all such direction is man-instituted and, therefore, man-directed! Only the Spirit of God can properly lead a person as to the particulars of which I speak.

PAUL

Paul was a controversial person. He minced no words in exclaiming the Gospel of Jesus Christ, which infuriated the Jewish Sanhedrin, etc. At the same time, it seems that the mother Church in Jerusalem was not nearly so bold respecting Jesus Christ and His Power to save. It is not my intention to take away from the Twelve Apostles or even of James, the Pastor of the Church in Jerusalem, because these men were some of the godliest who have ever lived.

However, I think it is obvious in Scripture that the mother Church in Jerusalem little knew what to do with Paul. As well, it is my personal thought that if it had not been for the Apostle Paul, the proper Message of Jesus Christ would have been ultimately so weakened and diluted that it would have soon been of no consequence!

As a result, it is not easy or simple, at least for most Believers, to support a man like Paul. As stated, he was controversial, having problems with the authorities almost everywhere he went. As well, he suffered terribly for the Cause of Christ.

However, he saw untold thousands of souls brought to a Saving Knowledge of Jesus Christ, plus baptized with the Holy Spirit, as well as bondages of every nature broken by the Power of God. He pushed the darkness, at least in some places, to the very extremity of the Roman Empire. Regrettably, most looked at the obvious controversy but not so much at the obvious fruit!

ALEXANDRIA

The phrase, *"Born at Alexandria,"* which speaks of Apollos, proclaims the mightiest city in the Roman Empire at that time, other than Rome itself. It was located in Egypt on the Mediterranean Sea, about 100 miles northwest of modern Cairo.

It was built by Alexander the Great under the direction of Dinocrates, the celebrated architect of the temple of Diana at Ephesus. Ptolemy Soter founded the famous academy here called, *"The Museum,"* in which learned men devoted themselves to philosophical studies. Some of the most celebrated schools of antiquity flourished here.

One of the Seven Wonders of the Ancient World was located at Alexandria. It was the Tower of Pharaohs. The Septuagint, which is the Greek Version of the Old Testament, was translated here in 285 B.C.

Continuing to speak of Apollos, the phrase, *"An eloquent man, and mighty in the Scriptures, came to Ephesus,"* gives us no reason as to why he came, but, at the time, whether he knew it or not, he was being led by the Holy Spirit.

The word, "*Eloquent,*" in the Greek Text is "*logios,*" and means, "*To be fluent, i.e. an orator.*" Such demands that he was trained in the Alexandrian schools. He was well educated, probably to the extent of an earned doctorate in our modern recognition system. Above that, he was a scholar, as well, in the Scriptures, at least according to the Light he presently had! However, that Light was about to be greatly increased!

FERVENT IN THE SPIRIT

"This man was instructed in the Way of the Lord; and being fervent in the spirit, he spoke and taught diligently the Things of the Lord, knowing only the Baptism of John" (Acts 18:25).

The "*Way of the Lord,*" refers to the Lord Jesus Christ. However, the knowledge of Apollos, although proficient as far as it went, was greatly limited respecting Grace and the Baptism with the Holy Spirit.

Whatever he had learned about Jesus was evidently from those who were deficient themselves. In other words, they told him all they knew, which obviously blessed him greatly, but it seems their knowledge was limited. Consequently, if he had been excited heretofore with only a partial knowledge of Christ, that joy was about to multiply manyfold.

The phrase "*And being fervent in the spirit,*" spoke of his own spirit and not necessarily the Holy Spirit.

As stated, he was so thrilled by what he did know about Jesus, which evidently spoke of His Birth, Life, Ministry, Death, and Resurrection, that he could not help but proclaim what he did know with great exuberance.

The phrase, "*He spoke and taught diligently the Things of the Lord, knowing only the Baptism of John,*" speaks of Repentance and Water Baptism. While he certainly was Saved, as should be obvious, and, as well, consecrated to the Lord, still, he, as millions of others, could make precious little advancement spiritually due to not being baptized with the Holy Spirit.

PRISCILLA AND AQUILA

"And he began to speak boldly in the synagogue: whom when Aquila and Priscilla had heard, they took him unto them, and expounded unto him the Way of God more perfectly" (Acts 18:26).

The first phrase of Verse 26 proclaims the style and method of most synagogues.

In most, if not all, synagogues, a special place was set aside for guests who desired to minister or felt they had something to say. The rulers of the synagogues could invite the guest to speak, which they did most of the time.

Apollos boldly and grandly portrayed Jesus Christ from the Scriptures, at least as far as he knew.

"Whom when Aquila and Priscilla had heard," presents that which was all in the Providence of God.

The Lord knew the hunger of this brother's heart and so would arrange this Divine appointment, for that is what it was!

"They took him unto them, and expounded unto him the Way of God more perfectly," pertained, no doubt, to the full complement of Salvation by the Grace of God exclusively, correct Water Baptism, and the Baptism with the Holy Spirit with the evidence of speaking with other Tongues.

THE WAY OF GOD MORE PERFECTLY

How many presently, and, in fact, has always existed, desperately need to know the *"Way of God more perfectly"?* As Apollos, they are Saved but can little grow in Grace because of a lack of Scriptural knowledge, or mostly, the problem of erroneous teaching respecting the Baptism with the Holy Spirit.

Satan, of course, does everything within his power to keep people from hearing the Gospel of Jesus Christ. If they do have the privilege of hearing the Good News, he will do all he can to keep them from accepting the free Salvation as offered by the Lord.

In fact, the Parable of the Sower bears this out dramatically so (Mat. 13:1-15).

However, if they do accept Christ, Satan will do all within his power to stunt their spiritual growth. He does this by causing them to hear and believe false teaching and error, or else, to not hear the total Message of Salvation by Faith in Christ and the Baptism with the Holy Spirit with the evidence of speaking with other Tongues (Eph. 2:8-9; Acts 2:4).

If he can succeed in doing this, he knows that the leaven of error, if not rooted out, can never remain static, but must enlarge until it ultimately corrupts the whole!

Thankfully, despite all of his education and eloquence, Apollos had a humble, teachable spirit, which received readily from God's Messengers, Aquila and Priscilla.

WHICH HAD BELIEVED THROUGH GRACE

"And when he was disposed to pass into Achaia, the brethren wrote, exhorting the Disciples to receive him: who, when he was come, helped them much who had believed through Grace" (Acts 18:27).

The area specified in Verse 27 refers to Greece, which was across the Aegean Sea and Corinth in particular!

The phrase, *"The brethren wrote, exhorting the Disciples to receive him,"* tells us that despite the fact that

Paul had only been able to minister in the synagogue in Ephesus for probably one service before leaving, at least the seed of a Church was now established.

It seems obvious that Priscilla and Aquila were very instrumental in the growth here which is evident. It would have hardly been possible for the word, *"Brethren,"* to be used were there not a goodly number of men already in the Faith, even though continuing in the synagogue.

As well, Apollos probably stayed for some time, maybe even several months, and was, no doubt, a great help in further establishing the Work.

So, when he felt led of the Lord to go to Corinth, the brethren recommended him, and rightly so.

THE GRACE OF GOD

The phrase, *"Who, when he was come, helped them much who had believed through Grace,"* tells us several things:

• It seems that Apollos had understood precious little, if anything at all, at the outset respecting the Grace of God, which is the Foundation of Salvation in Christ.

However, upon having this great Doctrine expounded to him, he was now very proficient in this most excellent Message. It seems that Priscilla and Aquila had done their work well.

• As a result of what he had learned, especially considering his background, Apollos could be of great blessing, which he was to the Believers at Corinth.

• Quite possibly, the first efforts by the Judaizers of attempting to add Law to Grace may have already begun at Corinth.

We do know that just a little later this became an extensive problem at Corinth and elsewhere as well!

Consequently, new Converts, as well as others who were not too well versed in the Word, could easily be swayed, and some were.

So, I think it is obvious that the Holy Spirit directed Apollos to this Church because of its very need, in which he was a tremendous help.

How beautiful is the Working and Administration of the Holy Spirit! As well, how wonderful it is when perplexing problems are so easily solved when the Holy Spirit has His Way and people, such as Apollos, can be led and directed according to the Will of God!

GREETINGS FROM PRISCILLA AND AQUILA

"The Churches of Asia salute you. Aquila and Priscilla salute you much in the Lord, with the Church that is in their house" (I Cor. 16:19).

The phrase, *"With the Church that is in their house,"* either speaks of the meeting place for the Church at Ephesus or one of the meeting places. In fact, most all Churches in those days were located in houses.

Not long after this, by taking advantage of relaxations toward Jews by Rome, it seems that Priscilla and Aquila went back to Rome.

PRISCILLA AND AQUILA, HELPERS OF PAUL

"Greet Priscilla and Aquila my helpers in Christ Jesus:"

The great Apostle went on to say, *"Who have for my life laid down their own necks: unto whom not only I give thanks, but also all the Churches of the Gentiles"* (Rom. 16:3-4).

The phrase, *"Who have for my life laid down their own necks,"* refers to Priscilla and Aquila. How they risked their lives for Paul is not exactly known.

It may have been at Corinth at the time of the Jewish insurrection against Paul (Acts 18:12), or at Ephesus at the time of the tumult raised by Demetrius, the silversmith (Acts 19:23), when Paul had been in eminent danger, which is probably the case.

At any rate, they were used in some way in which they greatly endangered themselves, but obviously, the Lord protected them. They realized the tremendous value of the Apostle Paul.

Regrettably, not many then did, and not many now do either!

Great Women OF THE BIBLE

NEW TESTAMENT

Chapter Eleven

PHEBE AND THE
ELECT LADY

PHEBE AND THE ELECT LADY

PHEBE

"I commend unto you Phebe our sister, who is a servant of the Church which is at Cenchrea" (Rom. 16:1).

The phrase, *"I commend unto you Phebe our sister,"* presents the first name of the 28 mentioned in Verses 1 through 16 of the Sixteenth Chapter of Romans. Twenty men are mentioned and eight women.

It is interesting that the first name is that of a woman and that she was a Deaconess of the Church at Cenchrea, and some even say its Pastor.

Ministry in the primitive Church was not confined to men.

Incidentally, Cenchrea was the port of Corinth and about nine miles from that city.

A DEACONESS

It is assumed that Phebe was a widow on the grounds that she could not, according to Greek manners, have been mentioned as acting in the independent manner described, even if her husband had been living or if she had been unmarried.

The phrase, *"Who is a servant of the Church which is at Cenchrea,"* presents this woman as very active in that particular Church. It was probably an extension of the Church at Corinth.

"Servant" in the Greek is *"Diakonos,"* a word that could be used in either the masculine or feminine gender. Our words, *"Deacon"* and *"Deaconess,"* are derived from it, showing that it's Scriptural for a woman to serve in this capacity as well as a man. The word means, *"A servant as seen in his activity,"* and can refer, as stated, also to a Minister of the Gospel.

Paul is commending this dear lady to the Church at Rome for several reasons, the foremost being that this Epistle was carried by her over the long and dangerous journey to Rome.

Renan says: *"Phebe carried under the folds of her robe the whole future of Christian Theology."* The Roman letter was written at and sent from Corinth. God's Watchful Care was over both the bearer and the letter.

Paul calls Phebe, *"Our sister,"* that is, *"Christian Sister."*

It appears that Phebe may have had business at Rome, perhaps of a legal kind.

Paul took advantage of her going to send the letter by her, desiring also to enlist the aid of fellow Christians at Rome in furtherance of her business, whatever it might be.

Her having business at Rome, and her having been *"a succourer of many,"* suggests the idea of her being a lady of means.

A HELPER TO MANY

"That you receive her in the Lord, as becomes Saints, and that you assist her in whatsoever business she has need of you: for she has been a succourer of many, and of myself also" (Rom. 16:2).

Paul is saying to those in Rome that they should receive Phebe into companionship and fellowship.

The idea was more than a mere reception, but rather that she was to be received in every capacity and not be barred from any type of spiritual intimacy.

In other words, this was a woman who could be trusted and loved the Lord extensively. What a privilege to be recommended thusly by the Apostle Paul.

"And that you assist her in whatsoever business she has need of you," suggests, as we have stated, that

she may have had business in Rome of a legal nature. They were to assist her anyway they could in whatever endeavors she sought.

The phrase, *"For she has been a succourer of many, and of myself also,"* lends credence to the idea that her house was always open to Ministers of the Gospel, a place where Paul had evidently frequented when in the vicinity.

One can tell from Paul's statements that the times the weary Apostle was able to avail himself of her hospitality were refreshing indeed!

THE ELECT LADY

"The Elder unto the elect lady and her children, whom I love in the truth; and not I only, but also all they who have known the Truth" (II Jn. 1:1).

The phrase, *"Unto the elect lady and her children,"* probably means exactly what it says, a Christian woman of some prominence in the Church. This would have been at Ephesus.

The Apostle addressed his letter to her and her children and mentioned the fact that in his travels, he met her other children and reported that they were ordering their behavior in the sphere of the Truth.

He also sent greetings from the children of this elect lady's sister.

The word, *"Lady,"* in the Greek is *"Kuria."* It is the feminine form of *"Kurios,"* which means, *"Lord, Master."* It was a common name in those days. It is the Greek form of the name *"Martha,"* which means, *"Mistress."* It is believed that this lady was a devout Christian who lived near Ephesus.

It also seems that her home was the meeting place of the local Church, there being no church buildings in those days.

ELECT

The word, "*Elect,*" from the Greek is "*Eklektos,*" and means, "*One picked out, chosen.*" The reference is to the fact that this lady was one of the Elect of God, one of the Chosen-out Ones of God, chosen-out from among mankind by the Sovereign Grace of God for Salvation.

However, the word, "*Elect,*" is not meant to refer to some special designation regarding this woman, but one might say that it is honorary, even as "*the Elder*" was honorary, other than John's original Calling.

Some have claimed that John was actually addressing a Church, thereby, referring to it as, "*Elect lady and her children.*"

However, the general consensus of the entirety of the Text as it regards the letter militates toward the fact that this individual was actually a prominent woman. She was a married woman, for her children are also mentioned.

No husband is mentioned, so possibly, her husband was dead. Quite possibly, the Church was actually in her house, which was the custom in those days, there being no church buildings.

The word here rendered, "*Children,*" would include in itself both sons and daughters, but as the Apostle immediately used a masculine pronoun, it would seem more probable that this woman's children were sons only. In other words, she had no daughters.

In any event, the use of such a pronoun proves that at least some of her children were sons. Of their number and character, we have no information except that a part of them, or possibly all of them, were Christians.

Great Women of the Bible

NEW TESTAMENT

Chapter Twelve

WOMEN IN THE HOME

WOMEN IN THE HOME

I think it would be obvious from the account given in the New Testament that the Holy Spirit makes no distinction between men and women in the Work of God, other than what Paul said:

"Wives, submit yourselves unto your own husbands, as unto the Lord" (Eph. 5:22).

Verse 22 presents the great Christian Law of mutual subjection or submissive consideration as it is now unfolded in its bearing on three particular relations, which lie at the foundation of man's social life — those of husbands and wives, parents and children, and masters and servants.

The relation of husbands and wives as the most fundamental, which is really the topic of this effort, is taken up before the others, and the Christian duty of the wives is set forth first.

Many people have falsely accused the Apostle Paul of being a male chauvinist. This incorrect perception arises because some contemporaries view him from a modern-day perspective rather than trying to view him from his own day.

To be frank, his statements do not enter into culture or time for the simple reason that this which he wrote was given to him by the Holy Spirit and is, therefore, the Word of God, which puts it in a class above modern or ancient thought.

Actually, his statements were extremely radical for his era in which the female gender formerly occupied an inferior status in Greek, Jewish, and Roman cultures. Instead of being a male chauvinist, Paul was, in reality, the very opposite, actually, a liberator of the female gender.

He made it cogently clear that God considers males and females totally equal in the Church (Gal. 3:28).

SO, WHAT IS THE MEANING IN VERSE TWENTY-TWO?

The Holy Spirit through the Apostle is relating to the spiritual leadership of the family, the oldest human institution in God's Creation.

The New Testament makes it poignantly plain that different functions exist in the Church (Rom. 12:5-8; I Cor. 12:27-31; Eph. 4:11). The same principles apply to the home.

In the Christian home, the believing wife needs to submit voluntarily to the spiritual leadership of her *"own"* husband.

The Bible does not condone the dangerous idea that women in general should submit to men in general. Remember, Paul was speaking about the ideal Christian home.

What happens when the wife is a Believer and her husband is not? She obviously cannot yield to him for spiritual leadership.

The Apostle Peter gave instructions about this kind of situation (I Pet. 3:1-7). So did Paul when he wrote I Corinthians (I Cor. 7:12-16).

On the other hand, in the Book of Ephesians, Paul dealt with a case where both parties are sincere Believers. In the latter environment, the husband is to fill the role of spiritual leader, and the wife is to fill a supportive role.

Is one more important than the other one? Of course one is not!

AS UNTO THE LORD

The phrase, *"As unto the Lord,"* proclaims in the Greek Text that the submission is to first be to Christ as Lord and Master and not to the husband.

If the husband's supremacy had been in view, it

would have been expressed in a different manner, so say the Greek scholars.

The idea is that just as Christian wives are to be submissive to Christ, so should they be to their husbands. Consequently, much is said here.

This completely shoots down the erroneous theory, to which we have already alluded, that Christian wives are to obey their husbands in all things, even unsaved husbands, etc.

The qualifying factor is, *"As unto the Lord."*

The Lord always comes first, and any request or demand made by an unbelieving husband must be evaluated in the Light of Scripture. If it violates the Word of God, it must be rejected out of hand.

Of course, that would be the same even if the husband was Saved. No authority overrides the Word of God in any case.

THE LOFTY LEVEL

"For the husband is the head of the wife, even as Christ is the Head of the Church: and He is the Saviour of the Body" (Eph. 5:23).

The marriage relationship is now set out as being a reflection of the relationship between Christ and His Church.

This is to raise it to an unimaginably lofty level.

In I Corinthians 11:12, Paul had already marked out a hierarchy in which God is seen as the Head of Christ, Christ as the Head of the man, and the man as the head of the woman.

Here he looks at it from another angle. If the head of the woman is the man, and the Head of the Church is Christ (Eph. 1:22; 4:12, 16), then it is permissible to draw an analogy between the wife's relationship to her husband and the Church's relationship to Christ.

Thus, marriage is interpreted in the most sublime terms. It is compared with the Marriage of the Lamb to His Bride.

Unless we take the next comment as an aside that bears no relation to the analogy Paul is presenting, it must be assumed that there is an attendant parallelism. It remains true, of course, that Christ is the Saviour of His Body, the Church, in a unique manner. In fact, the word, "*Saviour*," is never used in the New Testament except of Christ or God.

Having recognized and safeguarded that vital truth, we may legitimately pursue the analogy and assume that Paul regards the husband, even to an infinitely lesser degree, as the protector, even the spiritual protector, in a sense, of his wife.

THE HUSBAND, THE WIFE, CHRIST, AND THE CHURCH

The phrase, "*For the husband is the head of the wife, even as Christ is the Head of the Church,*" suggests that the obedience the wife renders to her husband is to be regarded as obedience rendered to Christ.

The idea is that the husband is to represent to her Christ as the Head of the whole Christian Body. The reason for this is found in the relation of headship.

In the marriage union, the husband holds the same relation, namely, that of headship, as Christ holds to the Church, and the headship of the one represents the headship of the other.

Every personal relationship has some element of submission in it. In the natural order of things, the husband occupies a position of priority. Paul fully recognizes this in calling wives to "*submit yourselves*" (I Cor. 11:2-16; Col. 3:18).

In unrelated marital situations, male and female

by Creation are equal, but in the family setting, the husband must assume certain Divinely-ordained prerogatives, and the wife must gladly accept this relationship.

Bruce writes: *"Wives are not inferior to their husbands, either naturally or spiritually. But Paul recognizes a Divinely-ordained hierarchy in the order of Creation, and in this order the wife has a place next to her husband."*

In that case, wives must be willing to surrender to their husbands in order that the husband may exercise the authority which is his responsibility.

Many modern marriages have been wrecked because wives have been unwilling to recognize this fact as it relates to the husband's labor, location of the home, and discipline of the children.

This deference by the wife is done as unto the Lord, that is, as part of her duty to the Lord, and only as long as the situation, whatever it might be, remains Scriptural.

In other words and as we have previously stated, the wife is to submit to nothing that is unscriptural. Consequently, it is assumed that Paul speaks here in terms of Christian families where this kind of submission should be both feasible and possible.

SAVIOUR OF THE BODY

The phrase, *"And He is the Saviour of the Body,"* refers to the Lord Jesus Christ.

The idea, I think, is that the husband is to be the head of the wife and in that, he is like Christ; but Christ is also that which the husband is not, namely, saviour of that whereof he is head.

However, even though the husband cannot be the saviour of his wife in redemptive terms, he can be her protector and provider.

Any sacrifice and self-giving that create a sense of well-being and security will normally evoke a free and loving submission from his wife.

The idea is, "*The husband must find the pattern of his conduct in the conduct of Christ toward His Church.*"

The full meaning of Verse 23 is actually found in the latter portion of Verse 25. Christ loved the Church and gave Himself for it, and, likewise, the husband is to do the same toward his wife, thereby, emulating Christ.

THE CHURCH, WIVES, AND HUSBANDS

The true Church as the Bride of Christ readily acknowledges His Authority and seeks to please Him in every respect.

When marriage is seen in the Light of this higher relationship between Christ and His Body, the wife finds no difficulty in submitting to her husband, for he too has obligations to her in the Lord, even as the next Verses in this Chapter proclaim.

THE CHURCH IS SUBJECT UNTO CHRIST

"*Therefore as the Church is subject unto Christ, so let the wives be to their own husbands in everything*" (Eph. 5:24).

The phrase, "*Therefore as the Church is subject unto Christ,*" is meant to serve as an example.

Unfortunately, the Church as a whole is not too very much subject to Christ, which brings on untold difficulties and problems.

Likewise, if the wife abrogates God's Ordered Arrangement of the husband being the head of the wife, assuming that the husband is Scriptural in his conduct and attitude, the same type of problems will be brought about in the marriage just as in the Church.

However, we must quickly add, for the husband to expect such allegiance from his wife in the marriage duties, he must, at the same time, conduct himself toward her as Christ does toward the Church.

Only as he properly does this can he expect proper submission from his wife.

IN EVERYTHING?

The phrase, *"So let the wives be to their own husbands in everything,"* presupposes that the husband is conducting himself even as Christ. Then, there is no difficulty whatsoever for the wife to be subject to her husband in *"everything."* Otherwise, the situation may not be as smooth as it ought to be.

However, even though the husband does not conduct himself as properly as he should, as far as possible, the wife should still make every effort to submit herself in her obedience, which is actually unto the Lord.

Of course, with a husband acting less and less like Christ, submission becomes more and more difficult.

But yet, the dedicated, consecrated wife (dedicated to the Lord, and if properly dedicated to the Lord, she will, as well, be properly dedicated to her husband), will still do the best she can toward obeying this injunction by the Holy Spirit because her first allegiance is to the Lord.

In other words, she will not allow a rebellious husband to keep her from doing what is right, at least as far as is possible to do so.

SUBMISSION AS FAR AS POSSIBLE

One of the oldest excuses in the world for not properly obeying the Lord is to blame our situation on others.

What others do really doesn't matter as far as we are concerned.

We are to do right, at least as far as we are able to do right, irrespective as to what other people may or may not do. Many erroneously take the position that if someone slights them in some way or does something bad to them, this gives latitude for them to do something negative in turn. It doesn't! So, whatever type of husband the wife has, she should do her best to be as submissive as possible in order to obey the Lord. However, she should never take the position to where she violates her conscience or does something that is contrary to the Word of God.

In fact, the Holy Spirit again and again gives qualifiers in all of these Passages that should amply explain what is being said and done. So, there is no need for anything to be misinterpreted.

However, despite that, some preachers have taken the position in interpreting this Verse that a Christian wife should obey her husband irrespective as to what he might ask her to do, Saved or unsaved.

In other words, if he asks her to go out to a nightclub with him, she should go. Nothing could be further from the truth. Even an elementary examination of these Scriptures proclaims the very opposite of that.

HUSBANDS AND THEIR WIVES

"Husbands, love your wives, even as Christ also loved the Church, and gave Himself for it" (Eph. 5:25).

The phrase, *"Husbands, love your wives,"* refers to the *"agapao"* love, which is *"the love that God is"* (I Jn. 4:8). It was the love that God showed at Calvary (Jn. 3:16) and the love that the Holy Spirit produces in the heart of the yielded Believer (Gal. 5:22).

This is a self-sacrificial love, a love that impels

the one loving to give himself in self-service for the well-being of the one who is loved.

There are really four types of love that the husband should have for his wife:

1. "*Eros*": this is a love of passion.
2. "*Stergo*": this is a love of satisfaction.
3. "*Phileo*": this is fondness and affection.
4. "*Agapao*": this is, as stated, the God kind of love, which must saturate the other types of love, which brings them into the context of that which is godly.

The first three can be had by any unsaved person, but not the fourth. For the first three to be proper, in other words, to be sanctified, they must be saturated with the fourth.

At first glance, it may seem somewhat superfluous for the Holy Spirit to remind a Christian husband that he should love his wife. However, it is not the fact of love of which the Holy Spirit through the Apostle is speaking here, but rather the kind of love that is required, which is the God kind, i.e., "*Agape.*" That being the case, the husband will have no problem conducting himself toward his wife as he should, and the wife will have no problem submitting to such a husband.

THE LOVE OF CHRIST FOR THE CHURCH

The phrase, "*Even as Christ also loved the Church,*" presents the qualifier. If a husband conducts himself accordingly toward his wife, she will have no problem whatsoever submitting to him, even as she should.

Chrysostom commented: "*Have you seen the measure of obedience? Hear also the measure of love. Would you desire that your wife obeyed you as the Church does Christ? Then care for her, as Christ cares for the Church.*"

Christ's Love for the Church is the supreme example of

all loves and, in this instance, the love which a husband must demonstrate toward his wife.

Barry said: *"Only so far as the husband shows the like love in perfect sympathy, and chivalrous forbearance, in abhorrence of tyranny, in willingness to self-sacrifice, has he any right to claim lordship."*

GAVE HIMSELF

The phrase, *"And gave Himself for it,"* presents the great Sacrifice, which characterizes the God kind of love. In other words, this type of love always gives oneself.

In the highly Christ-centered theology of Paul, Christ is the norm for the whole of life.

Here, sacrificial, self-giving love constitutes the very essence of Christian living.

If *"walking in love"* is necessary for the whole life, it follows that it is compulsory for this particular relationship in life. Thus, the application is, as Christ gave Himself up for His Church, a husband must be willing to make any sacrifice, even the sacrifice of his own life, if necessary, for the well-being and happiness of his wife. The Supreme Affection of Christ involves passion, undying devotion, sensitivity to need, and self-denial. With such love, husbands must love their wives. In respect to this, Bruce remarks, *"By setting the highest of standards for the husband's treatment of his wife, Paul gave to the limit in safeguarding the wife's dignity and welfare."*

If one is to notice, the Lord is not a dictator over His Church. In fact, He gives the Church a tremendous autonomy (freedom). As long as the Church remembers that He is the Head, and accordingly, that He is guiding the Church, a tremendous amount of freedom in that capacity is offered. The same should go for the proper husband for the proper wife.

Great Women of the Bible

NEW TESTAMENT

Chapter Thirteen

WOMEN IN THE CHURCH

WOMEN IN THE CHURCH

Paul said, *"Let your women keep silence in the Churches: for it is not permitted unto them to speak; but they are commanded to be under obedience, as also says the Law"* (I Cor. 14:34).

The phrase, *"Let your women keep silence in the Churches,"* refers to the manner of services as conducted at that time.

The women normally sat on one side while the men sat on the other, which some few Churches still do.

With many things taking place which were unusual and different, even as Paul had been addressing, it was quite usual for the women to speak out in the service and ask their husbands as to the meaning of certain things, etc.

Paul was telling them, even as the next Verse proclaims, that they should not do this, thus interrupting the service.

Women were relatively uneducated in those days; therefore, it was not unusual for them to seek information wherever it could be found.

These Verses make much more sense when the Bible student views them in the totality of the Chapter and in light of the immediate context. Unfortunately, they are taken out of context in many church circles and used by some male chauvinists to teach that God does not permit women to function in public ministries.

However, the context (related Verses) lends itself more to the subject of demeanor.

PROPER INTERPRETATION

The truth is, women were free to pray and prophesy (preach) in the Church (Joel 2:28-32; Acts 2:16-21; 21:9). Proper interpretation of Scripture is comparing Scripture with Scripture on the same subject.

When that is done, the full meaning of what Paul is here saying becomes more obvious.

The phrase, *"For it is not permitted unto them to speak,"* refers to their calling out to their husbands across the Church, or wherever they were worshipping.

If the word, *"Speak,"* is to be taken literally, then it would not be proper for a woman to pray in Church, prophesy in Church, preach in Church, teach in Church, or even sing in Church. Actually, it would not even be proper for the woman to say anything in any capacity, which is absurd!

In some churches which teach that women are not supposed to preach, etc., it is satisfactory for them to teach little children; however, if it's wrong for one, it is wrong for the other. The truth is, it's not wrong in either case.

The phrase, *"But they are commanded to be under obedience, as also says the Law,"* refers back to Genesis 3:16 and the Creation model.

The idea of Paul using the *"Law of Moses"* as an example means that Genesis 3:16 was not in any way changed when the Law of Moses was given some 2,000 years later. Neither has it been changed yet and will not be changed until the Resurrection.

The *"obedience"* of which Paul here speaks refers to the command of the Lord concerning the man being the head of the woman, which we have already discussed (Gen. 3:16; I Cor. 11:3). This is the Creation model and is to be respected.

LEARN ANYTHING?

"And if they will learn anything, let them ask their husbands at home: for it is a shame for women to speak in the Church" (I Cor. 14:35).

The phrase, *"And if they will learn anything, let them ask their husbands at home,"* tells us plainly what Paul was speaking about respecting women keeping silent in the Church.

Once again, he was telling the women not to call out in the Church to their husbands sitting across the way, asking about certain things, but wait until they got home and then ask. It has nothing to do with a woman preaching, praying in Church, etc.

The phrase, *"For it is a shame for women to speak in the Church,"* refers to that particular manner. As stated, if it is to be taken literally, then it would not be permissible for a woman to even open her mouth in Church in any capacity.

However, Paul was not talking about silly things of that nature, and neither is he meaning that it is wrong for a woman to preach, to sing, etc.

Inasmuch as this is a very important subject, and we might quickly add, a subject with diverse opinions, I think it would be wise to take a closer look.

THE WOMAN'S ROLE IN THE CHURCH

This is not an issue that can be resolved by a study of words alone.

We must look at the situations as they involve women as given to us in the Word of God in order to come to a Scriptural conclusion.

As previously stated, the only sure way to interpret Scripture is to compare Scripture with Scripture on the same subject.

To build a doctrine on one particular Scripture is not Scriptural within itself. The Word plainly tells us, *"In the mouth of two or three witnesses (occasions or Scriptures) shall every word be established"* (II Cor. 13:1; Deut. 19:15; Mat. 18:16).

THE SIGNIFICANCE OF WOMEN

Despite the reality of life in a male-dominated culture, women played a surprisingly significant role in the Early Church.

The reason undoubtedly is that in Christ, women as well as men are the recipients of Spiritual Gifts for ministry.

Thus, the contribution of women to the total ministry of the Body of Christ is basic to the health and growth of the whole congregation.

Specific lines of New Testament evidence show that an important place was given to women in the life of the Church. A few facts are worth noting.

THE MANNER IN WHICH WOMEN
ARE USED BY THE LORD

Women played a critical role in the establishment of several New Testament congregations (Acts 16:13-15, 40; 17:4, 12).

As well, women are identified by name and called "*fellow workers*" by Paul (especially Romans, Chapter 16, where seven women are identified by name). The inclusion of women in a ministry team is a significant departure from Jewish practice. The naming of Priscilla before her husband Aquila, as we've already stated, is also extremely significant (Rom. 16:3).

Women are also seen participating through prayer and Prophecy in Church meetings, even as we have recently studied (I Cor. 11:5).

Although the Old Testament foretold a day when sons and daughters would prophesy as the Spirit was poured out on "*both men and women*" (Joel 2:28-32; Acts 2:17-18), the participation of women in Church gatherings was totally different than Old Testament tradition; tradition, I might quickly add, which was, most of the time, man-devised and not from God.

DEACONESS

Phebe, as previously stated, is identified in Romans 16:1 as a Deaconess, and other evidence suggests that women may have participated with men in the diaconate (serving with them).

Despite the clarity of evidence in each of these areas suggesting that women participated freely in the life of the Early Church and were recognized as significant contributors of ministry, there are still some areas that need further investigation.

WOMEN AND CHURCH OFFICES

Most of the offices mentioned in the New Testament were ordinarily filled by men.

This seems especially true when one speaks of an Apostle.

There is no record of any woman being an Apostle even though women do stand in the Office of the Prophet (Prophetess) (Ex. 15:20; Judg. 4:4; II Ki. 22:14; II Chron. 34:22; Neh. 6:14; Isa. 8:3; Lk. 2:36; Acts 21:9).

The word, *"Prophesy,"* as used of the daughters of Phillip in Acts 21:9, speaks of the Office of the Prophet and not the simple Gift of Prophecy. *"Prophesy,"* as it is used here, in the Greek is *"propheteuo,"* and means, *"To foretell events."*

Actually, I think the New Testament bears out the fact of women serving in all of the five-fold ministry offices, with the exception of *"Apostle."*

As stated, there is no record of such in the New Testament. However, at the same time, there is no Scripture that says that such could not be.

DEACONESS

We have mentioned Phebe, with Paul describing her as *"a servant of the Church which is at Cenchrea"* (Rom. 16:1).

"Servant," as it is here used, in the Greek is *"diakonon."* It means several things, with one being the Pastor of a Church. So, there is a possibility that Phebe was actually the Pastor of the Church at Cenchrea and not merely a Deaconess. It stands to reason that if women stood in the Office of the Prophet, which they did, and these other offices, as well, at the same time, they could preach, sing, and testify the Gospel in any manner in which the Lord would desire to use them.

As we have already stated, there were women Prophetesses in the Old Testament, of which the evidence is plentiful, and at least one woman served as Judge in Israel when that office was the highest in the land (Judg., Chpts. 4-5).

Consequently, I hardly think that women would have a lesser role under the New Covenant, which is a far better Covenant, but rather a greater role, which I believe is borne out.

WOMEN IN THE WORSHIP SERVICE

The most controversial New Testament Passages regarding women have a common context; they deal with issues related to worship.

However, to understand these Passages, we need to interpret them in the total context of a gathering in which women did take part, for Paul wrote about women praying and prophesying when the congregation gathered (I Cor. 11:5).

Within this framework of participation, the Passages and the most likely interpretations follow:

The most obvious Passage is that which we are now studying, I Corinthians 14:34-36. Women are to *"remain silent in the Church"* to the extent that they *"are not allowed to speak."* Any questions should be held till they are at home and can *"ask their own husbands."* This very blunt instruction has been interpreted in several ways. Let's look at them:

Even though we have already dealt with this subject, I think it would be helpful to go a little deeper into this most important question.

NO FEMALE PARTICIPATION?

Some claim this decisively rules out any female participation in the worship services, especially of preaching, etc. However, such a view violates what Paul said about women praying and prophesying in I Corinthians 11:5.

Consequently, inasmuch as the Holy Spirit does not contradict Himself, we know this particular interpretation is grossly wrong.

A CORRUPTION OF THE TEXT?

Some claim that this statement concerning women was added by someone other than Paul. That is also foolish because it says, in essence, that the Holy Spirit was not powerful enough to safeguard the Text.

So, we have to rule that out also.

AN ANTI-FEMININE VIEW?

Some claim that this is but another example of Paul's inconsistence and reflects his culture-bound, anti-feminine view; however, Paul did not have, as is overly obvious, an anti-feminine view.

As well, to claim that Paul was inconsistent is to claim that the Holy Spirit is inconsistent, which is foolishness indeed!

Everything Paul wrote regarding the Scriptures, as well as everything all other Bible writers wrote, was inspired by the Holy Spirit, which guarantees against error, contradiction, inconsistency, or mere personal viewpoints.

MISUNDERSTANDING?

Some claim that Paul's statements in I Corinthians, Chapter 11, are misunderstood, and women are not to speak in Church.

My answer to that is: how can one misunderstand Paul's simple statement in I Corinthians 11:5, *"But every woman who prays or prophecies ...?"*

THE CORRECT ANSWER

The prohibition in I Corinthians 14:34-36 must be seen and answered in the context of which it is given, as dealing with a specific problem in the Church rather than reflecting a pattern in Church meetings as a whole.

This last option is most in keeping with higher view of Scripture and with careful attention to the Text.

In I Corinthians 14:26-40, Paul was dealing not only with disorderly meetings but also with the question of proper display of the Gifts.

As is obvious, at that particular time, there was much confusion in the Church at Corinth, which evidently precipitated some women constantly asking their husbands the meaning of certain things.

With men and women sitting on opposite sides of the meeting place, wherever that was, that would have created disorder, hence, Paul saying, *"If they (women) will learn anything, let them ask their husbands at home ..."* (I Cor. 14:35).

PAUL'S ADMONITION IN I TIMOTHY

What did Paul mean by the statement, *"Let the women learn in silence with all subjection. But I suffer not a woman to teach, nor to usurp authority over the man, but to be in silence"?* (I Tim. 2:11-12).

The Eleventh Verse of I Timothy, Chapter 2, once again deals with the same question dealt with at Corinth. Women were not to call out to their husbands for Scriptural explanations during the service.

If one looks closely at Paul's statement respecting the right of the woman to teach, it plainly says, *"Nor to usurp authority over the man."*

The idea is that the woman does not have power over the man. To do so is to violate the Creation model.

Women should not dictate to men, but they do have the right to exercise their privilege to teach, preach, prophesy, pray, and do other things under the authority of men.

As should be obvious, the key is in not exercising authority over men.

The Greek word for *"usurp"* is *"authenteo,"* and means, *"To have power over it."* So, women are not to have power over men, at least as it regards the Work of God.

However, under the authority of men, they can do anything they feel the Lord has called them to do.

"Do you hear them coming brother,
"Thronging up the steeps of light,
"Clad in glorious shining garments,
"Blood-washed garments pure and white?"

"Do you hear the stirring anthems,
"Filling all the Earth and sky,
"'Tis a grand, victorious army,
"Lift its banner up on high!"

"Never fear the clouds of sorrow,
"Never fear the storms of sin,
"We shall triumph on the morrow,
"Even now our joys begin."

"Wave the banner, shout His Praises,
"For our victory is nigh!
"We shall join our Conquering Saviour,
"We shall reign with Him on high!"

BIBLIOGRAPHY

CHAPTER 1: Zechariah and Elizabeth
H.D.M. Spence, *The Pulpit Commentary*, Grand Rapids,
Eerdmans Publishing Company, 1897, Book of Luke.

CHAPTER 1: The Angel Gabriel
Anthony Wilhelm, *Christ Among Us: A Modern Presenta-
tion of the Catholic Faith for Adults*, Harper Collins,
New York, 1996.

CHAPTER 1: The Angel
H.D.M. Spence, *The Pulpit Commentary*, Grand Rapids,
Eerdmans Publishing Company, 1897, Book of Luke.

CHAPTER 1: Mary
H.D.M. Spence, *The Pulpit Commentary*, Grand Rapids,
Eerdmans Publishing Company, 1897, Book of Luke.

CHAPTER 1: Ceasar Augustus
H.D.M. Spence, *The Pulpit Commentary*, Grand Rapids,
Eerdmans Publishing Company, 1897, Book of Luke.
George Williams, *Williams Complete Bible Commentary*,
Kregel Publications, Grand Rapids, 1994, pg. 744.

CHAPTER 1: The Land of Israel
H.D.M. Spence, *The Pulpit Commentary*, Grand Rapids,
Eerdmans Publishing Company, 1897, St. Matthew
2:23.

CHAPTER 1: His Mother
H.D.M. Spence, *The Pulpit Commentary: Vol. II*, Grand
Rapids, Eerdmans Publishing Company, 1978.

CHAPTER 3
George Williams, *William's Complete Bible Commentary*,

Kregel Publications, Grand Rapids, 1994, pg. 816.

CHAPTER 3: The Faith of Mary Magdalene
H.R. Reynolds, *The Pulpit Commentary*, Eerdmans Publishing Company, Grand Rapids, 1897, Book of John.
Ibid.

CHAPTER 4
H. R. Reynolds, *The Pulpit Commentary*, Eerdmans Publishing Company, Grand Rapids, 1897, Book of John.
Ibid.
Ibid.
Ibid.

CHAPTER 7
H.D.M. Spence, *The Pulpit Commentary: Vol. I*, Grand Rapids, Eerdmans Publishing Company, 1978.
George Williams, *William's Complete Bible Commentary*, Grand Rapids, Kregel Publications, 1994, pg. 784.
Ibid.

CHAPTER 9
Hervey, *The Pulpit Commentary*, Eerdmans Publishing Company, Grand Rapids, 1897, Book of Acts.

CHAPTER 10
Stanley M. Horton, *Acts: A Logion Press Commentary*, Springfield, Gospel Publishing House, 1981, pg. 304.
Ibid.

CHAPTER 11
Marvin R. Vincent, *Vincent's Word Studies in the New Testament Part 3*, 1905, pg. 177.

CHAPTER 12

F.F. Bruce, *The Epistle to the Ephesians,* Old Tappan, 1961, pg. 114.

A New Testament Commentary for English Readers, 1884, pg. 52.

F.F. Bruce, *The Epistle to the Ephesians,* Old Tappan, 1961, pg. 115.

About Evangelist Jimmy Swaggart

The Rev. Jimmy Swaggart is a Pentecostal evangelist whose anointed preaching and teaching has drawn multitudes to the Cross of Christ since 1956.

As an author, he has written more than 50 books, commentaries, study guides, and The Expositor's Study Bible, which has sold more than 2 million copies.

As an award-winning musician and singer, Brother Swaggart has recorded more than 50 Gospel albums and sold nearly 16 million recordings worldwide.

For nearly six decades, Brother Swaggart has channeled his preaching and music ministry through multiple media venues including print, radio, television and the Internet.

In 2010, Jimmy Swaggart Ministries launched its own cable channel, SonLife Broadcasting Network, which airs 24 hours a day to a potential viewing audience of more than 1 billion people around the globe.

Brother Swaggart also pastors Family Worship Center in Baton Rouge, Louisiana, the church home and headquarters of Jimmy Swaggart Ministries.

Jimmy Swaggart Ministries materials can be found at **www.jsm.org.**

NOTES

NOTES

NOTES

NOTES

NOTES